THE FREEMASONS

By the same author

THE FREEMASONS

A History of the

World's Most Powerful

Secret Society

JASPER RIDLEY

Arcade Publishing • New York

FIRST U.S. EDITION 2001

Library of Congress Cataloging-in-Publication Data

Ridley, Jasper Godwin.
 The freemasons : a history of the world's most powerful secret society / Jasper Ridley. —1st U. S. ed.
  p. cm.
 Includes bibliographical references and index.
 ISBN 1-55970-601-5 (hc)
 ISBN 1-55970-654-6 (pb)
  1. Freemasons—History. I. Title.

 HS403 .R54 2001
 366'.1'09—dc21   2001045745

Published in the United States by Arcade Publishing, Inc., New York
Distributed by AOL Time Warner Book Group

Visit our Web site at www.arcadepub.com

10 9 8 7 6 5 4 3 2 1

EB

PRINTED IN THE UNITED STATES OF AMERICA

To my grandchildren
Owen, Abigail and Anna

Contents

Acknowledgements

I wish to express my gratitude to everyone who has helped me while I was writing this book.

Her Majesty the Queen graciously permitted me to quote from a letter of Queen Victoria in the Royal Archives at Windsor.

I must thank first and foremost the Librarian and staff of the Library and Museum of Freemasonry at Freemasons' Hall in London. Although I am not a Freemason they allowed me to work in their library on sixty-three days, and gave me the benefit of their expert knowledge and efficient assistance, without, of course, making any effort to influence the opinions about Freemasonry which I would express in my book. I thank them, and all my Freemason friends, for the encouragement which they have given me, as a non-mason, to write an objective book on the subject.

I thank Hugh Barnes-Yallowley, Dr Charles W. Hollenbach and James Young for reading and advising me on the typescript; Lieselotte Clark, Marlies Evans, Antonia Fraser, Anita Garibaldi, John Hamill, Emina Kurtagić, Branko Markić, Ljubica Simić, Dr Michael Smith and Signor Salvatore Spinello for their help with the research and for the information which they gave me; Sarah Christensen, Wendy Hawke, Commander Michael Higham (the former Grand Secretary of the United Grand Lodge of England), Charles Hodgson, Duška Jovanović, Branka Kolić, Ruth O'Brien, Robert Pynsent, Ingrid Price-Gschlössl, my daughter Barbara Ridley, Denise Sells, Jasna Srdar, Derek Stuckey, George H. Vincent, S. F. N. Waley, Anthony West (a member of the Board of General Purposes of the United Grand Lodge of England) and Sharon Willett of Press Ahead for their help in various ways; the Librarian and staff of Canning House; the Inner Temple; the Istituto Italiano di Cultura in London, the Kent County Library at Tunbridge Wells (whose recent decision to remain open on Saturdays and Sundays has made it possible for me to finish this book on time); the London Library; and the Libraries of the University of California at San Diego and Berkeley, California; my publisher Benjamin Glazebrook and the staff at Constable and my agents Curtis Brown of London; the staff of the Carpenters' Company of London; my wife Vera for reading and advising me on the typescript and for her help in compiling the bibliography; and her and my son John and Henry Hely-Hutchinson for correcting the proofs; and Mrs Helen Baz for compiling the index.

The Master, Fellows and Scholars of Churchill College in the University of Cambridge kindly permitted me to use information in the Churchill Archives in the College.

The Secretary of the Ars Quatuor Coronatorum Lodge kindly allowed me to quote several passages from their *AQC* publications and from Knoop and Jones's *The Genesis of Freemasonry* and *Early Masonic Pamphlets*.

I have been kindly allowed to quote a passage from *Wellington at War* edited by the late A. Brett-James.

Jasper Ridley

Tunbridge Wells,
13 August 1999.

Introduction

In Britain in 1999 the Freemasons are once more under attack. The accusation levelled against them is that they are a secret society of men who take the most solemn oaths, enforceable by horrible penalties, to further their own interests against those of the 'cowans' (non-masons); who recognize each other by secret signs; and who then extend favours to each other even though this conflicts with their public duties. It is therefore improper that Freemasons should be in positions of authority, particularly in the police force or the judiciary. Police officers will help masonic criminals to escape. When judges are sitting in court, the prisoner in the dock, or a witness in the witness-box, will make a secret sign to the judge, who, recognizing him to be a mason, will give judgement in his favour, because the masonic oath overrules his public duty as a judge.

The masons, on the other hand, deny that they are bound by oaths to help their masonic brothers at all costs. They say that the oath to help a brother is subject to the overriding duty to obey the law, and that a brother must never be helped to break the law.

Which of these arguments is correct? If we examine the history of the Freemasons in the last 300 years, it is quite clear that the Freemasons are right, and that fears that they constitute a society whose members help each other to break the law, are unfounded. During 250 years of wars, revolutions and political upheavals, masonic oaths and obligations to help their masonic brothers, except in a very few cases where special circumstances existed, have counted for nothing when they have come into conflict with national allegiance, class interest, ideological zeal, or the personal ambition of the mason.

The anti-masons and their supporters in the media demand that Freemasons should be compelled to disclose the names of their members. If it had not been for the reforming enthusiasm of earlier

MPs, this would have been unnecessary; for by the Unlawful Societies Act of 1799 Freemasons were required to give their names to JPs. They duly complied with this requirement until it was abolished in 1967 by the Criminal Law Act at a time when a large number of obsolete Acts of Parliament were repealed by the Statute Law Revision Acts. As the Unlawful Societies Act 1799 was designed primarily to suppress Radical organizations and trade unions, the MPs abolished it without pausing to reflect on what the consequences might be. Now they wish to re-enact some of its provisions. The Freemasons do not really object to this – they were happy enough to comply with the Act until 1967 – but they do object to being singled out as different from a golf club or any other similar association.

The fear of the anti-masons that a Freemason police officer or judge cannot be trusted to do his duty because of his masonic oath, is based on an extraordinary *naïveté* of which both masons and anti-masons are often guilty. Both sides agree that there are good masons who carry out commendable charitable work, but that there are also bad eggs in the masonic basket, and that it is with the activities of the bad Freemasons that they are concerned. A man who is prepared to put on fancy dress and swear an oath which he realizes is weird, horrific and antiquated, because he thinks that it will help his career to do so, will not perform this oath if he thinks that if he does so, and is caught and found out, it will harm his career. This has been shown repeatedly in the history of Freemasony in Britain, France, the United States and every country in the world.

THE FREEMASONS

CHAPTER 1

◆

The Masons

THE masons were different. In the Middle Ages, from the thirteenth to the fifteenth centuries, in England, France and Central Europe, there was a general feeling that the masons were
different from other people. Most of the population were serfs, working on the lands of their feudal lords, and they never travelled beyond
their native village, except to walk along the King's highway to the
nearest market town; but some of the more enterprising among them
travelled much longer distances, going on a pilgrimage to the tomb
of St Thomas Becket in Canterbury, or to the shrine of Our Lady
of Walsingham in Norfolk, or occasionally going to France to serve
the English King in his wars against the French.

In the towns, craftsmen made things, and traders bought and sold
them. Weavers made cloth, goldsmiths made rings and jewellery, and
carpenters built wooden houses for the local inhabitants or the town
council. But the masons were different. They worked in stone, and
very few buildings were built in stone. Only the castles of the King,
and of those noblemen to whom he gave permission to 'castellate'
and build castles, and the cathedrals, abbeys and parish churches,
were built of stone. So the King, some of his nobles, and the Church
were the masons' only employers, though occasionally an important
bridge would be built of stone.

London Bridge, which until the eighteenth century was the only
bridge over the Thames below Kingston, was originally built of
wood; but after it was destroyed in 1176 it was decided to rebuild
it in stone. The people made up a song about it:

> London Bridge is falling down.
> How shall we build it up again?

Build it up with silver and gold,
Dance over my lady lea;
Silver and gold will be stolen away,
With a fair lady.
Build it up with iron and steel,
Dance over my lady lea;
Iron and steel will bend and bow,
With a fair lady.
Build it up with wood and clay,
Dance over my lady lea;
Wood and clay will wash away,
With a fair lady.
Build it up with stone so strong,
Dance over my lady lea;
Then 'twill last for ages long,
With a fair lady.

It did indeed last for ages long. After they had finished building it in 1209, it lasted 623 years, and when it was demolished in 1832, it was not because of any fault in the structure, but because the stone pillars on which the bridge was built were too close together to allow the larger ships of the nineteenth century to pass beneath.

And who was the 'fair lady', the 'lady lea' over whom the people danced when they crossed the bridge or entered the houses which were built on both sides of the bridge? Everyone knew all about her. She was a young virgin who had been walled up alive in one of the stone columns of the bridge by the masons when they were building the bridge, as a human sacrifice to appease God's wrath and induce Him to preserve the bridge from destruction by gales or floods. It was one of many lies about masons which people have spread and believed for more than 800 years, from 1176 to 1999.

The masons travelled all over the country building cathedrals in the county towns, castles at strategic points, and abbeys sometimes near towns and sometimes on the Yorkshire moors and in other places in the depths of the country.

The building of cathedrals provided the masons with a good deal of work. In France, 80 cathedrals, 500 large churches, and many more parish churches were built between 1050 and 1350.[1] In England, the building of cathedrals often took more than a hundred years. The work required a considerable amount of labour, both skilled and unskilled. Unskilled workers were needed to clear away the rubble for the building of the foundations, and to bring the stone and mortar to the site. The French regulations for the building of cathedrals of 1268, which were drawn up after consultations with the craftsmen's guilds, laid down that 'masons, mortar-makers and plaisterers may have as many assistants and valets as they please, provided they teach them nothing about their trade.' Three masons might have five assistants working for them.[2]

Many serfs seized the opportunity to escape from the lands where they were forced to work for their lords and go to a town where a cathedral was being built, knowing that if their lord did not recapture them within a year and a day they would be free from serfdom. Some gentlemen and noblemen came as volunteers to do the unskilled work as an act of piety. In some places, Jews were compelled to do the work as a penance on Holy Saturday.[3]

The masons were skilled workers. There were two kinds of masons – the 'hard hewers' or 'rough masons' who laid the ordinary hard stone from Kent and elsewhere of which the cathedrals were built; and the more highly-skilled masons, who carved the fine façades on the cathedral face. They worked in the softer, chalky stone which was found in many parts of England between Dorset and Yorkshire and in other countries of Europe. This softer stone was called 'free-stone', and the skilled masons who worked with it were called 'free-stone masons', which was often shortened to 'freemasons'.[4]

Near the place where they were working, they erected a hut which they called their 'lodge'. They kept their tools in the lodge, and ate their dinner there during the time they were allowed for their dinner break in the middle of the day. But they did not sleep in the lodge. They took rooms in an inn, or other lodgings, in the town, and often stayed there for several years.[5]

The freemasons, though they travelled from all over the country to their place of work, were not a bunch of unemployed tramps going everywhere to find employment. They were known for their skills, and were invited to come by the bishops and deans of chapters who were undertaking the building of the cathedral. While they were working on a cathedral they sometimes received offers from other parts of England, or from France or Germany, to leave the job and come, for higher rewards, to work on another cathedral. The bishops and deans who employed them tried to prevent this by imposing a term in their contract which prevented the freemasons from leaving to seek employment elsewhere until the work was finished; but the freemasons often refused to agree to such a condition.

When the King was building a castle or essential fortifications, he used his powers of impressment to force masons to work for him. In the 1540s, Henry VIII built fortifications on the Kent coast to guard against a possible French invasion. Masons from as far away as Somerset and Gloucestershire were obliged to come and work there, and masons from Gloucestershire, Wiltshire and Worcestershire were forced to help build Henry's magnificent new palace of Nonesuch, near Esher in Surrey. Sometimes masons in Kent were ordered to go to Berwick to work on fortifications against the Scots, and were sent twelve shillings and eightpence (63p) to cover the expenses of their 304-mile journey from Maidstone. Sometimes the authorities did not trust the masons to turn up to work as directed, and arrested them and forcibly carried them to the required destination. Cardinal Wolsey adopted this method to obtain masons to build his Cardinal College at Oxford, which after his fall was renamed Christ Church.[6]

But usually the conscription of masons and other workers was undertaken, not directly by the King or the government, but by a corporation, or trade guild, to which the King had granted a charter and instructions to regulate the craft. The guild was composed of the leading employers in the trade, but was sometimes directly controlled by a royal official. In the case of the masons, they were under the control of the Masons' Livery Company in London, which was almost certainly already in existence by 1220.[7] There was a guild of masons in Chester, Durham, Newcastle and Richmond in Yorkshire.[8]

In Scotland the masons' guilds were even older than in England. The Masons' Company of Glasgow was granted a charter, and the power and duty of regulating the trade, by King Malcolm III Canmore in 1057, the year in which he won the throne by defeating and killing Macbeth. There was a guild of masons, or joint guilds which included masons, in Edinburgh, Elgin, Irvine, Kirkcudbright, Rutherglen, and probably also in Aberdeen and Dundee.[9]

Medieval Europe was a highly disciplined and regulated society. In England, Parliament laid down the maximum wage which every class of workers was permitted to receive and the number of hours a day which they were required to work in summer and winter; the fabric and colour of the clothes which dukes, earls, gentlemen and the common people were allowed to wear; the number of courses which they were permitted to eat at dinner; the fast days on which they were not allowed to eat meat or eggs; and the games that they were allowed to play.[10]

Life was regulated for the masons too. Their duties were laid down in directives from their controlling guilds, which were known as 'Charges'. First of all came the mason's duty to God; he must believe in the doctrines of the Catholic Church, and must reject all heresies. Next came his duty to the King, whose sovereignty and laws he must obey. Third was his duty to his master, his employer, the master-mason for whom an apprenticed mason worked. He must not betray his master's secrets; he must not seduce his master's wife, daughter, or maidservant; he must not 'maintain any disobedient argument' with his master, his dame, or any freemason. Then there were the general moral duties: not to commit adultery or fornication, not to stay out late at night after 8 p.m. frequenting inns and brothels, and not to play cards except during the Twelve Days of Christmas. In this the Charges repeated the provisions of Acts of Parliament which laid down the rules about playing cards for every class below the rank of noblemen.[11]

The masons' wages and working hours, like those of other workers, had been laid down in the Statutes of Labourers which were passed after the series of plagues, which became known as the Black Death, reached Western Europe from the East in 1348, and in some parts of England killed between one-third and one half of the population. The result was a shortage of labour which increased the bargaining power of the survivors. Parliaments consisting of peers in the House of Lords and a House of Commons for which only gentlemen, merchants and employers had the vote, passed Acts which laid down, not a minimum, but a maximum wage. Employers and their workmen could agree that the workman should work for as little as the workman was prepared to accept; but it was made illegal for the employer to pay his workmen more than the maximum laid down in the Act. Employers and workmen who paid and received more than this were fined. The fine of 20 shillings for each offence imposed on the workman amounted to nearly six months' wages.[12]

The wages of a mason for a working day of fourteen hours in summer, from 5 a.m. to 7 p.m., with a total break of two hours for meals and rest, were sixpence a day. In winter the working day was from dawn to half-an-hour before sunset.[13]

These working hours, which were the minimum laid down by the statutes, did not apply when Henry VIII's officials rounded up the masons from all over England and forced them to work on the King's fortifications and palace. Then the masons worked for the hours that they were ordered to work, and sometimes worked throughout the night.[14]

But masons and other employers often made secret illegal agreements under which the masons were paid more than sixpence a day. The labour shortage was so acute, especially in the case of skilled workers, like the freemasons, and their bargaining power was so great, that they and their employers were prepared to risk the consequences of breaking the law. The masons formed trade unions, whose members agreed that they would not work for less than wages which were well above the legal maximum. These trade unions were illegal, and their meetings, and the decisions taken at the meetings, had to be kept very secret.

The law about the maximum wage for masons was so widely ignored and broken that it became virtually unenforceable, and usually no serious attempt was made to enforce it. Henry Yeveley, who was one of the most famous master-masons between 1356 and 1399, earned on an average well above sixpence a day. He became wealthy enough to buy two manors. His great contemporaries, William Wynford and Richard Beke, the chief mason of London Bridge from 1417 to 1435, became equally wealthy.[15]

In 1425, when the Duke of Bedford was Regent for his three-year-old nephew King Henry VI, the government and Parliament made an attempt to enforce the law. A statute was passed which declared that masons had been violating the law, and had formed illegal combinations to force their employers to pay them excessive wages. More severe penalties were imposed by the Act on masons who attended meetings of illegal trade unions;[16] but within two or three years the Act, like the earlier statutes, was no longer enforced.

In France, as in England, the masons, especially those who did the ornamental carvings in freestone, were the élite of the labour force employed in building cathedrals. They joined an organization which had no parallel in England, the Compagnonnage. The Compagnons who belonged to it welcomed workmen from nearly all the various trades, including masons, and organized their travels to their different places of work. The surviving records all refer to the journeys of the Compagnons in central and southern France; but the Compagnons were probably also active in the Paris area and the north of France.

They tried to negotiate for all the workers of the different trades, and were the nearest medieval equivalent to a modern Trade Union Congress.

The French kings and governments did not approve of this. Laws and royal decrees against the Compagnonnage were issued in 1498, 1506 and 1539; and local bylaws banned them in Orleans in 1560, in Moulins in 1566, and in Blois in 1579. A statute of 1601 forbade the Compagnons to greet one another in the street or for more than three of them to go together to an inn; and in 1655 the doctors of the Sorbonne, the divinity college of the University of Paris, proclaimed that the Compagnons were wicked men who were offending against the laws of God. But the Compagnons continued to work secretly for the interests of their members.[17]

In Germany and Central Europe, the Steinmetzen (stonemasons) were likewise the élite of the labour force employed in building cathedrals. Their activities were regulated by their trade corporations. They developed a national organization which covered the whole of Germany and Central Europe. There were important lodges of the Steinmetzen in Vienna, Cologne, Berne and Zurich, but they all accepted the leadership of the stonemasons of Strasbourg. In 1459 the Emperor Maximilian I issued a decree giving legal effect to the code of conduct drawn up by the leadership of the masons in Strasbourg. The control of Strasbourg over the German masons continued until 1681, when Strasbourg was captured by the armies of Louis XIV of France and annexed by France.[18]

The freestone masons were less successful in Scotland than in other countries in maintaining their privileged position in the building trade. As there was no soft freestone in Scotland, the freestone masons were unable to carry on their skilled work there. The regulations about apprenticeship were modified in Scotland by the 'entered apprenticeship' system. In England and other countries, no one was permitted to carry out the work of a master-mason until he had served a fixed period of apprenticeship. In Scotland an apprentice could become an entered apprentice after a much shorter period of apprenticeship; and an entered apprentice was allowed to perform most of the work of a master mason.

The Scottish freestone masons tried to strengthen their position by having a code word which they revealed to all qualified master masons, but not to entered apprentices or anyone else. This enabled the master masons to recognize each other, and as far as possible to exclude the entered apprentices from carrying on the work of a master mason. The code word became known as the 'Mason Word'. It was probably 'Mohabyn', which has links with the word 'marrow', meaning 'mate' or 'comrade', which was in use in Scotland until the nineteenth century.

The weight of evidence suggests that the Mason Word originated in about 1550. It spread across the Border into the most northern counties of England, but it was unknown south of Durham, or in any other country in Europe. The English masons had their secrets which they discussed at their illegal trade union meetings; but they had no need of any word or sign to disclose their identity to each other. In England, France and Central Europe, everyone knew who was a freestone mason.[19]

—————— ◆ ——————

CHAPTER 2

The Heretics

HOWEVER wicked the masons might be in forming their illegal trade unions, they were perfectly law-abiding and respectable as far as religion was concerned. They did not challenge the almost universal belief that the authority and doctrine of the Roman Catholic Church must be accepted without question. The two Saint Johns – St John the Baptist and St John the Evangelist – were their patron saints, and the feast days of St John the Baptist on 24 June and of St John the Evangelist on 27 December were the two days in the year which the masons celebrated. They also revered St Barbara, who protected masons against lightning, and the Four Crowned Martyrs. They were four masons in Roman times who had refused to renounce Christianity, and by order of the Roman Emperor were locked alive in a lead coffin and thrown into a river. Forty-two days later their bodies were rescued by a Christian who hid them in his house.[1]

The masons were as closely tied to the orthodox religion as all the other livery companies and trade guilds. The charter of the Masons' Company of Newcastle required them to act the play *The Burial of Our Lady St Mary the Virgin* in the plays performed on Corpus Christi Day every year; and the Masons' Company of Chester acted with the Goldsmiths' Company in *The Destroying of the Children by Herod*.[2] The first of the Charges imposed on masons by their guilds required them to do their duty to God by avoiding all heresy. They believed that the handful of dissidents who challenged the authority of the Church were heretics who should be severely punished.

As early as the beginning of the thirteenth century small religious sects at Albi in the south of France were opposing the Catholic

Church and were being denounced and persecuted as heretics. By the end of the fourteenth and the beginning of the fifteenth centuries, John Wycliffe in England and Jan Hus in Bohemia were alarming the authorities. In England new Acts of Parliament enacted that heretics were to be burned alive. Hus himself was burned at Constance in South Germany in 1415, and several 'Lollards', as the heretics were called, were burned in England.

The Lollards and their successors in the sixteenth century, who followed Luther, Calvin and Zwingli and other German and Swiss reformers, came to be known colloquially as 'Protestants'. They challenged orthodox Catholic doctrine on a number of points. They believed that in the communion service the wine as well as the bread should be given to the laity, and not reserved for the priest alone. They believed that priests could lawfully marry. They believed that men attained salvation by faith – by the correctness of their beliefs – and not by works, at a time when it was generally accepted that the 'works' which would ensure that men and women went to heaven and not to hell was to give money to priests and monks to pray for their souls.

Above all the Protestants disagreed with the Catholic Church over the nature of the presence of Christ in the consecrated bread and wine. Their theologians had all been trained in the philosophy of Aristotle which distinguished between the accidents and the reality of an object. The accidents were its appearance, shape, feel, smell and taste; but the true inner reality was something different. There was no doubt that the consecrated bread and wine looked, felt, smelt and tasted like bread and wine; but the Catholic Church believed that it really was the body and blood of Christ.

Catholics and Protestants disagreed as to the nature of Christ's presence in the bread and wine; and the Protestants disagreed with each other about this. Was it a real, corporal presence, as Catholic doctrine taught? Or was it a real, but a sacramental, presence? Or was it not a sacramental, but a spiritual, presence? Or not a spiritual, but a figurative, presence? Or was Christ not present in any sense at all? Was the sacramental bread, as the most extreme Protestants believed, simply bread, a 'vile cake'? Despite their disagreements about the nature of the presence, they were all agreed on one point: anyone who had the wrong belief about it should be put to death by torture.

That great sixteenth-century intellectual, Sir Thomas More, put the matter very clearly. He believed that heretics should be burned alive, that 'Princes should punish them, according to justice, by most painful death', both as a punishment for their heresy and as a deterrent to others.[3] A painting which was formerly in the Prado Museum in Madrid shows the holy work of a Catholic saint from an earlier period. The picture is called 'St Dominic converts a heretic'. It shows a naked heretic tied to a post while the saint, with a halo around his head, holds the flame of a torch up against the heretic's penis.

In England burning alive was considered to be a sufficient punishment for a heretic. Sometimes his friends, having bribed the executioner, were allowed to supply the heretic with a bag of gunpowder to tie around his neck, so that when the flames of the fire reached the gunpowder, it would explode and immediately kill the burning heretic and thus end his sufferings. Sometimes a heretic was strangled and killed before he was burned. But if the wood was damp, and the fire burned slowly, the heretic's agony could be prolonged; sometimes he burned for three-quarters of an hour before he died.[4] In France a heretic was often tortured before he was burned, especially if he had refused to recant.

In England the masons in their London livery company, and in their other organizations, approved of the action of the government in burning the small minority who challenged the authority of the Pope and the Church of Rome. Then in 1533 Henry VIII repudiated the Papal authority because the Pope would not grant him a divorce from his wife, Queen Catherine of Aragon, which would allow him to marry his mistress, Anne Boleyn. He persuaded his Parliament to pass an Act which declared that he himself, the King, and not the Pope, was the Supreme Head of the Church of England; anyone who denied this was a traitor and was to be hanged, drawn and quartered. This meant that the traitor was to be hanged but cut down while still alive; he was then to be castrated and disembowelled and his entrails were to be burned before his eyes, he being still living; only then was he to be put to death by having his head cut off. But while Catholics who refused to repudiate the Papal, and accept the royal, supremacy, were hanged, drawn and quartered, Protestants who denied the Real Presence and believed in other heresies were still burned alived. The Masons' Company and the other city livery companies accepted the royal supremacy over the Church, and believed that it was right that Papists should be hanged, drawn and quartered and that Protestants should still be burned alive. But a very small number of individuals did not approve of killing and torturing heretics and traitors and other dissidents. Some of them rejected the most fundamental truths of the Christian religion. They kept their views very secret. In October 1539 an eighty-year-old professor of the Sorbonne admitted on his deathbed that he had been an atheist for sixty years since he was aged twenty, and did not believe in God, though he had kept this secret during his lifetime, as he did not wish to be burned as a heretic.[5] There was a rumour that one of the Cardinals in the Vatican also admitted on his deathbed that he had always been an atheist.

The English Protestant writer, John Foxe, held unorthodox views about burning heretics. In 1563 he published the first edition of his *Book of Martyrs*, in which he gave the names and described the sufferings of the Protestant martyrs who had been burned during the reign of the Catholic Queen Mary Tudor. He did not approve when the Protestant Queen Elizabeth I burned Anabaptists as heretics, and unsuccessfully tried to persuade her to pardon them. He admitted, a little shamefacedly, that he was too tender-hearted, and could not bear to see even animals killed or tormented.[6]

The London Protestant merchant, Richard Hilles, in the 1540s, went even further. When he left Henry VIII's England to travel on business to the Frankfurt fair in Germany, he ventured to write letters to his Protestant friends in Switzerland which he would not have risked writing in England. He disapproved of burning any-one as a heretic, however strange and outrageous his opinions; he did not approve of traitors being hanged, drawn and quartered, or that the property of convicted traitors was forfeited to the King, so that their innocent children were made to suffer for their father's crime.[7]

The people who held these advanced beliefs in favour of religious toleration were obliged to keep their views very secret. If they had been found out, they would have been punished much more severely than masons who attended meetings of illegal trade unions.

When the Protestants had won power in England, Scotland and the Netherlands, they inflicted cruel punishments on Catholic fanatics who obeyed the call of Philip II of Spain and the Pope to assassinate heretical sovereigns. In England Elizabeth I reluctantly accepted the advice of her Secretary of State, Lord Burghley, that it was illegal to impose a more cruel form of death than hanging, drawing and quartering; but she was satisfied when Burghley assured her that with an efficient executioner, death by hanging, drawing and quartering could be very painful and prolonged.[8] In Scotland, Catholics who murdered the Protestant Regents were broken on the wheel.

When William the Silent, Prince of Orange, was assassinated by the Roman Catholic zealot Balthazar Gérard in 1584, William's Calvinist followers tortured Gérard for four days before he was executed. First they carved pieces out of his flesh with the points of quill pens and poured salt and vinegar into the wounds; then they tortured him by distorting his limbs on the rack; and finally, on the day when he was to be executed, they cut off his hands, and applied red-hot irons to the wounds before he was eventually put to death by being torn apart by wild horses after four hours of torture. They falsely told him that his attempt to assassinate William and been unsuccessful, so that he should believe that his sufferings had been in vain.[9]

Twenty-six years later, another Catholic fanatic, François Ravaillac, assassinated Henry IV of France because, although Henry had renounced his Protestantism and converted to Roman Catholicism, he had ended thirty years of civil war by issuing his Edict of Nantes which granted religious toleration to the Protestants. After Ravaillac had been tortured to induce him to name his accomplices, and the bones in his legs had been broken, they threatened that if he persisted in denying that he had any accomplices they would fetch his innocent old father and mother from Angoulême and torture them before his eyes to make him speak. When he was taken to the place of execution, his right hand, which had held the dagger with which he had killed the King, was burned off, and hot lead, boiling oil and scalding water were poured over the wounded stump on his hand. He was kept alive in agony for half an hour before being fastened to the horses that were to tear him apart. The horses were sluggish, but at the third attempt they tore him in pieces, and he died.[10]

It was about the time that Ravaillac suffered in 1610 that a new religious sect, which became known as the Rosicrucians, arose in Germany. Their doctrines were first expounded in a book, *The Universal and General Reformation of the Whole Wide World*, which was probably already circulating in manuscript in 1610, though it was first published in Kassel in the Rhineland in 1614.[11] It described how a member of the sect, while wandering in the woods, had come across the grave of Christian Rosenkrantz, deep in a very overgrown part of the forest. He found, on a little table beside the tomb, three books which Rosenkrantz had written. From this it appeared that Rosenkrantz had been born in 1384 and had lived to what was then the almost unheard-of age of 106 before dying in 1490, after travelling in the East and imbibing its wisdom. In his books, Rosenkrantz wrote about his vision of a future Paradise in which men believed in a God, or Supreme Being, who attached no importance to the subtleties of sixteenth- and seventeenth-century religious controversies, and whom people of differing religions could worship, while granting religious toleration to all.

Many people believed that Christian Rosenkrantz had never existed, and that the whole story about finding his tomb, and the three books in which Rosenkrantz expressed his theories, had in fact been written by Johann Valentin Andreae, a German Lutheran theologian. Certainly Rosenkrantz's doctrines, his fantastic visionary ideas and his Deism, seemed to have some links with Lutheranism, and his books contained a fierce attack on the Roman Catholic Church as the great religious persecutor. Within a few years of the publication of the books in 1614 and 1615, some German Rosicrucians had visited England, where they found a few English philosophers who were sympathetic to their ideas.

The most enthusiastic of these English sympathizers was Robert Fludd, a young gentleman from Bearsted in Kent who had studied medicine at St John's College, Oxford. He was also interested in mathematics, alchemy, philosophy and theology. He was very friendly with another student at St John's, William Laud. Both Fludd and Laud were members of the Church of England and had no intention of becoming Roman Catholics; but they did not hate Roman Catholics, as many Protestants did, and saw no reason why Protestants and Catholics should not be friends. In 1598, when he was 24, Fludd went abroad and for six years stayed with aristocratic Catholic families in France, Italy, Spain and Germany. He found that he could be very friendly with them without agreeing with their religious opinions. When he returned to England he qualified as a doctor of medicine, but spent much of his time reading and writing about alchemy, philosophy and religion.

He was attracted by the doctrines of the Rosicrucians. In 1616, the year after the publication of the second of the Rosenkrantz books, *The Reputation of the Brotherhood*, he wrote two pamphlets supporting the Rosicrucians. He now believed not only that Protestants and Catholics could be friends, but that their dogmas should be replaced by a simple religion which merely accepted the existence of God and the need to lead a moral life and do good.

His friend at Oxford, Laud, engaged in ecclesiastical politics, and in due course became Bishop of London and Archbishop of Canterbury. He was not the first or the last progressive intellectual who was so disgusted by the intolerance of the revolutionary opposition groups that he became their persecutor as an agent of royal despotism. As Charles I's Archbishop of Canterbury, he sat in the Court of Star Chamber, sentencing Puritan writers and their supporters to be whipped through the streets of London from Temple Bar to Westminster Palace Yard, to stand there in the pillory, and to have their ears cut off. After the revolution of 1640 he was arrested, condemned as a traitor, and beheaded, to the joy of all the opponents of Charles's tyranny. His friend Fludd did not live to see his downfall – he had died in 1637.[12]

There were more people now than there had been in the sixteenth century who were shocked by the horrible cruelties committed by both sides in the name of religion. At the beginning of the seventeenth century, after the savage thirty years of religious wars in France, the Netherlands and Ireland, it seemed as if Europe had had enough of religious warfare, and that Catholics and Protestants might agree to live together in peace. Then another war of religion, the Thirty Years' War, broke out in Bohemia and raged throughout Germany from 1618 to 1648, before Catholics and Protestants agreed to end it by a compromise peace, with some states being Catholic and some Protestant; but by this time about one-third of the population of Germany had died in the war.

In England, Scotland and Ireland the Civil War between King and Parliament, which began as a religious war and very largely remained so, caused far less loss of life than the Thirty Years' War in Germany; but it convulsed British society. It ended with the Restoration of Charles II in 1660, when an intolerant government of supporters of the Church of England persecuted Roman Catholics and Protestant Nonconformists, while at the same time intellectual societies, like the Royal Society, which were devoted to scientific research and non-religious interests, flourished under royal patronage. The people who believed in religious toleration, in the possibility of friendship between men of different religions, and in a simple faith in God and morality without theological complications, were still a small minority of the population; but they were becoming a growing force among the intellectuals. Some of them became Rosicrucians; some did not join any movement or organization; and some became Freemasons.

———— ◆ ————

CHAPTER 3

The Seventeenth Century

BETWEEN about 1550 and 1700, the Freemasons changed. They ceased to be an illegal trade union of working masons who accepted all the doctrines of the Catholic Church, and became an organization of intellectual gentlemen who favoured religious toleration and friendship between men of different religions, and thought that a simple belief in God should replace controversial theological doctrines. In the language of the time, the 'operative masons' were replaced by 'admitted masons' or 'gentlemen masons' as they were usually called in Scotland. In later times these admitted masons were called 'speculative masons', but this term was not used before 1757.[1]

No one really knows how this change came about. Masonic historians have written long and learned books giving their explanations, which have been refuted by other masonic historians in equally long and learned books, while the anti-masonic writers, with their popular best-sellers, have put forward their own theories. Some of the explanations have been far-fetched and almost ridiculous. Others have been very convincing and are supported by a great deal of plausible evidence, but there is equally strong evidence which suggests that the explanation is wrong.

There was a long tradition of trade guilds accepting as members men who had no connection with the trade. The livery companies of the City of London – the oldest one was the Weavers, which was founded in 1155 – originally consisted of members of the trade. But from the earliest times the liverymen's sons, if they had been born after their father joined the livery, could become liverymen by patrimony. In the Middle Ages a man usually followed his father's trade, but sometimes he did not; and this did not prevent him from joining the livery. Apart from this, the livery companies could admit as liverymen men who had no connection with the company, either by birth or occupation; and they often did so.

By the fourteenth century the great livery company, the Taylors and Linen Armourers (who later changed their name to 'the Merchant Taylors') were admitting as liverymen country gentlemen who sold them wool for export to the Netherlands. They even admitted King Edward III as a liveryman, after they had lent him money to pay for his wars which they knew he would never repay. For the gentlemen, it was an advantage to become more closely associated with the City of London, while for the livery company there was great social prestige in having gentlemen members in the very regimented society of fourteenth-century England with its class distinctions – gentlemen who, unlike their social inferiors, were allowed, if they owned land worth £20 a year, to wear a gold ring, a silk shirt, and red or velvet garments.

In Scotland, it was very usual for influential gentlemen to be invited to join a trade guild. It became so common for the Scottish masons to invite the gentlemen of the St Clair family at Rosslyn to join their guild, that the St Clairs wrongly claimed that they had a hereditary right to exercise authority over the masons of Scotland. King James IV joined the Edinburgh Guild of Merchants in 1505; and sixty years later the Earl of Moray, the illegitimate half-brother of Mary Queen of Scots, when Regent for the infant King James VI, joined the Bakers' Company in Glasgow.[2]

By the sixteenth and seventeenth centuries, it was reading the Bible which made so many gentlemen wish to join the masonic lodges. The Catholic Church had rightly regarded the translation of the Bible into English, and the reading of the English Bible by the people, as the greatest threat to its authority. Sir Thomas More and the other official persecutors had been zealous in burning copies of the English Bible and the Protestants who distributed them. If people read the Bible, they would regard the Bible, not the Church, as the authority which they must obey.

It was not good enough for the Church to tell the people that they must obey the Pope because it was stated in the Gospels that Christ had said to St Peter: *'Tu es Petrus, et super hanc petram aedificabo ecclesiam meam'*[3] – a pun which was lost in the English translation 'Thou art Peter, and upon this rock I will build my Church'; for the readers of the Bible could question why this passage meant that 1,500 years later, the Bishop of Rome was Supreme Head of the Church. They would point out that there was nothing in the Bible that stated that Peter was ever at Rome, just as they pointed out that Christmas should not be celebrated as a feast of the Church because there was nothing in the Bible that said that Our Lord was born on the twenty-fifth day of December. There were passages in the Bible which had revolutionary implications, as John Knox pointed out in his lengthy marginal notes in the English translation of the Bible which he and his colleagues published in Geneva in 1560. These passages showed that the prophets of God had deposed wicked kings, and, in Knox's words, that 'Jehu killed two Kings at God's commandment'.[4]

The Protestants read every one of the 860,000 words in the Bible to find texts which would denigrate the doctrines and authority of the Catholic Church. In the Second Book of Chronicles they read of how King Solomon decided to build a temple, how he asked Hiram, King of Tyre, to send him architects and masons to work on the temple, of how the work was completed; and they read about the length, width and height of the temple.[5] As everything in the Bible was the Word of God, these measurements were not inserted unnecessarily, or to satisfy the idle curiosity of the reader; they must have some profound theological implications.

Although the Presbyterians and the Protestant extremists rejected anything which was not in the Bible, the masons were prepared to add many stories, which were not in the Book of Chronicles, about the building of Solomon's temple. They told the story, not of Hiram, King of Tyre, but of another Hiram – Hiram Abiff, who knew the secret of the temple. Three villains kidnapped him and threatened him with death if he did not reveal it; and as he would not betray his trust, they murdered him. When Solomon found out about this, he wondered what was Hiram Abiff's secret, and if it had died with him. He sent three masons to find Hiram's body and the secret, and told them that if they could not discover the secret, the first thing that they saw when they found Hiram's body should henceforth be the secret of the temple. The masons eventually found Hiram's body, and when they opened his coffin, the first thing they found was his hand; and as they did not find the secret, the handshake and the other signs of recognition which the masons henceforth adopted became the new secret.[6]

As part of the ceremony in which a Freemason is raised to the third degree and becomes a master mason, he participates in the re-enactment of the story of the murder of Hiram Abiff. He swore an oath that, like Hiram, he would not reveal the Freemasons' secrets, and agreed that if he broke his oath, it would be right to put him to death by cutting out his heart, liver and other entrails. The horrific penalties which the candidate agreed should be inflicted on him if he broke his vow of secrecy bear a close resemblance to the punishment which traitors endured in the disembowelling part of the sentence of hanging, drawing and quartering.

The masonic tradition told other stories about the origin and development of Freemasonry. In 1723, after the formation of the English Grand Lodge, they were published by the prominent Freemason, James Anderson, in his *Book of Constitutions*; but they were almost certainly circulating, and believed, before the end of the seventeenth century. God Himself was a mason; had He not built heaven and earth in six days? Adam was a mason. It was masons who built the Tower of Babel; and when God had ordained that the peoples should speak different languages, He had told the masons to communicate by secret signs with masons who spoke different languages. Noah was a mason, though he had built the ark of wood, not stone. Abraham was a mason. He invented geometry, and when he was in Egypt he met a Greek slave named Euclid. Abraham taught Euclid geometry, and Euclid wrote down what Abraham had told him, and through Euclid's writings the world learned geometry.

The story continued: masonry was introduced into Britain in Roman times by St Alban; but after the death of the Four Crowned Martyrs it disappeared from Britain until it was reintroduced by King Athelstan at York in the tenth century. It was afterwards protected by other sovereigns. Queen Elizabeth I did not like the masons because, being a woman, she could not be admitted as one of them; but James I, Charles I, Charles II and William III were masons. Obviously masons were something very special, and God's favourites; just as God had created men to be above the animals, so He had created masons to be above other men.[7]

All this was absolute nonsense; but it was flattering to the masons, who believed what they wished to believe.

The learned men of the seventeenth century were greatly interested in Solomon's temple. Theologians, philosophers and other scholars wrote long books about it in Latin. The mathematician and scientist, Isaac Newton, was particularly impressed by the temple. Many of his 470 books and writings are on theological subjects, and he wrote several about the temple. He considered that Solomon was the greatest philosopher of all time. He seems to have believed that his reading about the measurements of Solomon's temple had helped him to formulate his law of gravity and he was sure that from these measurements it was possible to foretell that Christ's Second Coming would take place in 1948, and the dates of other portentous events during the next four hundred years.[8]

And there was also the Mason Word. The people had heard about the Mason Word, and wondered what it was. There was no good reason why they should be interested to know the code word which the Scottish masons had invented to enable them to distinguish between master masons and entered apprentices; but after the people had read and heard about Solomon's temple and all the stories about the secret initiation ceremony and the oath taken by the Freemasons, the Mason Word acquired a romantic and sinister fascination. They had also heard about the Rosicrucians – the brethren of the 'Rosy Cross', as they called them – and confused the Freemasons, the Rosicrucians, and witchcraft. A poem published in Edinburgh in 1638 referred to the Freemasons of Perth:

> For we be brethren of the Rosie Cross;
> We have the Mason Word and second sight;
> Things for to come we can foretell aright.[9]

The Presbyterian minister of a parish in Kirkcudbrightshire was worried in 1695 about the connection between Freemasonry and witchcraft. He had been informed that a local mason had met the Devil, and had donated his first child to him in return for being told the Mason Word: but after investigating the matter, the minister was convinced that the allegation was untrue, that the mason had never encountered the Devil, and did not know the Mason Word.[10]

Sir Robert Moray was one of the few men who had links with both the Rosicrucians and the Freemasons. He was a good Presbyterian, but, like other Scottish gentlemen of an adventurous disposition, he went to France in the 1630s and volunteered for the army of the Catholic King Louis XIII. Louis' Prime Minister, Cardinal Richelieu, sent him to fight with the French army on the Protestant side in the Thirty Years War, because Richelieu thought that it was in the national interests of France to oppose the Habsburg Holy Roman Empire and the King of Spain. After distinguished service in the French army, Moray returned to Scotland and fought for the Scottish Covenanters when they revolted against the attempts of Charles I and Archbishop Laud to force them to adopt a less Protestant form of Church service than that laid down in John Knox's service book. The Scots were victorious, and invaded England. While their army was stationed at Newcastle, Moray, who was Quarter-Master-General of the army, was initiated on 20 March 1641 into an Edinburgh masonic lodge, some of whose members were at Newcastle with the army. It was the first recorded case of admission to a military lodge which afterwards became a common practice in the army.[11]

The Scots won their war against Charles I, and Charles's defeat precipitated the revolution of 1640 and the outbreak of the Civil War in England. The Scots at first remained neutral in the English Civil War, and then came in on the side of Parliament against the King on condition that Parliament made England a Presbyterian state; but Robert Moray, like the Marquess of Montrose, was one of the minority of Presbyterians who, having fought against Charles I in the war of 1640, fought on Charles's side in the English Civil War. After Charles's defeat and capture, Moray escaped to France, but returned to England at the Restoration of Charles II, and was one of the founders of the Royal Society. Moray was a friend and patron of Thomas Vaughan, the Welsh Rosicrucian, who published the first English translation of the *Fama Fraternitatis*, which was supposed to have been written by Christian Rosenkrantz.[12]

The English antiquarian, Elias Ashmole, whose collection founded the Ashmolean Museum in Oxford, was a London solicitor. He fought for Charles I in the Civil War, and at the end of the war in 1646 he was taken prisoner by the Roundheads in Lancashire. While he was a prisoner he was initiated as a Freemason at Warrington on 16 October 1646. His father-in-law, Colonel Henry Mainwaring, who was an officer in the Roundhead army and a landowner in Cheshire, was initiated into the lodge at the same time. Ashmole continued all his life to be interested in Freemasonry, and recorded in his diary that he attended a meeting of a Freemasons' lodge in the hall of the Masons' Company of London in 1682.[13]

Masonic lodges, with accepted masons as members, were spreading all over England. Robert Plot, the Keeper of the Ashmolean Museum and professor of chemistry at Oxford University, who was not a Freemason, wrote about Freemasonry in his native county in his *Natural History of Stafford-shire* in 1686. He noted that it was spreading all over England, but faster in the moorlands of Stafford-shire than elsewhere;

> '... for here I found persons of the most eminent quality, that did not disdain to be of their *Fellowship*. Nor indeed need they, were it of that *Antiquity* and *honor*, that is pretended in a large parchment volum they have amongst them, containing the *History* and *Rules* of the craft of *masonry*.'[14]

In London, some eminent intellectuals, and several members of the Royal Society, were Freemasons; but many were not. Ashmole, Sir Robert Moray, and perhaps Inigo Jones, were Freemasons, but Isaac Newton was not. There has been a great dispute as to whether Sir Christopher Wren was a Freemason, and the evidence is contra-dictory; but a recently-discovered document seems to confirm that he was initiated as a Freemason in 1691, but never played an active part in the affairs of the craft.[15]

In Scotland, too, more gentlemen masons were joining. John Boswell, the laird of Auchinleck, who was initiated as a member of an Edinburgh lodge on 8 June 1600, may have been admitted merely because the masons thought it useful to have a gentleman as a member of their lodge; but in a lodge in Aberdeen in 1670, of the 49 master masons only 10 were operative masons; 4 were noblemen, 3 were gentlemen, 8 were lawyers and professional men, 9 were merchants, and 15 were tradesmen.[16]

Another theory has been put forward to explain the growth of Freemasonry in Scotland. This claims that the Freemasons were the Knights Templars, the military order which had been established to defend the Christian kingdom in Palestine. In 1094 the Pope launched the First Crusade, calling on Christian Europe to liberate Jerusalem, the city where Christ had lived and died, from the Muslim infidels. In July 1099 the Crusaders captured Jerusalem, and massacred most of the Muslim inhabitants of the city. They then established a Chris-tian kingdom in Jerusalem and the surrounding country which they called Outremer.

It was of course necessary to defend the Kingdom of Outremer against the attempts of the Muslims to recapture it, and in 1118 the Pope authorized the formation of a body of military knights who were called the Knights Templars. For 160 years the Knights

Templars defended Outremer against the Muslims, but with only partial success. In 1187 the Muslims, under their leader Saladin, overran Outremer and captured Jerusalem; and all the attempts of the Crusaders to recapture it were unsuccessful until the Holy Roman Emperor, Frederick II, went on the Sixth Crusade in 1228, at a time when he was engaged in a bitter power struggle against the Pope, who had excommunicated him and was offering financial help to the Muslims to enable them to defeat the Emperor's crusade. But Frederick, whose tolerant attitude on religious questions made him as willing to enter into friendly negotiations with the Muslims as he was with the Jews, made a treaty with the Sultan which gave him the right to occupy Damascus, Nazareth and Jerusalem for ten years; and without fighting a battle he became the only Christian leader to enter Jerusalem since Saladin captured it. While Pope Gregory IX committed the great sin of invading the territory of a ruler who was absent on a crusade, and ravaged Frederick's provinces in Northern Italy, Frederick crowned himself King in Jerusalem, as no bishop or priest was willing to crown him in view of the Pope's censures.

At the expiry of the ten-year treaty, the Muslims re-entered Jerusalem in 1239, and no Christian crusader ever entered it again. The next crusade was led by a far more pious and obedient son of the Church than Frederick II – by St Louis, King of France, who told his favourite, Jean, Sieur de Joinville, that the only way in which a good Christian should argue with a Jew was by driving his sword up to the hilt into the Jew's entrails. St Louis' two crusades failed. The last Crusade was abandoned in 1276. After this, there was nothing left for the Knights Templars to do.

During their stay in Outremer, the Templars had been in contact with Muslims and Jews, and became interested in their legends. They learned the stories about the building of Solomon's temple in Jerusalem. Some of them, like the members of other medieval monastic orders, became corrupted. The rumour spread that they engaged in unnatural vices, including homosexuality, and that they indulged in satanic anti-Christian practices; it was said that when new recruits joined the Templars, they spat on the crucifix during their initiation ceremonies, and denied Christ.

In 1305 King Philip IV of France (Philippe le Bel) decided to suppress the Templars and seize all their valuable property. Two Templars confessed to the authorities that they had indulged in immoral and satanic practices. The Pope was sceptical; for two years he refused to believe the King's allegations against the Templars. But as more and more of the arrested Knights Templars confessed their crimes, he agreed to order a thorough investigation of the Order. The Inquisitors interrogated more than 500 Templars and other witnesses in France; but they also pursued their inquiries in other countries, including England, where they examined 68 witnesses in London, Lincoln and York. In Scotland, 2 Templars and 41 other witnesses were questioned by the Bishop of St Andrews.

The Templars were found guilty of most of the crimes of which they were accused. The aged Grand Master, Jacques de Molay, and three of his highest officers eventually confessed, and after being held in prison for many months they were brought before the cardinals in the cathedral of Notre Dame in Paris on 11 March 1314, and sentenced to life imprisonment. Two of them accepted the judgement of the court, but Molay and the Provincial Grand Master of Normandy retracted their confessions, proclaimed that they were innocent of all the crimes with which they were charged, and that they deserved to die for having falsely accused their Order. The cardinals adjourned the proceedings till next day, saying that they would then deal with the two obstinate Templars; but news of what had happened was brought to King Philippe le Bel in his nearby palace of the Louvre. He ordered that Molay and the Provincial Grand Master of Normandy should immediately be burned alive as relapsed heretics on a little island in the River Seine between the royal gardens and the church of the Hermit Brothers of St Augustine; and the sentence was carried out the same evening.[17]

Although many of the Knights Templars were executed, sentenced to long terms of imprisonment, or pardoned after confessing their crimes, there is no doubt that some of them disappeared and escaped. What happened to them? All that is definitely known is that the King of Portugal, unlike the other European sovereigns, found the Templars not guilty of the charges against them. He granted political asylum to those of them who reached Portugal, and allowed them to reconstitute themselves under another name.

But in later centuries other rumours spread about the Knights Templars. It was said that old Jacques de Molay, though suffering from the effects of torture, was in full possession of his senses in the final days before he was burned. He succeeded in summoning a secret meeting of his higher officers in his prison cell and appointed four deputies who were to continue governing the Order in the

South, the North, the East and the West. The South was to be governed from Paris, the North from Stockholm, the East from Naples, and the West from Edinburgh.[18] Some of the Templars escaped to Scotland, where Robert Bruce was conducting his war of independence against King Edward II of England, and had been excommunicated by the Pope for having killed his rival claimant to the throne, Comyn, in a church. Bruce secretly granted asylum to the Knights Templars.

On 24 June 1314 – three months after Molay and his companion were burned – Bruce defeated Edward II at the Battle of Bannockburn. Our knowledge of precisely what happened at Bannockburn is a little hazy, because the earliest surviving account was written by a Scottish chronicler nearly sixty years later; but according to his story, at the decisive moment in the battle, the Scottish 'ghillies' – the servants who carried out routine duties in the Scottish camp – walked to the top of the hill overlooking the battlefield to see what was going on. The English saw them, and, wrongly believing that a new Scottish army was about to join in the battle, ran away. According to another theory, this new army was not the camp ghillies, but the Knights Templars to whom Bruce had granted asylum; they now showed their gratitude to Bruce by fighting for him at Bannockburn.

After the battle the Knights Templars took refuge in one of the islands off the west coast of Scotland. They stayed there for eighty years, but at the end of the fourteenth century moved to the east coast and settled in Aberdeen, where they called themselves Freemasons. By the sixteenth century they had moved again, going south to Edinburgh.[19] The story of their participation in the Battle of Bannockburn is certainly nonsense; and although it is not impossible that the accepted Freemasons in Scotland were descended from the Knights Templars, it is very unlikely.

Both the Freemasons and their enemies have been eager to believe that the Knights Templars were the ancestors of the Freemasons. Some Freemasons have thought that it was more romantic to be descended from a persecuted religious order of chivalry than from the trade unions of operative masons. On the other hand, the Catholic writer the Abbé Barruel, who in 1797 wrote a book blaming the Freemasons for the horrors of the French Revolution, argued that the Freemasons of 1789 were the heirs of the fourteenth-century Templars who had been rightly punished by their King and the Pope. He believed that the Freemasons were taking revenge for the justifiable actions of Philippe le Bel by guillotining Philippe's descendant, the saintly King Louis XVI.[20]

Barruel pointed out that the Templars were condemned after a legal process which lasted for several years; that the Pope at first refused to believe that they were guilty; and that he was convinced only when the evidence of guilt was overwhelming. The Templars confessed that they had spat on the crucifix, that they had worshiped a devil's head instead of Christ, that they indulged in saturnalian drinking parties on Good Friday, and that they threw new-born babies into the flames. Although torture was a regular procedure in criminal investigations in fourteenth-century France, only one of the Templars confessed under torture, and he said exactly the same as 200 other Templars who had confessed freely without torture. Barruel argued that the Templars were either guilty, or were too cowardly to deny their guilt. 'What glory is there for the Free-masons to claim as their fathers those people who, if they were not the most monstrous criminals, were at least the most cowardly of men?'[21]

Another Catholic anti-masonic writer in the eighteenth century, the Abbé Larudan, believed that that the Templars, when they were in the East defending Outremer, had come under the influence of the Hashish-eaters, the Arab sect who, under the influence of the drug *hashish* (cannabis), committed mass murder, and introduced a new word, 'assassin', into European languages. Larudan believed that the Knights Templars and their descendants the Freemasons, had learned their murderous habits from the Assassins.[22]

There seems to be no doubt that in the examination of the Templars the usual procedure was adopted. The suspects were first examined without torture; they were then threatened with torture, and shown the instruments of torture; and it was only if they still refused to confess that torture was finally applied. It is also clear that in most cases the moral pressure applied in the first stage, and the mere threat of torture, were enough to induce the Templars to confess. But it is also clear that in a few cases torture was applied, and twentieth-century readers will not be impressed by the argument that those who confessed under threat of torture, or even only under prolonged examination without the threat, were necessarily guilty of the crimes with which they were charged.

An even more preposterous version of the Templar story has recently been put forward by a writer whose vivid imagination and style is unfortunately not based on sufficient historical knowledge to make his theories plausible. According to his story, Jacques de Molay was crucified, not burned, and the face on the Turin shroud, which the Catholic Church claimed, until recently, was the face of Jesus, is that of Molay.[23] In fact, though the Roman Catholic Church in the Middle Ages resorted to all kinds of cruel practices, crucifixion was not, and could not have been, used, as the Church would never have allowed wicked sinners and heretics to have the honour of suffering the same death that Christ suffered on the cross.

It is not impossible that some Templars escaped to Scotland in the years after 1314, that their descendants found their way to Aberdeen and then to Edinburgh, and that they joined Freemasons' lodges; but they played no part in the development of speculative Freemasonry in Scotland and England. Although there are significant similarities between the regulations and procedures of the Knights Templars and the Freemasons, there are also important differences;[24] and the ideas of the speculative Freemasons in the eighteenth century had nothing in common with those of the Templars. The fourteenth-century Templars were not deists; they were not even Protestant heretics. But the story of the Templars did make a contribution to the ideas of the eighteenth-century Continental Freemasons; and here the Abbé Barruel was not entirely wrong. The martyrdom of Jacques de Molay was another example of the injustice and oppression of Catholic absolutism, and another reason for replacing it with a tolerant and enlightened deism and for overthrowing the Catholic monarchies.

CHAPTER 4

Grand Lodge

THE Restoration of 1660 brought to power the Cavaliers, or the Tory party as they later became known, and the rule of the Church of England, which persecuted both Roman Catholics and Protestant Nonconformists. The dissidents were not burned – no one was burned for heresy in England after 1612 – but the persecution was nevertheless severe, and many Catholics and Nonconformists suffered imprisonment and death. Although the King was himself a secret Catholic, he allowed his Protestant government in England to have Jesuits and other Catholic priests hanged, drawn and quartered on trumped-up charges of high treason. Nonconformist ministers were ejected from their benefices and their homes, for the Five Mile Act made it a criminal offence punishable by imprisonment for a former Nonconformist minister to live within five miles of any town where he had once had a benefice.

In Scotland the religious persecution was more severe, for there the Presbyterians rose in revolt against the Anglican government and murdered the Archbishop of St Andrews. The government sent soldiers into the Presbyterian strongholds in the south-west to crush the rebellion. The troops stopped people at random in the streets, the country lanes and the fields, and ordered them to say 'God save the King'. Those who refused were immediately shot without any kind of trial. Sometimes the soldiers tied their Presbyterian prisoners to posts that they had erected at low tide on the seashore, where the prisoners waited till the sea came in and drowned them.

This practice was commemorated in one of the most famous of Scottish folk songs.

Oh I'll take the high road, but ye'll take the low road,
And I'll be in Scotland before ye;
For me and my truelove will never meet again
On the bonnie, bonnie banks of Loch Lomond.

They had been to England to contact their Nonconformist allies across the Border, and on their return journey to Scotland she took the high road over the Cheviot Hills and arrived safely; but he took the low road along the coast, and was caught by the government soldiers, tied to a post on the seashore, and drowned.

Other Presbyterian prisoners were imprisoned in Dunnottar Castle on the east coast near Stonehaven, where they were tortured, for though torture had been abolished in England it survived in Scotland for another thirty years. Many of the prisoners died of starvation in the dungeons of Dunnottar. The older people afterwards remembered those terrible years as 'the Killing Time'.

In 1685 Charles II died, and was succeeded by his brother James, who was openly a Roman Catholic, though he upheld the rule of the Church of England, of which he was the Supreme Governor. He suspended the laws against Roman Catholics in England, but increased the severity of the persecution in Scotland. Then he changed his policy; he used his royal power of dispensation to grant religious toleration to both Roman Catholics and Nonconformists. He hoped to win the support of the Nonconformists, whose political allies were becoming known as the Whigs, against their Church of England persecutors; but the Quaker, William Penn, was the only Nonconformist leader who fell into James's trap and supported him. The others were too suspicious of Roman Catholics; they remembered the persecution of Protestants in England under Mary Tudor 130 years before, and more recently abroad by foreign Catholic sovereigns. Instead they made a united front with the Church of England against James, and invited James's son-in-law, William of Orange, to come from the Netherlands with an army to get rid of James. William landed in Devon, and in December 1688 James fled to France. In England it was a bloodless and 'glorious' revolution. There was armed Catholic resistance in Scotland and Ireland, but by 1690 it had been defeated.

The Revolution of 1688 introduced religious toleration for everyone except Roman Catholics and Unitarians. The Catholics were not persecuted as they had been in earlier times, but they were unable to play any part in public life, either as MPs, judges, army officers or at the universities, unless they took an oath that they did not believe in the Catholic doctrine of transubstantiation. This oath had to be taken by anyone who applied for any official position. The applicant was also required to swear that he had not been given a dispensation by the Pope allowing him to perjure himself by falsely swearing that he rejected transubstantiation. This was a remarkably silly provision, because if he had been granted a Papal dispensation to swear falsely that he did not believe in transubstantiation, he might also have been granted a dispensation to swear that he had not been granted a dispensation.

Not surprisingly, many Catholics believed that the Freemasons had played an important part in bringing about the Revolution of 1688, and in later years the Freemasons themselves were very ready to claim the credit for it. But in fact the masons played no part at all in the Revolution. None of the leading figures in the Revolution were Freemasons – not William III, nor his Whig Lord Chancellor Lord Somers; not Lord Churchill, the commander-in-chief of James II's army, who deserted James at a critical moment during the Revolution, and was rewarded by being created Earl of Marlborough; not the seven bishops whose acquittal by a London jury, when they were prosecuted by James II for sedition, sparked off the Revolution; not George Savile, Marquess of Halifax, and the other leading dignitaries who signed the invitation to William of Orange to invade England and make himself king. While the Revolution was taking place, the Freemasons were quietly attending their lodge meetings; but after it had succeeded, they were able to take advantage of the new situation, which was much more favourable for them.

John Toland, an Irish Presbyterian from Londonderry, was not a Freemason, but he went further than any mason in advocating deism. After studying at Oxford and travelling abroad, he published a book in 1690 which he could not have published before the Revolution. In his *Christianity not Mysterious*, he advocated a simple belief in God and in the moral teaching of Jesus Christ without any discussion about transubstantiation or any other controversial issue between Protestants and Catholics.

Although many people in England strongly disapproved of his book, no one there took any action against him; but Toland's fellow-Presbyterians in Ulster were less tolerant, in the year when William III and the Protestant Cause finally triumphed over James II at the

Battle of the Boyne, and discriminatory laws against Catholics were being rigorously enforced. Toland was prosecuted for blasphemy in the Irish courts, but the proceedings dragged on, and eventually he and his publishers withdrew the book. They received no further punishment.

Toland founded a philosophical society at Oxford, the Socrates Society, and wrote another book, *Panchristicon*, explaining the society's attitude.

Question: Under what auspices do we open this Society?
Answer: Under the auspices of Philosophy.
Question: To whom must this assembly, to whom must all our thoughts, words and actions be continually directed?
Answer: To the three-fold aim of the wise, Truth, Freedom, Virtue.[1]

Freemasons were becoming unpopular in certain quarters. In 1698 a leaflet attacking the Freemasons was distributed in the streets of London. The author's name was given as 'Mr Winter', but no one has been able to find out anything about him; and his leaflet had so little effect that it disappeared without trace until it was discovered by masonic historians in 1937. There seems to be very little doubt that the writer was a High Anglican Tory.

He told 'all godly people in the City of London' that he must warn them 'of the Mischiefs and Evils practised in the Sight of God by those called Freed Masons ... For this develish Sect of Men are Meeters in secret which swear against all without their Following. They are the Anti Christ which was to come, leading Men from fear of God.' It was the secrecy of the masons, and their secret oaths, which alarmed Mr Winter, as it was to alarm all the anti-masons during the next 300 years. If the Freemasons were a lawful and reputable society, why the secrecy? Men do not hide their virtues and their good deeds; it is their vices and crimes which they wish to conceal.[2]

But if the masons' secrecy aroused the suspicions of the anti-masons, it fascinated the masons themselves. They liked to believe that they, and they alone, knew important secrets. The seventeenth century was a period of new discoveries, in geography, medicine and science. Were there even more important new discoveries that God had revealed only to the Freemasons? Men became convinced that the masonic secrets were the secrets that they had always wished to discover. The Welsh clergyman and poet, Goronwy Owen, believed that if he joined a Freemasons' lodge, he would discover the legends of the ancient Welsh Druids. The distinguished eighteenth-century antiquarian, Dr William Stukeley, wrote in his autobiography that he had joined the Freemasons out of curiosity, 'suspecting it to be the remains of the mysteries of the ancients'.[3]

When Queen Anne died in 1714, Georg Ludwig, the Elector of Hanover, became King George I of England, Scotland and Ireland, under the provisions of the Act of Settlement of 1701 which vested the crown in the descendants of James I's Protestant granddaughter, the Electress Sophia of Hanover, as long as they were Protestants; but if any of her descendants became a Roman Catholic, or married a Roman Catholic, he could not succeed to, or continue on, the throne. It was the triumph of what people called 'the House of Hanover and the Protestant Succession'. Next year the supporters of James II's Roman Catholic son, who was a refugee in Lorraine and claimed to be King James III of England, launched a Jacobite rebellion in Scotland which was suppressed without much difficulty. A small number of Scottish Jacobites were executed.

The Freemasons decided that the time had come to take an important step forward, and in 1717 four London lodges decided to found Grand Lodge. There were more than four lodges in London, and there were lodges in York and elsewhere in England; but these four London lodges decided to act on their own and found a national Grand Lodge which would have authority over all the lodges in England. The four lodges were the lodge that was afterwards named Lodge No. 1, which met at the Goose and Gridiron alehouse in St Paul's churchyard; Lodge No. 2, which met at the Crown alehouse in Parker's Lane, near Drury Lane; Lodge No. 3, which met at the Apple Tree tavern in Charles Street, Covent Garden; and Lodge No. 4, which met at the Rummer and Grapes tavern in Channel Row, Westminster. Each of the first three lodges had about 15 members. Most of them were operative masons, or carpenters, or connected in some way with the building trade, though they included a few gentlemen. Lodge No. 4 had 70 members; they were nearly all gentlemen, and a few were noblemen.

The members of the four lodges held a meeting at the Apple Tree tavern in Charles Street, Covent Garden, the meeting place of Lodge No. 3, in February 1717, and decided to form a Grand Lodge. They met on St John the Baptist's Day, 24 June 1717, at the Goose and Gridirion alehouse in St Paul's churchyard, the meeting place of Lodge No. 1, and by a show of hands elected Anthony Sayer, 'gentleman', of Lodge No. 3, as their Grand Master.[4]

Two men, one a Scotsman and one a Frenchman, seem to have played the leading part in the foundation of Grand Lodge, though there is no written record that either of them were initiated as Freemasons until a few years later. The Scotsman was the Reverend James Anderson, from Aberdeen, where he was born and educated, and became a minister of the Presbyterian Church of Scotland in 1702, when he was aged 23. In 1709 he moved to London, and became the minister at Nonconformist chapels in Glasshouse Street, Swallow Street, Piccadilly, and Lisle Street in Leicester Fields. He wrote a long book, *Royal Genealogies, or the Genealogical Tables of Emperors, Kings and Princes from Adam to this time*. It was a translation of a German work with some additions taken from another English author. None of his written works have any value or interest except for his *Book of Constitutions of the Antient and Honourable Fraternity of Free and Accepted Masons*, which he wrote at the orders of Grand Lodge in 1723 and elaborated in a second edition in 1738.[5]

The Frenchman was a more important figure. Jean Théophile Desaguliers was the son of Jean Desaguliers, the pastor of a French Protestant congregation in the village of Aitré near La Rochelle. It had been a strongly Protestant district for more than a hundred years. When the Protestant leader, Henry of Navarre, converted to Roman Catholicism because he thought that Paris was worth a Mass, and became King Henry IV of France, he granted religious toleration to his Protestant followers throughout most of France; but under his grandson, Louis XIV, the rights of the Protestants were gradually whittled away, and in 1685 Louis revoked the Edict of Nantes. Many French Protestants fled abroad, and came as refugees to England and the Protestant cantons of Switzerland; but Louis then forbade them to emigrate without government permission. Anyone who was caught trying to leave the kingdom illegally was sentenced to serve for five years as a slave in the galleys. Protestant pastors were allowed to leave, but they were not allowed to take their children with them. The children had to remain in France to be educated as Roman Catholics.

Jean Desaguliers and his wife were given permission to leave France, but they knew that they would not be allowed to take their two-year-old son, Jean Théophile, with them. They decided to smuggle him out of the country. As they boarded an English ship at La Rochelle, they carried a barrel containing their linen. Their son was sleeping in the barrel hidden under the linen. They silently prayed that he would not awake and cry out as they calmly, without any outward sign of nervousness, walked past the soldiers on the quay-side. Jean Théophile slept soundly and was not discovered, and the three of them sailed safely in the English ship to Guernsey in the Channel Islands.

They lived for some years in Guernsey, where Jean Desaguliers was pastor to French Protestant refugees. Then he moved to London with his family. He was ordained into the Church of England and became the minister to a congregation of French Protestant refugees in Swallow Street, Piccadilly. He was afterwards a schoolmaster in Islington. His son, Jean Théophile, was 16 when his father died in 1699. He completed his education with a tutor in Sutton Coldfield, and then went to Corpus Christi College, Oxford. He studied theology, but was also interested in scientific projects.

In 1702 England and the Netherlands, and the Habsburg Austrian Empire, went to war with Louis XIV because Louis was supporting the claim of his grandson to the throne of Spain. In the War of the Spanish Succession, Louis's armies were for the first time repeatedly defeated by the Austrian general, Prince Eugène of Savoy, and by the British under John Churchill, Duke of Marlborough. After defeating the French at Blenheim, Ramillies and Oudenarde, Marlborough and Eugène invaded the north of France and won another victory over the French at Malplaquet. In the south of France, the Protestants took the opportunity to rise in revolt, but were brutally suppressed by Louis's troops.

At such a time, John Théophilus Desaguliers found it difficult to concentrate on his theological studies. He wished to play his part in the struggle against Louis XIV. Using his scientific knowledge, he designed a new type of gun for use in siege warfare, and sent his design to the War Office in London. The artillery experts were impressed, the gun was manufactured, and it was used by Marlborough's army against the French forts in Flanders. When Louis XIV was forced, for the first time, to make an unsatisfactory peace, Desaguliers felt that he had made his contribution to the defeat of Papist absolutism.

He was ordained into the Church of England, and through his

contacts in Oxford was appointed to benefices in Middlesex, Norfolk and Essex, and became chaplain to the Duke of Chandos. He lectured in experimental philosophy at Oxford. By the time he was 30 he had married and had acquired a house in London, and was lecturing in London on natural philosophy and on Isaac Newton's theories. In 1714 he was elected a Fellow of the Royal Society, and was later appointed Curator of the Society. In 1717 he lectured before King George I at Hampton Court.[6]

He probably became interested in Freemasonry because he thought that it was the best method of furthering the tolerant deism in religion in which he believed. He had a shrewd understanding of the society which had been established in his country of adoption by the Revolution of 1688 and the accession of the House of Hanover; he knew that England had become a nation ruled by the great landed aristocracy. If the nobility could be persuaded to become Freemasons, then Freemasonry would flourish as a society of deists, free from persecution or harassment.

He had no difficulty in persuading his many friends among the English aristocracy to become Freemasons. It was in line with the traditions of the aristocracy and the ruling class. For centuries the Christian Church had upheld the class structure of society while teaching that men of all social classes were equal in the sight of God. In His infinite wisdom, God had ordained that some of His beloved children should be princes and rulers, and others, whom He loved just as much, should be subjects; some should be rich and some should be poor, some masters and slaveowners, and some slaves; but the rulers should realize that their privileged position had been given them by God, and should humble themselves before God. So for centuries, Christian Kings had 'crept to the cross' on Good Friday, advancing on their knees to a statue of Christ; and they had washed the feet of beggars on Maundy Thursday. An organization in which all the members were brothers, but which treated aristocratic brothers with obsequious flattery, had great appeal to many English aristocrats, who were famous throughout Europe for their readiness to fraternize with their social inferiors. They were happy to join a society which had its historic links with famous Biblical figures, which accepted the House of Hanover and the Protestant Succession, but also avoided religious and political controversy, and held meetings where supporters of conflicting religions could meet together as personal friends.

In 1723 the principles of Masonry were published by Anderson in his *Constitutions*; but though Anderson had been instructed by Grand Lodge to write the *Constitutions*, his draft was discussed and amended by a committee of fourteen of the leading members of Grand Lodge, including Desaguliers.[7] It is unlikely that Anderson was personally responsible for the principles of Freemasonry laid down in his *Constitutions*. They stated the loyalty of the Freemasons to the House of Hanover; but, subject to this, they avoided all declarations of political allegiance, and forbade political discussions in the lodges. They emphasized the dominant role of the aristocracy in Freemasonry, and, where religion was concerned, they put forward principles which came close to deism.

The *Constitutions* stated that 'King George I entered London most magnificently on 20 September 1714, and after the rebellion was over, A.D.1716', the members of the four lodges decided to form Grand Lodge. In referring to 1716, Anderson was using the Old Style Julian Calendar by which, until 1752, the year began on 25 March. The meeting at which it was decided to form a Grand Lodge was held in February 1717. Anderson then states that at this first meeting, the members present decided 'to choose a Grand Master from among themselves, till they should have the honour of a Noble Brother at their Head'.[8]

On 24 June 1717, at the first annual meeting of the new Grand Lodge, Sayer was elected Grand Master, and the members present 'paid him homage'. Next year, on 24 June 1718, Brother Payne was elected Grand Master, with Captain Josiah Elliot, an army officer, and Mr Jacob Lamball, carpenter of the City of London, as his Grand Wardens. On 24 June 1719 John Theophilus Desaguliers was elected Grand Master, and in 1720 Payne was chosen as Grand Master for the second time. This was the last occasion on which a commoner was elected Grand Master. On 24 June 1721 the Duke of Montagu was chosen as Grand Master, and thereafter, for the next 278 years, every Grand Master has always been either a nobleman or a member of the royal family. At this annual meeting of Grand Lodge in 1720, it was decided that the Grand Wardens should no longer be elected, but should be appointed by the Grand Master, who could appoint a Deputy Master and two Grand Wardens to assist him, 'according to ancient custom, when Noble Brothers were Grand Masters'. At the next meeting of Grand Lodge, on 25 March 1721, Mr Payne proposed that his successor as Grand Master should be 'our most

Noble Brother John, Duke of Montagu', who should take office on 24 June; and 'they all expressed great joy at the happy prospect of being again patronised by noble Grand Masters, as in the prosperous times of Free Masonry'.[9]

John Montagu, second Duke of Montagu, was aged 31, but was already one of the great personages in the state. He had acted as High Constable at the coronation of George I, and was colonel of a regiment of the Horse Guards. The year after he was elected Grand Master, he was appointed Governor of the St Lucia and St Vincent Islands in the West Indies, but he remained in London and appointed a deputy to carry out his duties in the West Indies. As a boy of 15, he had been present with Marlborough at the siege of Menin, and he afterwards married Marlborough's youngest daughter, Lady Mary Churchill. He was reputed to be the richest man in England.[10]

The Freemasons were not so fortunate with their choice of a Grand Master in 1722. They chose Philip Wharton, Duke of Wharton, though he was only 24. His father, Thomas Wharton, the first Marquess of Wharton, had been a zealous Whig supporter of the Revolution of 1688. He had written the words of the song *Lillibullero*, which he set to the tune of a song in Purcell's opera *The Indian Queen*. The song, which described the plans of Irish Catholics to conquer England for James II and massacre English Protestants, had spontaneously become the song of the Revolution. Thomas Wharton claimed that he had 'sung a King out of three kingdoms'. When his son Philip was born, William III was his godfather, and Princess Anne, the future Queen Anne, was his godmother.

But Philip Wharton was brought up on the Continent, and came into contact with Jacobites, including the Pretender, James III, who offered, if he regained his English kingdom, to make Wharton a duke. When Wharton returned to England, he married, but soon separated from his wife, and established a reputation as a notorious libertine and member of the Hellfire Club, whose members indulged in scandalous orgies. Concealing his links with the Jacobites, he took his seat in the Irish House of Lords, though at 19 he was still under age. In his speeches in the Irish Parliament he strongly supported the House of Hanover, and soon after he had succeeded his father as Marquess of Wharton, George I created him Duke of Wharton.

He had great personal charm and knew how to fascinate women. He enjoyed participating in convivial societies, and became an active liveryman of the Wax Chandlers' Company. He took it into his head that he wished to become Grand Master of the Freemasons, and used his influence and charm to secure his election. The Freemasons were not altogether happy about him, but he was, after all, a duke, and he was chosen as Grand Master in 1722. The Duke of Montagu challenged the legality of his election; but Desaguliers persuaded Montagu not to endanger the unity of the Freemasons by protesting against it, and Montagu agreed to accept Wharton on condition that Wharton appointed Desaguliers as his Deputy Grand Master. Next year the Earl of Dalkeith was elected as Grand Master. Wharton challenged the validity of Dalkeith's election, but Grand Lodge supported Dalkeith and expelled Wharton from the craft. Wharton then formed another society, the Gormogones, which he hoped would rival the Freemasons; but no one took the Gormogones seriously.

Soon afterwards Wharton went abroad to escape his creditors, and resumed his contacts with the Jacobites. In Parma he met James III, who created him Duke of Northumberland. Wharton then went to Spain, and urged the King of Spain to declare war on England. The King of Spain appointed him colonel of an Irish regiment in the Spanish army, and Wharton took part in an attack on Gibraltar, in which he was wounded. In England he was denounced as a traitor; he was expelled from the House of Lords, and his property was confiscated. Despite his quarrels with the English Freemasons, he founded the first Freemasons' lodge in Spain. He made an unsuccessful attempt to change sides again, and to offer his services to Horace Walpole, the British ambassador in Paris, who was an active Freemason; but Horace Walpole refused to see him. Wharton became a Roman Catholic, and when he died in a Franciscan monastery in Paris in 1731, he was only 33.[11]

Despite their unfortunate experience with Wharton, the Freemasons continued to flourish under the other noble Grand Masters who followed him. When Dr William Stukeley decided to become a Freemason soon after Grand Lodge was formed, he at first found it difficult to find enough Freemasons to constitute the number necessary to take part in the initiation ceremony; but things were very different after it was known in London that a succession of dukes and lords were Grand Masters. The number of lodges under the authority of Grand Lodge increased from the original four in 1717 to 126 in 1735.[12]

Under the protection of the aristocracy, the Freemasons could safely declare their religious principles. Although some masonic historians have denied that Anderson's *Constitutions* advocated deism, it came close to doing so. The statement about religion is completely different from the charges of the Roman Catholic operative masons of the Middle Ages.

A mason is obliged by his tenure to obey the moral law; and if he rightly understands the Art, he will never be a stupid Atheist, nor an irreligious libertine. But though in ancient Times Masons were charged in every country to be of the religion of that country or nation, whatever it was, yet 'tis now thought more expedient only to oblige them to that religion in which all men agree, leaving their particular opinions to themselves; that is to be good men and true, or men of honour and honesty, by whatever denominations or persuasions they may be distinguished; whereby Masonry becomes the centre of union, and the means of consolidating true friendship among persons that must have remained at a perpetual distance.[13]

This opened the Freemasons' lodges to anyone who believed in God, or the 'Great Architect of the Universe' as He is called in Anderson's *Constitutions*.[14] Roman Catholics were not excluded. They could not be MPs, army officers, or hold any public position in the state; but they would be welcome in a Freemasons' lodge. Jews were also welcome, though they were at first a little reluctant to join. Jews had been admitted, perhaps as early as 1724, and certainly by 1732.[15]

The article on the duty of obedience to the King and his government was unusual.

A mason is a peaceable subject to the civil powers, wherever he resides or works, and is never to be concerned in plots and conspiracies against the peace and welfare of the nation. If a brother should be a rebel against the state, he is not to be countenanced in his rebellion, however he may be pitied as an unhappy man; and if convicted of no other crime, though the brotherhood must and ought to dismiss his rebellion, and give no umbrage or ground of political jealousy to the government for the time being; they cannot expel him from the lodge, and his relation to it remains indefeasible.[16]

This provision, while clearly repudiating treason, sedition and rebellion against the state, shows a very tolerant understanding of those who refuse to obey the existing government: the Freemasons were determined that the rights and wrongs of the rebels' activities should not be discussed in the lodge. It was very different from the violent and abusive denunciations of traitors in which commentators indulged in Tudor times, and would similarly indulge in the totalitarian dictatorships of the twentieth century.

The ban on religious and political discussion in the lodge appealed to many people who were disgusted by the bitterness of the controversies of the seventeenth century.

> The next thing that I shall remember you of is, to avoid politics and religion. Have nothing to do with these, as you tender your own welfare. . . . Ours is the best policy, it is honesty; it is the policy of the holy Jesus, who never disturbed governments, but left them as he found them, and rendered to Caesar the things that were Caesar's. . . . It is the same thing in relation to the religion we profess, which is the best that ever was, or will or can be . . . for it is the law of Nature, which is the law of God, for God is Nature. It is to love God above all things, and our neighbour as our self; this is the true, primitive, catholic and universal religion agreed to be so in all times and ages.[17]

The succession of noble brothers who served as Grand Masters in the years following 1723 very largely succeeded in reassuring the public that the Freemasons were not a dangerous and subversive organization. Occasionally someone suggested that their lodges might be a meeting place of Jacobite agents, but very few people took this suggestion seriously. The Mayor of Canterbury in 1732 issued a proclamation against the Freemasons; but this was exceptional, and the Mayor was widely condemned for his action.[18] There were still many critics of the Freemasons, but they ridiculed, rather than feared, them.

Unlike in earlier years, the Freemasons now went out of their way to draw public attention to themselves. On their feast day, 24 June, every year, they went in procession through the streets of London and Westminster, dressed in their masonic robes and aprons, with the Grand Master at their head. They hired a London theatre for a special performance of a Shakespeare play, or Farquhar's *The*

Recruiting Officer, which the Grand Master and the other brothers attended. A special prologue and epilogue were written for the performance and spoken by a well-known actor and actress, who praised the Freemasons, and stated what an honour it was to perform before the noble Duke the Grand Master and his brothers. The Freemasons were already engaging in a good deal of charitable work; but they succeeded in establishing a reputation of being what in fact they very largely were – a social club where middle-class gentlemen and tradesmen fraternized with members of the aristocracy.

The critics ridiculed the Freemasons for their ceremonies, for the masonic robes in which they went in procession, for their claims to be descended from the masons who built Solomon's temple and for the other historical assertions made in Anderson's *Constitutions*. Another accusation was now made against the Freemasons. Women were not admitted to their lodges, and they were often denounced as women-haters. This is a significant accusation. No one in the 1720s expected women to be admitted to Parliament, to local government bodies, to juries, to the legal or medical professions, or to the universities. But women did play a leading part in social life, particularly in aristocratic circles; they were the centre of attention at balls, dinner parties, and other social functions. If people were surprised that women were excluded from masonic lodges, it was because they regarded the meetings at the lodges, not as religious, political or educational meetings, but as social gatherings.

The Freemasons explained that women were not admitted to their lodges because, historically, women had never been operative masons; because the presence of women would distract the men from attending to the serious business of the lodge; and to prevent anyone from suggesting that immoral conduct took place in the lodge. Sometimes an additional reason was given: that women, with their tendency to gossip, could not be trusted to keep the secrets of the lodge.

The Freemasons were anxious to rebut the accusation that they hated women or that they were bad husbands. When they hired the Theatre Royal in Drury Lane for a special performance of Shakespeare's *Henry IV Part II* on 30 December 1728, the epilogue, composed for the occasion, was spoken by the actress, Mrs Thurmond. She described how at first she had been taken aback to find that her husband was a Freemason; but when he returned home from the lodge meetings, he was always particularly kind and affectionate.

Ye married ladies, 'tis a happy life,
Believe me, that of a Freemason's wife.
Though they conceal the secrets of their friends
In love and truth they make us full amends.[19]

The critics asked what the Freemasons did in their lodges that they did not wish their wives to know. A scurrilous and very obscene poem entitled *The Free Masons: an Hudibrastick Poem*, accused them of having sex with the famous prostitute, Sally Salisbury.[20] Others suggested that they were homosexuals who committed sodomy in the lodges.

A more subtle criticism of the Freemasons was made in *The Free Masons' Accusation and Defence*, which was published anonymously in 1726. It purported to be letters from a country gentleman to his son, a young man studying law at the Temple in London, and the son's replies. The father writes in alarm that he has heard that his son intends to become a Freemason. He asks his son the usual question: if the practices of the Freemasons are good, and not evil, why are they at such pains to keep them secret? He also informs his son that Freemasons have always been an assembly of trouble-makers against whom an Act of Parliament was passed in Henry VI's reign in 1425. The son writes to his father that today Freemasons are not trouble-makers, but gentlemen, and noblemen of the highest rank, and that he has been invited to join them by his friend Sir Thomas, who is the master of a lodge. The father then changes his line of argument. It may be all right for noblemen and wealthy gentlemen, in possession of a large fortune, to dissipate it in riotous living in Freemasons' lodges; but hardworking law students should avoid such follies. The correspondence ends with the son respectfully disagreeing with his father's assessment of the Freemasons, but promising that out of respect for his father's wishes he will not join the lodge.[21]

There is little doubt that the letters of both the father and the son were written by the same author, and that he intended the weight of the arguments to be against, and not for, the Freemasons; but it is difficult to see why his publication, with its reasoned statements, should have angered the Freemasons as much as it did.[22]

Desaguliers went to Edinburgh to establish contact with the Scottish Freemasons, and was admitted as a brother in a Scottish lodge. While he was there, he used his scientific and engineering knowledge to advise the Provost of Edinburgh how to improve the city's water supply. When he returned to London he suggested improvements to the ventilation of the House of Commons. He was appointed tutor to George II's son, Frederick, Prince of Wales.[23]

The English Grand Lodge had begun to organize lodges among English residents abroad, and they were joined by those natives in these foreign countries who were attracted by Freemasonry. In 1731 Desaguliers and the Earl of Chesterfield went to The Hague, where Desaguliers presided at a meeting of a lodge in which Francis, Duke of Lorraine, who was related to the Holy Roman Emperor, Charles VI, was initiated as a Freemason.[24] Some months later, the Duke of Lorraine came to London, and when he was entertained by the Freemasons at a banquet at the Devil's Tavern near Temple Bar, he brought the Prince of Wales with him as a guest. The Freemasons saw to it that the presence of His Royal Highness the Prince of Wales and His Serene Highness the Duke of Lorraine was duly reported in *The Daily Post* of 4 December 1731.[25]

The Freemasons enjoyed an even greater triumph on 5 November 1737, when the Grand Master, the Earl of Darnley, with Desaguliers and other leading brothers of Grand Lodge, went to the Prince of Wales's palace at Kew and initiated the Prince as a Freemason.[26] Next year, when the Prince of Wales was on holiday in Bath, Darnley and Desaguliers and the others went to Bath and held an Extraordinary Lodge at the Bear Tavern for the Prince's benefit on the King's birthday, which was duly reported in the *St James's Evening Post* of 30 October 1738.[27]

The Freemasons resorted to every means to obtain favourable press publicity and to reveal the identity of the noble and royal brothers who joined them; but at the same time they continued to emphasize that they had secrets which they would never reveal to non-members. They would not abandon the secrecy, because this was one of the factors which made men wish to become Freemasons. The prospect of joining a society which held the vital secrets of the universe that God had revealed to the Freemasons alone, was as attractive as the possibility of sitting next to a duke or other noble brother at dinner.

Some of the Freemasons' critics wondered if they really had any secrets at all. Someone suggested this to the philosopher, John Locke, who, unlike many of his fellow-philosophers, was not a Freemason. 'Even if this were its whole secret', said Locke, 'namely that it has no secret, yet it is no small feat to keep that a secret.'[28]

The Freemasons were in the habit of singing at their banquets.

Four of their songs were actually included in Anderson's *Constitutions*. They told of the masons' links with the great Biblical figures, with Adam and Noah, as well as with many English Kings:

> Great Kings, Dukes and Lords have laid by their swords
> That our mystery to put a good grace on;
> And ne'er been ashamed to hear themselves named
> As a free or an accepted mason.[29]

Other songs were published in various song books. Some repudiated the idea that Freemasons did not like women. 'No mortal can more the ladies adore than a free and an accepted mason.' 'We love our country and our King – We toast the ladies, dance and sing.'[30]
They sang about how

> God himself I'll prove for to be
> The first Great Master of masonry.
> He took up his compass with masterly hand,
> He stretched out his line and he measured the land,
> He laid the foundations of earth and sea
> By the first rules of masonry.[31]

The Freemasons were very sure of themselves. When their enemies accused them of being sodomites, they did not deign to deny these lies. Why should they worry? As God had created Man to be above the animals, so he had created masons to be above other men.[32] Masons were 'brothers of Princes and fellows of Kings'.[33] So let the bottle go round again! Fill the glasses to the brim!

> We'll be free and merry
> Drinking port and sherry.
> And let it, let it run the table round,
> While envy does the masons' foes confound![34]

Masonry had changed since the days when hard-working operative masons stopped working on the cathedral face, and climbed down to enjoy an ample but simple dinner in the wooden hut that they called their lodge. It was to change again in the next 140 years. During this time two French Freemasons wrote two songs which were very different from the drinking songs in Anderson's *Consti-tutions* and the other masonic song books of the 1730s. *'Allons enfants de la patrie, Le jour de gloire est arrivé'* wrote Brother Rouget de Lisle in 1791; and in 1872 Brother Eugène Pottier wrote: *'C'est la lutte finale, groupons-nous et demain, L'Internationale sera le genre humain!'*[35] These two masonic songs, *La Marseillaise* and *L'Internationale*, would in turn arouse the greatest enthusiasm and fear throughout Europe and the world as the anthems of international revolution.

◆

CHAPTER 5

The Pope's Bull

THE news of the formation of Grand Lodge and the activities of the English Freemasons spread quickly throughout Europe. By the 1730s, masonic lodges had been formed in the Netherlands, France, Germany, the Austrian Empire, several of the Italian states, Spain and Sweden. Many of them were formed directly by representatives of English Grand Lodge who travelled to the foreign country for this purpose; others were formed independently of Grand Lodge by local residents, but under the inspiration of the English example. Some later German historians have tried to prove that the German masonic lodges of the eighteenth century had a German origin; but this is untrue. The eighteenth-century Freemasons in Germany and France had no links at all with the German Steinmetzen or the French Compagnonnage, which by then had ceased to exist like the medieval lodges of the operative masons in England.

Freemasonry had the same appeal to the aristocracy and the middle classes in Europe as it had in England; but on the Continent another factor was involved. Freemasonry was English; and whereas in England the patronage of the English aristocracy ensured its respectability and very largely disarmed all suspicion of its activities, in the other countries of Europe this was both an attraction and a reason to fear the Freemasons. To the European intellectuals England was the country of the Revolution of 1688, where constitutional government and the rule of law had replaced the arbitrary despotism of an absolute monarch. In France Louis XIV had said 'I am the State'. In England, the division of powers between the Executive, the Legislature and the Judiciary ensured that none of them could claim that it alone was the State. In England the King and his government could govern the realm only subject to the laws which had been passed by

Parliament; and neither King nor Parliament, but only the judges, decided whether the agents of the Executive had acted within the laws that the Legislature had made. In France, the King could issue a *lettre de cachet* ordering anyone to be imprisoned without trial for many years in the Bastille or some other prison; in England the writ of habeas corpus ensured that no one could be unlawfully imprisoned except when convicted by a jury, or otherwise under process of law as established by the independent Judiciary in the courts of law. In England the rule of the King had been replaced by the rule of the aristocracy.

Most of the foreign philosophers and other intellectuals who so greatly admired the English constitution had never been to England. The English intellectuals themselves, who knew the reality, were less favourably impressed. They knew about the corruption in public life, which had led the Prime Minister, Sir Robert Walpole, to say about the MPs in the House of Commons: 'All those men have their price'; about the unrestrained coarseness and scurillity of the free English press, of which the attack on the Freemasons in the Hudibrastick poem was only one example; of the improper exercise of influence by the aristocracy in the administration of justice in the law courts, of which Henry Fielding, who was himself a JP in Middlesex, wrote in his novels; of the criminal underworld, and its links with corrupt lawyers and prison warders, which Gay treated lightheartedly in his *Beggar's Opera*; of the poverty and degradation of the poor in London, which the Freemason William Hogarth described in his paintings. Most of the foreign admirers of England did not know about these things. Those who did thought that, with all its faults, corrupt aristocratic-dominated England was better than the royal despotisms of Europe.

So the foreign intellectuals and the nobility were eager to join English Freemasonry; but their governments were worried. In addition to the general suspicion of a secret society, there was especial fear of a secret society which was linked to constitutional Protestant England. In England the presence of the nobility was a guarantee of the respectability of the Freemasons; in Europe, the King and his officials knew that the nobility sometimes made revolutions against the King, as the English nobility had done in 1688.

The first government to take action against the Freemasons was not a Catholic despotism but Protestant Holland, after a rioting mob in Amsterdam had attacked a Freemasons' lodge in the city. Four years after Desaguliers and the Earl of Chesterfield had held a lodge meeting at The Hague at which the Duke of Lorraine had been initiated, the President and Council of Holland, Zeeland and Friesland, meeting at The Hague on 12 December 1735, issued a proclamation stating that 'certain persons here at The Hague, under a specious pretence of belonging to a so-called Fraternity of Freemasons, meeting together under a Grand Master', had formed an illegal association; for 'it is in no way to be supposed that the study of architecture is the sole and principal object of their meetings'. The real object was faction and debauchery, and they were illegal. The authorities must prevent such meetings from being held, and anyone who allowed a room in his house to be used for a Freemasons' meeting was committing an offence.[1]

The English Freemasons took up the cudgels on behalf of the Freemasons in The Hague. On 30 December they sent a formal protest, in which they tried to identify the Freemasons with the royal house of Nassau. They wrote that the Council of Holland, Zeeland and Friesland were Republicans, the heirs to the faction of De Witt which had been overthrown by William of Orange in 1672, before he became King of England, when he established his personal rule in the Netherlands in place of the republic. They accused the Council of acting against the Freemasons because they thought that the Freemasons were planning ways of upholding the authority of the Prince of Orange.[2]

In various states of Italy, the masonic lodges were established by the English Jacobite refugees, many of whom were Roman Catholics. The Revolution of 1688 had broken out because James II issued his Declaration of Indulgence granting religious toleration to Roman Catholics and Nonconformists; during his short rule in Ireland, in 1689, he had granted religious toleration; and James III was repeatedly assuring the English Protestants that if he became King of England he would not burn or otherwise persecute the Protestants. The Protestants did not believe him; they thought it was a trick, a political tactic on his part. Their attitude was understandable in view of the persecuting record of Roman Catholic sovereigns from Philip II of Spain to Louis XIV of France; but in fact the Old Pretender, as they called James III, was certainly sincere. If he had regained his kingdom he would not have persecuted Protestants, and might well have become a Protestant himself in order to win popularity with the majority of his subjects.

Sincerely or no, the Jacobite leaders had been saying for thirty years that they believed in religious toleration, and this made it easier for their followers to think that they could join a Freemasons' lodge, and accept the Freemasons' doctrine of friendship with Protestants and religious toleration, without betraying the Jacobite cause or their Roman Catholic faith. One of the most prominent Jacobite leaders, Charles Radclyffe, Earl of Derwentwater, was an active Freemason. His brother, the previous Earl of Derwentwater, had been prominent in the Jacobite rebellion of 1715, in which Charles himself had also taken part when he was still very young. The Earl was sentenced to death for his treason and beheaded on Tower Hill. Charles was also imprisoned in the Tower, but broke out of the prison with a few of his young friends, and escaped. He now took his brother's title of Earl of Derwentwater, though in England he was the traitor, Charles Radclyffe, who after his escape was sentenced to death by an Act of Attainder.

Derwentwater and his fellow-Jacobite Freemasons were shocked when, on 28 April 1738, Pope Clement XII issued a Bull against the Freemasons. It stated that Freemasons had formed lodges 'in which men of no matter what religion and sect, content with a certain affectation of natural virtue, are mutually bound together in a close and exclusive league'. They took oaths on the Bible to preserve their secrets under threat of horrible penalties if they broke these oaths. Like the other anti-masons, Pope Clement asked: why the need for secrecy if the Freemasons were doing good and not evil? They were libertines and miscreants, 'for assuredly if such people were not doing evil they would never have so much hatred of the light'. The Pope therefore forbade Catholics to become Freemasons on pain of excommunication.[3]

The Pope's Bull was enforced in many Catholic countries, but not in all. The Pope himself, of course, enforced it in his Papal States in Italy. It was immediately enforced in Portugal. A lodge of Irish Catholic refugees had been formed in Lisbon. As soon as they heard about the Pope's Bull, they dissolved their lodge, and informed the Inquisition of what they had done. The Inquisition appointed a commission in July 1738 to investigate the conduct of the members of the lodge. The commissioners reported that they were all good Catholics who had not done anything in the lodge that was immoral, and that their masonic oaths did not apply to questions of religion, or interfere with their loyalty to the King and the state. As the members had already dissolved the lodge as soon as they heard of the Papal Bull, the Inquisition decided to forgive them and not to punish them. The government in Spain was slower to act, but in 1740 the Freemasons were banned, and the lodge that the Duke of Wharton had formed was disbanded.[4]

The Freemasons' lodge in Florence had been formed in 1733 by Charles Sackville, Earl of Middlesex (afterwards Duke of Dorset). He was a staunch supporter of the House of Hanover and the Protestant Succession, and a friend of Frederick, Prince of Wales; but the lodge was composed largely of English Jacobite Catholic refugees in Florence, though there were also a few Italian brothers. The lodge dissolved itself as soon as the Papal Bull was issued. The secretary, Tommasso Crudeli, who was a Florentine, was arrested by the Inquisition, and questioned about masonic activities. It was widely believed in England that he had been tortured, but although this was untrue, he was held in the prisons of the Inquisition in harsh conditions for two years. He told the Inquisitors nothing that they did not know already.[5]

While the Inquisition was conducting this drive against the Freemasons in Tuscany, a new Grand-Duke had appeared. He was none other than Brother Francis, Duke of Lorraine, whose initiation as a Freemason by Desaguliers at The Hague in 1731 had been so widely reported in the press in England. The Holy Roman Emperor, Charles VI, had been making plans for his successor as Emperor. In theory the Emperor was elected by the nine German Princes and Archbishops who were Electors of the Holy Roman Empire; but for more than 200 years they had always elected a prince of the House of Habsburg. If Charles VI had had a son, he would have arranged for him to be chosen as Emperor by the Electors; but he had only a daughter, the Princess Maria Theresia. She would be entitled to inherit his kingdom of Hungary, which, in the absence of a male heir, could descend to a woman; but no woman could succeed as Holy Roman Emperor. Charles VI therefore planned to marry Maria Theresia to his relative, Francis, Duke of Lorraine, who would be elected Emperor after Charles's death. His wife Maria Theresia would have the title of Queen of Hungary.

Charles VI had recently had a set-back. He had backed the Polish nobleman, Stanislaus Leszczyński, whose daughter had married King Louis XV of France, to be chosen as King of Poland, who was always elected, on the death of the last King, by a Council of Polish nobles. But while France and the Emperor supported Stanislaus, other Polish nobles, and Russia, worked to secure the election of Augustus, Elector of Saxony, who was the last King's son. Both parties disputed the validity of the election, and the dispute led to a war in 1733–4 which has been remembered in history as the War of the Polish Succession, The Russian army overran Poland, and the Elector of Saxony became King Augustus III of Poland.

Charles VI now suggested to Francis, Duke of Lorraine, that he should resign his hereditary independent duchy of Lorraine so that Charles could give Lorraine as a consolation prize to Stansilaus Leszczyński. Francis would be compensated by marrying the Emperor's daughter, and in due course becoming the next Holy Roman Emperor. In the meantime, Francis would become Grand Duke of Tuscany, which was in effect a vassal state of the Habsburgs, as soon as the aged Grand-Duke, the last of the House of Medici, died without an heir.

Things did not go quite according to plan. In 1735 Francis resigned as Duke of Lorraine, and Stanislaus took over there. In February 1736 Francis married Maria Theresia, and took up his residence with her in Vienna. After a few months they went to live in Florence, and next year, when the old Grand-Duke died, Francis became Grand-Duke of Tuscany on 5 July 1737. He resided sometimes in Florence and sometimes in Vienna.

Charles VI died in October 1740. Frederick the Great, who became King of Prussia a month later, immediately claimed the Duchy of Silesia, which was part of the Habsburg territories, while the nobles and people of Hungary supported Maria Theresia as their Queen. The war between Frederick and Maria Theresia, which lasted for eight years, became not only a European war – the War of the Austrian Succession – with France supporting Frederick and Britain Maria Theresia, but also spread to India and North America, where the British and French fought against each other. During the war, Frederick the Great persuaded the Electors to set aside Charles VI's plan, and elect the Elector of Bavaria, who was fighting on Frederick's side, as the Holy Roman Emperor Charles VII in January 1742. But Francis's ambition was only temporarily thwarted; when Charles VII died in 1745, he was elected as the Holy Roman Emperor Francis I. His wife had meanwhile appointed him to be co-Regent with her of Hungary and all the hereditary Habsburg territories. Francis lived for the most part in Florence till he died in 1765.

He had been Grand-Duke of Tuscany for two years when the Inquisition in Florence arrested Brother Tommasso Crudeli because he had been the secretary of the now-dissolved Freemasons' lodge. Here was an opportunity for his masonic brother the Grand-Duke to do something to help a brother in distress. But like other eminent Freemasons, the Grand-Duke Francis did not take his masonic oaths too seriously. They must certainly not be allowed to jeopardize his chances of becoming Holy Roman Emperor. So while Grand Lodge in England contributed £21 to relieve Crudeli from distress, and English public opinion became indignant at the untrue reports that he had been tortured, the Grand Inquisitor in Florence, who was repeatedly questioning Crudeli, did and said nothing about the fact that their Grand-Duke was a Freemason; and the Grand-Duke did nothing to help Crudeli.

The Duke of Newcastle, the British Foreign Secretary, did much more for Crudeli than did the Grand-Duke. Newcastle was not a Freemason, but he knew that he and his Prime Minister, Sir Robert Walpole, would win political popularity in England if he was seen to be acting vigorously to help a victim of the Inquisition, who was being persecuted for no other offence than that of being a Freemason, a society to which so many English noblemen belonged. He asked the government of Tuscany to release Crudeli from prison. The Tuscan government referred the British request to the Inquisition, who courteously informed the Duke of Newcastle that they could not understand why the British government should be interested in Crudeli, as he was not a British subject. Newcastle replied, equally courteously, that while it was true that Crudeli was not a British subject, and that the British government had no right to interfere in his case, he hoped that the government of Tuscany would see the advantages of remaining on friendly terms with Britain, where public opinion would be outraged if they felt that Crudeli was being ill-treated by the Inquisition. As the British plea was unsuccessful, Newcastle put the same arguments forward to the Pope's government in Rome, and the Pope intervened with the Inquisition in Florence in favour of Crudeli. He was released from prison in 1741, after being held there for two years, and banished from Florence to his native village. Some years later, he was allowed to return to Florence, where he died after a peaceful old age in which he had nothing to do with the Freemasons.[6]

The activities of Francis I's masonic brothers were to be an embarrassment to him in Austria as well as in Tuscany. By the 1730s, Freemasons' lodges had been established in Bohemia, and within a few years also in Austria and Hungary.[7] The first Freemasons' lodge in Vienna was formed in 1742. The members of the lodge decided to hold a special meeting on 7 March 1743 at which some distinguished foreign brothers would be present. But someone heard about it and told the police, who thought that this sounded dangerous and subversive – a meeting of a secret society of men who admired constitutional and Protestant England and had been condemned by the Pope.

The chief of police persuaded Maria Theresia to send a troop of soldiers from the army, fully armed, to raid the premises and arrest the malefactors. Without knocking or waiting to be given permission to enter, they broke down the doors of the meeting place, and rushed in with their swords drawn. They called on the Freemasons to surrender their weapons at once, and all of them handed in their swords to the master of the lodge, who gave them to the soldiers' commanding officer. He was astonished, and visibly taken aback, to find that out of about twenty Freemasons present, 13 were Austrian or foreign noblemen, including the German Prince of Hesse-Rheinfeld, Count Starhemberg from Bohemia, Lord Hamilton from England and a French gentleman, Monsieur du Vigneau.

The soldiers removed the masonic insignia to police headquarters. They released the Prince of Hesse, Lord Hamilton, du Vigneau and all the princes and foreigners, and ordered Starhemberg and the other Austrian noblemen to remain in their homes under house arrest. The lower-class masons were arrested and taken to the city jail, where they remained for twelve days; but on 19 March, which was the saint's day of Maria Theresia's infant son (the future Emperor Joseph II), she commemorated it by granting an amnesty, and all the Freemasons were released from house arrest and the prison. Maria Theresia forbade them ever to meet again, under threat of very heavy penalties. They were careful to comply, and the lodge did not meet again even to dissolve itself.[8]

The Freemasons believed that it was the Jesuits who had incited Maria Theresia to order the raid on the lodge, and this is very possible. All her life she was under the influence of the most reactionary sections of the Catholic Church, and pursued an anti-liberal policy in religious and civil matters. She introduced new discriminatory legislation against Jews, who were excluded from most professions.

John Coustos was a Swiss by birth;[9] he was born in 1703, the son of a Protestant family in Berne, who emigrated first to France and then to England, where they arrived when John was aged 13. He became a diamond-cutter by trade, married an English woman, and before 1730 had been initiated as a Freemason in a London lodge; but in 1735 he went to Paris, where he lived for five years. He became the master of a lodge in Paris and initiated the Duke of Villeroy as a mason.

In 1740 he decided to emigrate to Brazil, and went to Portugal, intending to sail from Lisbon; but he liked Lisbon and stayed there, carrying on his trade as a diamond-cutter. He founded a Freemasons' lodge in Lisbon; all the members were foreigners, and most of them were French. He afterwards said that he did not know that Freemasons' lodges were illegal in Portugal; but it is difficult to believe that he was speaking the truth, even allowing for the fact that he was not in Portugal at the time when the decree was published, with such publicity, after the Papal Bull of 1738.

He did sufficiently well as a diamond-cutter to arouse the jealousy of Madame Leruitte, the wife of a goldsmith in the same district of Lisbon, and in October 1742 she denounced him to the 'Holy Office' (the Inquisition) as a Freemason who was organizing a Freemasons' lodge. The Inquisition did not take action immediately; but in 1743 the Portuguese government launched another drive against the Freemasons, and a new decree was promulgated making Freemasonry punishable by death.[10] The Inquisition then acted against Coustos, who was arrested on 5 March 1743. He was questioned at length about the procedures and the other secrets of the masonic lodge. He afterwards claimed that, like Hiram Abiff, he was true to his masonic oath of secrecy and told the Inquisitors nothing; but their official records show that in fact he told them a good deal.

But they wished to know more, and believed that he had not told them all he knew; so they decided to torture him. After their official surgeon had certified that he was in good enough health to endure torture, the Inquisitors obtained an order from their superiors allowing them to torture him, and this was read out to him. He was then taken to the torture chamber at 10 a.m. on 25 April 1744. The official records of the Inquisition, written by the Lord Inquisitor, his deputies and his clerk, describe what happened next.

He was administered the oath of the Holy Gospels, on which he placed his hand, and was charged to tell the truth and keep it secret, all of which he promised to do, and he was at once told that, from the nature of the chamber in which he found himself, and the instruments present therein, he would readily understand how arduous and thorough would be his examination, which he could avoid by truly and faithfully confessing his sins, and on declaring he had nothing more to say he was sent below, and the Doctor and Surgeon and the other Ministers of the torture approached the Bench where they were given the oath of the Holy Gospels, on which they placed their hands, and promised faithfully and truly to carry out their duties, and the torture prescribed for the accused was then ordered to be executed, and stripped of those clothes which might impede the proper execution of the torture, he was placed on the rack and the binding up commenced, and he was then informed by me, the notary, that if he died during the operation, or if a limb was broken, or if he lost any of his senses, the fault would be his, and not of the Lords Inquisitors and other Ministers, who had judged his case according to its merits, and being bound for the occasion he was given the full torture prescribed, which lasted more than a quarter of an hour, all of which took place and is attested to by the said Lords Inquisitors and Deputies.

Written by Alexandre Henrique
Manoel Varejão e Tavora
Joachim Jansen Moller

Felipe de Abranches
Clerk[11]

The Inquisitors gave judgement on 21 June 1744. They held that he, being a Protestant heretic resident in Portugal, had offended all good Portuguese Catholics by forming a Freemasons' lodge in which they proclaimed the heresy that they had the best religion because they believed in religious toleration. In view of his belated recantation, he was not sentenced to death, but was ordered to make a public recantation and then to serve for five years as a slave in the galleys. He was also required to sign a declaration that he would not reveal anything that had happened to him while he was a prisoner of the Inquisition.[12]

The British ambassador then intervened on his behalf. After the

Portuguese government had originally questioned whether Coustos was a British subject, as the ambassador insisted, they accepted the British claim. At the same time, Coustos's Portuguese lawyer petitioned the Inquisition to show mercy to Coustos, bearing in mind that he was a foreigner, that he did not know that Freemasonry was illegal under Portuguese law, and that his family in a faraway country were suffering destitution in his absence. His lawyer wrote to the Cardinal Grand Inquisitor that Coustos 'hopes, having confidence in the great charity with which this holy and merciful tribunal is actuated, and for so great a favour, that prayers will be said to Our Lord for the life and health of Your Eminence and the other gentlemen' of the Inquisition.[13]

A sentence of banishment from Portugal was substituted for the five years in the galleys, and Coustos was released. He returned to England and broke his promise to the Inquisition not to reveal what had happened to him in their prison. He wrote a book which was published in London in 1746. In *The Unparalleled Sufferings of John Coustos*, he described, with illustrations, how he had been tortured by the Inquisition. The book created a great sensation in England. It increased the British hatred for the Inquisition and for foreign Roman Catholic despots, and boosted the popularity of the Freemasons in Britain.[14]

The Papal Bull was a great disappointment for Charles Radclyffe; but, for all his interest in Freemasonry, he was a Catholic and Jacobite first and a Freemason only second. He left Italy and went to live in Paris, perhaps because the persecution of Freemasons was less intense there. Before long he was involved in the second Jacobite rebellion, the '45. Soon after 'Bonnie Prince Charlie' had landed in Scotland, and was marching from Edinburgh into England, the Earl of Derwentwater set out in a French ship with a fresh supply of arms for the Jacobites. He sailed to the east coast, intending to land at Montrose; but his ship was captured by a warship of the British navy, and Derwentwater was taken prisoner. There was very little doubt in the minds of the authorities that the arms in the ship were destined for the Jacobites; but as there might be difficulties in proving this, he was taken to London and executed on Tower Hill in December 1746 under the old Act of Attainder which had been passed against him after his escape from the Tower thirty years before.

The French government tried to help him. They claimed that he had become a naturalized Frenchman through his long residence in France, and so could not be deemed a traitor if he took arms in a French ship to the allies of the King of France. The British government rejected this plea.[15]

Some of the Jacobite Freemasons believed that Derwentwater might be saved, that some of his noble brothers in England, who held such influential positions both in Grand Lodge and in the British government, would help a fellow-mason; but of course none of them had any intention of doing so. Was not George II's son, the Duke of Cumberland, who had led the army that defeated the rebellion, himself a Freemason, like Derwentwater? Cumberland had earned the title of 'Butcher Cumberland' because he ordered the wholesale slaughter of the Jacobite prisoners after his victory at Culloden. He would not have refrained from killing them if someone had told him that there were Freemasons among them.

Derwentwater was granted the privilege, as a nobleman, of being beheaded and not hanged, drawn and quartered. This was considered by the British government to be an act of great generosity on their part, because by English law he was no longer a nobleman, as his title of Earl of Derwentwater had been forfeited by the Act of Attainder of 1716. But in any case the sentence of hanging, drawing and quartering was now automatically commuted to death by the axe or by simple hanging. No one was hanged, drawn and quartered in England after the Papist priests who suffered during the so-called 'Popish Plot' in 1679–81.

On the scaffold, Derwentwater, in the last words which a condemned man was always invited to speak, declared his continued devotion to the Catholic faith and the Jacobite cause. He died, as everyone would have expected, with great coolness and courage.[16]

CHAPTER 6

Germany and France

FREEMASONRY flourished in Germany, and aroused the inter-est of Frederick, the Crown Prince of Prussia, who afterwards became King Frederick II of Prussia and is known in history as Frederick the Great. His father, King Frederick William, was the son of the first King of Prussia, who had converted the Electoral Duchy of Brandenburg into a kingdom. King Frederick William was a strange man with a violent temper, and was almost certainly mentally unbalanced. His great interest was to collect giants; he formed a regiment in his army of men between seven and nine feet in height whom he assembled from every country in Europe. He aimed to build up a strong army which would make Prussia one of the most powerful military nations in Europe; but he knew that this would take time, and that he would have to leave to his son Frederick the task of making use of the military machine which he was patiently building.

But his son was a bitter disappointment to him. The King thought that he was an effeminate and decadent intellectual, not a manly Prussian soldier. The Crown Prince preferred speaking French rather than German; he enjoyed reading French books, French plays, and French works of philosophy and liberal politics. He enjoyed playing the flute, and sitting around in his room in a silk dressing gown instead of riding or hunting or watching army manoeuvres in military uniform. Worst of all, he was very friendly with a number of young army officers, especially with Lieutenant Katte. His father was con-vinced that he was a homosexual and was carrying on a homosexual love affair with Katte.

The King became increasingly impatient with his son. One day he broke into the Crown Prince's bedroom early in the morning, tore up his silk dressing gown, and threw his flute and his French books into the fire. After this Prince Frederick and Katte decided to run away. They planned to escape together when they were sent to join the King on army manoeuvres near the Prussian border. But someone betrayed their plans to Frederick William. The Crown Prince and Katte were arrested, tried and convicted by a court martial of attempted desertion from the army, and were sentenced to death. In the case of the Crown Prince, the sentence was commuted to imprisonment for life in a fortress; but the King was determined that the death sentence on Katte should be carried out.

Katte was beheaded in the courtyard immediately beneath the window of the room in the prison where the Crown Prince was confined. On the King's orders, the jailers dragged Frederick to the window and held him there by force, compelling him to watch the execution of his friend. He waved to him, and called out, 'Forgive me, Katte'. 'There is nothing to forgive, Prince', replied Katte. As the axe fell, and Katte's severed head was held up for Frederick to see, the Crown Prince fainted.

But Frederick William had no other son, and no near relative to whom he could leave his kingdom; so after a few weeks he released Frederick from his prison, and eventually restored him to his position at court as Crown Prince. Frederick decided not to risk enraging his father again; he dissembled his feelings about him, and waited for the King to die. He pretended that he had lost his interest in French culture and in music; and he was not dissembling when he showed great interest in his father's military projects, and a readiness to use his father's army to further Prussia's greatness when he came to the throne. The King believed that his son had learnt his lesson, and was a reformed character.

In the summer of 1738 Frederick William and the Crown Prince travelled to Holland and met Count van der Lippe-Bückenburg and other guests at a supper party in The Hague. The conversation turned to Freemasonry. Frederick William inveighed fiercely against it, while Count Lippe tried to defend it. Crown Prince Frederick also said a few words in support of the Freemasons, but quickly desisted when he saw how this angered his father. But afterwards he privately approached Lippe and told him, in the strictest confidence, that he would like to be initiated as a Freemason if this could be done without King Frederick William's knowledge. Lippe suggested that the Crown Prince's initiation should take place at Brunswick on the

King's and the Crown Prince's return journey to Berlin. The famous Freemason, Dr Bielfeld, would come with them and take part in the initiation and he would bring with him the masonic aprons and furnishings which they would need for the ceremony.

When they reached the frontier between Holland and Brunswick, the Brunswick customs officials asked them to open their baggage. This was very embarrassing, because if the customs officials saw the masonic equipment, it would be difficult to prevent the King from hearing about it and discovering what was happening. Lippe adopted a haughty attitude. He gave the customs official a ducat, and asked him if he realized that he was dealing with personages of high rank who would never defraud the Brunswick customs but would naturally resent it if their word was doubted and they were required to open their baggage. The customs official let them through without opening the baggage.

They decided to hold the meeting of the lodge, at which the initiation would take place, at Kron's Hotel in Brunswick on the night of 14–15 August 1738. They found a room which they thought was suitable; but it was divided by only a thin wooden partition from the next room, which was the bedroom of a Hanoverian nobleman. The Freemasons were afraid that this nobleman would hear what was happening in the next room and would talk about it, and that Frederick William would find out. But someone told them that the Hanoverian nobleman was a heavy drinker who got drunk quite easily. Several of the Freemasons visited the nobleman in his room, one after the other. He offered each of them a glass of wine, drank heavily himself with every one of them, and was soon completely drunk. He fell fast asleep, and did not awaken for hours, having been completely oblivious to what was happening in the next room.

The Crown Prince was admitted by Bielfeld with the usual initiation ceremony; Frederick insisted that no part of it should be waived in his case. He was accompanied by his friend Captain Wartensleben, who also wished to join the craft, and was initiated at the same time as the Crown Prince.[1]

King Frederick William never discovered that his son had become a Freemason. Two years later he died, and a Freemason with strong homosexual instincts, who loved French culture and speculative philosophy, with progressive liberal ideas on religion and politics, and who was also one of the great military commanders of his age, had become King of Prussia.

The reaction to the Papal Bull in France was complicated. Louis XV, like his great-grandfather Louis XIV, prided himself on being 'the most Christian King'; but in France the tyrannical and persecuting Catholic Church was a Gallican Church, claiming to have independent national authority, and the King did not allow it to become too subservient to the Pope. The Kings of France had firmly established, and had forced the Pope to accept, that no Papal Bull was to be enforceable in France until the King consented to it.

The position of the French nobility had greatly changed during the previous hundred years. In the sixteenth century the great noble houses of Guise and Bourbon, with their power bases in eastern and south-west France, had torn the kingdom apart by thirty years of civil war; and the fighting between the nobility had started up again in the days of the Fronde, when Louis XIV was a child. But when he came of age, and established his absolute royal authority, he destroyed the political power of the nobles by bribing them to renounce it. He encouraged them to come to his court at Versailles, to hold honorific and well-paid sinecure offices – to carve for the King at dinner, or to attend his *petit levé* when he dressed in the morning, and hand him his shirt, his coat and his wig. He hoped that when the nobles were not engaged in these duties at court, they would be staying in their great mansions in Paris. He wished to prevent them as far as possible from living on their lands in the country, where they could enrol their tenants in a private army and begin a new civil war.

The King governed France through middle-class civil servants, who were mostly lawyers. The provincial *Parlements* had limited powers, most of which were judicial rather than legislative; but the King could veto all their decrees. The government was administered by the *intendants*, who had absolute authority in their districts, and were subject only to the directives of their superiors, the *surintendants*, who were themselves subject only to the King's Council, where the King presided in person, and might either accept or reject the advice given to him by his councillors.

The nobles had the privilege of having their seigneurial courts in which they exercised a civil and a criminal jurisdiction over their tenants; but the presiding judges in the seigneurial courts were the same middle-class lawyers who presided in the King's courts, which could on appeal overrule the decisions of the seigneurial courts. The nobles also had the privilege of being allowed to ask the King to imprison anyone they did not like for as long as they wished in the Bastille or some other prison, though it was up to the King whether he granted or refused their request. Normally he would grant it only when a nobleman asked him to imprison, for a short time, the nobleman's son to prevent him eloping with a young woman of whom his father did not approve.

By far the greatest privilege of the nobility was to be exempt from the obligation to pay taxes. It made them the richest class in France. The King thought that this was a price well worth paying if it stopped them from launching a civil war.

The attitude of the nobility was changing. While they enjoyed their privileges, some of them had a guilty conscience about it; and they were beginning to regard the lower classes in a more sympathetic way. In 1699 Charles Perrault published a book of short stories about men and women who encounter fairies good and bad. He called one of his stories *Cinderella*. It was about a girl who worked among the cinders in the kitchen, which she was forced to do by her unkind ugly sisters. A kind fairy-godmother arranges for her to go to a ball at the King's palace, where the King's son, the Prince, falls in love with her at first sight. As she leaves the ball she loses one of her slippers.* The Prince finds it, and searches everywhere throughout the kingdom till he discovers Cinderella among the cinders in the kitchen, finds that the slipper fits her foot only, and asks her to marry him as he kneels to her in the kitchen; and they live happily ever after.

Cinderella is not, in fact, a working-class girl; she is the ill-treated daughter of a middle-class family. But this detail seems to have been completely overlooked by Perrault's readers. The story was seen as a revelation of how a good and kind girl from the lowest social class could win the love of a handsome prince by her virtues, and that their love could triumph over class prejudice. A hundred years earlier the aristocracy would have considered the story ridiculous, and perhaps subversive; but the French nobles of 1699 found *Cinderella* very moving, and it immediately became one of the most popular stories of all time.

The French nobles also read more serious books – the writings of Montesquieu, showing the advantages of the English constitution

---

* But it was not a glass slipper. The slipper was made of squirrel fur, *vair*. The English translator confused the word with *verre* (glass), and mistranslated it.

over the French absolute monarchy; the satirical works of Voltaire, and later of Rousseau; and the works of the Encyclopaedists, who published the first Encyclopaedia in the 1760s. It is not surprising that many of them asked to become Freemasons; but the official attitude about this was confused and uncertain. The King and his government had no objection if the nobility attended meetings of masonic lodges and discussed philosophy there; it might even be a good thing if it kept them out of mischief, plotting against the monarchy. But if middle-class intellectuals – lawyers, journalists, school and university teachers – and tailors and other artisans formed a secret society which held secret meetings, and bound each other by secret oaths, this might constitute a serious threat to the government and the régime, particularly if the Freemasons looked to Protestant and constitutional England for guidance. At any rate, King Louis XV was certain about one thing: whatever he did about the Freemasons, he would do what he and his government wanted to do, not what the Pope ordered him to do.

In 1737, a year before Clement XII's Bull against the Freemasons, Louis XV issued a proclamation banning the Freemasons in France. He also announced that a nobleman who joined a Freemasons' lodge would not be received at court. But two years later, just after the Pope had issued his Bull and Freemasonry had been banned in Tuscany, Austria, Spain and Portugal, Louis XV was persuaded by the young Duke of Antin, who was very attracted by Freemasonry, to allow Antin to assume the title of Grand Master of the *Grande Loge Anglaise*, as the French Grand Lodge was known. Several other noblemen then joined the Freemasons. It was even rumoured in high society, though the rumour was certainly false, that Louis XV himself wished to join. Unlike the English Freemasons and their imitators in the other countries of Europe, many of the French lodges admitted women; and some of the most beautiful and pursued of the ladies of French high society were admitted as *Franc-maçonnes*.

The chief of the Paris police was much more worried about the situation than the King and his ministers; and the Church was unhappy that the Pope's Bull was being ignored in France. In 1744 the police carried out a raid on a masonic lodge in Paris while a lodge meeting was in progress, and detained the Freemasons present. Many of them were noblemen, and they were immediately released with apologies; the middle-class and lower-class brothers were carted off to prison but were soon released, perhaps because of the intervention of some of their noble brothers with the police and the authorities. The police saved their face by prosecuting the owner of the premises where the lodge had been held, and he was sentenced to pay a fine. No other proceedings were taken against the Freemasons.[2] This angered the Church, but they could do nothing about it. The doctors at the Sorbonne issued a statement in 1745 denouncing the Freemasons; but this achieved nothing.[3]

It was not the Freemasons who would constitute the greatest threat to the Church's authority and the absolute monarchy in France. François Marie Arouet de Voltaire was not a Freemason; he was far too much of an individualist to join any society. He got into trouble at an early age when he ventured to write an article in a newspaper poking fun at a nobleman. The nobleman's lackeys beat up Voltaire in the street, and the nobleman obtained a *lettre de cachet* from the King imprisoning Voltaire for a short spell in the Bastille. When he was released he came to England, and, like the other French intellectuals, preferred aristocratic England, with its vices, to the tyranny of State and Church in France. He believed above all in freedom of speech, and made the famous comment: 'I disapprove of what you say, but I will defend to the death your right to say it'.[4]

Voltaire's somewhat flippant and cynical wit did not make him by nature a crusader, but an episode which occurred when he was already 68 changed his attitude. In 1761 a Protestant family named Calas were living in Toulouse. Since the Revocation of the Edict of Nantes they were forbidden to hold or attend any Protestant religious service; but no one could prevent them from worshipping privately as Protestants in their homes; in the more tolerant atmosphere of the mid-eighteenth century, the persecuting measures of the time of Louis XIV were no longer enforced, to the disappointment of the more intolerant Catholics.

The Calas family consisted of a father and mother and two teenage sons. But a Catholic maidservant who worked in the house had grown very fond of the younger son, and she persuaded him to convert to Roman Catholicism. He continued to live in the house with his parents, though the elder son had left to look for work elsewhere in France. One day, when the younger son was aged 16, he was found dead, hanged, in his room. Perhaps his father had been unkind about his conversion; perhaps he found the conflict of loyalties to his family and to his new-found faith too unsettling an experience to bear, and, like other unhappy teenagers in other centuries, had taken the easy way out. The local Catholic population in Toulouse had another explanation. His father and mother and brother had murdered him because he had become a Catholic. There were angry demonstrations outside the Calas house, and Monsieur and Madame Calas were taken into custody.

The Catholic Church fanned the flames of the popular anger. The local priests preached from the pulpit that the boy had been murdered by the Protestants. He was buried with full solemnities as a martyr for the Catholic faith. Monsieur Calas was prosecuted for murder, and Madame Calas for being an accessory. As Calas stoutly denied his guilt, the prosecutor demanded that he be questioned under torture. He appealed against the sentence of torture to the *Parlement* of the province of Toulouse; but with the priests and the bishop denouncing the Protestant murderers more loudly than ever, the *Parlement* dismissed the appeal. Calas and his family wrote to the King's Council in Paris, but they would not intervene.

Calas was tortured on the rack, but still refused to confess. The court then pronounced judgement: he was guilty of murder and heresy, and was sentenced to be broken on the wheel, to have all his bones broken by blows with a hammer and then left to die after as long as it pleased God to allow him to linger in pain. Then his body was to be burned. Again Calas appealed against the conviction and the sentence to the *Parlement* of Toulouse, and again urged the government in Paris to intervene. No one would defy the popular clamour, and the sentence was carried out, without any mitigation, on 9 March 1762. Calas's only consolation was that the court found his wife not guilty of being an accessory to the murder. His eldest son was found guilty of being an accessory although he had not been at home at the time; but in his case the sentence of the court was banishment from France.

Madame Calas would not let the matter rest there. She knew that an innocent man had been sentenced to undergo a painful death, and she was determined to fight on to have him posthumously exonerated. She approached all the friends she could think of who might have influence and would be prepared to help her, but all her efforts were unsuccessful. Then someone suggested that she write to Voltaire. He looked into the case, and the more he studied the evidence, the more convinced he became that there had been a gross miscarriage of justice. He wrote to the King's Council in Paris; he visited all the courtiers and aristocrats who had told him that they admired his books. It took him five years to convince them, but in 1767 the King's Council, acting as the supreme Court of Appeal, ruled that Calas was innocent and had been unjustly convicted. It was a complete vindication, but it came too late.

Voltaire, like other intellectuals of the period, had thought that the worst days of religious persecution were over, and that the cruel punishments of the sixteenth and seventeenth centuries were no longer applied in practice; but now it was clear that the evil had only been lying dormant, and was still there, ready to be revived at any moment. The time for writing witty books had passed, and the time for a crusade had come. It was now that he launched his famous slogan *'Ecrasez l'infâme'* – crush the shameful thing. Voltaire always denied that by *'l'infâme'* he meant Christianity, the Catholic religion, or even the Catholic Church; he meant 'persecuting and privileged orthodoxy'.[5] But everyone knew what was the 'persecuting and privileged orthodoxy' which was dominating Europe in the 1760s. The *'infâme'* which must be crushed was the Catholic Church.

———— ◆ ————

CHAPTER 7

English Grand Lodge:
'Wilkes and Liberty!'

BY 1750, the men who had founded Grand Lodge had died. Anderson died in 1739 and Desaguliers in 1743. Their funerals were attended by the Grand Master and many of their masonic brothers, and were well reported in the press, which also published ample obituaries about them.[1] The last days of the first Grand Master, Anthony Sayer, were not so happy. He had been dwarfed by the succession of noble brothers who followed him as Grand Master after 1720, and he ended his days in the relatively humble position of the Tyler standing on guard outside the door in his local lodge. On several occasions he petitioned Grand Lodge for a pension, but had to ask several times before he was awarded £15 (about £450 in today's values) in April 1730.

Four months later, he was summoned to appear before Grand Lodge charged with having committed grave irregularities 'notwithstanding the great favours he hath lately received by order of the Grand Lodge'.[2] His offence had apparently been to have secretly founded a lodge without the authority of Grand Lodge. On 15 December 1730 he was examined by the members of Grand Lodge, including Desaguliers. Some of them thought that he had been guilty of clandestine activity; but as the majority considered that his conduct was merely irregular, he was let off with a warning 'to do nothing so irregular for the future'.[3]

It was eleven years before Sayer ventured to petition Grand Lodge for money, and he was then granted another two guineas from the General Charity. But he carried on a reasonably successful trade as a bookseller in Covent Garden,[4] and when he died in 1742 the Freemasons did at least give him a good funeral. The hearse was followed 'by a great number of gentlemen of that Honourable Society of the best quality' from the Shakespeare Head Tavern in Covent Garden to Covent Garden church.[5]

A new generation of masons was ready to take over. There was no shortage either of scholastic masonic philosophers or of members of the aristocracy who were prepared to fill the office of Grand Master. Year after year, one noble brother followed another. Among the philosophical scholars, William Preston and Thomas Dunckerley played an important part. Dunckerley was born in 1724.[6] His mother was the wife of a serving man in the Duke of Devonshire's household at the Duke's London residence at Somerset House in the Strand. Dunckerley was an intelligent and enterprising lad, and went into the Royal Navy as a gunner. He did well in the Navy, becoming a respected petty officer. He became a Freemason, and formed naval lodges in several ships in which he served, and in Canada, where he was stationed for some months. He became a prominent leader of Freemasonry.

From time to time during his naval career, important people intervened and used their influence on his behalf; but it was not until he was 36 that his mother, on her deathbed, told him her great secret. His father was the Prince of Wales, who afterwards became King George II. The Prince had seen her and fallen in love with her when he was visiting the Duke of Devonshire. After that, he came again and again to Somerset House, spending the night with her on fifteen occasions. George II died in October 1760, only a few months after the death of the serving-man's wife whom he had loved. When Dunckerley left the Navy, George III granted him a pension, and several members of the royal family helped him financially.

Dunckerley wrote books about Freemasonry, and helped to further its development, using his contacts with the royal family and the aristocracy to ensure that their patronage continued. He used his influence to improve the moral tone of the lodges, and to counter the masons' reputation for gormandizing and engaging in drinking orgies.

He introduced a rule banning smoking in the lodges.[7] In 1717 the aristocracy smoked tobacco in long clay pipes, and pipe-smoking was a feature of the banquets in Freemasons' lodges. But in the 1770s George Brummell – Beau Brummell – a friend of the Prince of Wales, became the arbiter of fashion in high society in London, Tunbridge Wells and Bath. He thought that smoking was vulgar, and succeeded in making it unacceptable in society for 80 years. Smoking also disappeared in Freemasons' lodges. During the Crimean War, British officers acquired the habit of smoking cigars and cigarettes from their French allies, and by the 1860s cigar-smoking was popular with many aristocrats, and especially with Edward, Prince of Wales, the future Edward VII. It was duly introduced into Freemasons' lodges. In smoking, as in other matters, when royalty and the aristocracy led the way, the Freemasons followed.

Freemasonry became complicated during the eighteenth century. A new rite, the Royal Arch, had developed by about 1750. Its origin is obscure. Some believe that it was invented by the Chevalier Ramsay. Andrew Ramsay[8] was born in Ayr in 1686, the son of a Scottish baker. As a young man he served in Marlborough's army in Flanders during the War of the Spanish Succession, and after leaving the army he remained in the Netherlands, and became friendly with the famous French author, François de Salignac de La Mothe Fénelon, Archbishop of Cambrai, who converted him to Roman Catholicism. Ramsay had contacts with many English Catholic Jacobites in Italy, and at one time was tutor to the Old Pretender's infant sons in Rome; but he was not an active Jacobite agent, and declared his allegiance to the House of Hanover. In 1716 he settled in Paris, but sometimes visited England, and it was on a visit to England that he was initiated as a Freemason in Westminster in 1730.

In Paris he became known as the Chevalier de Ramsay, having been granted the title of Chevalier of the Order of St Lazarus by the Duke of Orleans. He was appointed Orator to the French Grand Lodge, and wrote the speech which he was to have delivered as Orator in 1737; and though he did not, in fact, deliver the speech, it was printed and widely read in Paris in the 1740s. In it he claimed that the Freemasons were descended from the Knights Templars of the medieval kingdom of Outremer.

Although Ramsay's name has been widely associated with the Royal Arch, some masonic historians believe that the Royal Arch originated in Ireland, while others think it began in France.[9]

In the admission ceremony to the Royal Arch, the initiate is told the name of God, the Great Architect of the Universe. This is one of the most closely guarded secrets of the Freemasons. In recent years they have published many of the secrets that they have guarded for centuries, but not the name of God, which is revealed to the members of the Royal Arch. Renegades from Freemasonry have published it, and it is now generally known that the name is Jahbulon, with the

'Jah' standing for Jehovah, the 'Bul' for Baal, and the 'On' for Osiris.

The anti-masons have made great play with the masons' worship of Jahbulon. The Egyptian God, Osiris, might be acceptable, but the masons' worship of Baal outrages them. The bishops of the Church of England who have become Freemasons are asked to explain how they can reconcile their Christian beliefs with a worship of Baal, who is regarded in the Bible as absolute evil; and these bishops have been very embarrassed by the question.

The references to Baal in the Old Testament are vague and confusing. The author of the Book of Numbers can only with difficulty find words to express the wickedness of the Midianites who worshipped Baal. While the other wicked acts of some erring Israelites, such as the worship of the Golden Calf, are fully described, all details are avoided in the denunciation of the unparalleled sin of the Midianites in worshipping Baal; for they had broken the First Commandment, the greatest of all the Ten Commandments: 'I am the Lord thy God . . . Thou shalt have no other gods before me . . . For I, the Lord thy God, am a jealous God'. This was the unforgivable sin of the Midianites. They worshipped Baal, not Jehovah.

So Moses decided to exterminate the Midianites. He told the Jews to kill them all, including the women and children. But the Israelites suffered from the fault that Himmler and Mussolini in the twentieth century called 'sentimental humanitarianism'. They killed all the men but spared the women and children. Moses was very angry. 'And Moses was wroth with the officers of the host. And Moses said unto them: "Have ye spared all the women alive? . . . Now therefore kill every male among the little ones, and kill every woman that hath known man by lying with him. But all the women children that hath not known a man by lying with him, keep alive for yourselves".' This time the Israelites obeyed orders.[10]

By including the name of Baal in the composite name of God, the members of the Royal Arch were identifying themselves with the victims of Moses' savagery. They were making a protest against the Judaeo-Christian violence and religious persecution which had been responsible for so much suffering in the past 3,000 years. No one knows who thought of the name 'Jahbulon'; but it is unlikely to have been Ramsay, with his sympathy for Roman Catholicism and the Christian Knights Templars of Outremer.

Many new degrees of Freemasonry were developed. Originally there were three masonic degrees. An initiate was admitted as an apprentice mason, then he was raised to be an entered apprentice, and in the third ceremony he became a master mason. Now new degrees were added till there were 33 degrees to which a mason could be raised, though only the first three degrees were under the control of Grand Lodge, and the Grand Master himself might have attained only to the third degree.

During the eighteenth century other masonic rites developed in various parts of the world, of which the most important was the so-called Scottish Rite. It had never, in fact, existed in Scotland, but had originated in France, and was called the *Rite Ecossais* – the Scottish Rite – because the Scotsman, the Chevalier Ramsay, was thought to have started it. All the degrees of all the various rites add up to some 1,400 different degrees, with their own procedures and differences.[11] Some, like the Knights Templars, are specifically Christian, and their ritual contains express references to Christ; other degrees have the deistic concept of the Great Architect of the Universe. The Lodge of Israel is a Jewish form of masonry. All the brothers in their various rites and degrees have one thing in common: they are all Freemasons. All must believe in some kind of God, a Great Architect of the Universe; and in all meetings of the lodge the Book of the Sacred Law must lie open throughout the proceedings. In England the Book of the Sacred Law is the Bible; but it can be the Roman Catholic New Testament, the Jewish Old Testament, the Muslim Koran, or the holy book of any religion.

Freemasonry developed in Scotland and Ireland along the same lines as in England, with a Scottish and an Irish Grand Lodge, and Grand Masters who were high-ranking members of the aristocracy. According to legend, one of the first masonic lodges in Ireland was in Viscount Doneraile's house near Cork in 1710. While a lodge meeting was in progress in the house, Lord Doneraile's seventeen-year-old daughter, Elizabeth St Leger, walked into the room; and the members of the lodge decided that, as she had witnessed their proceedings and learned many of their secrets, she had better be initiated as a member of the lodge, and she became the only woman Freemason. After her marriage to Richard Aldworth, she was known as 'our sister Aldworth' to the Freemasons, and she continued to patronize and help them till her death at the age of 80.[12]

There are several similar stories of a woman who was admitted by accident to a Freemasons' lodge and thereby become the only woman Freemason. There was Miss Havard at Hereford in 1770;

Isabella Scoon at Newstead, near Melrose in Scotland, in the eighteenth century; and Mrs Bell, the landlady of the Crown Inn at Newgate in London, who on New Year's Day 1770 forced her way into a room in her inn where a meeting of a military regimental lodge was being held. Mary Sproule, of Sussex in New Brunswick in Canada, early in the nineteenth century overheard the proceedings at a meeting of a lodge of American Freemasons who had supported George III during the War of Independence and had come to Canada after the war. When they realized what she had done, they shouted at her: 'You listened in to the initiation ceremony!' 'I didn't listen', she replied, 'but you talked so loud.' They decided to admit her to the lodge, and she became Canada's only woman Freemason.

There was a woman who hid herself in a cupboard in a room in the inn on Chatham Pier during a lodge meeting in 1861. Catherine Sweet of Brading Green, Virginia, secretly watched every lodge meeting for a year in 1907 before she was at last discovered. The masons locked her in her room for a month while they discussed what to do. They eventually decided to make her a mason, so that if she broke her initiation oath and revealed their secrets, they could apply against her all the terrible penalties referred to in the initiation ceremony.

All these almost identical stories are probably apocryphal. But the story of Countess Hadig Barkoczy is true. She quite openly joined a lodge in Hungary in 1875, and the brothers in the lodge welcomed her; but when the Grand Orient of Hungary, the controlling body in the country, heard about it, they expelled her from the lodge and the craft, and suspended all the brothers of the lodge for three months as a punishment for having admitted her. In all these stories, the point is made that the woman who improperly gained admission to the lodge became the only woman Freemason in the world; but this, in any case, is untrue, because women have been admitted to masonic lodges in France at various times since the middle of the eighteenth century.[13]

Among a series of noble brothers who were Grand Masters of Irish Grand Lodge was Garret Wesley – the family later changed the spelling of their surname to Wellesley – second Baron and first Earl of Mornington, who was Grand Master in 1776. His eldest son, Richard Colley Wesley, the second Earl, who later became Governor-General of India and Marquess of Mornington, was Grand Master in 1782–3. The first Earl's younger son Arthur, the second Earl's brother, afterwards became Duke of Wellington and the victor of Waterloo. On 7 December 1790 he was initiated as a Freemason at Trim in Ireland, the country where his father and brother had been Grand Master.[14]

Not every lodge in England was pleased at being under the authority of Grand Lodge. Some grumbled, but accepted the position, and did not contest the control of Grand Lodge and its noble Grand Master. But a few lodges revolted, broke away from the other masonic lodges, and continued in existence independently of Grand Lodge. Most of these independent lodges collapsed and disappeared after a few years.

In 1751 Grand Lodge faced a more serious revolt. It resulted in the lodge in York, which had been taught by tradition and by Anderson's *Constitutions* that King Athelstan had established a mason's lodge at York in the tenth century, declaring that they were senior to Grand Lodge in London and would not accept its authority. A number of lodges all over England departed from Grand Lodge in London and adhered to Grand Lodge in York, including Lodge No. 1 in London, which was one of the original four lodges that had formed Grand Lodge in 1717. The Grand Lodge in York and their followers called themselves the Ancient Grand Lodge, and contemptuously dismissed Grand Lodge in London and its supporting lodges as 'the Moderns'.

The division between the Moderns and the Ancients, between London and York, lasted for 60 years.[15] The Ancients in York took the precaution of inviting dukes and other noble brothers to be their Grand Masters. The Duke of Atholl, who was Grand Master of the Ancients for 28 years, could stand up to the noble Grand Masters of the Moderns in London. From time to time there were suggestions that a reconciliation would be desirable which would re-unite the masonic movement; but personal dislikes and a refusal to compromise prevented any progress towards reunification.

On several occasions Grand Lodge in London was confronted with embarrassing situations. For nearly 300 years, from 1717 to 1999, the English Freemasons have been particularly eager to avoid becoming involved in politics, and above all in revolutionary politics, like the masons on the Continent of Europe and in North and South America; but they only just avoided it in the case of John Wilkes. Born in 1727, the son of a wealthy distiller in Camberwell, south London, Wilkes in his youth acquired the reputation of being something of a rake. After marrying, at his father's suggestion, a woman ten years older than himself, and acquiring through her a property in Buckinghamshire, he separated from her, and was involved in litigation with her because of his failure to carry out the financial terms of their separation agreement. He became friendly with disreputable noblemen, and joined their drinking clubs; if rumour was correct, satanical ceremonies were performed in some of these clubs. But Wilkes also became a journalist, and the accession of George III brought about a change in his career, and perhaps in his character.

The Freemason Frederick, Prince of Wales, died in 1751, before he had succeeded to the throne; but his son succeeded as George III at the age of 22 when George II died in 1760. George III put an end to the rule of the Whigs which had lasted for 46 years. Unlike his great-grandfather and his grandfather, George I and George II, he spoke perfect English and never spoke German. He believed that a King should rule as well as reign, and he was determined not to allow his kingdom to be governed by a succession of Whig ministers while he himself played no part in politics.

Unlike so many of his contemporaries and other members of his family, George III was virtuous. In the 450 years since Henry VIII, 15 Kings have been Supreme Head or Supreme Governor of the Church of England. Nine of them, and possibly 10 – the case of George V is doubtful – have been adulterers and have had mistresses. Of the other six, Edward VI died at the age of 15, and James I was a homosexual who committed sodomy, not adultery. The remaining four did not have mistresses because they were virtuous and were loyal to their spouses; they were Charles I, George III, perhaps George V, and George VI.

George III realized that it was no longer possible in 1760 for him to ignore Parliament and govern without the support of the House of Commons, as earlier sovereigns had tried to do. Instead, he set about building a political party in the House of Commons of MPs who became known as 'the King's Friends'. By bribes and offers of honours, which were at the King's disposal, he succeeded in gaining the support of these MPs and ousted the Whigs from office. He dismissed the Secretary of State, William Pitt, who had been the organizer of victory in the Seven Years War, and appointed Tory Prime Ministers – first Lord Bute and later Lord North. To the indignation of Pitt and the Whigs, George III and the new Tory government opened peace negotiations with France, and in November 1762 signed the Treaty of Paris on less advantageous terms for

Britain than Pitt had hoped to obtain. Britain's ally, Frederick the Great, although abandoned by Britain, had been militarily so successful in Germany that he was able to impose very good terms in the Treaty of Hubertusburg which ended the Seven Years War in February 1763.

Wilkes had obtained, through the influence of the Whigs, a seat in the House of Commons for Aylesbury, and he had also started a newspaper which he called *The North Briton*. He adopted this title out of mischievousness to annoy the Scots, for in many articles in the paper he mocked them. He annoyed Dr Johnson by ridiculing some of the ponderous pronouncements in Johnson's *Dictionary*; but he appeased Johnson's indignation when he used his influence to free Johnson's black servant who had been press-ganged into the Navy.

Wilkes's article in the notorious Number 45 of *The North Briton* was much more serious. It commented on George III's speech at the opening of the Parliamentary session in 1763 when the King said that the Treaty of Paris had been responsible for the favourable terms which Frederick the Great had obtained in the Treaty of Hubertusburg. Wilkes wrote that this was a deliberate lie; and while he criticized the King's Tory ministers, who had presumably drafted the King's speech, he clearly hinted that the King himself had consciously told a lie.

George III was very angry, and ordered that Wilkes be arrested and prosecuted for seditious libel. Wilkes was arrested as he was walking home from the Temple to his lodgings in Westminster, and imprisoned in the Tower. The King's officers then broke into his rooms and searched them for incriminating documents. Wilkes brought proceedings for habeas corpus in the Court of Common Pleas, claiming that the King's officers had acted unlawfully as he, being an MP, was privileged from prosecution for seditious libel, and that the officers had not obtained a warrant which entitled them to search his rooms. The court ordered him to be set free, and awarded him a substantial sum in damages for wrongful arrest; but the King's Friends in the House of Commons passed a resolution condemning his article in No. 45 of *The North Briton* as a seditious libel, and ordering it to be burned. They expelled him from the House of Commons and declared his seat vacant.

Although Wilkes, being no longer an MP, could not now claim Parliamentary privilege, he reprinted his article in No. 45 of *The North Briton*. He was again prosecuted for seditious libel. After being wounded in a duel with one of the King's supporters, he fled to Paris, where he was welcomed by Diderot and the French intellectuals of the Enlightenment; but he returned to England in 1768, and surrendered himself to the judgement of the court. He was sentenced to 22 months' imprisonment in the King's Bench prison.

While he was in prison there, he stood as a candidate in a Parliamentary by-election in Middlesex, and was elected. The House of Commons expelled him again, and declared the seat vacant. Although he was still in the King's Bench prison, he stood again, and was elected; and when he was expelled, he was re-elected a third time. The House of Commons declared his election void. By this time, a great political campaign in support of Wilkes had been launched throughout the country. His supporters raised the cry 'Wilkes and Liberty!'

For the fourth time an election was held for the Middlesex seat. The King's Friends nominated Colonel Luttrell as their candidate. He was supported by the Fox family and an important section of the Whigs, who were becoming tired of the continuing trouble with Wilkes. Luttrell and his supporters spent an unprecedented amount of government money on the election campaign in a determined effort to defeat Wilkes; but when the result was declared, Luttrell received 296 votes against 1,149 votes for Wilkes. The House of Commons then declared that Luttrell had been elected MP for Middlesex. Public indignation against the Tory government and the King became stronger than ever, and the cry 'Wilkes and Liberty!' grew louder.

At this point, Wilkes applied to become a Freemason. The officers and members of the Jerusalem Lodge in London accepted him enthusiastically. London Grand Lodge were not so enthusiastic, but they did not wish to resist the pressure of opinion in the Jerusalem Lodge, especially as the master of the lodge, Thomas Dobson, was a Past Assistant Grand Master of Grand Lodge. The Provincial Grand Master, Brother Maschall, and the Grand Secretary, Brother French, were equally ardent supporters of Wilkes. So Grand Lodge granted a dispensation to the Jerusalem Lodge to admit Wilkes in prison, and on 3 March 1769 Maschall and French, both of them Grand Officers of Grand Lodge, went with Dobson and other members of the Jerusalem Lodge to the King's Bench prison, and Wilkes was duly admitted. This was reported in *The Gazeteer and New Advertiser* of 6 March.[16]

Some members of Grand Lodge were worried. Such a demonstration in support of Wilkes was not the way to win the favour of the King and the Tory government and to induce more members of the royal family to become Freemasons. So on 10 March *The Gazeteer and New Advertiser* published a statement by Grand Lodge denying that Wilkes had been granted a special dispensation to be initiated in prison, or that any Grand Officer was present at the ceremony.

But Dobson wanted everyone to know that the Freemasons supported Wilkes and Liberty. On the same day, 10 March 1769, he inserted a statement in *Lloyd's Evening Post*:

> It is thought proper to acquaint the public that I, in the presence of two Grand Officers and by virtue of a Dispensation dated February 2, 1769, signed by the deputy Grand Master, did make Mr Wilkes a Free and Accepted Mason. The Dispensation may be seen by any mason at the Jerusalem Lodge No. 24, on a lodge night.
>
> Thomas Dobson, Master[17]

Grand Lodge did nothing. When, 12 years later, in November 1781, an Army captain, who was the master of a regimental lodge and a past officer of Grand Lodge, initiated and raised some prisoners in the King's Bench prison, Grand Lodge ruled that it was 'inconsistent with the principles of masonry' that masons should be admitted, or raised to higher degrees, in any prison or place of confinement.[18] But none of these prisoners was a Wilkes.

After serving his sentence, Wilkes was released from the King's Bench prison. He was nominated for the office of Lord Mayor of London. The Court of Aldermen, who did not wish to antagonize the King, refused to elect him. This raised a storm of protest in the City, where there was strong support for Wilkes and Liberty, and the Court of Aldermen eventually gave way to the pressure, and Wilkes became Lord Mayor.

It was a triumph for Wilkes, and the collapse of the attempts by George III and his Friends to harm him. They still hated Wilkes, and vilified him; they denounced him as a profligate rake, and for publishing his friend Thomas Potter's *Essay on Woman*, a sexually explicit book, which they said was obscene. But they could do him no further injury, and their resistance collapsed. After his term as

Lord Mayor ended, he was elected Chamberlain of the City for life. He was again elected MP for Middlesex in the general election of 1774; this time the House of Commons did not expel him, and he remained MP for Middlesex for 16 years. In 1782 the Whigs won a majority in the House of Commons, and the House voted to rescind and invalidate all the resolutions against Wilkes which it had passed when the King's Friends controlled it in the 1760s.

He retired from political life in 1790, and lived quietly till his death seven years later. He had not only successfully withstood the tyranny of George III but had come closer than anyone else between 1717 and 1999 in drawing the English Freemasons into the radical political activity which the Freemasons pursued in most other countries in the world.

◆

CHAPTER 8

Troubles and Scandals

THE Freemasons, having survived John Wilkes, did not expect to be involved in any similar controversy when they initiated Dr William Dodd.[1] He was born in 1729, the son of the vicar of Bourne in Lincolnshire. After a successful university career at Cambridge, where he obtained a BA degree, with honours in mathematics, Dodd was ordained in the Church of England, and received other academic degrees. He became the tutor to the children of several members of the aristocracy and obtained three ecclesiastical benefices, as well as being appointed a canon of the Priory church of St John in Brecon. He lectured at ecclesiastical colleges, and wrote a number of theological books, including his *Commentary on the Bible* and *Sermon to a Young Man*. He also established a reputation as a popular preacher. He took an interest in charitable projects, and founded the Magdalene Home in Streatham for 'fallen women' – that is to say, prostitutes who were induced to abandon prostitution and come to live in the Home. In 1763 he was appointed one of George III's chaplains.

But people who knew Dr Dodd well were not altogether happy about his way of life. They thought that he must be living beyond his means. He had a wife to keep who had no independent income; he had a town house in Southampton Row and a country house in Ealing. He gave extravagant parties, and established a reputation for ostentation. When he won £1,000 in a state lottery, he spent it on building a chapel in his name. It was difficult to see how he could afford to maintain his lifestyle.

He wrote a novel called *The Sisters*. Some of his fellow-clergymen, and other conventional people, were shocked that he, a churchman, should have written a novel in which sex played such an important part. One writer commented that 'he descended so low as to become the editor of a newspaper'.[2] Adverse rumours about him were beginning to circulate. There was talk about a pretty servant girl who worked in his house, and about his connection with a well-known London prostitute.

Extravagance was not Dr Dodd's only fault. Despite his theological learning and his intellectual abilities, he could sometimes do very stupid things. In February 1774 he heard that the vicar of St George's, Hanover Square, had been appointed Bishop of Bath and Wells. This very well-endowed living in Hanover Square was therefore vacant. Dr Dodd thought that it was just what he wanted and needed. The presentation to the living was in the gift of the Lord Chancellor, Lord Apsley. So Dr Dodd wrote an anonymous letter to Lady Apsley, offering to pay her £3,000 if she would persuade her husband to give the Hanover Square benefice to a person whose name would be given to her later. Lady Apsley was indignant at this attempt to bribe her. She told Apsley, who ordered an inquiry to try to trace the writer of the letter. Dodd had not taken any effective precautions to hide the fact that he had written it, and it was traced to his house. When he was questioned about it, he replied so evasively that his questioners had no doubt that he had written it. The Lord Chancellor told the King, who insisted that Dodd should be dismissed from his post as a royal chaplain.

It is extraordinary that Dodd was able to survive the disgrace. He turned to one of his closest friends, his former pupil Philip Stanhope, who had just succeeded to his father's title of Earl of Chesterfield. Chesterfield stood loyally by his tutor, and appointed Dodd to another living, the vicarage of Wing in Bedfordshire, which was in Chesterfield's gift. Dodd was perhaps helped by a misfortune which may have turned out to his advantage and won him sympathy. When he and his wife were returning in their carriage from Barnet to London, they were attacked near St Pancras by a highwayman who fired a shot at the carriage. The shot broke the glass window, but did not injure them. The highwayman was caught, and after Dodd had given evidence for the prosecution at his trial, he was sentenced to death, and hanged.

Dodd succeeded so well in hushing up the scandal about his attempt to bribe Lady Apsley that when he applied to join a Freemasons' lodge at St Albans, the brothers had no hesitation in accepting him; and Grand Lodge almost immediately conferred a special distinction on him. Grand Lodge had decided to build a hall on the site of the inn in Queen Street, Covent Garden, which had been their headquarters since the formation of Grand Lodge in 1717. The foundation stone of the new hall was laid on 1 May 1775. On the same day it was announced that Dr Dodd had been appointed Grand Chaplain of the Freemasons; this was a new office which was created specially for him. The new hall was finished in a year, and on 23 May 1776 the dedication ceremony took place. Dodd preached the sermon, which made a very favourable impression. Eleven days later, at the Great Feast on 3 June, he was reappointed Grand Chaplain for a second year.

Dodd then went off for a holiday to Paris. Rumours reached England that he was leading a dissipated life there; he certainly spent money in Paris. When he returned to England he was heavily in debt. On reaching London, in January 1777, he gave a party at which Wilkes was one of the guests, and this was reported in the press. On 2 February he preached a sermon at the Magdalene Home in Streatham which he had founded for fallen women. It was a particularly moving sermon, and none of his admirers knew that it was the last time that he would ever preach. Two days later, he contacted a moneylender, and asked for a loan of £4,200, offering as security a bond issued by Lord Chesterfield. Dodd had in fact forged Chesterfield's signature on the bond.

The moneylender paid over the £4,200 to Dodd; but there were circumstances which made him suspicious about the bond, and he took it to Lord Chesterfield, who told him that his signature had been forged. Dodd offered to repay the money, and hoped that the matter would be hushed up; but Chesterfield was very angry. He had treated Dodd as a friend, he had presented him to several lucrative livings, and had continued to help him even after Dodd had been involved in the attempt to bribe Lady Apsley; yet Dodd had repaid his kindness by trying to cheat him out of £4,200. He insisted that Dodd be prosecuted.

Dodd was tried for forgery in the Court of King's Bench before three judges and a jury, who found him guilty. He was sentenced to be hanged, for forgery was a felony punishable by death. Thirty thousand people signed a petition for his reprieve; but the judges advised the King that it would set a bad example, and would lead to accusations of favouritism, if Dodd, who had held a prominent position in society, were pardoned; and George III may have been prejudiced against Dodd because it had been reported in the press that Wilkes had attended his party in January. Some people said that the Freemasons would use their influence to save Dodd; but after he had been convicted, Grand Lodge announced that on 7 April 1777 it was 'resolved unanimously that the said doctor be expelled this society'.[3] The greatest effort to help Dodd was made, not by the Freemasons, but by Dr Johnson, who helped organize the petition for a reprieve. Johnson was not a Freemason, though many eighteenth-century authors were – Pope, Gibbon, Johnson's friend Boswell, Robert Burns and Sir Walter Scott.[4]

A great crowd came to Tyburn to see Dodd hanged on 27 June. A story was told that after his body had been cut down from the gallows, the Freemasons seized it and took it to a house where Dodd, who was not quite dead, was restored to life, and that the Freemasons then smuggled him to safety in France.[5] Others said that the thousands of spectators who had come to watch the execution blocked the roads and prevented the Freemasons' carriage, with Dodd's body, from reaching the house in time to save him.[6]

The story of Dr Dodd ended in tragedy; but the public had a good laugh at the Freemasons about the case of the Chevalier d'Éon.[7] Charles Geneviève Louis Auguste André Timothée Déon de Beaumont – or d'Éon, as the family was usually called – was born on 5 October 1728, the son of a respected family of the *petite noblesse* of Tonnerre in Burgundy. As a young man he was sent to study law in Paris, but in 1755 he was offered a post in the diplomatic service at the French embassy in St Petersburg. Here he was entrusted with an important secret duty. The French government had been alarmed at the success of the British ambassador, Sir Charles Hanbury Williams, in extending British influence in Russia through his contacts with influential people at the court of the Empress Elizabeth. D'Éon was told to spy on Williams, to discover his contacts, and if possible to find means of compromising him with the Russian government.

D'Éon carried out his duties efficiently; but when the Seven Years War broke out he asked to be transferred to the army. He was given the command of a regiment in the French army that was fighting in Germany on the side of Maria Theresia against Frederick the Great, and he distinguished himself by his courage in several engagements. In April 1757 he fought in the Battle of Prague, which Frederick the Great called the bloodiest battle of the age. Frederick was eventually victorious, after both the Prussians and the Austrians had suffered

[83]

very heavy losses. D'Éon was sent to carry the news of the defeat to the government in Paris. He had a fall on the journey and broke his leg; but he hastily had it treated, and continued his journey with his leg in splints, arriving in Paris thirty-six hours before the Austrian officer who brought the news to the Austrian ambassador there.

In 1762 negotiations to end the war began in London between the British and French governments. D'Éon was appointed a member of the French delegation. Pitt and the Whigs wished to continue the war in North America and India until Britain and Prussia had completely defeated the French and the Austrians; but the Tories were ready to agree to a compromise peace immediately. Some of the Tory leaders were in secret contact with the French government and were receiving bribes from them. D'Éon was given the task of making secret contact with these Tories in London and in paying over the money to them. The Tories took office and signed the Treaty of Paris with France.

After the war, diplomatic relations between Britain and France were resumed, and d'Éon was appointed First Secretary at the embassy in London. Louis XV also awarded him a very high decoration for his bravery during the war – the Cross of the Military Order of St Louis. But d'Éon was on bad terms with his ambassador, the Comte de Guerchy, and their hatred for each other grew so bitter that eventually d'Éon left the embassy, taking important documents with him. These documents included letters which revealed the names of the Tory MPs and other influential figures in England to whom d'Éon had paid bribes on behalf of the French government. They also included the plans for a French invasion of England, though peace had been made before the plan could be put into operation.

Guerchy demanded that d'Éon return the documents. D'Éon refused, and, having broken completely with the French government, settled down to the life of a gentleman in London. He knew that the Tory MPs to whom he had paid the subsidies would be as eager as the French government to prevent him from publishing the documents, and he intended to hold on to them for the moment and then sell them to the highest bidder. The Tory MPs offered him £40,000 for the documents, but d'Éon turned down the offer. He hoped to get more than this from Louis XV.

Guerchy sent his agents to steal the documents from d'Éon's house in London, but they were unsuccessful. Guerchy then tried to kidnap d'Éon and bring him to the French embassy, but he failed again. D'Éon brought a criminal prosecution for attempted kidnapping against Guerchy before a Middlesex Grand Jury; Guerchy pleaded diplomatic immunity, and the judge upheld his plea.

But a strange rumour was circulating in London – that the Chevalier d'Éon was a woman who for years had been masquerading as a man. The rumour first began in 1764, but it was another five years before it became the talk of London. D'Éon indignantly denied and ridiculed the suggestion. No one knows how it originated, but d'Éon was sure that it had been started out of malice by Guerchy.

D'Éon was friendly with many noblemen and gentlemen in England, and he wished to do the fashionable thing and become a Freemason. He applied to join the Lodge of Mortality which met at the Crown and Anchor in the Strand; it had become the favourite lodge of French residents in London. The lodge, like all the English masonic lodges, had rules which laid down who were eligible and ineligible to join. The persons admitted as members of a lodge must be 'good and true men, freeborn and of mature and discreet age, no bondsmen, no women, no immoral or scandalous men, but of good report ... hale and sound, not deformed or dismembered at the time of their making; but no woman, no eunuch'.[8] This followed the rules of the operative masons of the Middle Ages, who excluded cripples, either because cripples were physically incapable of doing the work of an operative mason, or because of the medieval prejudice against cripples and hunchbacks, who were regarded as a manifestation of evil.

No one in the Lodge of Mortality had any doubt about the propriety of admitting d'Éon.

But within a year the rumour that d'Éon was a woman had really taken off. All London was talking about it, and people began to bet on it. Soon it became a fashionable subject for a bet, and in 1769 and 1770 higher and higher sums were wagered. It was said that the total amount that had been wagered on d'Éon's sex amounted to £120,000. In order to evade the legal restrictions on wagers, they were disguised, in accordance with the usual practice, as insurance policies. A syndicate was formed which offered what they called 'Policies of Insurance on the Sex of Monsieur le Chevalier (or Mademoiselle la Chevalière) D'Éon'.

Those who believed that d'Éon was a man relied on two main

arguments: his gallant record of bravery as an officer in the French army during the Seven Years War, and the fact that he was a Freemason; because everyone knew that the Freemasons did not admit women. On the other side, those who thought that he was a woman pointed out that he had not married and was not known to have a mistress. He never pursued women, which was certainly unusual for an eighteenth-century officer and gentleman.

How could anyone know if he had won or lost his bet? How could it be proved that d'Éon was a man or a woman? The obvious and only way was to ask him to submit to a medical examination; but d'Éon indignantly rejected the idea. He was offered £25,000 if he would agree to be medically examined, but he refused. Some people who had wagered a great deal of money then thought of kidnapping him and forcibly examining him. D'Éon, fearing the worst, suddenly left his house and disappeared. This sparked off more rumours; people said that he had disappeared so that no one could discover that he was a woman. Others asked if he himself had started the rumour, and had secretly wagered on it: would he one day allow doctors to examine him and establish his sex, so that he could collect the money that he had won by his bet?

After disappearing for some months, d'Éon reappeared at the end of June 1771, and swore an affidavit before the Lord Mayor. He swore that he had never betted on his sex, that he had always objected to the betting that had gone on, and that he had refused an offer of £25,000 to prove his sex. But the rumours and the betting continued. From time to time someone publicly challenged d'Éon to prove that he was a man, but he never responded.

Meanwhile the French government continued their efforts to recover the documents that d'Éon had taken from the embassy. They brought extradition proceedings against him in the English courts, asking that he be sent to France to be tried for theft and treason; but the courts rejected the application. Louis XV then authorized his agents to try to kidnap d'Éon; but again the attempt failed.

Matters finally came to a head in 1777 when a man who had bet that d'Éon was a woman brought an action in the courts to recover his money, for he claimed that he could prove that he had won his bet. The law about wagers, then as now, was complicated, but it was not unlawful to sue to recover a bet, as it later became by the Gaming Act 1845. The case was heard before the Lord Chief Justice, Lord Mansfield, and a jury in the Court of King's Bench on 1 July

1777. The issue was simple: could the plaintiff prove, to the satisfaction of the jury, that d'Éon was a woman? The plaintiff put forward the usual argument that d'Éon had never been known to pursue a woman; but he relied chiefly on the evidence of two French witnesses – one a journalist and one a doctor – who testified on oath that d'Éon was a woman.

Against this, the defendant could only argue that the fact that d'Éon had fought so bravely in the Seven Years War, and was a Freemason, proved that he was a man; but this was not very convincing in the face of the contrary evidence of the two French witnesses. The fact that d'Éon refused to go into the witness box and give evidence for the defendant seemed to suggest that he was afraid of being asked to submit to a medical examination which he knew would prove that he had deceived the world into thinking that he was a man, and that really he was a woman.

The jury gave their verdict that d'Éon was a woman, and Lord Mansfield gave judgement for the plaintiff. The defendant appealed to the full Court of King's Bench, who allowed his appeal on a technical point, because a recent statute had enacted that wagers of this kind did not come within the definition of an insurance policy. But as far as the public was concerned, this did not matter. Before waiting for the hearing of the appeal, the world had accepted the verdict of the jury that d'Éon was a woman.

The new King of France, Louis XVI, seized his opportunity to strike at d'Éon. On 19 August 1777 he issued a royal decree, 'De Par le Roi', at Versailles, in which he ordered that d'Éon 'is hereby required to lay aside the uniform of a dragoon which she has been in the habit of wearing and to resume the garments of her sex, and is forbidden to appear in any part of the kingdom except in garments belonging to a female'.[9]

Louis XVI's decree did not, of course, have any force of law in England; but d'Éon was now prepared to accept the verdict of the world that he was a woman. He made a bargain with Louis XVI, which was negotiated through the French author, Pierre Augustin Caron de Beaumarchais. D'Éon agreed to hand over all the documents that he had taken from the embassy in London, and the French government would pay him £3,000, and also the pension to which he was entitled for his services as a French officer and diplomat. He also agreed that he would never again dress in man's clothes in any country in the world.

Already before Louis XVI's decree, on 6 August 1777, d'Éon appeared in London dressed as a woman. He then returned to France. On 13 August he put on his dragoon's uniform for the journey, but this was the last time that he ever wore men's clothes. He retired to his family estates in Burgundy, where he lived for eight years dressed as a woman.

The revelation, which was universally accepted, that d'Éon was a woman not only enabled many gamblers to win their wagers and a great deal of money, but also provided a splendid opportunity for critics to poke fun at the Freemasons. The masons, so renowned for their refusal to admit women to their lodges, had been fooled into admitting a well-known officer and gentleman who had turned out to be a woman in disguise. One writer mocked 'our brethren (I mean sisters)' the masons, who, at one of their lodges in the Strand, 'had admitted a woman called Madame D'E—'.[10] But the Freemasons had already expelled d'Éon on the grounds that he was a woman; they had acted as soon as they heard the verdict of the jury in the Court of King's Bench.

In France 'la Chevalière d'Éon', as she now called herself, became very religious. She entered one of the most devout and respected orders of nuns. In 1785 she asked Louis XVI's permission to go to London to settle the debts which she had incurred during her residence there. Perhaps the story of the debts was an excuse to obtain the King's permission to leave France, because, after reaching London, she stayed there for 25 years and never returned to France. During these 25 years she always wore woman's clothes. Towards the end of her life she lived in great poverty, and was bedridden. She died on 21 May 1810.

During her last illness she was attended by two doctors. One was a famous French surgeon, Père Elisée. He had come to England as a refugee during the French Revolution; when he returned to France after the Restoration of the Bourbons, he became surgeon to King Louis XVIII.

Elisée and his colleague had a shock when they laid out d'Éon's body for the funeral. They saw that he was a man – a complete man, with no deformation of his male sexual organs. His masculinity was conclusively proved, as it could have been at any time during his life if he had agreed to submit to a medical examination like that to which his body was subjected after his death.

Elisée realized that no one would believe him if he reported that d'Éon was a man. He insisted on informing the authorities in England, so that they could verify it for themselves, before d'Éon's corpse was buried. The body was inspected by the Earl of Yarborough and the distinguished admiral Sir Sidney Smith, who was a Freemason; they were accompanied by some twenty other witnesses. They all saw for themselves that d'Éon was a man, but invited an independent witness, the eminent surgeon Thomas Copeland, to examine the body and confirm their sensational report about d'Éon's sex.

The revelation cannot have come as a surprise to any surviving members of the masonic lodge who were present when d'Éon was admitted. They must have known that he was a man. During the initiation ceremony the new member is required to bare his chest; and although this is not done in order to ascertain his sex, but for symbolic masonic reasons, it would have enabled everyone present to see that d'Éon was a man, not a woman. Yet the Freemasons remained silent about this, and expelled him when he himself admitted that he was a woman and agreed to wear women's clothes, at a time when the public were laughing at the Freemasons for having been duped by d'Éon. It shows the eagerness of the masons to preserve the secrets of the initiation ceremony and their reluctance to arouse further antagonism by defying the prevailing public opinion.

There remained the mystery for the people of 1810, which still remains a mystery for us today, as to why d'Éon agreed to be publicly exposed as an impostor, and to wear women's clothes for the last 33 years of his life, when he could at any time have proved that he was a man. It has been suggested that he became so pressurized by the continual accusations that he was a woman, that in the end he came to believe it himself; but modern psychology may have more plausible explanations. It seems clear that it is for students of sexual fantasies, rather than for a historian, to explain the underlying mystery of the Chevalier d'Éon.

CHAPTER 9

The American Revolution

D URING the seventeenth century, English settlers went to the North American colonies. Some went to Virginia to cultivate tobacco by the labour of black slaves who had been abducted from their homes in Africa and sold to English and other slave traders by their local chiefs; others were Puritans, like the Pilgrim Fathers, who refused to live in James I's Anglican England, and landed near Boston in 1620. The Presbyterians were as intolerant in Massachusetts as they were in Scotland and Ireland; they persecuted the more radical Protestant sects, as the Presbyterians in Britain persecuted Cromwell's Independents.

The Independents left Massachusetts, and went to Rhode Island, and Massachusetts remained an intolerant Presbyterian state. The Presbyterians in Massachusetts went further than other persecuting régimes in introducing the death penalty for Quakers, and hanged six of them. In 1692 they hanged nineteen innocent people – fourteen women and five men – and pressed one innocent man to death* at Salem, having falsely accused them of witchcraft in what came to be regarded as one of the most scandalous cases of a miscarriage of justice induced by mass hysteria.[1]

It is very possible that some of the English emigrants to North America in the seventeenth century were Freemasons, and that they opened masonic lodges there; but there is no record of Freemasonry in North America before the establishment of Grand Lodge in England. After 1717, English Grand Lodge exported Freemasonry to

---

* Under the old English law, which applied in Massachusetts, if an accused person refused to plead either guilty or not guilty, his trial could not proceed, but he was 'pressed' by having heavy weights pressed on him until he either agreed to plead or died under the pressure.

North America as it did to the European Continent. When the settlers in the American colonies heard that in England Freemasonry was becoming very fashionable among the highest ranks of society, they wished to follow the English example and form masonic lodges on their side of the Atlantic. Lodges had been established in Boston and Philadelphia by 1730.[2]

The spread of Freemasonry in North America was facilitated by the formation of military lodges, which had greatly developed since the days when Sir Robert Moray was initiated into a military lodge during the occupation of Newcastle by the Scottish Presbyterian army in 1641. After the creation of Grand Lodge, military lodges were established which moved about from place to place with the regiment. The Freemasons were as determined to be as respectable where military lodges were concerned as they were in their choice of noble brothers as their Grand Masters. The consent of the commanding officer of the regiment had to be obtained before a military lodge could be formed, and he could order the closure of the lodge.[3] It was for the commanding officer to decide who could be admitted to the lodge, and in the eighteenth century few commanding officers allowed other ranks to join; they thought that it would be contrary to good military discipline to allow fraternization in the lodge between officers and NCOs.

Grand Lodge introduced the rule that civilians could not join a military lodge, because they wished the local inhabitants to be initiated in their own fixed lodges; but this rule was often waived in practice, and many regimental lodges invited the local gentry to join. When the regiment moved on, the local residents continued to attend the meetings of the lodge, and then asked Grand Lodge to constitute them as a new affiliated lodge. With many British regiments stationed along the Atlantic seaboard of North America, from Nova Scotia and Canada to South Carolina and Georgia, lodges grew rapidly in the American colonies.

English Grand Lodge exercised their control over the American lodges by appointing a Provincial Grand Master, who, under the authority which he derived from Grand Lodge in London, could create local lodges in his area and exercise discipline over them. The first such appointment in the American colonies was when a Provincial Grand Master was appointed for New York, New Jersey and Pennsylvania on 5 June 1730. Another Provincial Grand Master was appointed for New England in April 1733,[4] and in the course of the next 40 years Provincial Grand Masters were appointed for Virginia, Georgia, and North and South Carolina.

Benjamin Franklin was born in Boston in 1706, only 14 years after the Salem witchcraft trials. His father was a candlemaker who had emigrated to Boston from England. Benjamin became apprenticed as a printer to his brother James, who was also a journalist. James revolted against the intolerance of Presbyterian Massachusetts, and criticized it in his newspaper. He was arrested and his newspaper suppressed. Benjamin then decided to leave Boston and go to Philadelphia, where the Quakers had established a far more tolerant form of Nonconformity, though they owned black slaves, like all the other white residents in the colonies.

When Benjamin Franklin was 18, he went to London, arriving on Christmas Eve 1724, and staying there for eighteen months. We need not take too seriously the allegation that he led a dissipated life in London merely because he admitted that on one occasion, 'being at this time under no Religious Restraints', he attempted to seduce a young woman, which was certainly not an unusual action for a young man in London in 1725. He did not particularly enjoy his time in London; he had hoped to meet the aged Isaac Newton, but never did. He was happy to set off in July 1726 on the two-and-a-half-months' sea voyage to Philadelphia.[5]

He did not become a Freemason in London, but after his return to Philadelphia he joined the St John's lodge at Tun Tavern in Water Street in 1731, and by 1734 had become master of the lodge. He pursued his trade as a printer in Philadelphia, and in the same year 1734 he published an American edition of Anderson's *Constitutions* of 1723, 'Reprinted by B. Franklin in the year of Masonry 5734. Price stitch'd at 2s. 6, bound 4s.'[6] The masonic year was based on the calculation by the seventeenth-century theologian, Archbishop James Ussher, who had reckoned that God had created the world in 4004 BC, except that the Freemasons ignored the four years and treated the creation of the world and the beginning of the masonic calendar as 4000 BC. The price of 2 shillings and sixpence (12½p) for the paperback, and of 4 shillings (20p) for the hardback, was of course given in English sterling, which was the currency in force throughout Britain's American colonies.

Franklin became a very active and enthusiastic mason, filling many masonic offices. In 1749 he was Provincial Grand Master of Pennsylvania. For sixteen years from 1737 to 1753, he was in charge of the post office in Philadelphia. Like other educated eighteenth-century gentlemen, he did not confine his interests and studies to either the sciences or the arts. In 1751 he invented the lightning conductor. He wrote and published many books designed to further popular education.*

Freemasonry had its critics in America as in Britain. The stricter Protestant sects did not like the tolerant deism, and, as in England, it was both criticized for its secrecy and ridiculed for its ceremonies and ritual. Soon after the Philadelphia lodge was formed, it was involved in an unfortunate scandal. An apothecary in Philadelphia, Evan Jones, had a young apprentice, Daniel Rees, who was eager to become a Free-mason and discover the mysterious secrets of the craft. Jones and his other apprentices decided to play a trick on Rees. They pretended to be masons, and dressed up in fancy costumes, like devils; and after making Rees take an oath of obedience to the devil and kiss the pos-teriors of the other apprentices, Jones dropped some burning brandy on him, and Rees suffered burns from which he died some days later.

Jones was prosecuted for manslaughter, and was branded on the hand. When the story came out at the inquest and the trial, many people blamed the Freemasons and their ceremonies for Rees's death. Franklin was more closely involved in the affair than he would have wished. When Jones told him of the trick that they intended to play on Rees, Franklin at first treated it as a good joke. Then he realized that the joke was in bad taste, and decided to warn Rees, but was unable to contact him. Franklin gave evidence for the prosecution at Jones's trial for manslaughter,[7] and published a statement in the press denying that Jones and the others were in fact Freemasons, and strongly criticizing their behaviour.[8] The Freemasons survived the scandal, and the mockery of their critics, and by the 1740s were well established in Philadelphia.

In America, as in England, Freemasonry attracted two different types – the philosophical intellectuals and the gentlemen who thought that a masonic lodge was a useful and agreeable social gathering. Franklin was one of the first kind, with his ideas on freedom of worship and religious toleration, which in his case came closer to deism than it did in any of the leading brothers in English Grand Lodge in the 1720s

---

* Fay, *La Franc Maçonnerie et la révolution intellectuelle du xviiie sièle* 114–25. During the Second World War, Fay was appointed by Pétain as Chief of the organiz-ation for the Suppression of Secret Societies – that is to say, the Freemasons – and in this capacity he co-operated with the German occupation authorities, the Gestapo, and the Nazi anti-masonic organization in Berlin. His shameful record under Vichy does not alter the fact that his book on eighteenth-century Freemasonry (first pub-lished in 1935) is an erudite and impartial work of scholarship.

and 1730s. But in Fredericksburg in Virginia a man of a very different type was initiated as a Freemason in November 1752.

George Washington of nearby Mount Vernon was in fact too young to become a mason, for he had been born (under the Old Style calendar which was then in force in the American colonies as it was in England) on 11 February 1731, which by the new Gregorian calendar that had just been introduced in September 1752, was 22 February 1732. In his early years, Washington never took Freemasonry very seriously; for him, as for so many other colonial gentlemen, it was originally just a social club. After he was raised to the third degree in August 1753, he only twice in his life attended a meeting of his Fredericksburg lodge. It was only after the Revolution, when he was President of the United States and the Freemasons had come to be regarded as the men who had made the Revolution, that he attended, in his masonic apron, the laying of the foundation stone of the Capitol in the new city of Washington, DC, in 1793.[9]

He was a perfect gentleman, a slave owner who was always kind to his slaves, very tall, about 6ft 3in in height, as he informed the tailor in London from whom he ordered his clothes, very well-built and broad, weighing 220 lbs or nearly 16 stone, but carrying himself with so much dignity that he did not look in any way disproportioned, not even with his enormous hands, which, according to his friend La Fayette, were the largest hands that he had ever seen. He was interested in surveying, and, apart from supervising his estate, he was employed by the government of Virginia surveying the undeveloped land in the west of the state near the border with Ohio which marked the beginning of that vast unexplored territory that was called 'the West'. He was afterwards granted a commission in the Army and fought under British command against the French and their 'Indian' (native American) allies in the Seven Years War, which is known in the United States as the French and Indian Wars.

In 1757 Benjamin Franklin went to London for a very different reason than he had gone there on his last visit 32 years before. He was now representing the interests of the state of Pennsylvania in London. He stayed in Craven Street, near Charing Cross in Westminster, for five years, contacting the English Freemasons and making friends with eminent English intellectuals. He also went to Edinburgh, where he met Adam Smith and other Scottish men of learning, and was awarded an honorary doctorate by the University of St Andrews. He returned to Philadelphia in 1762, but two years later set off again for London. This time he stayed in London for ten years, engaging in the most difficult and controversial negotiations with the British government; these negotiations – though no one realized it at the time – would culminate in the American Revolution and the Declaration of Independence. During these negotiations he showed that he was a very tough and ruthless champion of the American cause, and an opponent of the British monarchy.

Franklin and the Americans stood for the principle that had been adopted by the English parliament in their struggle against Charles I – no taxation without representation. George III, who had been reluctantly forced to admit that in England he could only rule by building up a party of his supporters in the House of Commons, was certainly not prepared to relinquish his monarchical powers of government in the American colonies. The struggle came to a head over the Stamp Act passed by the English Parliament, which enacted that every legal document in the American colonies must bear a stamp, for which a tax must be paid to the English government. Resistance to the Stamp Act broke out in America, and Franklin in London encouraged it.

The British Governor of Massachusetts was Thomas Hutchinson, who was in favour of taking firmer action to suppress resistance in the colonies than the government in London was prepared to do. Hutchinson wrote private letters to a friend who was an MP in London, in which he expressed these opinions and made adverse comments about leading politicians in Massachusetts and Pennsylvania. Franklin managed to get hold of these letters, and sent copies of these provocative passages to his supporters in North America, who published them. This caused an outburst of indignation against Hutchinson, and violent demonstrations in North America, especially in Boston. These demonstrations, and the opposition of the Whigs in England, induced George III's government to repeal the Stamp Act, but at the same time they maintained their right to impose taxes in America if they wished. The protests in the colonies culminated in the Boston Tea Party in December 1773, when the British government imposed a tax on all tea imported into the American colonies, and sent three ships loaded with tea to Boston harbour. Some men dressed as 'Red Indians' (native Americans) boarded the ships and threw the tea into the water.

In London, Franklin was summoned before the Privy Council and denounced as the man responsible for all the trouble in the American colonies. By 1775 the colonists were preparing for armed resistance. Franklin thought that it was time for him to leave England, and he sailed for Philadelphia in March. When he landed there on 5 May, he heard that fighting had begun a fortnight earlier.

It is a well-established legend in the United States that the Freemasons made the American Revolution; that it was the Boston Freemasons who instigated the violent resistance to the British authorities; that it was the Freemasons who, disguised as 'Red Indians' threw the tea into the water in the Boston Tea Party; that it was the Freemasons who issued the Declaration of Independence; that they provided the leadership of the revolutionary struggle during the War of Independence; and that, after the victory, it was the Freemasons who drafted the Constitution of the United States in 1787. This theory does not please some British Freemasons, who admire, or at least sympathize with, George III, and are almost as embarrassed to find Freemasonry associated with the American revolutionaries as with the nineteenth-century revolutionaries in France, Italy, Spain and South America; though they are a little reluctant to offend their American allies in Nato, and are particularly cautious about criticizing that revolutionary Freemason, George Washington.[10] But recent objective studies have shown that the influence of the Freemasons in the American Revolution has been exaggerated.

There are three reasons for this. Men who were not in fact Freemasons but were, rightly or wrongly, accused of associating with them, have been listed as Freemasons. Others who later became Freemasons but were not yet Freemasons when they engaged in their revolutionary activities, have also been included; and the role of the anti-revolutionary Freemasons has been ignored. In fact, of the 55 men who signed the Declaration of Independence, only 9 were certainly masons; and of the 39 who approved the Constitution of the United States in 1787 only 13 were, or became, masons; 2 of them became masons after 1787, and only 3 were already masons before the outbreak of the Revolution in 1775.[11] Many became Freemasons during the war, for by this time they had heard that it was the Freemasons who had begun the Revolution; and the revolutionary army continued the practice of the British army of having military lodges with no territorial limits. Thirty-three of the general officers of the American Continental Army, and eight of Washington's aides and military secretaries, were Freemasons.[12]

There has been particular interest and disagreement as to the part played by the Freemasons in the Boston Tea Party. On the evening of Thursday 16 December 1773, either 60 or 200 men dressed as native Americans – there are conflicting accounts as to the numbers – came out of the Green Dragon Tavern near the port of Boston, where the St Andrews Freemasons' lodge met once a month on a Thursday. The 'Indians' boarded three British ships which were anchored at Griffins Wharf in Boston harbour. They broke open 340 chests containing tea and threw the tea into the water. The value of the tea was about £10,000 (£300,000 in terms of 1999 prices). The 'Indians' then returned to the Green Dragon Tavern, and were never seen again. Many people believed they were the Freemasons of St Andrews Lodge, who had come to the Green Dragon for their weekly meeting carrying their bags, which contained, not their usual masonic aprons, but the Red Indian costumes, which they had taken away with them after returning to the Green Dragon.[13]

Recent research has challenged this well-known story. The St Andrews Lodge at Boston had been formed in 1752, and met regularly at the Green Dragon Tavern. They held their usual monthly meeting on Thursday 9 December 1773, when 14 members and 10 visitors attended, and as they had not finished their business, they adjourned for a week till 16 December. But on 16 December only 5 members attended. The minutes of the lodge for 16 December record the names of these 5 members, and beneath there is an entry: 'Lodge closed (on account of the few Members present) untill to Morrow Evening'.

It has been suggested that this entry in the minutes was added later, in order to conceal the fact that the lodge met on 16 December, and instead of transacting masonic business, raided the British ships in the harbour and destroyed the tea; but an examination of the original minute book of the lodge has convinced one learned masonic historian that this is unlikely. His theory is that, as the members of the St Andrews Lodge did not meet on 16 December, the room in which they would have met was used by another organization, the North-east Caucus of the local Sons of Liberty, a political group composed largely of radical artisans. He concedes that some members of the St Andrews Lodge were members of the Sons of Liberty and that some of the men who raided the ships may have been members of the lodge; but it was the Sons of Liberty, not the St Andrews masonic lodge, who planned and carried out the Boston Tea Party.[14]

Revolutionary ideas were spreading throughout the colonies.

Patrick Henry, in Virginia, was particularly outspoken. As early as 1765 he was calling for volunteers to undergo military training so as to be ready to fight for liberty. He inspired and shocked the members of the Virginia Legislature by his fiery oratory. 'Tarquin and Caesar had each his Brutus. Charles I had Cromwell, and George III . . .' There were loyalists in the Virginia Legislature, and at this point they interrupted Henry with indignant shouts of 'Treason!' But Henry continued: '. . . and George III may profit by their example. If that be treason, make the most of it.' Ten years later he was calling on the people of Virginia to fight for freedom against the British. 'Is life so dear or peace so sweet as to be purchased at the price of chains and slavery? Forbid it, Almighty God! I know not what course others may take, but as for me, give me liberty or give me death!' This time no one interrupted him with cries of 'treason!' Patrick Henry was probably not a Freemason, but it was not only Free-masons who were revolutionaries.

In Philadelphia, the Continental Congress met in Carpenters' Hall in 1774; they could not meet in the State House because British officials, who were loyal to the King, had offices there.[15] They proclaimed a boycott of British goods, and formed a 'Continental Association' to enforce it. To the disappointment of the extremists, they did not go so far as to declare independence. But in April 1775 the war began when General Gage, the British Commander-in-Chief in North America, sent troops from Boston to Lexington and Concord to attack the Americans, who were preparing for war. Gage offered an amnesty to the revolutionary leaders, but excepted the Massachusetts Freemason, John Hancock, for he was 'too flagitious and mature to admit of any other consideration'. The revolutionaries in Boston heard that the British were coming, and sent the Freemason Paul Revere on his famous ride to Lexington to warn them. In June 1775 the British troops met the American volunteers at Bunker Hill, and exchanged fire with them. The Americans fell back, but the British lost one-third of their men. The war had begun.

Benjamin Franklin had a clear and logical mind. He knew that if it came to open war, the Americans would not easily be able to defeat the British army. He hoped to be able to persuade the French to intervene on the American side. Some of the Americans had doubts about this. There was great sympathy in England for the American cause, and the Whigs were very largely on their side. One of their most ardent supporters was the Freemason Edmund Burke. This

British sympathy would be alienated if the Americans became the allies of France, the national enemy of Britain. But Franklin had no doubt that French arms would be more useful than British sympathy.

The French government was pursuing the policy which great powers always pursue when they wish to injure a hostile state without any risk to themselves. France had lost Canada and India to Britain in the Seven Years War. This trouble in America would be the opportunity for the French to regain what they had lost. When they heard what was happening there, they sent Julien Achard de Bonvouloir to encourage the Americans to resist; but they did not wish to be involved until they were sure that the Americans would win.

After Franklin returned to Philadelphia from London, he and his colleague John Jay had three secret meetings in December 1775 with Bonvouloir in Carpenters' Hall.[16] Bonvouloir was encouraging, but would not commit the French government.

By the summer of 1776 the Continental Congress had issued the Declaration of Independence. This was largely due to the English radical revolutionary, Thomas Paine, who came to America from England and wrote his book, *Common Sense*, in which he urged the Americans to overthrow the monarchy of George III and declare a republic. Contrary to what has often been stated, Paine was not a Freemason, though he was interested in Freemasonry, and in later life wrote a book about it, in which he repeated the inaccurate myth that it had originated with the ancient Welsh Druids.[17]

As the British officials had now left, the Congress met in the State House, which today is called Independence Hall. The Declaration of Independence was issued on 4 July 1776. It was drafted by Thomas Jefferson, who was not a Freemason. The President of the Congress was Hancock, who signed first. He was asked why he had signed in such large handwriting. He replied that it was so that George III could read it without putting on his spectacles.[18]

Franklin persuaded Congress to send delegates to France to negotiate with the French government in Versailles. He and his colleagues sailed for France, and arrived safely in December 1776.

King Louis XVI found an easy way of helping the Americans. A young nobleman, Marie Joseph Paul Yves Roch Gilbert du Motier, Marquis de La Fayette, was a typical member of the young, progressive aristocracy who believed in ideals of freedom, constitutional government and religious toleration; and he had become a Freemason. The King gave him permission to raise a band of volunteers to fight for freedom in America. The ruthless realist Franklin realized that this was not enough; he must try to persuade the French government to declare war on England.

It took him eighteen months of argument to achieve this. His personality, his charm, and his links with some of the French Freemasons made him popular in Parisian society and at Versailles; but it would not have brought France into the war if news had not arrived of the surrender of General Burgoyne and his army to the Americans at Saratoga. This convinced the French government that the American revolutionary army was a serious fighting force; and the fact that soon afterwards the British General Sir William Howe captured Philadelphia seemed only a temporary set-back after the triumph of Saratoga. In February 1778 France declared war on Britain, and in June 1779 Spain came into the war on the French side, though the Spanish government did not recognize the United States as an ally because of their fears of American designs on the Spanish territory of Florida and Louisiana.

The higher-ranking leaders of American Freemasonry were loyal to the King. Of the 7 Provincial Grand Masters, 5 supported George III, and condemned revolutionary agitation against the established authority.[19]

The Pennsylvania lawyer, Joseph Galloway, who was probably a Freemason, was a great friend of Benjamin Franklin. When Franklin went to London, he entrusted his documents to Galloway. On his return to America in 1775, Franklin visited Galloway, who had retired to his estate in the country, and urged him to join the revolutionary struggle against George III; but for the first time Galloway could not agree with Franklin, and told him that he would remain loyal to the King. When the British forces marched on Philadelphia, Galloway went to Howe's headquarters and offered his services; and when Howe captured the city he appointed Galloway as Superintendent of Police and in charge of the civil government. The British held Philadelphia for only nine months, and when they evacuated it, Galloway went with them and sailed to England. He never returned to America, and lived in England until his death in 1802. In 1788 the Pennsylvanian Assembly pronounced him guilty of high treason and ordered that his property be confiscated.[20]

It is not surprising that the British Army officers, who joined regimental lodges in the American colonies, did their duty and were loyal to the King. One prominent Freemason in the British administration was Sir William Johnson, who was probably one of the men responsible for spreading the so-called Scottish Rite on the American continent. In the 1750s, he was given the duty of contacting the tribes of native Americans in the West, beyond the River Ohio, who were still independent and had little contact with the white Americans. Some of these tribes were fierce fighters, especially the Mohawks, and the British government hoped to enlist their support against the French during the Seven Years War.

Johnson was an imaginative and enterprising man, and became intimate with the chief of the Mohawks. The chief's daughter became Johnson's mistress – Johnson gave her the English name of Molly – and Johnson took an interest in her young brother Thayendangea.[21] He gave the boy the name Joseph Brant. Joseph was brought up in Johnson and Molly's household, and when he grew up he fought with Johnson in several battles against the French. Johnson appointed him as his secretary, and before Johnson died in 1774 Joseph Brant had been thoroughly accepted by the British administration in America. In 1775 he went to England, and next year was initiated as a Freemason in a London lodge; he was the first native American to become a Freemason. He then returned to America to rouse the Mohawks to fight for the British against the American rebels.[22]

Another American loyalist was Colonel Sir John Johnson, a Free-mason who had been initiated in a military lodge. After the war, the victorious revolutionaries confiscated all his property in their territory. He went to England, and was afterwards sent to Canada, and appointed Superintendent-General of Indian Affairs in North America. He was Grand Master of the Provincial Grand Lodge of Quebec in 1787.[23]

The British had another imaginative and daring officer to deal with the native American tribes. Colonel John Butler probably originally became a Freemason in a British military lodge stationed in New York; but, with his unconventional attitude and his desire to establish contacts outside British regimental circles, he joined a civilian lodge at Albany in New York State, and later became the secretary of the fashionable St Patrick's Lodge at Johnstown, New York.

When the War of Independence broke out, Colonel Butler offered to form a unit composed of some British soldiers and native American Mohawks to fight as guerrillas against the American revolutionaries. They became known as 'Butler's Rangers'. His son, Captain Walter Butler, was one of his officers; but he relied chiefly on Joseph Brant and the Mohawks. Butler did not feel bound to observe the gentlemanly rules of eighteenth-century warfare; he was waging war against rebels, and encouraged the Mohawks to fight with their usual methods, with bows and arrows and tomahawks, and to kill and torture their prisoners.[24] The white Americans were indignant, and thought that the action of the British government in letting loose the Mohawks was even more dastardly and criminal than the use by the British of the 'savage Hessians' whom they had recruited in George III's territories in Hanover and elsewhere in Germany.

Butler and the Mohawks attacked and massacred the Americans in several bloody encounters; the prisoners who were captured alive were handed over to the Mohawks and tortured to death. But, according to the story which was published some 30 years later, when Colonel John McKinstry of the American revolutionary army, who was a Freemason, was captured by Brant's Mohawks, he had already been tied to a tree, waiting to be ritually sacrificed by the Mohawks, when, as a forlorn hope, he gave a masonic recognition sign. Brant saw it, and ordered him to be unbound. He then took him to Canada, where he was set free and sent back to rejoin the American army. After the war, Brant visited him at his house in Greendale, New York, and in 1805 they went together, with the author William Stone, to a meeting of a masonic lodge at Hudson, New York. Stone, who wrote about McKinstry's escape in his book *The Life of Joseph Brant*, stated that McKinstry always spoke well of Brant, and expressed his gratitude to him.

The story is a little suspect, because Stone wrote that it took place at the Battle of The Cedars on 20 May 1776, when Brant was still in England; and, to make the story believable, it has been suggested that it took place, not at The Cedars, but at the Battle of Oriskany, in what is now the State of New York, on 4 August 1777, when Brant was certainly present in command of his Mohawks with the army of the Freemason, Sir John Johnson. An almost identical story is told about Lieutenant Jonathan Maynard and Major John Wood, who were captured by Brant's Mohawks on 30 May 1778 and 19 July 1779; in both cases they were about to be tortured to death by the Mohawks when they gave a masonic sign, which Brant recognized. He ordered the Mohawks to set them free, and took them to Canada, where they were held as prisoners of war for some months, and then exchanged for British prisoners of the Americans.[25]

The simple primitive Mohawk took his masonic oath seriously;

but unfortunately for Lieutenant Thomas Boyd of the revolutionary army (who had joined the revolutionary military lodge No. 19 in Pennsylvania during the war) when he was captured by Butler's Rangers and Brant's Mohawks on 13 September 1779, Colonel Butler was present. Boyd gave the masonic sign, and Brant as usual ordered him to be set free; but Butler knew that masonic obligations were overruled by the duty of an army officer to serve his King, and must not be invoked to protect rebels. Butler asked Boyd to reveal the whereabouts of the forces of the American General Sullivan. As Boyd refused to tell him, Colonel Butler ordered his son, Captain Walter Butler, to deliver Boyd to the Mohawks for torture. Boyd died under the torture, and Butler's Rangers moved on, leaving Boyd's unburied body where he had died. It was later recovered by the Americans, and the Grand Lodge of Pennsylvania directed that Boyd should be given a masonic funeral.[26]

The Americans told many stories of Colonel John Butler's atrocities, of the captured revolutionaries whom he had hanged or allowed to die of starvation. They would have shown him no mercy if he had fallen into their hands; but he managed to escape to Canada, where he became a charter member of St John's Lodge of Friendship No. 2, and later became Master of the lodge. He was the first Grand Master Warden of the Provincial Grand Lodge of Upper Canada. He initiated many of his former comrades in his Butler's Rangers as members of the lodge. Brant joined it for a time before returning to his Mohawk people in Ohio.[27]

As well as enlisting the support of the native Americans in the West, the British tried to win the support of the black slaves in the South. The planters and slave-owners of Georgia and the Carolinas supported the war against Britain; if they had noticed Jefferson's Declaration of Independence, with its statement that all men are created equal, they assumed that this meant all white men, and excluded black slaves as effectively as it excluded women. This was a serious error on their part. Jefferson's statement 'that all men are created equal' was remembered by the men who liberated the slaves and won equal civil rights for women and blacks. The year 1776 was a necessary prerequisite for 1863, 1922 and 1964.

When the British captured Savannah and Charleston they encouraged the slaves of rebel masters to run away and come to the British there; the British could find work for them to do on the fortifications and as labourers and servants to the garrison. They welcomed the slaves who reached their lines, and even initiated some of them into Freemasons' military lodges,[28] though no black had hitherto been permitted to join any masonic lodge in the North American colonies. This was flagrant hypocrisy on the part of the British. They had slaves in their West Indian territories, and still played a leading part in the slave trade – the three-way trade from Liverpool to the West African coast with commodities for the African chiefs; then from the African coast to the West Indies with slaves which the native African chiefs had sold to them; and back from the West Indies to Liverpool with sugar. Bills to abolish the slave trade were rejected in the House of Commons, and above all in the House of Lords, on the grounds that abolition would harm British trade in the face of foreign competition.

When the Americans and the French besieged Yorktown in the final stages of the war, the British garrison, running short of food, drove all the blacks out of the town, to die of starvation between the lines, or to be recaptured and punished as runaway slaves by their masters in Georgia. In some cases, individual British officers treated slaves who escaped to their lines as captured enemy property, or war booty, and sold them into slavery to planters in the British West Indies, where they were treated at least as harshly as in Georgia or South Carolina.

On the other hand, the spirit of freedom which animated the American revolutionaries, to some extent at least, led them to have doubts about the propriety of slavery and their treatment of the blacks. Black slaves were accepted into the revolutionary army, and granted their freedom as a reward for their war service. By 1779, about 15 per cent of the revolutionary army were blacks. At the end of the war slavery was abolished in the northern states of Vermont, Massachusetts and New Hampshire, and plans for the gradual emancipation of slaves had been accepted in Connecticut, Rhode Island and Pennsylvania.[29]

The heroic Nathan Hale was not a Freemason, though he is another who has been falsely claimed by the masons as a brother; they had confused him with another Nathan Hale who fought in the revolutionary army and died in 1780. The non-mason Nathan Hale was sent by Washington to spy behind the British lines on Long Island. The British caught him, and hanged him on 22 September 1776 at a place which today is at the junction of Market Street and East Broadway in New York City. He asked to be allowed to have a Bible and to talk to a chaplain before he was hanged; but General

Howe, who had ordered his execution, refused his request, saying that there was no time to waste before dispatching him. His last words were: 'I regret that I have only one life to lose for my country'.[30]

Benedict Arnold was a Freemason. He was initiated into a lodge at New Haven, Connecticut, in 1763. He was chiefly responsible for the first great American victory in the War of Independence, when the British army under General Burgoyne surrendered to the Americans at Saratoga in 1777. But his personal enemies in the American political administration in Philadelphia accused him of acts of indiscipline, and malpractices. He was censured for these, and in his exasperation decided to desert to the British.

General Howe sent a British officer, Major André, to meet Arnold. André was caught behind the American lines and treated as a spy; but his captors merely glanced at his documents and, without reading them properly, sent them to their general, Benedict Arnold. He realized what had happened, and hastily crossed to the British lines. He was denounced as the arch-traitor by the Americans, and was promptly expelled by his lodge in Connecticut; for the masonic rule that a lodge does not become involved in politics did not apply in revolutionary America.

As André had been captured behind the American lines, he was treated as a spy; but Washington sent Aaron Ogden, who was a prominent political leader among the Americans and a Freemason, to contact the British General Sir Henry Clinton and offer to release André if the British handed over Benedict Arnold to the Americans. But Clinton refused to do a deal, and André was tried by a court-martial; one of his judges was the Freemason Samuel Parsons. He was sentenced to be hanged. Washington refused his request to be executed by a firing squad, and the sentence of death by hanging was carried out under the supervision of the Freemason Jonathan Bancroft.

After the war, Benedict Arnold went to London. The British paid him £6,315 in compensation for the forfeiture of his property in America; but, according to the Americans, they despised him as a traitor, and he died in obscurity in London in 1801. The Americans said that he died bitterly regretting his treason, and that his last words were: 'Let me die in the old uniform in which I fought my battles for freedom. May God forgive me for putting on any other'.[31]

John Paul Jones was a Freemason. He was born John Paul, the son of a gardener at Kirkbean, in Scotland, in 1747. As a boy he longed to go to sea, and managed to get apprenticed to a ship-owner at Whitehaven in Cumberland, who, like many others, was engaged in the slave trade. Paul went to sea when very young. He was returning from a slave-trading journey to the West Indies when both the captain and the mate fell ill and died. The crew, left without leaders in a plague-ridden ship, did not know what to do; so young Paul took command, and managed to steer the ship back to port at Whitehaven. When he was 23 he became a Freemason, joining a lodge in Kirkcudbright in November 1770. Soon he was off to sea again, sailing as mate in a ship which traded in black slaves between the islands in the West Indies, with his base on the island of Tobago.

He acquired a reputation in Tobago for daring and brutality. He ordered a lazy carpenter, who refused to work, to be flogged. The carpenter sued him for assault in the courts in Tobago, but lost his case. A story was told about him, that he had found the carpenter asleep and had poured turpentine over him and set him on fire. This story was probably untrue; but Paul became very unpopular with the blacks in Tobago when he killed a mutinous sailor who had threatened him with a cudgel. Paul hastily left Tobago to avoid being lynched by the infuriated natives. He sailed to North Carolina, where he became very friendly with a local Freemason named Jones. Paul changed his name to John Paul Jones out of respect for his friend. He left the British merchant navy and settled in North Carolina; but he failed in his efforts to start a business on land, and was living in poverty when the War of Independence broke out in 1775.[32]

Jones offered his services to the Americans, asking to fight in their navy against the British at sea. They appointed him as mate in a warship, and after he had given proof of his skill and courage, they gave him the command of a ship, *The Providence*, in which he fought several successful engagements against the British Navy. In the summer of 1777, he was appointed captain of *The Ranger*, a frigate with 26 guns, and ordered to sail to France with the news of the victory at Saratoga. When France came into the war, the French gave him the command of a squadron of seven ships. He changed the name of *The Ranger* to *Le Bonhomme Richard*, as a tribute to Benjamin Franklin's *Poor Richard's Almanack*, which had been translated into French and was a best-seller in France; but *Le Bonhomme Richard* flew the American flag.

The British denounced Jones as a traitor and a pirate, and would probably have hanged him if they had caught him; but he had no intention of being caught. His exploits, which were naturally exaggerated in wartime propaganda, aroused the greatest enthusiasm in America. The British had been fighting, destroying property, occupying towns, and killing Americans on American soil, thinking that Britain was safe from any counter-attack; but here was John Paul Jones striking at them in their own home waters.

Many of his exploits were unsuccessful, because he was too adventurous, or the other captains in his squadron were too timid, and sometimes just because of bad luck. His plan to destroy the British ships at anchor in Belfast Lough failed because the wind changed. He entered the harbour at Whitehaven, which he knew so well in his younger days, but he failed to set on fire the ships in the harbour. He landed on St Mary Isle in the Bay of Kirkcudbright, intending to capture the Earl of Selkirk; but the Earl was not at home, and his raid achieved nothing except to give his men an opportunity to plunder. They stole Lady Selkirk's silver plate. Jones bought it from them, and returned it to Lady Selkirk.

But the Americans and the French celebrated his successes, not his failures. He was acclaimed in France when he captured the British ship, the *Drake*, and brought her as a prize to Brest; they overlooked the fact that his 40 guns on the *Bonhomme Richard* easily outgunned the *Drake*.

Sailing around Scotland from the west to the east coast, and dodging a British squadron off Cape Wrath, he planned to enter Leith harbour and bombard the town; but this also failed, because his captains were too slow in coming up, and by the time they arrived the wind had changed. Sailing south from Leith, he decided to enter the Tyne and burn the shipping there; but again he had to wait for his captains, and by the time they arrived the wind once more had changed. But his setbacks at Leith and Tynemouth were the prelude to his greatest triumph.

He continued his voyage south in the *Bonhomme Richard*, accompanied by the *Alliance* and the *Pallas*. On 23 September 1779, off Flamborough Head, he encountered two British ships, the *Serapis* and the *Countess of Scarborough*, under Captain Sir Richard Pearson who had been sent to intercept him. The *Alliance* made off without fighting. The *Pallas* engaged the *Countess of Scarborough* – they were both smaller ships, with 20 guns – leaving Jones in the *Bonhomme Richard* with his 40 guns to engage the *Serapis*, whose 44 guns had a longer range than Jones's. Only desperate daring could save the situation, but this was a quality which Jones possessed. After three-and-a-half hours' fighting, with the *Bonhomme Richard* badly damaged, he managed to close with the *Serapis*, so that the two ships were too close to use their guns. He jumped on board the *Serapis*, and threw two handgrenades down the hold; they ignited some explosives, causing great damage. When the terrified gunner of the *Serapis* came up on deck, Jones killed him with a blow from the butt of his pistol. Sir Richard Pearson in the *Serapis* then struck his colours, and surrendered. The *Countess of Scarborough* had already surrendered to the *Pallas*. As the *Bonhomme Richard* was sinking, Jones transferred his crew to the *Serapis* and sailed away, leaving Sir Richard Pearson to explain what had happened at his court martial.*

John Paul Jones had a great reception when he returned to Philadelphia. He then went to Paris, and here too he was greeted as a hero. King Louis XVI gave him a gold-hilted sword, and Queen Marie Antoinette received him in her box at the opera.[33] But after the end of the American War of Independence, there was no work for him to do in France; so he went to Russia and offered his services to Catherine the Great. She appointed him a rear-admiral in her navy, and sent him to fight against the Turks in the Black Sea; but the Russian admirals were jealous of him, and told a story of how he had sexually assaulted a girl of fourteen. He strongly denied this accusation, and after he had persuaded Catherine the Great that it was untrue, she received him in audience and awarded him the Order of St Anne. He returned to Paris, and died there of dropsy, aged 45, in 1792.[34]

It is certainly an oversimplification to say that the Freemasons made and led the American Revolution. Some revolutionaries were Freemasons, and some were not. Thomas Jefferson, John Adams, Alexander Hamilton, Thomas Paine, Nathan Hale and Patrick Henry were not Freemasons; and some Freemasons supported George III, among them such merciless enemies of the Americans as Colonel John Butler. But it is not surprising that a brotherhood which included Benjamin Franklin, George Washington, John Hancock, James Madison,†

---

* Sir Richard was completely vindicated by the court martial, which ruled that he had fought gallantly and had sunk the *Bonhomme Richard*, but had finally been forced to strike his colours by an exceptionally skilful and daring enemy.
† Madison was almost certainly a Freemason, and probably joined the society in 1795, although there is disagreement about the date of his initiation and the lodge to which he belonged.[35]

James Monroe, Paul Revere, John Paul Jones and La Fayette has been given the credit, and the blame, for its part in the American Revolution and the creation of the USA.

◆

CHAPTER 10

The Magic Flute

T HE French Freemasons wished to become as respectable as the English Freemasons. If English Grand Lodge could have noble Grand Masters and royal brothers, why should not the French Freemasons do likewise? In 1738 they had the young Duke of Antin as their Grand Master, and when he died in 1743 Louis de Bourbon-Condé, Count of Clermont and Abbé of St Germain des Près, one of the greatest noblemen in France, was elected Grand Master defeating two other candidates of the highest rank, the Prince of Conti and Marshal Saxe; fourteen months later, Saxe became a national hero after his victory over the British at the Battle of Fontenoy. The Freemasons changed their name from the *Loge Anglaise* to the *Grande Loge de France*; and in 1773 they changed it again to the *Grande Loge Nationale*, or *Grand Orient*.[1]

By the 1770s they were aiming higher, and looking for a royal Grand Master. They had encouraged the rumour that Louis XV himself was a Freemason, but this was untrue; nor could they persuade Louis XVI to join. His brother, the Count of Provence, who afterwards became King Louis XVIII, was interested, and it has often been said that he was a mason; but the weight of evidence seems to suggest that he never joined. Louis XVI's younger brother, Charles, the Count of Artois, did join. He was initiated as a Freemason in 1778.[2]

It is remarkable that the Count of Artois, who 46 years later became King Charles X, should have become a Freemason. By the time he became King in 1824, the Freemasons in France, and in many other countries, were regarded as a revolutionary and left-wing force; but Charles X was a diehard enemy of revolution, and a champion of the extreme right wing. He was in many ways more intelligent than other members of his family. His intelligence led him to be interested in Freemasonry, to see the logic of its deism, and the intellectual challenge which it represented. This same intelligence led him to realize that concession and weakness encourage opposition, and that the best way for him and his family to retain their throne and power was to suppress, at the outset, all revolutionary movements and all signs of resistance to the régime. He had already adopted this attitude in 1778. The Count of Artois was the leader of the group of courtiers and ministers who were urging Louis XVI to make no concessions, and to reject all demands for reforms.

The Freemasons had hoped to persuade the Count of Artois to become their Grand Master, but he refused; and they looked for another suitable candidate for the position. They approached the 'Very Respectable and Very Illustrious Brother, Louis Philippe of Orleans, Duke of Chartres'.[3] He was the son of Louis XVI's cousin, the Duke of Orleans, and his great-grandfather had been Regent of France when Louis XV was a child. When they asked the Duke of Chartres to accept the position of Grand Master, he at first refused and said that he was too busy. They tried again, but he refused for a second time. The third time that they asked him, he accepted. The Freemasons were delighted. They had the King's cousin, the Duke of Chartres, as their Grand Master, and soon he would be Duke of Orleans. They thought that this would show how respectable they were; but it turned out to be the greatest mistake that they could have made.

In Prussia, Voltaire was making friends with Frederick the Great. Voltaire, unlike Frederick, was not a Freemason, but they both had the same deistic tolerance and the same sympathy for intellectual and political freedom; and they both opposed the intolerance of the Catholic Church. They also shared the same interest in cryptograms, which perhaps had a connection with Frederick's interest in the rituals of Freemasonry.

When Frederick invited Voltaire to supper at his palace of Sans-Souci at Potsdam, he wrote to Voltaire:

$$\text{`}\frac{\text{P}}{\text{Venez}} \quad \text{à} \quad \frac{6}{100}\text{'}$$

Voltaire replied, accepting the invitation, in the same style:

'G a'*

---

* *Venez sous P à cent sous six* = *Venez souper à Sans-Souci* (come to supper at Sans-Souci).

G grand, a petit = *J'ai grand appétit* (I have a hearty appetite).

The friendship between Frederick and Voltaire lasted for only two years. They then had a violent quarrel when they took different sides in a dispute about an official who was accused of corruption, and Voltaire wrote a sarcastic article ridiculing Frederick and his court. This enraged Frederick, and he showed that there was a limit to his tolerance and his belief in freedom of speech. He ordered that Voltaire was to be arrested and expelled from Prussia. Voltaire went to live in Switzerland and carried on writing his penetrating and brilliant books. He and Frederick were afterwards sufficiently reconciled to carry on a friendly correspondence about intellectual freedom and their opposition to the Catholic Church.

In February 1778 Voltaire came to Paris for the first time for 28 years. He received a great welcome from all his admirers among the Parisian intelligentsia. Benjamin Franklin, who four days earlier had seen his efforts crowned with success when France declared war on Britain, urged Voltaire to become a Freemason; and Voltaire agreed, perhaps only to please Franklin. He was initiated into a Parisian masonic lodge on 7 April 1778 at the age of 83, less than two months before his death on 30 May.[4]

In 1751 Pope Benedict XIV issued another Bull against the Freemasons; it reiterated the 1738 Bull of his predecessor Clement XII. Benedict issued his Bull at the suggestion of the Kings of Spain and Naples. The Kingdom of Naples, which was officially known as the Kingdom of the Two Sicilies, was the largest state in the Italian peninsula; it stretched from the frontier with the Papal States, some hundred miles south of Rome, to Calabria and all the south of Italy, and included the island of Sicily. It was ruled by the King of Spain and his family (the King of Spain's son, the heir to the throne of Spain, was King of Naples during his father's lifetime). In 1751 Ferdinand VI was King of Spain, and his son was King Charles VII of Naples. In 1759 Charles VII became King Charles III of Spain, and his son became King Ferdinand IV of Naples.

There had been rumours that some of the cardinals in the Vatican were Freemasons, and that Pope Benedict himself had been initiated into a masonic lodge.[5] Although these stories were quite untrue, they made it difficult for the Pope to resist the suggestion from the Kings of Spain and Naples that he should launch a new drive to suppress Freemasonry. The Bull of April 1751 was followed within a few weeks by decrees in both Naples and Spain suppressing the Freemasons.[6] The Portuguese government, as they had shown in the case of John Coustos, had already acted vigorously against them. The French government paid no more attention to the Papal Bull of 1751 than they had done to the Bull of 1738.

In the Austro-Hungarian Empire, Maria Theresia pursued her policy of suppressing Freemasonry, although the police usually turned a blind eye to the activities of the aristocrats who joined a Freemason's lodge. Her Freemason husband, the Emperor Francis I, died in 1765. Maria Theresia then arranged for their son Joseph to be elected as the Holy Roman Emperor Joseph II, and she appointed Joseph to be co-regent with her of the Kingdom of Hungary and all her Habsburg territories. Joseph could not exercise much influence as long as his mother was alive; but after her death in 1780 he became the sole ruler of the Austrian Empire, and he reversed her reactionary Catholic policy, and introduced progressive liberal reforms.

In the imperial capital, Vienna, Freemasonry was gaining increasing influence, not only among the intellectuals but also in all fashionable circles. Masonic aprons and other emblems were incorporated into women's clothes, and it became fashionable to wear white gloves. It was a reaction against the suppression of masonry for so many years under Maria Theresia.

Freemasonry was particularly strong among the musicians. The leading composer in the empire, Franz Joseph Haydn – old 'Papa Haydn', as the people called him – was a Freemason. He did not belong to the leading masonic lodge in Vienna, the Zur Wohltätigkeit lodge, but to a smaller lodge, the Zur Wahren Eintracht lodge. It was Haydn who persuaded his young colleague, Wolfgang Amadeus Mozart, to become a Freemason and to join, not the famous Zur Wohltätigkeit lodge, but Haydn's Zur Wahren Eintracht. Mozart arrived in Vienna in 1783 and was initiated in Haydn's lodge next year. There were several distinguished brothers in the lodge, including the philosophers Reichfeld and Ignaz von Born.

Mozart, like Haydn, became very interested in Freemasonry. Eight of his compositions had some connection with the subject. Three of them were written in 1785, soon after he had joined the lodge. These were his song 'Die Gesellenreise'; the 'Opening and Closing of the Lodge', which was probably specially composed for a new lodge, the Zur Neugekrönten Hoffnung; and his short cantata 'Maurer-freude' in honour of Ignaz von Born. Six years later, in 1791, he composed another short cantata written by his friend and librettist,

Johann Emanuel Schikaneder, for the consecration of a masonic temple on 15 November 1791. At about the same time he composed the cantata 'Die ihr des unermesslichen Weltalls Schöpfer ehrt' (Opus 619); and the 'Maurerische Trauermusik' on the occasion of the deaths of Duke Franz August of Mecklenburg-Strelitz and of Prince Esterhazy.[7] More important than any of these was his opera, *The Magic Flute*; but by the time that this was produced in 1791, the Freemasons were facing a very different situation.

Joseph's policy of introducing liberalism by the decrees of an autocratic sovereign was not entirely successful. He reversed his mother's measures against the Jews, extended popular education, and went some way towards establishing freedom of the press. Newspapers were allowed to comment freely on political matters, and even to criticize some of the Emperor's measures. But his policy of land reform and the abolition of serfdom, and his measures to restrict the power of the Church, encountered opposition from powerful groups, and were frustrated by the government bureaucracy. He felt that his plans for reform were being sabotaged.

He pursued a friendly policy with regard to the Freemasons. He declined their invitation to become their Grand Master, but told them that he approved of their activities.[8] But though the Emperor did not object if aristocrats and educated intellectuals talked in Freemasons' lodges, his Minister of the Interior and Chief of Police were very suspicious if lower-middle-class journalists and working-class artisans attended meetings of a secret society. In the Austrian Empire, as in France, this led to contradictions in the government policy towards Freemasons.

The problem was exacerbated by the emergence in Bavaria of the secret society which became known as the Illuminati.[9] In view of the interest and fear that they aroused, it is extraordinary that they were numerically so insignificant. The organization originally consisted of only five members. It was founded by Adam Weishaupt, a Jew by race who had been baptized a Roman Catholic and had become the professor of canon law at the Roman Catholic university of Ingoldstadt in Bavaria. Weishaupt's lectures at the university were a little suspect from the point of view of the orthodox Catholic clergy; but he went much further in the private internal publications which he issued to the Illuminati. He wrote these under the pseudonym 'Spartacus', the name of the Roman gladiator who had led a slave revolt in the first century BC and, after he had seriously alarmed the

Roman authorities and slaveowners, was defeated and killed in battle; many of his captured followers were crucified. Weishaupt believed that he and his handful of Illuminati could overthrow all governments of kings and bishops in State and Church, and then rule the world; for only the Illuminati could introduce a tolerant and libertarian régime on earth.

Weishaupt's Illuminati soon increased beyond the original five members, and at one time numbered 2,500. Weishaupt decided that they should infiltrate the Freemasons. There were obvious links between the Freemasons and the Illuminati; they both disapproved of religious persecution, and advocated tolerance and understanding between men of different religious views. But most Freemasons did not go along with all the doctrines of the Illuminati; many of them had no idea what these doctrines were, and some of them had not even heard of the Illuminati. When the Freemasons realized what were the ultimate aims of the Illuminati, some of them objected to being associated with them.

One of these was the prominent German Freemason, Baron Adolf von Knigge. He had originally been a friend of Weishaupt and one of his closest collaborators; but they disagreed about the direction which Freemasonry should take, and this disagreement led to a violent quarrel which split, and helped to destroy, the Illuminati. At the same time, the Bavarian authorities moved against the Illuminati. Weishaupt was denounced as a seditious and blasphemous propagandist; he was expelled from his chair at the university, and fled from Bavaria to avoid arrest and prosecution. In his hasty flight he left his papers behind, and they were found and published by the government of Bavaria. The documents created a sensation, as they showed that the Illuminati were planning revolution against every established government in Europe; and in the excitement the utter insignificance of the Illuminati, and the impossibility of their ever achieving their aims, were overlooked.

When, fifteen years later, the revolution of 1789 broke out in France, some people said that it was the work of the Illuminati; others, because of the association of the Freemasons and the Illuminati, blamed the Freemasons for the French Revolution. Interest in the Illuminati, and the picture of them as the dangerous secret centre of world revolution, revived at the beginning of the twentieth century, after the Russian Revolution of 1917 and the other revolutionary outbreaks which followed the First World War.

Two factors encouraged the counter-revolutionaries of the 1920s to see Weishaupt and his organization as the guiding force behind every revolution from 1776 to 1919: the fact that Weishaupt was a Jew, and that his pseudonym 'Spartacus' was also used by the German Communists, Karl Liebknect and Rosa Luxemburg, whose Spartacus League led the unsuccessful revolution in Berlin in January 1919. One of the foremost believers in the sinister influence of Weishaupt and the Illuminati was the British author, Mrs Nesta Webster,[10] who in 1920 formed her organization, the British Fascists, some years before Sir Oswald Mosley founded his British Union of Fascists and eclipsed Mrs Webster. Her book about the Illuminati won at least some degree of approval and support from Brother Winston Churchill, who had been initiated as a Freemason when he was a young Conservative MP for Oldham in 1901, though he never played an active part in the craft and allowed his membership to lapse in 1911. During his passionate anti-Bolshevik phase after the Russian Revolution, he was quite prepared to believe that Lenin and Trotsky were Weishaupt's heirs.[11]

The Illuminati influenced the policy of Joseph II towards the Freemasons. Unlike his father, he did not become a Freemason, though he was a far more active liberal reformer than Francis I; but the Freemasons had every reason to hope that he would pursue a friendly policy towards them, and their hopes appeared to be fulfilled when he abolished the laws against Freemasons that Maria Theresia had enacted. But Joseph II, like other progressive and well-meaning monarchs and statesmen, tempered his theoretical beliefs with political realism after he had come to power and was confronted with a potential menace. He could not ignore the warnings of his chief of police that meetings of a secret organization could be dangerous and that the Freemasons might constitute a revolutionary threat to his authority. Nor could he forget their association with the Illuminati.

But he had a more important and more calculating reason for distrusting the Freemasons. Frederick the Great was as progressive a ruler as Joseph II, and as sympathetic to the Freemasons; indeed, it was rumoured, correctly, that Frederick was a Freemason himself. Fredrick's kingdom of Prussia was the great enemy of the Austrian Empire, which had twice been defeated by Prussia in a long war. If there were another war between Austria and Prussia, would Frederick's friends the Freemasons act as Frederick's agents within the Austrian Empire?

To everyone's surprise, and to the dismay of the Freemasons, Joseph II issued an edict on 11 December 1785 which he wrote out in his own hand.[12] He declared that from all the information that he had received he believed that the activities of the Freemasons were beneficial; but there were obvious dangers in the existence of a secret organization, some of whose lodges might be used as a cloak for seditious revolutionary activities. So he declared that no more than one Freemasons' lodge should exist in any province of the empire; an exception was made in the case of the three capitals, Vienna, Budapest and Prague, and three lodges could be formed in each of these three great cities. Particulars of the officers, members and meeting places of all the Freemasons' lodges had to be given by the Freemasons to the police.

Although at the time the Freemasons were dismayed by Joseph II's edict, they afterwards looked at it in retrospect as beneficial, compared with what was soon to come within a few years. When Joseph died in 1790, the French Revolution had begun, and this everywhere increased the hostility of governments towards the Freemasons. Before 1789, despite all the talk about the Illuminati, the kings of Europe and the Conservatives were not seriously frightened of the Freemasons; but after the revolution had broken out, they believed that they had realized too late that it was the Freemasons who were responsible for the calamity, which they had been plotting for many years in the meetings in their lodges.

In the case of the French Revolution, as in the case of the American Revolution, some of the revolutionary leaders were Freemasons and some were not; and while the enemies of the revolution claimed that the Freemasons were responsible for it, some of the bitterest opponents of the revolution were themselves Freemasons, just as in the American Revolution some Freemasons had been ardent supporters of George III. Because of this, the leading English Freemasons, both in the eighteenth century and today, have protested that the Freemasons had nothing to do with the American and French Revolutions; but the popular belief, among Catholics and Conservatives in Europe, that the Freemasons were responsible is not entirely unjustified. Many of the revolutionaries were Freemasons, and their slogan of Liberty, Equality and Fraternity seemed to coincide with the Freemasons' attitude. The Freemasons claimed the liberty to worship any God whom they pleased. Dukes and noblemen, along with men of lower rank, were all members of the same lodges, thus showing their belief in equality; and they addressed each other as 'brother', because they believed in fraternity.[13]

In February 1790 Joseph II died and was succeeded as Holy Roman Emperor by his brother Leopold II. The Freemasons did not know what to expect from Leopold. He had succeeded his father, Francis I, as Grand Duke of Tuscany, and during Joseph's reign he had introduced liberal constitutional reforms in Florence and had tolerated Freemasonry; but now, in the new mood which followed the French Revolution, he was under strong pressure from many quarters to clamp down on all liberal reforms. He was advised to deal firmly with the Freemasons, not only by the Catholic Church and his chief of police, but also by his sister, Marie Antoinette, who was being held a virtual prisoner in her palace of the Tuileries in Paris by the government of Mirabeau and the Freemason La Fayette which had taken over in France. She managed to correspond secretly with Leopold, confiding in him her troubles and her anxieties that worse was to come.

On 17 August 1790 she wrote to warn Leopold about the Freemasons. 'Take good care, over there, about any organization of Freemasons. You must already have been warned that it is by this road that all the monsters here hope to achieve the same ends in all countries. O God, protect my country and you from similar misfortunes.'[14] By 'my country' (*ma patrie*) she obviously meant Austria, the land of her birth, and not France, the country whose Queen she was. And did she realize that her own father, Francis of Lorraine, the Emperor Francis I, had been a Freemason?

The Freemasons thought that it was time for them to fight back. Leopold's coronation as King of Bohemia was due to take place next year in Prague, on 6 September 1791; and the opera company would certainly be expected to produce an opera by Mozart for the occasion. Would it not be possible for Mozart to compose an opera about Freemasonry which would be pro-masonic propaganda?

The idea was put to Mozart by his librettist Schikaneder, who was an ardent Freemason. In the eighteenth century, librettists were not yet hampered by the modern law of copyright, and Schikaneder thought that they could produce an opera based on the popular fairy story by Christoff Martin Wieland, *Lulu, or the Magic Flute*. Mozart was not at all enthusiastic about the idea. He was very busy working on his masonic cantatas; and he could not visualize himself writing an opera based on a libretto about magic flutes.

Mozart thought that his kind of music required a libretto in the traditional style which was always adopted for comedy and farce. It should be a story about unfaithful wives turning the tables on unfaithful husbands, with people popping in and out of cupboards and jumping in and out of windows in full view of other people who somehow manage not to notice what is going on in front of their eyes. Mozart was sure that this was what the opera-going public would expect and he could give them what they wanted. It was true that he had once composed an opera with a more dramatic libretto which could be regarded as a tragedy rather than as a comedy, about a statue that came to life to punish a wicked sinner; but his *Don Giovanni* had been the story of the famous philanderer, Don Juan, and his 1,003 mistresses in Spain, and more elsewhere. He did not think that his admirers would want to see an opera based on a libretto about magic flutes.

Schikaneder appealed to Mozart as a Freemason to do his duty and compose a work which would be propaganda for Freemasonry. Mozart resented the suggestion that he was letting down the Freemasons. The other work on which he was so busily engaged was his cantatas for the masonic funerals of those famous brothers, the Duke of Mecklenburg-Strelitz and Prince Esterhazy. But Schikaneder pointed out that a masonic opera would have a far greater impact on the public than a tragic cantata at two masonic funerals. So Mozart reluctantly agreed to his proposal.

Schikaneder ran into a further difficulty when a rival opera company had the same idea of producing an opera based on Wieland's story and presented *Kaspar der Fagottist oder die Zauberzither* (Jasper the bassoonist or the Magic Zither). Schikaneder thought that he ought to make at least a few alterations in his libretto; and while he was working overtime on it, Mozart was even further behind with the music. The opera was not ready by 6 September, though Schikaneder had completed the libretto. Mozart finished composing the music on 28 September, and *The Magic Flute* opened in Vienna two days later. The first night was not a great success, and Mozart thought that his worst fears had been realized; but soon interest was aroused, and during October the opera was performed to great applause on twenty-four occasions.[15]

This explanation of how *The Magic Flute* came to be written was the story told by Schikaneder, to which he always adhered, and there is no real reason to doubt it; but, apart from all the other controversies about Mozart, there has been a dispute between Freemasons about the authorship of *The Magic Flute*. Karl Ludwig Gieseke, a Freemason who was the editor of a theatrical newspaper published in Regensburg, claimed that he, and not Schikaneder, had written the libretto of *The Magic Flute*. In 1819 he mentioned this to the author Julius Cornet, and in 1846 Cornet published Gieseke's statement in a book that he wrote about German opera. As Gieseke told Cornet twenty-eight years after the event, and his statement first appeared in writing after fifty-five years, there were very few people still living who remembered what had happened in 1791 and could testify as to who was speaking the truth. But there is confirmation that Gieseke had always claimed to be the author in a statement made by Schikaneder himself. In 1794 he wrote the libretto of Süssmayer's opera *The Mirror of Arcadia*, and in the preface he mentioned that a journalist had been impudent enough to claim to be the author of the libretto of *The Magic Flute*, though really it was he, Schikaneder, who had written it.[16]

The story sounds like an all-too-familiar dispute as to who first had the idea for a literary work, and one which is very difficult to decide when all the witnesses are dead; but at a time when many people in Vienna were talking about Wieland's *Lulu, or the Magic Flute*, it would not be surprising if more than one Freemason had the idea of turning it into a pro-masonic opera with music by Mozart. Perhaps the journalist said something to this effect, and made some off-the-cuff suggestions for a libretto, and Schikaneder, the professional librettist, actually sat down and wrote the libretto.

The Magic Flute was a success; but Mozart was exhausted, and had fallen ill. When his wife returned from a holiday in Baden, she found him in a dreadful state, and she insisted that he stop working and go to bed at once. He died on 5 December 1791; he was aged 35.[17] Soon people were saying that Mozart had been murdered, and the stories have continued right up to the present day, though there have been conflicting theories as to who the murderer was, and each of these stories is more absurd than the last.

The first story was that he had been murdered by the rival Italian composer, Antonio Salieri. When this allegation had been effectively disposed of, it was said that the murderers were Mozart's wife and her lover, or the husband of Mozart's mistress. Needless to say, it was not long before the story was spreading that he had been murdered by the Freemasons because he had revealed their secrets in *The Magic*

Flute. This is one of the most ridiculous stories that the anti-masons have invented. No masonic secrets are revealed in *The Magic Flute*; but the beneficial effects of a mysterious cult were emphasized, as the Freemasons wished.

The public realized that the reference was to Freemasonry, and recognized the characters portrayed on the stage. The wicked Queen of the Night, who persecutes the young hero and heroine, is Maria Theresia. The evil spirits who encourage her to do so are the Catholic Church. The all-wise, just and beneficial ruler Sarastro, punishing the wicked and protecting the good, is Joseph II, or any other well-meaning autocrat who protected the Freemasons.

But *The Magic Flute* was out of date almost before it was first performed. By 1791 the threat to Freemasonry, in Austria, Russia and Naples, no longer came from a Queen of the Night. It came from Sarastro himself, from a Sarastro who had been thoroughly frightened by the French Revolution and by Marat, Danton and Robespierre.

CHAPTER 11

◆

The French Revolution

I N France, the *ancien régime* had been in difficulties for some time. The government was confronted with financial crises which could not be averted by a succession of well-meaning and able Ministers of Finance who were obstructed by groups and individuals with influence at court. The chief trouble was that the aristocracy did not have to pay taxes; this was a privilege which had been granted to them in return for their relinquishing all political influence. They were no longer aggressive and cruel, as their ancestors had been. Many of them had mildly liberal ideas, read Voltaire, and became Freemasons. But they would not listen to the appeals of the King's ministers that they should voluntarily agree to pay taxes. When they met in their Assembly of Notables, they refused to make any concessions, and obstructed all plans for financial reforms.

A number of strange adventurers appeared at court; they were connected with Freemasonry, or claimed to be. The man who usually called himself the Count of St Germain first came to the French court in 1748; but after visiting Italy, Russia and other parts of Europe, he reappeared in Paris in the 1780s. No one knows who he really was. In Venice he called himself the Count of Bellamura; in Pisa, he was the Chevalier de Schoning; in Milan, the Chevalier Welldone; in Genoa, Count Soltikov. He told people that he was 500 years old, that he knew the secrets of ancient Egypt, that he could turn coal into diamonds; and he claimed, quite untruthfully, that he was the highest-ranking Freemason, though really he was not even a member of the craft. But he had charm, and even those who realized that he was a charlatan and an impostor tolerated him in society. He became friendly with Frederick the Great, and lived for a time at his court; but Frederick thought that he was 'a man no one has ever been able to make out'.[1]

Giovanni Jacobo Casanova de Seingalt also found his way to Paris after a life of scandal and adventure. Casanova was a Venetian aristocrat who decided to become a priest and entered a seminary; but it was not long before he was expelled for scandalous behaviour. Although he had a succession of love affairs with beautiful young girls, he was probably not much more of a womanizer than many other eighteenth-century gentlemen. The fathers and mothers of Venice who complained to the authorities about his conduct were worried, not that he would seduce their daughters, but that he would persuade their sons to become atheists and Freemasons. He himself became a mason when he joined a lodge in Lyons during a visit to France in 1750.[2]

By the time that he was 30, in 1755, the Venetian authorities were so alarmed that they set secret agents to watch him and to win his confidence by pretending to be his friend; and the reports of these agents convinced the Venetian Inquisition that he was a Freemason. His contacts with many foreigners made them suspect that he might be spying for a foreign government; and although they could find no proof of espionage, and his sexual misconduct was too common to be treated as a very serious offence, they could prove that he was a Freemason, which had been made a criminal offence in Venice after the Papal Bull of 1751. For a man with a reputation for frivolity, he was surprisingly brave and firm under interrogation; despite their strenuous efforts, the inquisitors could not get him to reveal any of the masonic secrets. He was sentenced to five years' imprisonment.[3]

A year later, he escaped by making a hole in the wall of the prison and blackmailing and tricking the prison warder into conniving at his escape.[4] He went to Paris, where he was welcomed and appointed director of a national lottery. Before long he was on the move, visiting all parts of Europe, and staying with Frederick the Great in Prussia and with Voltaire in Switzerland before returning again to Paris. But Louis XVI and his government did not approve of his financial speculations and his reputation for sexual immorality, and they expelled him from France. A Bohemian count, whom he had known in Paris, came to the rescue, and he ended his days working peacefully as the librarian in the count's castle in Bohemia.

Giuseppe Balsamo outshone St Germain and Casanova as a plausible and successful charlatan. He was born in Palermo in 1743, but no one was sure from what family he came; some said that he was a Portuguese Jew. He travelled all over Europe, and in 1776 arrived in London, where he called himself Count Cagliostro, and was initiated as a Freemason in a London lodge. He claimed to be the inventor of a new and superior Egyptian Freemasonry, with its own history, traditions and symbolism. He went to Germany, and came into contact with the Illuminati, and then to Lithuania, St Petersburg and Poland, before returning to Paris in 1785.[5]

During his travels he had met the Cardinal Louis de Rohan in Strasbourg. The Rohans were one of the most powerful families in France. Their family motto was '*Roi ne puis, prince ne daigne, Rohan je suis*' (I cannot be a King, I do not deign to be a Prince, I am a Rohan). The cardinal liked Cagliostro, and took him under his protection. Rohan was not a Freemason, but he was very sympathetic to Freemasonry, and he and his friend Georges Louis Phélypeaux, the Archbishop of Bourges, tried unsuccessfully to persuade the Pope to stop persecuting the Freemasons and to reach an agreement with them under which they would modify Freemasonry by making it more acceptable to Catholic doctrine.[6]

Marie Antoinette hated Rohan, because of things that he had done and written some years before when he was the French ambassador at the court of her mother Maria Theresia in Vienna. This piqued Rohan, who fancied himself as a seducer of beautiful women, and would have liked to satisfy his sexual desires and his political ambitions by becoming the Queen's lover. An unscrupulous adventuress, Jeanne de la Mothe, succeeded by an elaborate hoax in convincing Rohan that Marie Antoinette was in love with him and would grant him her favours if he gave her a valuable diamond necklace which had been made by well-known and respectable Parisian jewellers. Jeanne de la Mothe obtained possession of the necklace without paying for it; but eventually the jewellers, who had been told that the necklace was to be a gift from Rohan to the Queen, asked the King to pay them, and the whole story was revealed.

Marie Antoinette was furious, and at her insistence Rohan was arrested in the Chapel Royal as he was about to celebrate Mass for the royal family. He was charged with the crime of *lèse-majesté* for having attempted to violate the Queen's honour. Cagliostro was also arrested. He had nothing to do with the affair, but the authorities thought that as his friend Rohan was connected with a financial fraud, Cagliostro must be involved.

Rohan was put on trial before his peers in the *Parlement* of Paris. To Marie Antoinette's indignation, they found him not guilty. Jeanne de la Mothe was sentenced to be whipped, branded and imprisoned. Cagliostro was acquitted, but was imprisoned for a time under a *lettre de cachet* and then banished from France.[7] He went first to England, then to Central Europe, and finally to Italy.

After staying for a time in several Italian cities, he arrived in Rome in May 1789. The Roman Freemasons, who were banned by the Pope and were afraid to hold any lodge meetings, refused to meet him, because they believed that he had been associated with the Illuminati and was being watched by the Papal authorities. The Roman Inquisition was indeed very suspicious of him, particularly in view of the developments in France during the summer of 1789.[8]

On Sunday 27 December 1789 Pope Pius VI called a meeting after Mass which was attended by his Secretary of State Cardinal Zelada and by three other high officials. They decided to order the Governor of Rome to arrest Cagliostro.[9] He was charged with being 'an instigator and propagator of the Freemasons' sect' and a member of the Illuminati, who aimed at the 'total destruction of the Catholic Religion and monarchies'.[10]

Cardinal Zelada himself presided at the trial. Cagliostro did not deny that he was a Freemason and a member of the Illuminati; in fact he claimed that he was one of the leaders of the Illuminati. The trial lasted for more than fifteen months before the court gave their judgement in April 1791. They found Cagliostro guilty of being a Freemason and a heretic, and sentenced him to death by fire, but announced that the Pope, in his mercy, had commuted the sentence to imprisonment for life.[11]

Cagliostro served his sentence in the terrible Papal prison of Fort San Leo at Urbano. He was confined in a small cell which was very hot in the summer. The only light in the cell came from a small skylight. 'I do not believe', said Cagliostro, 'that God punishes sinners in Hell as cruelly as this.'[12] He went mad, and died after six years in his prison, a few months before Rome was occupied by the French revolutionary army which would have freed him. The Freemasons and the Radicals regarded him as a martyr and a victim of Papal torture.

In France the government's financial difficulties in 1788, and the refusal of the aristocrats in the Assembly of Notables to waive their privilege of exemption from taxation, drove Louis XVI to summon the States-General, which had last met 175 years before in 1614. The States-General consisted of the First Estate, the representatives of the clergy; the Second Estate, the representatives of the nobility; and the Third Estate, the representatives of the common people or, more accurately, of those members of the middle classes and independent craftsmen and artisans who owned sufficient property to be entitled to vote. During the election campaign for the States-General in the spring of 1789 the Abbé Joseph Emmanuel Sieyès wrote a pamphlet *What is the Third Estate?* He claimed that it was the only elected legislative body that had the right to govern France. His pamphlet was widely read with the greatest interest and excitement. The supporters of the monarchy and the old régime said that Sieyès was a Freemason, but this was untrue.

When the States-General met at Versailles on 4 May 1789, the Third Estate soon challenged the right of the First and Second Estates of the clergy and the aristocracy to participate in the government of France. Honoré Gabriel Riqueti, Count of Mirabeau, emerged as the leading spokesman for the Third Estate. He had had a tempestuous youth in which he had several times been imprisoned under *lettres de cachet* obtained by his father to prevent him from becoming involved in compromising love affairs, and had once been unjustly sentenced to death for rape; but he had succeeded in having this sentence reversed; and by the time that he was elected as a deputy to the Third Estate he had become a forceful orator and politician.

Mirabeau wished to preserve the monarchy, but to make it, as in England, a constitutional monarchy with limited powers. He saw himself as the friend and protector of the King and the royal family; but Marie Antoinette disliked and mistrusted him, and refused to cooperate with him. Mirabeau was not a Freemason, though many of his associates were, and he himself has often been accused of being a mason.

The conflict in the States-General led to the Third Estate proclaiming itself to be the National Assembly with full legislative powers. Louis XVI took no effective action against them, but the rumour spread in Paris that he was preparing a military coup to dissolve the National Assembly and arrest its leaders. The people of Paris replied by raiding the arms depot of the Invalides and, having obtained small arms, stormed the Bastille on 14 July 1789. The attack on the Bastille was led by Camille Desmoulins, another revolutionary leader who has been wrongly accused of being a Freemason.[13]

They found only five prisoners in the Bastille, which had almost ceased to be used as a prison; but its capture by the people of Paris was everywhere regarded as the overthrow of the symbol of tyranny. The Governor of the Bastille, who had surrendered after a short resistance, was immediately beheaded by his captors; and in the following weeks some ministers and officials who were particularly hated by the people were lynched and hanged on the lampposts in the streets of Paris. In August the National Assembly passed the declaration of the Rights of Man and abolished all the privileges of the aristocracy.

In October 1789 there was another rumour of a military coup when officers of the royal guard at Versailles gave an enthusiastic demonstration of loyalty to Marie Antoinette when she appeared at a banquet in which they were taking part. The people of Paris, led by the women, marched to Versailles and forced the King and Queen and their children to return with them to Paris, where they were held as virtual prisoners in their palace of the Tuileries.

The National Assembly had created a National Guard to protect the new régime, and had appointed La Fayette as the commander of the guard. He had become a Freemason before he led his volunteers to fight for the Americans in the War of Independence. He considered that the National Guard had two functions – to protect the National Assembly against a royalist coup and to protect the King and the royal family from the anger of the mob. It was La Fayette who persuaded the King and the royal family to go from Versailles to Paris with the women in October 1789, and it was he who provided the escort to protect them on their journey. The King's best chance of survival was to cooperate wholeheartedly with Mirabeau and La Fayette against the more extreme revolutionaries; but the Queen distrusted them both, and she persuaded the King to keep them at a distance.

By the spring of 1790 a conflict had broken out between the moderate revolutionaries and the extremists. The government of Mirabeau and La Fayette were determined to maintain law and order and repress revolutionary excesses; the extremists accused them of betraying the revolution and protecting the monarchy. While Mirabeau and the National Assembly were drafting a constitution on the English model under which Louis XVI would still be the head of the executive government and would retain a right to veto legislation, La Fayette's National Guards were protecting the property of the aristocrats and opening fire on the peasants who cried out for vengeance on the aristocratic oppressors and tried to burn their *chateaux* and their title deeds.

In the summer of 1790 there were mutinies in the army at Nancy and Metz when soldiers who supported the revolution rebelled against the harsh discipline imposed by aristocratic officers – for the old rule still applied, that no one could become an officer in the army unless he could prove that he was descended from an aristocratic family. After the government of the National Assembly had failed to suppress the mutinies by a mixture of promises and threats, the commander-in-chief in the eastern provinces, François Claude Amour, Marquis of Bouillé, decided to take action himself. He came from an old aristocratic family, and had a distinguished record of service in the Seven Years War and as Governor of the Antilles in the American War of Independence.

Bouillé sent troops to storm their way into Nancy and Metz and take possession of the towns. He executed 24 of the mutineers and imprisoned many more. There was an outcry from the revolutionary supporters, and Bouillé became especially hated by them; soon afterwards he was named in the song, *La Marseillaise*, as a leading example of a 'bloody despot'.* But the government of the National Assembly refused to remove Bouillé from his position, and La Fayette strongly supported his action in suppressing the mutinies as a necessary step to preserve law and order and save France from falling into anarchy.

The leading part in the criticism of Mirabeau and La Fayette was played by Georges Jacques Danton and Jean Paul Marat, though they were supported by Maximilien Robespierre, a deputy in the National Assembly. Marat was a Freemason; Danton and Robespierre were not, though it has often been said that Danton was. In the struggle between the moderate revolutionaries and the extremists, as in the American Revolution, there were masons and non-masons on both sides. There was no one whom the extremist Marat, the Freemason, opposed more strongly than the moderate Freemason La Fayette; and the non-masons Danton and Robespierre bitterly denounced the policy of the non-mason Mirabeau.

Marat was a Swiss, who was born in the canton of Neuchâtel in

* 'Mais le despote sanguinaire,
  Tous ces complices de Bouillé,
  Tous ces tigres qui sans pitié
  Déchirent le sein de leur mère . . . '

1743. In 1789 he was forty-six, older than Mirabeau and more than ten years older than Danton, Robespierre and most of the men who played a leading part in the French Revolution. Marat went to France and studied medicine. He travelled in the Netherlands, and spent several years in London, Newcastle, Edinburgh and St Andrews. He wrote a number of books both on philosophical and medical subjects, including a treatise on gleets (venereal diseases) and on diseases of the eyes which were well received by learned societies in Britain.[14] While he was in London he was initiated into a Freemasons' lodge.[15]

Like so many Continental radical intellectuals of his generation, Marat had been brought up to admire the English constitution; but when he arrived in London in 1769, at the height of the struggle for 'Wilkes and Liberty' and the attempts of the Tory government to suppress the American Revolution, he saw the corruption in English public life and the oppression of the lower classes by the nobility, and became very disillusioned. He wrote two books, *Reflections on the Faults in the English Constitution* and *The Chains of Slavery*, in which he criticized the English system of constitutional monarchy, though he stopped short of expressly calling for the establishment of a republic. A story was told during the French Revolution, which has been repeated by twentieth-century historians, that Marat was convicted of some non-political offence, such as theft, and served a term of imprisonment in an English jail; but there is no reliable evidence to support this story, which was almost certainly a libel by Marat's counter-revolutionary enemies.[16]

When he returned to France he became a very successful doctor, and was appointed as physician to the Count of Artois and to several noble families.[17] The stories told by Marat's enemies during the revolution that he was a quack doctor are as untrue as the imaginative accounts by biographers of how he bitterly resented being looked down upon by the aristocrats for whom he cared, and of how he lusted for beautiful aristocratic ladies who despised and repulsed him. In fact, he was well established in Parisian society as a successful middle-class professional man, and when the revolution broke out in 1789 he sacrificed his position and his comfortable existence for the sake of the revolution in which he believed.

His attacks on the government of the National Assembly for their anti-revolutionary policies, and particularly for the suppression of the mutinies at Nancy and Metz, led to his being prosecuted for sedition. After serving a short term of imprisonment he went into hiding in the cellars under Paris, and as a result caught a serious skin disease. He found a supporter in Danton, a thirty-year-old lawyer from northern France. Danton addressed a number of open-air meetings in Paris protesting against the order for the arrest of Marat. The government ordered the arrest and prosecution of Danton for sedition, and he fled to England.

The King had accepted the Declaration of the Rights of Man and the abolition of the privileges of the aristocracy; but he came into conflict with the revolutionaries on two points. Many of the more reactionary aristocrats, embittered by the loss of their privileges, left France and went as refugees to Germany and England and other countries, from where they carried on propaganda against the revolution in France. These émigrés included such eminent figures as the Count of Artois and the Marquis of Bouillé. Many of them openly called on the foreign governments to go to war with France and overthrow the revolution by force. Louis XVI refused to issue a statement denouncing the émigrés.

The second difficulty arose over the Church. Many of the parish priests in France welcomed the revolution; they were in close contact with the peasants, and often were themselves the children of peasant families. They were happy to see the abolition of aristocratic privileges and the liberation of the peasants from oppression. But in April 1791 Pope Pius VI issued a Bull which condemned the revolution in France and called on all Catholics to oppose it. This fateful and disastrous step was the beginning of nearly two hundred years of strife between the Roman Catholic Church and the supporters of radical revolution throughout the world. It also increased the hostility between the radical elements in Freemasonry and the Catholic Church.

The immediate effect in France was to split the clergy between those priests who followed the Pope's policy and those who were prepared to collaborate with the government. The National Assembly proceeded to reorganize the administration and the financial position of the Church in France. Those priests who were willing to accept the position were tolerated and encouraged; those who would not were driven out. King Louis would not condemn the priests who refused to collaborate with the government.

Mirabeau died in April 1791, but he was succeeded by Antoine Barnave, who pursued the same policy. In June the King and Queen tried to escape from France, intending to cross the frontier into the

Rhineland at Varennes, where Bouillé was waiting with an army to welcome and rescue them. The King and the royal family reached Varennes, but Louis had been recognized on the journey by a revolutionary supporter who, galloping ahead and taking a short cut, reached Varennes first and roused the inhabitants. They filled the town square in such large numbers that the King's carriage could not pass through them and advance that last half-mile to the safety of Bouillé's troops beyond the frontier.

The royal family returned to Paris under the protection of the National Guard. But La Fayette and the government still insisted on maintaining Louis XVI's authority. On 17 July 1791, a month after the attempted flight to Varennes, a revolutionary demonstration against the monarchy took place on the Champ de Mars in Paris. La Fayette ordered the National Guard to open fire on the demonstrators, and several of them were killed. The revolutionary opposition to the monarchy was suppressed. Marat remained in hiding and Danton stayed in London.

Foreign rulers had become very alarmed at the developments in France. In July 1790 the Spanish government received a report from their embassy in Paris stating that the Freemasons were planning revolution in every country in Europe. The writer explained that Freemasons were 'a sect of varied persons who profess different religions', who had originated in the lodges in England, and who included Jews as well as Christians. He enclosed a report in French on 'the Red Lodge unmasked'.[18] The revolutionaries in France had adopted as their emblem the 'red cap of liberty', and the word 'red' was used for the first time to describe revolutionaries. It has continued to be used in this sense for two hundred years.* The Spanish government received a very similar warning from their agents in Turin about the revolutionary plans of the Freemasons.[19]

By the summer of 1791 the European sovereigns were contemplating taking joint action to crush the revolution in France. In August 1791 the Emperor Leopold of Austria and King Frederick William of Prussia met at Pilnitz to discuss the possibility of joint action. King Gustavus III of Sweden thought that all countries of Europe should make war on France. He had established his royal dictatorship

---

* But it is incorrect to say that the terms 'Left' and 'Right', and 'Left Wing' and 'Right Wing', to denote the political position of a person or party, date from the French Revolution of 1789. They arose as a result of the position in which the deputies sat in the French National Assembly after the revolution of 1848.

over the Swedish nobility, restricting their power and winning the support of the middle classes and the popular forces. He was a Freemason; he had encouraged the formation of masonic lodges in Sweden and had become Grand Master of Swedish Grand Lodge.[20] But he believed that the revolution in France threatened all the kings of Europe.

Gustavus III's plan to organize a counter-revolutionary crusade against revolutionary France was cut short when he was assassinated by a group of Swedish noblemen. He was shot dead at a masked ball in the opera house in Stockholm in March 1792. His assassination gave Verdi the story of his opera *Un Ballo in Maschera*. The murdered King is the hero of Verdi's opera. This is ironical, because Verdi strongly supported the revolutionary movement in the Italy of the Risorgimento. He ignored the fact that the nobles who, for their own reasons, assassinated Gustavus III thereby rendered a service to the French Revolution.

The Empress Catherine the Great of Russia was also alarmed at the developments in France, and believed, like Gustavus III, that foreign powers should intervene to crush the French Revolution by force. This daughter of a minor German prince had married into the imperial Russian family, had survived and forestalled the plan of her husband, Tsar Peter III, to have her arrested and assassinated, and had persuaded the imperial guard to make a *coup d'état* and to depose and kill her husband and make her Empress. She fancied herself as a progressive ruler, encouraging the ideas of the liberal enlightenment, reading the books of Voltaire and the Encyclopaedists, and welcoming progressive writers to her court. In line with this policy, she had not objected to the development of masonic lodges in Russia. But she was a shrewd politician. She did not wish to antagonize the Russian nobility or take any measures to restrict their power over their serfs; and she believed that sovereigns, however progressive, must retain their absolute power and firmly repress any revolutionary movement. She is supposed to have said that 'Kings and princes should pursue their course, paying no more attention to the clamour of their subjects than the moon does to the howling of cats'.

According to a well-established tradition, Freemasonry had been introduced into Russia by Peter the Great. Soon after Peter became Tsar, he visited the Netherlands and England incognito, working in the shipyards and learning the ways of Western

Europe; and when he returned to Russia in 1698, he proceeded to modernize his empire on Western European lines. He is said to have joined a Freemasons' lodge when he was in London, and after he returned to Russia he ordered his trusted minister, François Lefort, a Swiss by birth, to found the first Russian masonic lodge in his newly-built capital of St Petersburg and to be the Master of the lodge.

The story is quite plausible. Peter might well have joined one of the lodges of admitted masons which existed in London before the formation of English Grand Lodge, and which were flourishing in the years after the Revolution of 1688; and if he introduced Freemasonry into Russia, this would be in line with his policy of defying and weakening the Russian Orthodox Church. This explanation of their origin was certainly believed by the Russian Freemasons at the beginning of the nineteenth century, when they used it in an attempt to persuade the Russian government not to suppress a society which had been founded by Peter the Great; but the more scholarly historians of Russian Freemasonry reject the story as a myth.

There is no doubt that English, Swedish and other foreign masonic lodges had been formed in Russia by the middle of the eighteenth century in the reign of the Empress Elizabeth, and that Russian lodges were formed under Catherine the Great; but though Catherine at first tolerated the Freemasons, she was always a little suspicious of them, and after the outbreak of the French Revolution she turned strongly against them. She subjected them to all kinds of restrictions and harassment, seizing some of their property and ordering prominent noblemen who had become Freemasons to leave St Petersburg and to remain on their country estates. Eventually, in 1794, she suppressed all masonic lodges in Russia.[21]

In Austria, the Freemasons' worst fears were realized under Leopold II; as the French Revolution developed, he abandoned his sympathetic attitude towards them. Attacks on the Freemasons were launched by Catholic propagandists and by a renegade Freemason, Leopold Alajo Hoffman, who became one of Leopold's trusted advisers.[22] Matters grew worse after Leopold died and was succeeded by Francis II. In 1794 Francis banned Freemasonry, and all the masonic lodges in the Austrian Empire were closed down.

In France, the revolutionaries who wished to go further than Mirabeau and La Fayette were divided into two groups, the Girondins and the more extreme Jacobins. They were so called because many of the Girondin deputies came from the province of the Gironde in south-western France, and the Jacobins met in the Jacobin Club in Paris. In April 1792 a government was formed of the more moderate section of the Girondins. They responded to the threats of foreign intervention by declaring war on Austria and Prussia. The Jacobins opposed the declaration of war, but Louis XVI and Marie Antoinette secretly welcomed it, because it provided an excuse for the Austrian and Prussian armies to invade France, to liberate the King and Queen, and to crush the revolution. Louis XVI and Marie Antoinette were in secret correspondence with the Austrians, and prayed for the success of their armies. On 20 June 1792 a revolutionary mob invaded the Tuileries, forced their way into the King's presence, and made him put a red cap of liberty on his head.

The Tuileries was defended by the King's Swiss Guard. The Jacobins in Paris decided that the time had come to storm the Tuileries, to imprison and depose the King, and to proclaim a republic. They called on the revolutionary city of Marseilles to send men 'who know how to die' to lead an attack on the Tuileries. Six hundred volunteers set out from Marseilles; their leader, François Joseph Westermann, was a Freemason. As they marched they sang the *Chant de l'armée du Rhin* which the Freemason Rouget de Lisle had composed a year before in honour of the French army on the Rhine. After the men of Marseilles had sung it on their march to Paris, the song became known as *La Marseillaise*.

The Prussian army was waiting on the northern frontier of France. Their commander was Field Marshal Karl Wilhelm Ferdinand, Duke of Brunswick. He was a very prominent Freemason, who had done much to encourage Freemasonry in Germany. Two days after the men of Marseilles arrived in Paris, Brunswick issued a manifesto to the French people. The draft had been secretly submitted to Louis XVI and Marie Antoinette; it had been approved by the Queen and, more reluctantly, by the King. Brunswick's manifesto called on the people of Paris to treat the King with proper respect; he warned them that he would punish 'the slightest outrage' to the royal family by 'military execution' and the 'total overthrow' of the city.[23]

The manifesto had the opposite effect from what Brunswick intended. It enraged the people of Paris against the King and Queen who, not unjustly, were held responsible for it. Marat had now emerged from hiding and took the lead in denouncing his masonic brother Brunswick in his newspaper *L'Ami du Peuple*. He called on the people to reply to Brunswick by arresting the King and Queen and the royal family and holding them as hostages who would suffer if Brunswick carried out his threats.

On 10 August the men of Marseilles, supported by revolutionary fighters from the Paris Jacobins, attacked the Tuileries after representatives of the Jacobins had escorted the King and Queen and their children to safety. The Swiss Guard repulsed the first attack, but at the second assault the revolutionaries succeeded in entering the palace and overpowering the Swiss Guard, who were summarily executed by the victors for their crime of having opened fire on the people. The King and Queen and the royal family were imprisoned in the Temple prison. Next day the National Assembly deposed the King and a few weeks later proclaimed the establishment of the republic.

La Fayette had been appointed commander-in-chief of the armies facing the Prussian and Austrian invaders. But when he heard of the events in Paris of 10 August, he issued a statement condemning the revolutionaries and expressing his support for the monarchy. The government in Paris denounced him as a traitor, and he deserted his post and fled to neutral territory in Liège. The authorities there handed him over to the Austrians, who imprisoned him. The government of the United States tried unsuccessfully to intervene on his behalf; but while he was regarded as a counter-revolutionary traitor by the revolutionaries in France, he was kept in prison for five years by the Austrians as a revolutionary who had rebelled against the King.

Danton, who had become Minister of Justice in the new revolutionary government that was formed after 10 August, called on the people to suppress the counter-revolutionary traitors in the rear as they prepared to repel the foreign invaders who had come to restore the monarchy. On 2 September revolutionary detachments broke into the Conciergerie prison and killed many aristocrats and other enemies of the revolution who were imprisoned there. Among the victims was the beautiful Princess Marie Thérèse Louise de Lamballe, who was an intimate friend of Marie Antoinette. She had joined one of the Freemasons' lodges which admitted women.[24] The news of the 'massacres of September' increased the indignation of the conservatives in Europe against the French revolutionaries, and, in many cases, against the Freemasons, who were being increasingly blamed for the revolution and its excesses.

The Austrian and Prussian armies invaded France. French volunteers, revolutionaries who were determined to defend the revolution against its enemies, rushed to enlist. Battalions of men who had more revolutionary enthusiasm than military experience hastened to the frontier. The armies met in the Battle of Valmy on 20 September 1792. The revolutionary volunteers defeated and routed the trained Austrian and Prussian troops. The German author Johann Wolfgang von Goethe who, like his colleague Gotthold Lessing was a Freemason, visited the Prussian army that was invading France. On the evening of the Battle of Valmy he said, 'A new epoch in world history begins here today'.[25]

The belief that the Freemasons were responsible for the French Revolution was confirmed by the conduct of the Grand Master of the French Grand Orient. The Freemasons had tried so hard to persuade the King's cousin, Philippe, Duke of Chartres, to become their Grand Master, and had been so pleased when he at last accepted. They had been even better pleased when their Grand Master, on the death of his father, succeeded to the title of Duke of Orleans. But after the revolution broke out, Philippe, Duke of Orleans, joined the Jacobins and was elected to the National Assembly. He renounced his title, and took the name of 'Philippe Egalité'. The Grand Master of the Freemasons was regarded by their enemies as a traitor to his family and his class, and a dangerous revolutionary leader.

In January 1793 the French revolutionary government decided to put Louis XVI on trial for treason because he had corresponded with, and helped, the enemy armies who were invading France. The King's trial outraged conservative opinion throughout Europe; but Danton said: 'The Kings of Europe are attacking us; let us throw down to them, as a challenge, the head of a King.' Louis was tried before more than 700 deputies of the National Assembly, which was now called the Convention. They reached their decision by majority vote. They were divided as to what to do about Louis. Some wished to find him guilty, but not to impose the death penalty; others wished to refer the decision to the people to decide in a plebiscite; others, to postpone the question indefinitely; but some were determined that Louis should be executed immediately.

During the third week of January 1793, the Convention voted four times on the issue. A resolution finding Louis guilty of treason, and rejecting the idea of an appeal to the people by a plebiscite, was carried by 426 votes to 278; the decision to impose the death penalty was carried by 387 to 314. Philippe Egalité voted to convict Louis and for the death penalty. A deputy then proposed that the question of what to do with Louis should be postponed indefinitely. This was defeated by 361 to 360, a single vote. Philippe Egalité voted against the proposal, so his vote decided the issue. On 20 January a resolution that the death sentence should be immediately carried out was passed by 380 to 310, and Louis was guillotined next day.[26]

The royalist supporters bitterly attacked Philippe Egalité for voting to put his cousin to death. Simplifying the voting figures, they declared that the decision to guillotine Louis had been carried by only one vote – Philippe Egalité's vote. For the enemies of the Freemasons, this was the final proof of their responsibility for the French Revolution. Their Grand Master, Philippe, Duke of Orleans, had ordered his Freemasons to launch the French Revolution because he wished to overthrow and kill his cousin, his lawful King, so that he could replace him. But the more the enemies of the Revolution denounced the Freemasons, and held them responsible for the American and the French revolutions, the more revolutionary the Freemasons became. If masonic lodges were places where revolutions were planned, that was where ardent young revolutionaries wished to be.

CHAPTER 12

———— ◆ ————

Loyalist and Revolutionary Freemasons

B Y January 1793 the attitude of politically-conscious people in Britain towards the French Revolution had changed. When the revolution broke out in 1789 most Englishmen were pleased; they thought that it would replace the absolute monarchy of France with a constitutional monarchy based on the English model in which the King would have limited powers and be subject to the powers of Parliament and the rule of law. When the Whig leader, Charles James Fox, heard about the taking of the Bastille, he declared that it was the greatest event which had occurred in the history of the world and by far the best. The Freemason Edmund Burke was one of the few English observers who disagreed with him. Burke had supported the American Revolution, but he was hostile from the first to the revolution in France. He was sure that it would soon pass under the control of extremists, and that France would fall into anarchy.

Four years later, most Englishmen had come round to Burke's opinion. The British government were indignant and alarmed when the French revolutionary government, in November 1792, offered to send their armies to fight on the side of the people of any country who rose in revolt against their tyrannical monarchs. They were alarmed when the French revolutionary armies invaded Belgium and occupied the Belgian Channel ports; and they were shocked at the execution of Louis XVI. In January 1793 Britain declared war on France and joined the coalition of European sovereigns who were fighting to destroy the French Revolution.

The English Freemasons in London Grand Lodge had achieved a great success in 1782 when they persuaded Henry Frederick, Duke of Cumberland, the brother of George III, to become their first royal

Grand Master. They did even better in 1790 when the Prince of Wales (who later became George IV) agreed to succeed the Duke of Cumberland as Grand Master; and in the same year the Prince of Wales's brothers, the Duke of Kent and the Duke of Sussex, were initiated as Freemasons.[1]

The Prince of Wales was not on very good terms with his father, George III. His friendship with Charles James Fox and with other Whigs placed him in opposition to the Tory government of William Pitt the Younger, and the Duke of Sussex was even closer to the Whigs. But the Whigs did not carry their opposition to the Tory government to the length of opposing the government's policy of war against revolutionary France, though a minority of the more extreme Whigs, among whom Lord Grey was prominent, did oppose the war. They were regarded with great suspicion by the government, who set informers and agents to watch them. Thomas Paine supported the French, as he had supported the American, Revolution, and in 1792 published his book *The Rights of Man*, for which he was prosecuted for sedition. He escaped to France during the trial in London, and was elected for a Calais constituency to the Convention.

The official Whigs were particularly anxious to dissociate themselves from Paine and from the minority in the Whig party who opposed the war against France. The English Freemasons were even more eager to do this, in view of the fact that the enemies of the Freemasons were accusing them of having fomented the French Revolution. The day after Britain declared war on France, Grand Lodge asked their Grand Master the Prince of Wales to present a letter on their behalf to the King, assuring him of the Freemasons' loyalty to him and to the throne, and their support for the war against France.[2]

Although the enemies of the revolution criticized the Freemasons as dangerous revolutionaries, the more extreme revolutionaries who now came to power in France denounced the Freemasons as too moderate. Soon after the execution of Louis XVI, the disagreements between the Girondins and the Jacobins came to a head. Danton tried to reconcile the two factions, but the Girondins refused all compromise. They particularly hated Marat, who attacked them in his newspaper *L'Ami du Peuple* and in the Covention, to which he had been elected. Relations there became very bitter. When Marat went to the rostrum to speak, he was the target of a violent hostile demonstration by the Girondin deputies; many of them tried to bar his way to the rostrum, yelling abuse at him and spitting in his face. The quarrel culminated in Marat's prosecution before the Convention on a charge brought against him by the Girondins of betraying the revolution; but the people of Paris rose in his support and stormed the session of the Convention, which acquitted Marat. This was followed by the arrest of many of the Girondin leaders.

In July 1793 a young Girondin woman, Charlotte Corday, gained admission to Marat's house by pretending that she wished to give him a list of names of Girondins to be guillotined. She found him sitting as usual in his bath to cure his skin disease, and she stabbed him to death. She was guillotined, and the Girondin party was suppressed.

In Lyons, the Girondins had gained control of the Freemasons' lodges. In the summer of 1793 the Girondins there defied the authority of the Jacobin government in Paris, and guillotined one of the local Jacobin leaders. The Lyons Freemasons played a leading part in the rising against the Paris Jacobins; but the Jacobins suppressed the revolt, and several of the leading Girondin Freemasons of Lyons were guillotined.[3]

The developments in Lyons were one of the factors which turned the Jacobin government against the Freemasons. Too many of the Girondins were Freemasons, and this reminded the Jacobins that the structure of Freemasonry, with its Grand Masters and hierarchical ranks, was undemocratic and conflicted with the revolutionary ideal of equality. Philippe Egalité went with the tide. In February 1793 he resigned as Grand Master of the Grand Orient, declaring that it was an inappropriate office for a revolutionary to hold.[4]

The number of victims of the guillotine increased. The guillotine was named after Dr Joseph Guillotin, a medical doctor who was a member of the Convention. He was a Freemason. He had said, in a speech in the Convention, that it was essential to have an instrument which could carry out the death penalty as quickly and as painlessly as possible, though it was not he, but some technicians, who had then constructed the guillotine. The words 'the guillotine' aroused fear and horror throughout Europe; but many of the enemies of the revolution who shuddered at 'the guillotine' had been in favour of executing revolutionaries by breaking them on the wheel and by resorting to other forms of torture.

In October 1793 Marie Antoinette was guillotined. In November it was the turn of the Girondin leaders. Philippe Egalité was accused of supporting the Girondins, and was guillotined at the same time. By the beginning of 1794 Robespierre had gained control of the government. In March he had Jacques Hébert guillotined for being too extreme and for worshipping the Goddess of Reason instead of the Supreme Being whom Robespierre had proclaimed as God. In April, Danton and Desmoulins and their supporters were guillotined for being too moderate.

Thomas Paine was accused of being a Girondin, and imprisoned in the Luxembourg prison. The public prosecutor, Antoine Fouquier-Tinville, who had prosecuted Marie Antoinette, Danton, and most of the other victims of the Reign of Terror, decided on 24 July 1794 that Paine should go to the guillotine after the usual formality of a trial. Next day, on Fouquier-Tinville's instructions, the jailer made a mark on the door of Paine's cell to indicate that he was to be among the next victims. But the jailer did not realize that he had made the mark on the inside, not the outside, of the door; so the guards, not seeing a sign on the outside of the door, did not come for Paine.[5]

Two days later, Robespierre made a great tactical error. He rose in the Convention and announced that he had a list of deputies who were traitors to the republic, and that he would give their names after the lunch adjournment. The members of the Convention became alarmed that their names might be on Robespierre's list, and they decided to destroy him before he could destroy them. As soon as he began to speak after the lunch adjournment, he was interrupted by the deputies who shouted him down and denounced him as a traitor. The Convention ordered his arrest, and he was guillotined next day.

The fall of Robespierre took place on 27 July 1794 which, under the revolutionary calendar, which had been introduced in France, was 9 Thermidor. It was the beginning of what was called the Thermidorian reaction. In the course of the next year a number of leading revolutionaries were guillotined, including Fouquier-Tinville; and the rule of the fanatical revolutionary zealots was replaced by a government of luxury-loving and corrupt politicians who enjoyed money, good living and beautiful mistresses. They set up a government which was known as the Directory. The rule of the Directory ended on 18 Brumaire (9 November) 1799 when Napoleon Bonaparte overthrew it and established himself as First Consul before taking the title of Emperor five years later. Under the Directory and

Napoleon, Freemasonry revived and again became first legal and then influential.

The fact that the Freemasons, in the final stages of the French Revolution, had been persecuted by the revolutionary extremists, did not prevent their enemies from denouncing them for having been responsible for the revolution. In 1792 the French Catholic writer, Le Franc, wrote a book *The Veil Lifted for the Inquisitive, or The Secret of the Revolution revealed by the Help of Freemasonry*, in which he attributed all the evils of the revolution to the Freemasons. Le Franc had just finished writing his book when he was arrested by the revolutionary government, imprisoned in the Conciergerie, and murdered in the Massacres of September.[6] But the Abbé Barruel succeeded in escaping from France to England. In 1797, when living in London, he wrote his *Memoirs devoted to the History of Jacobinism*. It was published in French by the French publishing company at 128 Wardour Street, Oxford Street, London,[7] which published books for the French royalist refugees in England. Barruel's book was not translated into English, but it formed the basis of a book in English by John Robison, professor of natural philosophy and secretary of the Royal Society of Edinburgh, which was published later in 1797. Robison's book was named *Proofs of a Conspiracy against all the Religions and Governments of Europe carried on in the Secret Meetings of Free Masons, Illuminati and Reading Societies*.

The Abbé Barruel informed his readers that 'about the middle of the century in which we live, three men met; all three of them were filled with a deep hatred of Christianity. These three men were Voltaire, d'Alembert, and Frederick II King of Prussia.'[8] At the meeting, according to Barruel, Voltaire and the philosopher Jean Le Rond d'Alembert, who was one of the editors of the *Encyclopaedia*, planned the course of events which were to lead to the French Revolution; for the attack on the Church was a prelude to the attack on the monarchy, the assault on the altar being a necessary preliminary to the assault on the throne.

Barruel thought that Frederick the Great perhaps did not appreciate that the throne could not survive if the altar fell, and did not realize that by destroying Christianity and the Catholic Church he would destroy the monarchies of Europe. This led to the triumph of the Jacobins, 'trampling underfoot the altars and the thrones in the name of that equality and that liberty which summon the peoples to the disasters of revolution and the horrors of anarchy'.[9]

Although Barruel believed that the French Revolution had first been planned by Voltaire, d'Alembert and Frederick the Great, he thought that the Freemasons had played a large part in it. He explained that for many years the Freemasons had had their secret words and their secret aims. People had wondered what these secret words and aims were, for the Freemasons had always carefully guarded the secrets. But on 12 August 1792, two days after the men of Marseilles stormed the Tuileries and overthrew the French monarchy, the Freemasons ran through the streets of Paris, openly announcing their secrets, which they could now reveal. The secret words were 'Liberty, Equality and Fraternity', and the secret aim was the overthrow of the French monarchy and the establishment of the republic. The Abbé Barruel had himself heard the victorious Freemasons boasting of their secrets on 12 August 1792; but in other countries they still kept their masonic words and aim secret, and the Abbé Barruel was now disclosing them in order to warn all governments of what the Freemasons were planning to do.[10]

The Abbé Barruel, in his book, expressed his thanks to the British government for granting him political asylum in Britain, and wrote that he realized that his allegations about the dangerous revolutionary activities of the Freemasons did not apply to the respectable English Freemasons.[11] Robison also excepted the English Freemasons from what he wrote about the Freemasons' revolutionary projects; but he believed that the revolutionary Continental Freemasons had their agents in England who were carrying on their preparations for revolution, though they were working in other secret organizations and not in the English Freemasons' lodges.[12] Pitt's government agreed with Robison. They were not worried about the activities of the English Freemasons, but they did have cause for alarm about the Freemasons in Ireland.

In Ireland, as in England, the Freemasons had originally been very respectable, and had found aristocrats to be their Grand Masters; but a revolutionary movement was forming in Ireland in the 1790s. Unlike many Irish political movements, it was not based on religious loyalties. There were revolutionaries among both the Catholics and the Protestants, who wished to overthrow the government of the King of England and were hoping that the French revolutionaries would send an army to liberate them. In 1797 they were expecting the French to come, and the people were singing the song

O the French are on the sea, says the Shan van Voght,
The French are on the sea, they'll be here by Saturday,
And then Ireland will be free, says the Shan van Voght.

Some of the revolutionaries joined Freemasons' lodges. The secrecy surrounding the lodges could form a good cover for the preparations of the Irish revolutionaries. The doctrines of Freemasonry, with its libertarian ideas in religion, appealed to revolutionaries in Ireland as it had done to revolutionaries on the Continent of Europe. The fact that the Pope had condemned Freemason did not deter those young revolutionaries who were nominally Catholics from becoming Freemasons; and the accusations of the enemies of the French Revolution that the Freemasons had been responsible for it attracted the Irish revolutionaries to the Freemasons. The government received reports that in many districts of Ireland lower-middle-class journalists and artisans were joining Freemasons' lodges and were using them as a cover for their revolutionary preparations.

The authorities were informed that John McBride, who lived in Clady near Londonderry, was a Freemason and a member of the revolutionary organization, the United Irishmen. When they raided his house on 21 February 1797 they found badges; on one side were masonic symbols, the square, the compasses and the All-seeing Eye, and on the other side were the slogans: 'Tear off your chains and be free! Irishmen unite!'[13]

The Chief Secretary for Ireland, the Honourable Thomas Pelham, was the son of Lord Pelham who afterwards became Earl of Chichester. He had no doubts about the loyalty of the Earl of Donoughmore, the Grand Master, and of the other members of Irish Grand Lodge. On 24 October 1797 he wrote to Donoughmore and asked for his help in dealing with revolutionaries who had infiltrated the Freemasons. 'Not being a Freemason, I cannot tell in what way your Lordship can check the doings of those who wish to make Freemasonry a political engine, but I am perfectly satisfied that whatever steps you may take will be better than I can suggest.'[14]

Lord Donoughmore informed the Chief Secretary that he was already taking steps to deal with the situation. He had sent a loyal Freemason, Mr Charles McCarthy, to inspect the masonic lodges in northern Ireland, and he enclosed a copy of McCarthy's report. McCarthy had found, in the lodges, members of a type which 'I did not much approve of. Impelled with a desire to be useful, I hereby beg leave to submit to Lord Donoughmore a plan that struck me at this critical time for the prevention of any unfortunate practices that the lower orders of the people may put into execution by being initiated into the mysteries of Masonry.' He told Donoughmore that one member, whose loyalty was doubtful, had been expelled from his lodge.[15]

Donoughmore sent his Deputy Grand Master, Dr Wade, to investigate the position in the northern lodges. 'On him I could implicitly rely', he told Pelham; 'he is a zealous supporter of the government'. Wade and Donoughmore decided that it would be advisable to suspend all new admissions to the Freemasons in Ireland until the dangerous political crisis had passed. They also urged all Freemasons to keep a careful watch on the activities of their masonic brothers, and to give the authorities the names of any Freemasons whom they suspected of being revolutionaries.[16]

The French did not send a fleet and an army to liberate Ireland. Napoleon Bonaparte decided instead to sail to Egypt to conquer the Egyptian province of the Turkish Empire and cut the British communications with India. When the revolt in Ireland broke out in 1798, it was suppressed.

Although the supporters of the French Revolution in Britain were not numerous, and opposition to the war could be curbed without much difficulty, Pitt's government kept a close watch on revolutionary opposition. The government were egged on by such patriotic Tory bodies as the Association for Preserving Liberty and Property against Republicans and Levellers, and by Tory journalists like the Freemason George Canning, who attacked the French revolutionaries and their British sympathizers in his newspaper, *The Anti-Jacobin*. The mutinies in the Navy at Spithead and The Nore, and the activities of the recently-formed trade unions, increased the government's alarm. Two Acts of Parliament were enacted to deal with the situation – the Unlawful Oaths Act 1797 and the Unlawful Societies Act 1799, which made it a criminal offence to take certain kinds of oaths, including an oath not to reveal the secrets of a society, and to belong to a society whose members took such an oath.[17]

The Unlawful Oaths Act and the Unlawful Societies Act could easily have been interpreted as applying to the Freemasons, and as banning their oaths and their meetings. But the Prince of Wales, the Grand Master, intervened with Pitt on their behalf. He was assisted by his Deputy Grand Master, Francis, Lord Rawdon, who had recently succeeded to his father's title of Earl of Moira. No one could suspect Moira of being a supporter of the French Revolution. He had probably been initiated as a Freemason in a regimental lodge when he was serving in the British Army in America during the War of Independence; he had fought for George III at the Battle of Bunker Hill, and had loyally served the British cause throughout the war. After succeeding to his father's title he had been promoted to the rank of Major General, and served under the Duke of York in the campaign against the French revolutionary armies in the Netherlands.[18]

The Prince of Wales and Moira assured Pitt that the Freemasons were loyal, and said that no one could suspect that a society, which included members of the royal family, was seditious. Pitt was sympathetic. Moira reported to Grand Lodge that the Prime Minister had 'expressed his good opinion of the society, and said he was willing to recommend any clause to prevent the new Act from affecting the society, provided that the name of the society could be prevented from being made use of as a cover by evilly disposed persons for seditious purposes'.[19] It was agreed that a clause should be inserted in the Act expressly exempting the Freemasons from the ban on secret societies provided that every masonic lodge supplied the local Justices of the Peace with the names of their members and the times and places of their lodge meetings.

Moira was most indignant that Freemasons in foreign countries were engaging in revolutionary activities. In his speech to Grand Lodge on 3 June 1800 he said that these people had 'resorted to the artifice of borrowing the denomination of Freemasons to cover meetings for seditious purposes'. But these 'profligate doctrines' would never have been tolerated in any English Freemasons' lodge.

'We aver, therefore, that not only such laxity of opinion has no sort of connection with the tenets of Masonry, but is diametrically opposite to the injunctions which we regard as the foundation stone of the lodge namely, Fear God and Honour the King. In confirmation of this solemn assertion, what can we advance more irrefragably than that so many of His Majesty's illustrious family now stand in the highest order of Masonry.'[20]

Moira served as Acting Grand Master for twenty-three years until 1813, when he was appointed Governor General of India. He was then created Marquess of Hastings.

In Naples, King Ferdinand IV continued from time to time to issue decrees against Freemasons, re-enacting the first decrees which followed the Papal Bull of 1751. But in 1768 he married Maria Carolina, the beautiful, intellectual and dominating daughter of Maria Theresia of Austria. Unlike her mother in Vienna and her sister Marie Antoinette at Versailles, Maria Carolina was sympathetic to liberal ideas, and used her influence on behalf of the Freemasons in Naples. She could not prevent Ferdinand IV from issuing new decrees against them, but it was probably thanks to her that the persecution of the Freemasons was relaxed, and that the decrees were not put into force. Several leading members of the aristocracy in Naples became Freemasons, and Maria Carolina became friendly with some of them.[21]

Maria Carolina's liberalism did not extend to the length of approving of any attempt by the Neapolitan liberals to deprive her husband of his throne; but this was what many of them were hoping to do. After the French Revolution broke out, they looked to revolutionary France and to the Jacobins in Paris for inspiration and help. Many of them became Freemasons, no doubt for the same reason that the Irish revolutionaries became Freemasons – because the enemies of the revolution had told them that the Freemasons were dangerous revolutionaries.

Maria Carolina was not the first or last liberal who, in the course of her life, moved from a liberal position to an extreme reactionary one. When she realized that the Freemasons and liberals were planning to overthrow the monarchy and establish a Jacobin republic in Naples, and when she heard that the Jacobins in Paris had guillotined her sister Marie Antoinette, she turned violently against them and blamed herself for having previously encouraged them by her tolerant attitude.

The Jacobins of Naples included a number of aristocrats, but derived their support chiefly from the middle-class intellectuals: the lawyers, journalists and university lecturers. They had some support among the urban artisans in Naples; but the people in the country districts, who were devoutly Catholic, had no sympathy for the Jacobin revolutionaries and were loyal to the monarchy. Some army and naval officers were secret sympathizers with the Jacobins. The most important was Admiral Prince Francesco Caracciolo, the highest-ranking officer in the Neapolitan navy.

The hopes and revolutionary enthusiasm of the Neapolitan

Jacobins rose as they heard the news of the victories of the French revolutionary armies, under their young general Napoleon Bonaparte, over the Austrian armies in northern Italy. Then in 1798 a Jacobin revolution broke out in Rome, and a French force came to their help and occupied Rome. They did not harm the Pope, or deprive him of his authority in his Papal States, but they held him as a virtual prisoner in the Vatican and forced him to comply with the directives of the commander of the French garrison. For the Neapolitan Jacobins, the revolution was coming closer.

Maria Carolina persuaded her husband to declare war on France. Britain, Russia and Turkey were also at war with France, and in the summer of 1798 the British, Russian and Turkish navies arrived to help the King of Naples against the French. The British fleet was commanded by Rear Admiral Sir Horatio Nelson, who was created Lord Nelson a few months later. He fell in love with Emma, Lady Hamilton, the wife of Sir William Hamilton, the British ambassador in Naples, and she fell in love with him. She was a close confidante of Queen Maria Carolina.

King Ferdinand marched against the French garrison in Rome, and succeeded in capturing the city; but it was not long before the French returned, and drove him out, and they quickly advanced on Naples. In January 1799 the Neapolitan Jacobins and Freemasons proclaimed the Parthenopaean Republic, and French troops arrived to help them.

Admiral Prince Caracciolo escorted the King and Queen from Naples to Palermo in Sicily, and then returned to Naples to fight against the rebels. The King and Queen did not know that he was a secret Freemason. When he reached Naples, instead of fighting against the Jacobins, he went over to their side and was chosen to be their leader.

In Palermo, Nelson was laying his plans to crush the Jacobin republic in Naples. His famous love affair with Emma Hamilton has usually been held responsible for the policy which he pursued towards the Jacobins, for it is suggested that Maria Carolina, who now hated the Jacobins, persuaded Lady Hamilton to incite Nelson to act against them. But quite apart from his love affair with Emma, Nelson was a convinced Tory. Already in 1794, when he was fighting against the French revolutionaries at Toulon in France, he had shown his hatred of Jacobinism by cutting down with his own hand the revolutionary Trees of Liberty in the French territory which was occupied by the British forces.[22] His ruthless policy towards the Neapolitan Jacobins had the approval of Pitt's Tory government in London.

While Nelson was preparing to overthrow the Parthenopaean Republic, he was forestalled by the Neapolitan Cardinal Fabrizio Ruffo, who had gone to Palermo with the King and Queen. Ruffo called on the Catholic peasants from the countryside to march against the godless Jacobins and Freemasons who had seized power in the city of Naples. He and his forces of counter-revolutionary zealots – they called themselves the Christian Army of the Holy Faith – were everywhere victorious, and the revolutionary forces were reduced to holding out in the fortress in Naples.

Caracciolo offered to surrender to Ruffo on condition that the lives of his men were spared and that they were allowed to sail to France. Ruffo agreed to these terms; and the Russian and Turkish admirals, and Captain Edward Foote, who was in command of the British squadron at Naples, also agreed to them. But when Nelson arrived from Palermo, he refused to be bound by the surrender terms; he said that Ruffo and Foote had no authority to agree to them, and he insisted that Ruffo hand over Caracciolo to him.

Queen Maria Carolina, through Lady Hamilton, was urging Nelson to show no mercy to the Neapolitan Jacobins. She particularly hated Caracciolo, for she felt that he had been guilty of a personal betrayal, having been so close to her and the King, and having deserted and gone over to the enemy.

Nelson convened a court-martial on board his ship *The Foudroyant* in the Bay of Naples, with a court consisting of Neapolitan naval officers, to try Caracciolo for treason. Caracciolo complained that the officers on the court-martial were his personal enemies, and asked to be tried by impartial British officers; but Nelson refused his request. He asked for an adjournment to allow him time to call witnesses in his defence, but Nelson again refused. He referred to the promise which Ruffo had given him that he and his men would be allowed to go free, but the court would not listen to this plea. After a trial which lasted most of the night he was found guilty and sentenced to death. Nelson ordered that he was to be hanged at dawn from the yardarm on *The Foudroyant*. Caracciolo asked Nelson to allow him to be shot, like a naval officer, by a firing squad; but again Nelson refused his request, and he was duly hanged at dawn from the yardarm.[23]

The hanging of Caracciolo, in violation of the surrender terms agreed with Ruffo, has been remembered by Italian radicals for two hundred years as a shameful act which has branded Nelson as a black villain in history. Nelson's conduct has been defended, or excused, by several of his biographers and admirers, in some cases very ably, though not entirely convincingly. Their chief argument is that he repudiated Ruffo's surrender terms before they were carried out, and that Caracciolo already knew, when he surrendered, that Nelson would not be bound by the terms; but this has been disputed.

Maria Carolina and the Neapolitan government carried out wholesale executions of the rebels, and many more were imprisoned in the Neapolitan dungeons that afterwards became notorious. One hundred and nineteen were hanged; they included several prominent intellectuals and Freemasons. Some of them had committed no greater offence than having agreed to serve in minor posts in the administration of the rebel government during the five months' rule of the Parthenopaean Republic.[24]

At the time, and to a considerable extent also today, opinion about Nelson's conduct has divided on national and political lines. It was condemned at the time by the English radical writer, Helen Maria Williams, as strongly as it was, and has been ever since, by French and Italian radicals. It has not diminished the admiration for Nelson felt by English Tories, by sailors, and by many other patriotic Englishmen.

———— ◆ ————

CHAPTER 13

Napoleon

THE struggle between the Roman Catholic Church and the French Revolution had culminated in the rising of the Catholic peasants in the Vendée in western France between 1793 and 1795, and a savage war of extermination between the Vendéeans and the Jacobins in which no quarter was given on either side. By 1794, both the Catholic Church and the Freemasons had been suppressed in France. But the Catholics and their enemies the Freemasons were again tolerated under the Directory; and their position improved still further after Napoleon Bonaparte had made himself First Consul by his *coup d'état* of 18 Brumaire in November 1799.

Napoleon was eager to make a settlement with the Papacy and the Catholic Church. He knew the hold that the Church had over the minds of the people of France and Italy, and wished to avoid another Catholic rising like the war in the Vendée. He thought that religion exercized a useful discipline over the people, and condemned atheism as 'a doctrine which destroys all social organisation and deprives man of all his consolations and all his hopes'.[1] But he did not wish the Catholic Church to become too powerful and to constitute a threat to his position; so he decided to allow the Freemasons to exist, because he knew that they were the enemies of the Catholic Church and could check and counterbalance the power of the Church. Nor must the Freemasons, any more than the Church, become too powerful. He said that if he tolerated the Freemasons, he would be able to make use of them; if he encouraged them too much, they might end by making use of him.[2]

Nevertheless, both as First Consul and later as Emperor, he did encourage the Freemasons to a considerable extent. It has been said that he himself was a Freemason, having been initiated into a military lodge in Malta in 1798, when it was temporarily occupied by the French and he called there on his way to Egypt; but there is no reliable evidence of this, and it is very unlikely.[3] The story that when he was Emperor he once secretly slipped into a meeting of a masonic lodge in Paris is also almost certainly a myth.[4]

When he was a prisoner on St Helena, he spoke his mind more freely on many subjects than he had done in his years in power. He became friendly with Barry O'Meara, the Irish surgeon on *The Bellerophon*, the ship which had taken him to St Helena, and he often confided in O'Meara in their talks on the island. On 2 November 1816 O'Meara asked him what he thought of the Freemasons. He said that they were 'a set of imbeciles who meet for a good meal* and perform fooleries. However, they do some good actions.' He agreed that he had encouraged the Freemasons 'for they fight against the Pope'.[5]

Although Napoleon himself did not become a Freemason, he permitted and encouraged his closest relatives, military commanders and political advisers to join. After he became First Consul, he appointed Jean Jacques Régis de Cambacérès, an able and cautious lawyer who had managed to survive and keep out of trouble under the Jacobins and the Directory, to be his Second Consul, and Cambacérès played the leading part in drafting the *Code Napoléon* which modernised the law of the *ancien régime* and has ever since remained the basis of French law and of the law of many other countries who adopted it as their model. Cambacérès was an ardent Freemason. When Napoleon abolished the Consulate and took the title of Emperor of the French, he appointed Cambacérès as his Arch-Chancellor. He also made him a Prince of the Empire and gave him the title of Duke of Parma.

Several of Napoleon's brothers had become Freemasons when they were young men, in the early days after the Revolution and before Napoleon had become prominent. But, as always, the police were suspicious of the Freemasons; a secret organization holding secret meetings could be a cover for the activities of the old Jacobin republicans or the royalists, both of whom opposed Napoleon's government.

---

* O'Meara quoted Napoleon as saying 'A set of imbeciles who meet *à faire bonne chère* and perform some ridiculous fooleries'. Chevallier translates O'Meara as '*C'est un tas d'imbéciles qui s'assemblent pour faire bonne chère et exécuter quelques folies ridicules*'.

It was probably the influence of Cambacérès which persuaded Napoleon to reject the warnings of his police, and instead of suppressing the Freemasons, to make them an organization of his loyal supporters.[6]

Four of Napoleon's brothers were Freemasons – Joseph, who became King of Naples and later of Spain; Louis, King of Holland; Lucien, Prince of Cannino; and Jerome, King of Westphalia, who annoyed Napoleon by marrying Elizabeth Patterson of Baltimore in the United States. Napoleon dissolved the marriage by imperial decree. Napoleon's brother-in-law and Marshal, Joachim Murat, who married Napoleon's sister Caroline and succeeded Joseph Bonaparte as King of Naples, and his stepson Eugène de Beauharnais, the son of Napoleon's wife Josephine by her first marriage, were Freemasons. So were 22 of Napoleon's 30 leading marshals, including Michel Ney, Duke of Elchingen and Prince of the Moskwa; André Masséna, Duke of Rivoli and Prince of Esseling; Jean Lannes, Duke of Montebello; Joseph, Count Soult; Jacques Macdonald, Duke of Taranto; Jean Baptiste Bernadotte, who became King Charles XIV of Sweden; and François de Kellermann, the victor of Valmy, who defeated the Girondin insurrection in Lyons. He was afterwards arrested and was lucky to escape the guillotine; but he survived to serve Napoleon, who created him Duke of Valmy. There were also the Arch-Chancellor of the Empire, Cambacérès; the Arch-Treasurer, Charles Le Brun; and the Minister of General Police, the Duke of Choiseul-Preslins. Joseph Bonaparte was Grand Master, and the others held various masonic offices.[7]*

In France, women had been admitted to masonic lodges since the beginning of the eighteenth century, and this tradition continued under Napoleon. An Empress Josephine lodge was formed in Strasbourg and in Milan. Josephine was the Grand Mistress of the lodge.[8]

If the English Freemasons were proud of their links with the royal family, and emphasized their loyalty to the throne and their support for the war against France, the French Freemasons outdid them in their devotion to Napoleon and the Bonaparte family, and their praise of the Emperor's military triumphs. In 1805 Napoleon concen-

---

* The position was complicated by the existence, in France as in England at this time, of two rival masonic organizations – the Grand Orient and the Rite Écossais. At one time Joseph Bonaparte was Grand Master of the Grand Orient and Louis Bonaparte was Grand Master of the Rite Écossais, and Napoleon's marshals held office in both organizations. The two bodies were united in December 1804.

trated his Grand Army* at Boulogne in preparation for an invasion
of England; he then decided that it would be too risky, with the
British navy commanding the Channel, and instead marched into
Germany against Britain's allies, Austria and Russia. On 2 December
1805, the first anniversary of his coronation as Emperor, he defeated
the Austrians and Russians at Austerlitz in Moravia; it was the most
brilliant of all his victories.

When the French Freemasons held their annual December feast –
which by age-old tradition was held on St John the Evangelist's Day,
27 December – news of Austerlitz had reached Paris, and the feast
was more a celebration of the Emperor's victory than anything to
do with masonry or the winter feast of St John. The highlight of the
occasion was the recitation of a poem which had been specially
composed by Brother Brunet:

> This is what gold and treason have achieved!
> Here you are alone, proud islander!
> Do you wish to prolong the rash struggle?
> Tremble, for the gods carry Napoleon.
> Yield, or soon this noble war cry will penetrate into Albion's
>   breast:
> Long live Napoleon!⁹†

Napoleon made the north of Italy a kingdom, which he called the
Kingdom of Italy, with himself as King; he took the title of Emperor
of the French and King of Italy, and in all his official proclamations
he referred to himself as 'the Emperor and King'. To the south of
his Kingdom of Italy he allowed the Papal States to continue for a
time, but held the Pope in the Vatican as a virtual prisoner. Then in
1810, growing tired of the Pope's haggling over the position of the
Catholic Church in France, he ordered Joseph Bonaparte to invade

---

* The phrase 'Grand Army', like many contemporary English translations, is a
mistranslation of 'Grande Armée'; but I have used it here as the term has become
accepted in English historical phraseology.
† *Vois ce qu'ont fait l'or et la trahison!*
   Te voilà seul, orgueilleux insulaire!
   Prolonges-tu la lutte téméraire?
   Tremble, les dieux portent Napoléon.
   Cède, ou bientôt ce noble cri de guerre
   Va retentir jusqu'au sein d'Albion;
   Vive Napoléon!

the Papal States. They were annexed to France; the French tricolour was hoisted over the Vatican, and the Pope was taken as a prisoner to France. He remained there for four years until he was liberated by the Allied advance.

After Austerlitz, Napoleon decided that he would not allow the Kingdom of Naples to continue on the Italian mainland as an enemy power and ally of Britain. He issued a proclamation, calling on his soldiers to avenge 1799, and sent his brother Joseph to lead an invasion of the Kingdom of Naples. King Ferdinand and Maria Carolina fled to Palermo. Napoleon made no attempt to conquer Sicily, which was protected by the British navy, but installed Joseph as King in Naples.

It was liberation and triumph for the Neapolitan Freemasons. King Joseph encouraged the formation of masonic lodges, which appeared even in the villages in Calabria and other Catholic areas.

But Napoleon, like all other autocratic sovereigns, was always a little afraid of the Freemasons. He felt, like Catherine the Great and Joseph II, that while Freemasons' lodges might be loyal, they might also be a cover for disloyalty and opposition to the régime. In 1811 he issued a decree which made it a criminal offence to form any organization of more than twenty people which met regularly for religious, literary, political or other objectives, unless the organization obtained the consent of the government and complied with government directives as to the time and place of meeting and other matters.[10] Under the provisions of this decree, permission to meet was granted to the Freemasons; but Napoleon ordered the Minister of the Interior to conduct an investigation to see if they were engaging in political activity in any part of France.

The Prefects conducted their investigations and sent their reports to the Minister of the Interior. With one exception, they all reported that the Freemasons in their districts were loyal and did not engage in any political activity. The one exception was in the canton of Geneva. In 1798 French troops had invaded Switzerland in order to fight the Austrian and Russian armies which were waiting there for the opportunity to attack France. At the end of the campaign, after they had driven out the Austrians and Russians, the French troops withdrew from every part of Switzerland except Geneva, which Napoleon decided should be annexed by France. The Prefect of Geneva reported that the Freemasons in the canton were using the lodges as a cover for revolutionary activity.[11]

This was the doing of the Tuscan revolutionary, the Marquis Felippe Buonarroti, who has been called the father of revolutionary socialism. He had come to Paris during the French Revolution, had become a friend of Robespierre, and was elected to the Convention as one of Robespierre's supporters. After the Thermidorian reaction and the establishment of the Directory, he became associated with François Babeuf – 'Gracchus Babeuf' – who believed that the French Revolution should go further and set up a régime based on economic as well as political equality, a socialist régime in which all goods would be held in common. Babeuf and his supporters tried to overthrow the Directory and seize power by an insurrection in 1797. The revolt was suppressed. Babeuf, who was regarded as the ringleader, was guillotined. Buonarroti was less directly compromised, and was merely banished.

He devoted the rest of his life to planning a socialist revolution, which he believed was the only way to introduce socialism. He thought that masonic lodges, with their secret meetings and secret identification signs, would be an excellent cover for a revolutionary organization. He deliberately set out to infiltrate the Freemasons' lodges. He thought that Geneva, with its population of independent artisans and watchmakers, would be a good place to start; but when Napoleon was informed of what was happening in Geneva, he deported Buonarroti from the canton and placed him under police surveillance in Grenoble; and he suppressed all Freemasons' lodges in Geneva. Buonarroti was more successful in Italy, after the fall of Napoleon, in infiltrating both the Freemasons and the local organization of the charcoal-burners, the Carbonari, who were a secret society with oaths of secrecy and secret signs of recognition. Both the Carbonari and the Freemasons in Italy became a cover for revolutionary activities.[12]

During the Napoleonic era, stories began to circulate of masonic solidarity, of masons who recognized each other by secret signs and then proceeded to help each other. These stories resemble those in America of masonic 'Indians' who saved white Americans when they were on the point of being ritually slaughtered by the 'Indians', after the prisoner had given a secret masonic sign. The stories told of masonic solidarity in Napoleonic Europe do not really establish that masonic loyalty was strong enough to override national loyalties or the call of duty.

There are stories of English and French Freemasons who allowed

French and English prisoners-of-war to escape after the prisoners
had given a secret masonic sign; of a French soldier, a mason, who
allowed a Russian Freemason prisoner to escape during Napoleon's
retreat from Moscow; and the Russian Freemason, General Platov,
set free a French prisoner-of-war in the campaign of 1807 because
they were both Freemasons.

There is the story of how, at the court-martial of a French officer
in Napoleon's army in Florence in 1807 on a charge of striking a
subordinate without cause, the prisoner was found 'not guilty', by
a majority of one, because he gave a secret masonic recognition sign
to one of the officers on the court, who was a Freemason. The
commanding officer of the regiment found out what had happened,
and reported it to Napoleon, who ordered that the decision of the
court-martial must stand, but that the officer who had been found
'not guilty' should be held in prison for a time and then discharged
from the army without a pension, and that his masonic brother on
the court should also be discharged from the army. The same thing
happened at a court-martial in Toulouse.[13]

These stories may well be true, but they show that although
masonic solidarity certainly means something, similar action might
have been taken even if the parties involved had not been masons.
A soldier sometimes shows mercy and comradeship to an enemy
soldier even if they are not Freemasons, and an officer sitting on a
court-martial sometimes shows injudicial and improper partiality
towards a defendant who is a personal friend, or someone with
whom he finds solidarity or affinity on the grounds of some common
association, such as membership of the same club, or on grounds of
racial or regional solidarity. But when high politics are involved, or
the political career of high-ranking individuals, masonic solidarity
gives way to national duty, class interest or political ambition.

In 1806 Napoleon, having decided that it was impracticable to
invade England, decided to ruin British trade by his Berlin Decree,
which he issued in Berlin after he had defeated Prussia and occupied
the city. The decree prohibited all the countries of Europe from
trading with Britain. He realized that he could only enforce the
boycott and prohibit illicit trade with Britain if all the coastline of
Europe was occupied by French troops or by states which were
satellites of France. He thought that he would have to occupy Spain
and Portugal, for though Spain had been France's ally against Britain
earlier in the war, and agreed to prohibit trade with Britain, he knew

that the Spanish government would connive at smuggling; and this would be even more likely in the case of Portugal, which had been the ally of England for more than four hundred years.

In 1807 he ordered Marshal Junot to cross the Pyrenees, march through Spain and invade Portugal. Junot occupied Lisbon, and the King of Portugal and the royal family escaped in a British ship to the Portuguese colony of Brazil; but the Portuguese rose in revolt and drove out the French. Junot's army had antagonized the Spaniards on its march through Spain, and Napoleon then decided to conquer both Spain and Portugal. He invited King Charles IV of Spain and his son, the Infante Prince Ferdinand, to Bayonne, and forced King Charles to abdicate and Prince Ferdinand to renounce his rights to the throne of Spain. Holding them both prisoners at Bayonne, he invaded Spain and entered Madrid. He installed his brother Joseph as King of Spain, and arranged for his brother-in-law Murat to succeed him as King of Naples; and he ordered Soult to invade Portugal.

In Spain and Portugal, the Freemasons were suppressed by the Inquisition as fiercely as they had been when Charles III issued his decree against them after the Papal Bulls of 1738 and 1751 and the Portuguese Inquisition had tortured John Coustos. King Joseph suppressed the Inquisition in Spain, and encouraged the formation of masonic lodges there, as he had done in his earlier kingdom of Naples. When Soult invaded Portugal, the Portuguese Freemasons looked on him as a liberator, and under the protection of Soult's army they formed Freemasons' lodges. For the first time in the history of Portugal, they could join these lodges openly.

Unfortunately, both in Spain and Portugal, the French army showed no consideration for the national feelings of the people, but treated them as a conquered nation. Ever since Napoleon had witnessed the demonstrations and revolutions in Paris under the Jacobins and the Directory, he had always acted on the principle that riots must be suppressed by 'a whiff of grapeshot'. He thought that Louis XVI was a coward for not having opened fire on the people who entered the Tuileries on 20 June 1792: 'If he had only turned the cannon on them and shot down five or six hundred, the rest would have run'.[14] Napoleon, by shooting down a few hundred demonstrators in Madrid and in the other Spanish and Portuguese towns and villages where there was any sign of resistance to the French, succeeded in uniting the Spanish and Portuguese people in a national struggle against the French, which completely nullified all the liberal reforms and the suppression of the Inquisition carried out by the Freemason King Joseph Bonaparte and his two Freemason Marshals, Soult and Masséna.

But in the province of Estramadura, in June 1811, a French officer, Captain de Castillon, a Freemason, allowed some Spanish Freemason guerrillas, who were hiding in a monastery, to go free; and they, in return, gave him some masonic emblems for him to show to save his life if he were captured by the guerrillas and happened to meet some Freemasons among them.[15] This story is more credible than many similar ones of masonic solidarity during the Napoleonic wars, because undoubtedly many French Freemasons, some of them old revolutionaries from the days of the republic, did not approve of Napoleon's oppression of subject peoples when he 'liberated' them from their old reactionary rulers.

The British government sent an army to Portugal under General Sir Arthur Wellesley, who had distinguished himself in a campaign in India. He built a strong defensive position to protect Lisbon from the French, and after repulsing the French attack he was able to take the offensive and drive Soult out of Portugal and back across Spain. He was rewarded for his victories by being created Viscount Wellington. Some of the officers in his army were Freemasons, having joined their regimental lodges. They were disconcerted to find that as they liberated Portugal from Soult, the Portuguese Freemasons who had formed masonic lodges under the protection of Soult's army were now arrested by the Portuguese authorities and handed over to the Inquisition, which was again active.

On St John's Day in winter, 27 December 1809, some British officers who were Freemasons went on a procession through the streets of Lisbon from the fortress where the garrison was stationed to the British-owned cotton-spinning factory. This alarmed the Portuguese Inquisition and government and many of the more reactionary elements among the population of Lisbon. When Wellington heard what had happened, he was most displeased, for it was the policy of the British government to stand united with the intolerant and persecuting Portuguese against the French who tolerated the Freemasons.

On 4 January 1810 he wrote from his headquarters at Coimbra to Colonel Warren Peacocke, the commanding officer of the British garrison in Lisbon, telling him that he had received a protest from the Portuguese Secretary of State about the masonic procession in Lisbon. 'I have to inform you that the procession, the insignia, and the existence of Freemasonry are contrary to the laws of Portugal; and adverting to circumstances which have recently occurred at Lisbon, and to the reports in circulation of the confinement of different individuals by the government, I should have believed it impossible that it was not already known that these proceedings were illegal.' The procession had been very offensive to many people in Lisbon 'who are at least equally attached to the laws of the country as we are to those of our own'. Wellington therefore ordered Colonel Peacocke to inform the commanding officers of all British regiments that meetings of British regimental masonic lodges, the display of masonic emblems, and masonic processions should cease as long as the army was stationed in Portugal.[16] Peacocke may not have known that Wellington was himself a Freemason; but Wellington had no sense of solidarity with the Portuguese Freemasons who had been arrested by the Portuguese Inquisition after the departure of the Freemason Soult.

In Spain, the united front of all Spaniards against the trigger-happy and exploiting French army and its firing squads caused further complications for Wellington. As he drove first Soult and then Masséna back across Spain to the Pyrenees, the first part of Spain to be liberated was the area in the south round Cadiz. In 1812 the Spanish Liberals, who were fighting against the French, met in Cadiz and drafted a liberal constitution. It abolished the Inquisition, granted freedom of speech and of the press, and religious toleration, legalized Freemasons' lodges, and established a Parliament with sovereign powers elected under a system of almost universal suffrage for men.

After Wellington had driven Joseph Bonaparte and the French army across the Pyrenees, King Ferdinand returned to Spain and took over the government. He repudiated the Constitution of 1812 which the Liberals had proclaimed at Cadiz, and re-established his royal absolutism. The Inquisition was restored, and Freemasons were arrested and sentenced to long terms of imprisonment.

In the struggle between Ferdinand and his former allies, the Spanish Liberals, the role of the British army was of decisive importance. Wellington intervened decisively on King Ferdinand's side. Both his own Tory sympathies and the policy of Lord Liverpool's Tory government in London made him support the King against the Liberals and allow Ferdinand to reintroduce his absolute monarchy, to bring back the Inquisition and imprison Liberals and Freemasons. The fact that Wellington was himself a Freemason was irrelevant.

It was perhaps because Wellington had encountered Freemasonry in its liberal and revolutionary form in Spain and Portugal that he was a little embarrassed about being himself a Freemason. The records of the lodge, which are still available, show clearly that Wellington, then Arthur Wesley – as his family still spelt their surname at the time – was initiated as a Freemason in a lodge at Trim in County Meath on 7 December 1790. He continued to be a member of the lodge until his membership lapsed in 1795. But the Irish Freemasons remembered that he was their brother and were proud of his association with them. In 1838 the members of a lodge in Dublin wished to call themselves the Wellington Lodge, and their master, Mr Carleton, wrote to Wellington to ask his permission to do this.

Wellington replied to Carleton in the third person but in his own hand. 'The Duke of Wellington presents his compliments to Mr Carleton. He perfectly recollects that he was admitted to the lowest grade of Free Masonry in a lodge which was formed at Trim in the County of Meath. He has never since attended a lodge of Free Masons.' In view of this, to call a Freemasons' lodge by his name 'would be a ridiculous assumption of the reputation of being attached to Free Masonry, in addition to being a misrepresentation'. So he hoped that the lodge would not be named after him.

Wellington was aged 69 when he wrote this letter. Thirteen years later, in the last year of his life, he went even further in repudiating Freemasonry in a letter to Mr J. Walsh, who wrote to him about his connection with the Freemasons. On 13 October 1851 he replied: 'Field Marshal the Duke of Wellington presents his compliments to Mr Walsh. He has received his letter of 7th ult. The Duke has no recollection of having been admitted a Freemason. He has no knowledge of that association'.[17]

CHAPTER 14

——————— ◆ ———————

The Restoration

THE French Freemasons continued to show their enthusiasm for Napoleon, despite his defeats in Spain and Russia. After the retreat from Moscow and the loss of 400,000 men in Russia, when Napoleon hastily took steps to build up a new army for the 1813 campaign, the Grand Orient Grand Lodge contributed 5,000 francs for buying cavalry horses for the army.[1] But when, after two more years of defeats, the Allies invaded France and restored Louis XVIII as King, the Grand Lodge of the Grand Orient turned against Napoleon. So did Napoleon's marshals, who accepted appointments in Louis XVIII's army and seats in his House of Peers. Ney, Masséna, Soult and Macdonald all took office under Louis XVIII.

The restored Bourbon monarchy chose Henry IV, the first Bourbon King, as their hero, for he had granted religious toleration by the Edict of Nantes, had expressed concern for the well-being of the poor, and had gained a reputation for tolerance and benevolence. The government decided to erect a great equestrian statue of Henry IV on the Ile de la Cité, near the cathedral of Notre Dame in Paris, and invited the public to subscribe to the cost. The Grand Orient Grand Lodge contributed.[2] It was just over a year since they had contributed to the cost of buying cavalry horses for Napoleon's army.

In April 1814, a fortnight after the Allies and Louis XVIII entered Paris, the Freemasons in Marseilles paraded through the streets carrying a bust of Louis XVIII.[3] Grand Lodge announced that the annual Feast on St John the Baptist's Day, 24 June, should be devoted to celebrating the return of the rightful King.[4]

King Joseph, who had lost his kingdom in Spain, had gone into exile in Switzerland. French Grand Lodge wrote to him, asking him

[162]

to resign as their Grand Master. He refused. This was embarrassing for Grand Lodge, for it would be difficult to find a reason for deposing him, apart from the true one, that the Grand Orient wanted to be on the winning side. They decided to appoint a commission of three officers to exercise the powers of the Grand Master. One of them was Napoleon's Marshal Macdonald, who was now supporting Louis XVIII.[5]

Then on 1 March 1815 Napoleon left Elba and landed in the south of France. The Freemasons' first reaction was to re-emphasize their loyalty to Louis XVIII. Marshal Ney offered to lead the troops that were sent to capture Napoleon; but when he and his men encountered Napoleon near Grenoble on 7 March, they went over to his side. On 20 March Napoleon entered Paris, and Louis XVIII fled to Brussels.

Ney was the only one of Napoleon's former generals who joined him. The others, like the Freemasons' Grand Lodge, kept quiet during the Hundred Days, and waited to see what would happen. Napoleon offered peace to the Allies, but they prepared for war, and as he, on his side, also prepared to fight them, he turned to the revolutionary and liberal forces that he had suppressed during his fifteen-year rule as First Consul and Emperor. He granted a liberal constitution, abolished the slave trade, and called on the people to show the revolutionary spirit of 1792 as they prepared to repulse the attempts of the foreign sovereigns to invade France and restore the Bourbons. Later, on St Helena, he admitted that if he had defeated the Allies and remained in power in France, he would have annulled all these concessions that he made to the liberals. He was joined by a few Freemasons who had been in opposition to him and in disgrace during his Empire;[6] but the Grand Lodge and most of the Freemasons waited to see what would happen. There were no more calls on Joseph Bonaparte to resign as Grand Master; he had returned from Switzerland to join Napoleon. Grand Lodge cancelled the celebration on the summer feast of St John in 1815.[7]

At the Battle of Waterloo, Napoleon himself was almost the only man who played a prominent part who was not a Freemason. For eight hours on the afternoon and evening of 18 June 1815 he tried in vain to destroy the British army; but the British, under the Freemason Wellington, stood firm and resisted the last desperate attack by the Imperial Guard which was led by the Freemason Ney. Just before 9 p.m. the Prussian army arrived to attack the exhausted French and to butcher them as they fled, defeated. The Prussians were led by their seventy-three-year-old commander, Field Marshal Gebhard von Blücher. He was a Freemason.[8]

The Allies went on to Paris, entering the city on 3 July, and bringing Louis XVIII with them. Napoleon, after a fatal hesitation for thirteen days, decided to try to escape to the United States; but as his ship left Rochefort, she was intercepted by the British warship *The Bellerophon*. Napoleon surrendered, and the Allied governments sent him as a prisoner to the island of St Helena in the South Atlantic.

The Allies and Louis XVIII reached Paris too late for the Freemasons to celebrate their summer feast of St John on 24 June; but as soon as Louis arrived they issued a statement welcoming the return of their lawful King.[9] Joseph Bonaparte, unlike Napoleon, had succeeded in reaching the United States, and spent the last twenty-nine years of his life in his house at Point Breeze in New Jersey. The French Freemasons again wrote to him asking him to resign as their Grand Master, but again he refused. The Freemasons decided not to elect a Grand Master for the time being, and did without one for thirty-eight years.[10]

Ney was arrested, and charged with high treason for having deserted to Napoleon during the Hundred Days. He pleaded that he was exempt from prosecution under the terms of the capitulation which Wellington had granted to the soldiers of Napoleon's army after Waterloo; it exempted them from all punishment. Wellington argued that the provisions of the capitulation did not apply to crimes committed by a soldier against the laws of France; he granted an interview to Madame Ney, but refused to intercede with Louis XVIII. He had no more sympathy for his masonic brother Ney than he had had for the Freemasons of Spain and Portugal.[11]

Ney was put on trial before a court-martial; the judges were his former colleagues, and included Masséna, Pierre Augereau and other masons, though Masséna tried unsuccessfully to be excused from serving on the court. As it turned out, they did not have to decide Ney's fate, for Ney claimed the right, as a peer of France, to be tried by the House of Peers. Here, too, some of his judges were fellow-marshals and Freemasons; but with one solitary exception the House unanimously found him guilty and sentenced him to be shot by a firing squad.[12]

Several people urged Louis XVIII to show mercy and commute the death sentence on Ney; but the foreign governments and their ambassadors, including the British Prime Minister Lord Liverpool, his Foreign Secretary Lord Castlereagh, and Wellington urged King Louis to deal firmly with the traitors of the Hundred Days and to make an example of Ney.[13]

The Duchess of Angoulême, the daughter of Louis XVI and Marie Antoinette, used her influence with Louis XVIII to dissuade him from commuting the death sentence on Ney. As a child, she had been in prison with her father and mother during the Revolution with her little brother the Dauphin, or Louis XVII, as the royalists regarded him. Her father and mother had been guillotined, and her brother had died as a child of nine or ten from ill-treatment by his jailer. She felt bitter towards all revolutionaries and their heirs, including Ney, and she pressed for the death sentence to be carried out. Some years later, she read a book which described Napoleon's retreat from Moscow in 1812 and the courage which Ney had shown during that campaign. She said that if she had read the book in 1815, she would have intervened in favour of commuting the death sentence on Ney.[14]

The sentence was carried out on 7 December 1815.

The position of the French Freemasons was not too comfortable under Louis XVIII, because of their reputation as revolutionaries and their support for Napoleon under the Empire. They were protected by Elie, the Duke Decazes, who was a Freemason. After a quiet career as a successful lawyer under Napoleon, he was appointed by Louis XVIII to be Minister of Police and later Minister of the Interior. He persuaded the King to pursue a liberal policy. With Louis's consent, he issued a circular to the Prefects and police, informing them that the King did not consider the Freemasons to be a dangerous organization.[15] It has often been suggested that Louis XVIII himself was a Freemason, and that he was initiated when he was Count of Provence in the 1770s; but there is no reliable evidence of this.[16]

There is no doubt that the King's brother, the Count of Artois, was a Freemason; but he was the greatest opponent of Decazes's liberal policy. He urged his brother to suppress the liberals, and criticized Decazes for his weakness. He was supported in this by the Allied governments, especially by Austria and Russia, which had formed the Holy Alliance to suppress revolution and liberalism everywhere in Europe, if necessary by armed intervention.

The Count of Artois was not the only reactionary Freemason. The writer Joseph de Maistre was a Freemason;[17] he had been initiated before the French Revolution. The political developments in France and Europe had convinced him that the danger of revolution must be combated by firm government and severe repression. With his clear mind and his brilliant powers of analysis he had the greatest contempt for woolly liberal thinking, though he could not withhold a grudging admiration for the revolutionary determination of the Jacobins. He became the leading conservative political philosopher of his time.

The Count of Artois's son, the Duke of Berry, had far more liberal ideas than his father; and Decazes and the Freemasons hoped that he would accept the position of Grand Master of the Grand Orient. But in 1820 the Duke of Berry was stabbed to death by a saddler named Louvel, who apparently had liberal revolutionary views, though he was not connected with any organization and had acted on his own initiative. There was an outcry of indignation from the conservatives, who blamed the liberals for the assassination and Decazes for having encouraged the liberals by his weakness and pro-liberal policy. He was forced to resign. The Freemasons held a public memorial service for the Duke of Berry at which they expressed their horror at his assassination. The murder ended Decazes's liberal policy and strengthened the position of the Count of Artois; but it did not lead to any new measures against the Freemasons.[18]

When Louis XVIII died in 1824, the Count of Artois became King Charles X. He pursued a more reactionary policy than Louis XVIII. But now an elderly Freemason reappeared on the political scene. When La Fayette was imprisoned by the Austrians in the Netherlands in 1792 he remained there for five years; all the efforts of President George Washington and the United States government to intervene on his behalf were unsuccessful. But after Napoleon had defeated the Austrians in northern Italy he forced them to agree to the Treaty of Campo-Formio in 1797. One of the conditions of peace on which he insisted was the release of La Fayette. This was a generous action on Napoleon's part, for he had a low opinion of La Fayette both as a general and a politician. He did not give him any employment under the Consulate or the Empire, and for nearly thirty years La Fayette lived quietly in France taking no part in politics. When Napoleon temporarily adopted a liberal policy during the Hundred Days, and many liberals and Freemasons who had formerly opposed him came out in his support, people wondered if La Fayette would do the same; but La Fayette did not join Napoleon during the Hundred Days, and remained quietly at home.[19]

He began taking an active part in politics once again after Charles X's accession. In 1824 La Fayette visited the United States, where they had not forgotten his services to the American cause during the War of Independence. He received a hero's welcome wherever he went in the United States, and was invited to address a joint session of the two Houses of Congress. It was the first time that a foreigner had been invited to do this, and for many years La Fayette had the distinction of being the only man so honoured, for it was not until the second half of the twentieth century that it became not unusual for a foreign statesman to be invited to address Congress.

When La Fayette returned to France he took an active part in French political life. As dissatisfaction with the policy of Charles X and his government increased, La Fayette embarked on a tour of French cities, attending great masonic banquets. These banquets were supposed to be merely masonic occasions, but they attracted large crowds of liberal opponents of the government; and La Fayette, in his speeches at the banquets, criticized government policy.[20]

But when the revolution against Charles X broke out in July 1830, neither La Fayette nor Grand Lodge had anything to do with it. The revolution was started by young Freemasons in lodges which had been taken over by revolutionary groups. The most important of these was a secret organization called *Aide-toi, le ciel t'aidera* (Help yourself and Heaven will help you). Most of its members were Freemasons. It was these young men who manned the barricades against the police and the army during the Three Glorious Days of 25–27 July 1830. In fierce street fighting, and at the cost of many lives, they first gained control of the working-class suburbs to the east of Paris, the traditionally revolutionary district of the Faubourg St Antoine, and eventually captured the Town Hall. Charles X abdicated and fled to England.[21]

A story was told about Charles de Talleyrand, who had served as a diplomat under the Jacobins, Napoleon and Louis XVIII, and would soon become the new King Louis-Philippe's ambassador in London. He was in his house with a friend during the Revolution of 1830, and looked out of the window at the fighting between the government forces and the revolutionaries that was going on in the street outside the house. 'Who is winning?' asked his friend. 'We are', replied Talleyrand. 'Who do you mean by "we"?' asked his friend. 'I am not sure yet', said Talleyrand. The Freemasons' Grand Lodge adopted a very similar attitude during the Glorious Three Days of July; but after the students and young revolutionaries of *Aide-toi, le ciel t'aidera* and their Freemasons' lodges had won, Grand Lodge acclaimed them as heroic fighters for liberty.[22]

The revolutionaries did not proclaim a republic, which might have alarmed the foreign powers of the Holy Alliance and Britain, and provoked foreign intervention against the revolution; instead, they invited Louis Philippe, Duke of Orleans, the son of Philippe Égalité, to become King. He was a more cautious and stable politician than his father, but he was much more liberal than his cousins Louis XVIII and Charles X. He invited liberals to form his governments and won the full support of the Freemasons.

In Italy the downfall of Napoleon had led to the restoration of the old régimes. In the north, his Kingdom of Italy was divided between Austria and the duchies of Parma, Modena and Lucca and the Grand-Duchy of Tuscany, which were granted to Habsburg relatives of the Emperor of Austria. Piedmont was restored as a kingdom to the House of Savoy. Only the republics of Genoa and Venice were not restored, for the victorious Allies did not like republics. Genoa was given to the Kingdom of Piedmont and Venice to Austria.

In the south, Murat was driven out of the Kingdom of Naples, which was given back to the Bourbons. In 1815 Murat landed in Calabria in an attempt to instigate a rising and regain his kingdom; but he was captured by an officer of the Bourbon army, and shot. Freemasons' lodges were suppressed; like their associated organization, the Carbonari, they continued to meet secretly.[23] In Austria Prince Clemens von Metternich was Chancellor and Foreign Minister for 39 years. He pursued a consistently reactionary policy and the Freemasons were utterly suppressed.[24]

In Russia, the suppression of the Freemasons by Catherine the Great was relaxed after her death. Her son, Paul I, who was so erratic and unpredictable that eventually his courtiers assassinated him, at one time seemed to favour the Freemasons, but then suppressed them again. Paul I was succeeded by his son Alexander I, a liberal, who had great ideas of introducing reforms into Russia; but, like all benevolent dictators, he was suspicious of secret societies which might be plotting against him.

At the beginning of his reign he re-issued the usual decree banning all secret societies; but in 1805 he was visited by Ivan Boeber, a member of the Imperial Academy of Sciences and a leading Freemason. He asked the Tsar to exempt the Freemasons from the law against secret societies and allow their lodges to meet. He stressed the loyalty of the Freemasons to Russia and to the Tsar and the good works which they performed. Alexander is supposed to have said to Boeber: 'What you tell me in regard to this institution suggests to me not only to grant it my protection but even to ask for myself to be admitted among Freemasons.' It was certainly believed at the time that Alexander was initiated as a Freemason, though this has been doubted. Many leading figures in Russian society were Freemasons, including Field Marshal Mikhail Larionovich Kutusov, the commander-in-chief of the Russian army in the war of 1812 against Napoleon, and General Count Alexander Ostermann Tolstoy, who distinguished himself by his gallantry at the Battle of Borodino. The poet Alexander Pushkin was a Freemason.[25]

Alexander I's attitude to Freemasonry in Russia was affected by the position in Poland. The first Freemasons' lodge in Poland was formed in 1735; but the Freemasons were immediately attacked by the Jesuits and the Roman Catholic Church, which was influential in Poland, and in 1738 King Augustus II issued a decree suppressing them. His successor, King Stanislaus Augustus Poniatovsky, was sympathetic to the Freemasons. He allowed the first Polish Grand Lodge to be formed in 1767, and ten years later he himself became a Freemason.

The partition of Poland between Catherine the Great, Frederick the Great and Maria Theresia in 1772, was followed by the further partitions of 1793 and 1796, which eliminated Poland as a country. It was a black day for the Polish Freemasons. Only Frederick the Great and his successors in Prussia tolerated them; they were suppressed in Austrian Poland in 1795 and in Russian Poland in 1797. Some of the leaders of the Polish resistance, whose fight against the invading Russian armies aroused the admiration of Liberals throughout the world, were Freemasons; but the most famous of all the heroes of Polish independence, Tadeusz Kosciuszko, was not a Freemason, though he was a personal friend of La Fayette.

When Napoleon defeated the Russians at Eylau and Friedland, and established the Grand Duchy of Warsaw under French protection in 1807, he permitted and encouraged the Freemasons, and in March 1810 the Grand Orient of Poland was established. After the defeat of Napoleon, Alexander I did not ban the Freemasons in that part of Poland which again came under Russia. When he visited Warsaw in November 1815 he was entertained at a banquet by the Polish Freemasons, and was made a member of the Polish Grand Orient. In 1816 General Alexander Rojnezky became Deputy Grand Master of the Polish Grand Orient, and he drafted a new constitution for the Freemasons which brought the organization to a considerable extent under the control of the Russian government. This aroused the resentment of patriotic Poles who did not like the Russians. In 1819 Major Victor Lukacinsky formed a rival masonic organization. It was free from Russian control and only Poles were admitted.[26]

This development in Poland was probably one of the factors which persuaded Tsar Alexander to change his attitude towards Freemasonry; though another was his general shift towards a reactionary policy which followed the formation of the Holy Alliance against revolution between Russia, Austria and Prussia. He asked Lieutenant General Egor Alexandrovich Kushelev, who was a senator and himself a prominent Freemason, to report to him on the masonic lodges in Russia.

Kushelev's report, in June 1821, stated that although true Freemasons were loyal subjects and their ideals and activities were praiseworthy, masonic lodges could be used as a cover for revolutionary activities, as they had been in the Kingdom of Naples; and the same was happening in Russia, especially in three of the St Petersburg lodges.

> This is the state, Most Gracious Sovereign, in which Masonic lodges now exist in Petersburg. Instead of the Spirit of Christian mildness and of true Masonic rules and meekness, the spirit of self-will, turbulence and real anarchy acts through them.[27]

Within a month of receiving Kushelev's report, Alexander I banned the publication of masonic songs and all other masonic documents. On 1 August 1822 he issued a decree suppressing the Freemasons throughout Russia. In November he issued a similar decree banning the Freemasons and all other secret societies in Russian Poland. These decrees were re-enacted by his more reactionary brother, Tsar Nicholas I, when Nicholas succeeded Alexander and clamped down on all potentially revolutionary organizations after the abortive insurrection of the Decembrists in December 1825.[28]

In Britain, Freemasonry continued to flourish under royal patronage.

In 1811 George III's periodical outbreaks of insanity became worse and more prolonged, and the Prince of Wales was appointed Prince Regent to exercise the royal powers on his behalf. The Freemasons felt that it was inappropriate that the sovereign or his regent should be their Grand Master, because the Grand Master had to go through the formality of being re-elected from time to time, and it would be improper for anyone to vote against the King. So the Prince Regent resigned as Grand Master of London Grand Lodge. The precedent was followed in 1901, and Edward, Prince of Wales, resigned as Grand Master when he succeeded to the throne as King Edward VII on the death of Queen Victoria.

The Prince Regent was succeeded as Grand Master of London Grand Lodge by his brother Augustus Frederick, Duke of Sussex, the sixth son of George III. The rival Antient Grand Lodge in York, who were always eager to equal London Grand Lodge in their choice of Grand Masters, persuaded another brother of the Prince Regent, George III's fourth son, Edward Augustus, Duke of Kent (who later became the father of Queen Victoria) to become their Grand Master. The two royal brothers were able at last to end the division between the rival Grand Lodges, which had lasted for sixty years. Using their royal influence, they succeeded, where others had failed, in forcing the two bodies to forget their differences and unite. The United Grand Lodge was formed in 1813. The Duke of Kent had no wish to continue as Grand Master, and he stood down, leaving the Duke of Sussex to become Grand Master of the United Grand Lodge, a position which he filled till his death in 1843.

The Duke of Sussex was close to the Whigs, and had liberal progressive views on many subjects. He strongly supported Catholic Emancipation, and he was sympathetic to the Jews, having studied Hebrew documents. He used his position as Grand Master to encourage Roman Catholics and Jews to become Freemasons.[29]*

Although the Earl of Moira, in his efforts to convince Pitt and everyone else of the Freemasons' loyalty to the throne, had referred to the presence of members of the Royal Family in Grand Lodge, the Duke of Sussex's loyalty to his brother, George IV, was questioned in

---

* For the successful attempt to form a masonic lodge in the Honourable Artillery Company at Armoury House in London, which the Duke of Sussex supported valiantly while he was both Colonel, and later Captain-General, of the Company, see a monograph on the setting up of the Fitzroy Lodge at Armoury House by Jean Tsushima, Archivist Emeritus of the HAC, which is in preparation.

some cases after the Prince Regent succeeded to the throne on the death of George III in 1820. George IV became very unpopular because of his attempts to divorce his wife, Queen Caroline, and his treatment of her. The Queen's barrister in the divorce proceedings, and her greatest political champion, was Henry Brougham. His support of the Queen, and of other liberal causes, aroused the hatred of George IV and the Tory government, but made him a hero of the Radicals. After the Whig election victory of 1830, he was appointed Lord Chancellor and played a leading part in forcing through the Reform Bill of 1832. Brougham was a Freemason.[30]

The Duke of Sussex was criticized for his conduct when he presided at a dinner given by the Arts Society in 1823. One of the guests was John Simmons, an ardent Tory and admirer of George IV. He believed that when the King's health was drunk, it should be accompanied by 'noise', by loud cheering, by the traditional 'three times three', with 'Hip, hip, hip hurrah!' repeated three times and then repeated three more times again on two more occasions. Simmons thought that to drink the royal toast in silence was an insult to the King. At the Arts Society dinner the Duke of Sussex proposed the King's health, but added 'No cheering.' Simmons was indignant, and shouted out: 'What? No cheering?' 'No cheering,' replied the Duke of Sussex. Simmons thought that this was an insult to 'the best of Kings'. He wrote an indignant protest to the Arts Society which resulted in his being expelled from the society.[31]

The Duke of Sussex and the Duke of Kent were both interested in the work and ideas of Robert Owen, the Socialist owner of a factory in Scotland where his employees were treated much better than they were by most factory owners. The first two decades of the nineteenth century were the period of the industrial revolution when the workers in the factories in Lancashire and Yorkshire worked in very harsh conditions. The trade unions were agitating for legislation which would prohibit children of seven from working fifteen hours a day in the factories; but the factory owners and the government rejected these demands, arguing that to limit the working day for children would harm British trade in the face of foreign competition.

Lord Liverpool's Tory government reacted to the agitation by a policy of severe repression. Trade unions were banned; their members were prosecuted under the Combination Acts and the Unlawful Societies Acts; the breaking of new machinery by 'Luddite' workers, who objected because the machinery caused unemployment, was made a capital offence carrying the death penalty; the writ of habeas corpus was suspended; and protests against the government were silenced by the Act which banned public meetings. But many members of the aristocracy sympathized with Owen's views; they received him in a very friendly way, and told him how much they regretted that they could do nothing to help the oppressed working man.

Owen often visited the Duke of Kent at the Duke's home in Kensington Palace, and occasionally the Duke went to Owen's house. The Duke of Sussex wished to meet Owen, and sometimes went to Kensington Palace when he knew that Owen would be there. Some Freemasons, whom Owen knew, tried to persuade him to become a Freemason. Owen was interested, and said that he would consider the idea. But the Duke of Sussex was against inviting Owen to join their society. He said to the Duke of Kent:

> No, by all that is good, were he to witness our ceremonies he would make us all to appear fools. His subjects are of a character too serious and extended for him to be occupied with our trifling amusements.

So Owen did not become a Freemason.[32]

During the period of political repression under Lord Liverpool's government, the Freemasons came under attack from a new quarter. Richard Carlile was the son of a shoemaker in Devon, and was educated at the village school. He became a convinced and reckless freethinker, prepared to suffer persecution in order to assert his right to criticize the Church of England and established religion. He wrote a number of pamphlets attacking religion, became the editor of a popular newspaper, *The Republican*, and opened a bookshop where he sold his own publications and the works of other freethinkers and rebels who criticized the monarchy and the Church of England and advocated republicanism and atheism.

In 1813 he married Jane, the daughter of a cottager in Gosport in Hampshire. Six years later they agreed to separate as husband and wife, but she continued to help him run his bookselling business. He said that he would have been unable to carry on without her help.

Carlile wrote a number of publications attacking the Freemasons, but the reason for his criticism is unclear. Like so many other critics he concentrated on the secrecy of the organization, arguing that a secret society is a sinister thing, though he once stated that he believed that the Freemasons' secret is that they have no secrets. He seems to have been influenced by the fact that so many high-ranking members of society, and the Royal Family, were Freemasons, for in his writings, and in the open letter on the subject that he wrote to George IV, he ridiculed the King and the other Freemasons for belonging to the society.[33]

He was repeatedly prosecuted, and sentenced to short terms of imprisonment, for publishing and selling atheist literature. In 1819 he was prosecuted again for selling in his bookshop a parody on the Book of Common Prayer; Thomas Paine's book *The Age of Reason*, in which Paine criticized religion; and other similar publications. He was sentenced to several years' imprisonment for each offence, the sentences to run consecutively, and to a further term of imprisonment for non-payment of Church rates and fines.

His wife was also prosecuted for helping him run the bookshop and sell the books. The Solicitor-General, Sir John Copley (later Lord Lyndhurst), in opening the case for the prosecution, described her as 'a person of wicked and dangerous mind and disposition'. She put forward a plea that she was an ignorant and uneducated woman who acted under her husband's influence. When accused of selling *The Republican*, she said:

'I was guided entirely by my husband. I do not feel myself a competent judge to decide on its propriety or impropriety as having been brought up as the daughter of an humble cottager in a sequestered part of Hampshire, I had reached the age of maturity without the least education.'[34]

Perhaps she was underestimating her intelligence and independence, thinking that the judge and the middle-class jury would approve of a wife who adopted this attitude. They might indeed have done so in other cases, but not when they were dealing with rebels who attacked religion, one of the cornerstones of the established order of society. She was sentenced to two years' imprisonment.

In 1825 Richard Carlile was still in prison, having served nearly six years for selling atheist books. On 30 June he petitioned the House of Commons, asking them to release him. The petition was presented by the Freemason, Henry Brougham.

Carlile was praised by his fellow-rebel, William Cobbett: 'You have done your duty bravely, Mr Carlile; if every one had done like you, it would be all very well'.[35] Carlile died in 1843. By this time, Lord Brougham and Vaux had become a reactionary, warning the peers and the world, in his speeches in the House of Lords, of the danger to society presented by American democracy.

Politically, there were Freemasons and anti-masons on both sides. Charles X, Joseph de Maistre, and the revolutionaries in Paris, Naples and Spain were Freemasons; the Catholic Church, the monarchs of the Holy Alliance, all the anti-revolutionaries of Europe, and the Radical freethinker Richard Carlile, were anti-masons. Being a Free-mason did not determine a man's political beliefs; but the political beliefs of the members of a lodge determined whether it was a body of loyal monarchists or an organization of Red revolutionaries.

——————— ◆ ———————

CHAPTER 15

The Case of William Morgan

I N September 1826, in the north-west part of the state of New York, William Morgan was probably murdered by Freemasons in order to prevent him from revealing masonic secrets. This was widely believed at the time, and triggered off a powerful anti-masonic movement which threatened to destroy Freemasonry in the United States. Freemasons today still deny that Morgan was murdered. It is true that the murder cannot be conclusively proved, but the other explanations of his disappearance are so improbable that it is much more likely that he was murdered by the Freemasons.

If so, this is the only case in the history of Freemasonry in many countries of the world in which such a thing has occurred. The Freemasons have often been accused of carrying out the secret oaths which are taken at the initiation ceremonies, when the initiate agrees to suffer death in a most grisly way if he reveals masonic secrets; but the only occasion when something like this has actually occurred is the case of William Morgan, who was not in fact killed by the methods suggested in the ritual, but was drowned in the River Niagara.

The Morgan case also shows that when it comes to murdering disobedient brothers who talk too much, as with the political attitude adopted by Freemasons, they act as they do, not because they are Freemasons, but because of the social surroundings in which they live. British noblemen and members of the Royal Family who become Freemasons continue to behave like British noblemen and members of the Royal Family, just as French, Italian, Spanish and Latin American revolutionaries who become Freemasons continue to act like French, Italian, Spanish and Latin American revolutionaries. Hoodlums and petty local bosses in the small towns of up-state New

York in 1826 happened in many cases to be Freemasons, but they continued to act like hoodlums and petty local bosses in the small towns of up-state New York.

In 1826 the little town of Batavia in the county of Genesee in the north-west of New York state was not far from the frontier of the Wild West, and the independent-minded inhabitants of the district were to a considerable extent free of control by a central government. They believed in the virtues of self-help, which easily spills over into crime. When a Justice of the Peace for Genesee county, who happened to be a Freemason, was asked whether he approved of the attempt by the Freemasons to burn the offices of the publisher of Morgan's anti-masonic book, he replied: 'If you found a man abusing your marriage bed, would you have recourse to law or take a club and beat his brains out?' This was the attitude of a law-enforcement officer in the county where the Freemasons murdered Morgan.[1]

William Morgan was a native of Culpepper county in Virginia. He left Virginia and lived for a time in Canada and in various parts of New York state, working in different occupations, before taking up employment as a stonemason in Batavia in Genesee county. He called himself Captain William Morgan, and claimed to have served with distinction in the War of 1812 against Britain; but some people believed that this was untrue, and that he had never been in the army.[2] He joined a Freemasons' lodge, but soon quarrelled with the other members, and left the society. He then let it be known that he had written a book in which he revealed the Freemasons' secrets, and had been paid a large advance for the book by David C. Miller, the publisher of a local newspaper.

The first reaction of the local Freemasons was to insert an advertisement in other local newspapers stating that 'a man calling himself William Morgan' had come to the village of Canandaigua in Genesee county, that he was a most undesirable character, and that everyone, particularly masons, who had dealings with him should be on their guard. The masons also organized a boycott of Miller's newspaper, and stopped advertising in it.[3]

Soon afterwards, a prominent local Freemason asked an innkeeper in a village six miles from Batavia to provide a cold supper for fifty men. He made no secret of the fact that after supper they intended to proceed to Batavia and attack the newspaper offices of David Miller, Morgan's publisher. Miller got to hear of it, and let it be known that he and his friends had armed themselves, and that he would be waiting for the Freemasons' attack.[4] The Freemasons then thought better of it, and decided not to proceed to Batavia. Instead, a few of them went there stealthily two nights later and tried to set fire to Miller's offices; but though they laid down bales of straw and saturated them with paraffin, Miller managed to put out the fire.[5]

Some Freemasons then went to Morgan's house and arrested him, claiming that he owed them money and that they were entitled to hold him in prison until he had paid off the debt. They took him to the local jail, and the jailer, who was a Freemason, took Morgan into custody. When Miller heard what had happened, he went at once to find the jailer and pay off any debt which it was claimed that Morgan might owe; but he could not find the jailer, who had deliberately made himself scarce. Morgan had been arrested on a Friday evening, and as the jailer went off for the weekend, no steps could be taken to procure Morgan's release until the Monday morning.

The Freemasons told Morgan that they would release him from jail if he handed over to them the manuscript of his book; but he refused to do this. They then went to Morgan's home, while he was imprisoned in the jail. Forcing their way in, and brushing past his indignant wife, they went upstairs to his room, ransacked it, and removed his papers; but they did not find the manuscript of the book in which he revealed masonic secrets.

On Monday morning Morgan was duly released, after Miller had given security for his alleged debt; but the Freemasons then alleged that Morgan had stolen a shirt and also owed money on a very small debt in Canandaigua. They took Morgan in a carriage to Canandaigua, about 50 miles east of Batavia, and put him in the local jail.[6] Meanwhile they had arrested Miller too, and detained him without alleging any specific charge against him; but he protested so strongly, and warned them of the serious consequences that they would incur for what they were doing, that they released him after a few hours.

On 13 September 1826 a Freemason named Lotan Lawson went to the jail at Canandaigua where Morgan was being held. He said that he was a friend of Morgan's and had come to pay off his debt and obtain his release. The jailer was out, but his wife, who had been left in charge of the jail, accepted the money offered, and released Morgan, who was a little reluctant to go with Lawson, but did walk out of the jail. In the street, Lawson invited Morgan to enter his carriage but Morgan refused. Two other Freemasons named

Chesebro and Sawyer then appeared, and they and Lawson forced the struggling Morgan to enter the carriage. People standing in the street heard Morgan cry 'Murder!' as the carriage drove off.

During the remainder of the day, the night, and next day, the carriage travelled 105 miles from Canandaigua to Fort Niagara on the River Niagara, the frontier between the United States and Canada. When the disappearance of Morgan was later investigated, the investigators were able to trace the route that Morgan and his kidnappers had taken, by Rochester, Gaines, Ridgeway, Lockport, Lewiston and Youngstown. On the journey the kidnappers were joined by Eli Bruce, the High Sheriff of Niagara county, who was a Freemason. At Youngstown the other Freemasons went into an inn for supper, leaving Bruce in the carriage with Morgan. Passers-by heard Morgan asking for water. Bruce said that they would bring him water, but they did not.

On the evening of 14 September they arrived at Fort Niagara. Until recently it had been occupied by the defence department of the United States Federal government, but they had given up possession a month before. Afterwards, inquiries were made as to how the Freemasons managed to get into the fort, and it appeared that the Federal government had handed over the key to a caretaker. He was a Freemason, and he allowed the Freemasons to take temporary possession of the empty fort.

Morgan was imprisoned in the room which had been the powder magazine, and was held there for several days. Once he was taken by four Freemasons in a boat across the River Niagara to the Canadian shore. The ferryman later revealed what had happened. He and two of the Freemasons were left to guard Morgan in the boat while the other two Freemasons went on shore to speak to some Canadian Freemasons who had arranged to meet them there. Apparently the Americans suggested that they should hand over Morgan to the Canadians for them to dispose of him as they thought best; but the Canadians refused to become involved. So the American Freemasons returned to the boat and took Morgan back to Fort Niagara, and imprisoned him again in the former powder magazine.

This was the last occasion on which anyone admitted seeing Morgan. The statements about what happened to him after this are all hearsay evidence of what the witnesses were told, or alleged that they had been told, by the masons in Fort Niagara. The Freemasons there decided that, as their Canadian brothers refused to become

involved, they had better murder Morgan, to prevent him from testi-
fying against them. One night between 17 and 21 September they
took him out on to the River Niagara in a boat, fastened metal
weights to his feet, and threw him into the river, where he drowned.[7]

Morgan's friends and acquaintances in Batavia and elsewhere in
Genesee county were informing the press and the public about his
disappearance. Miller was also using the incident to publicize
Morgan's book, which immediately became a best-seller; the Freemasons suggested, then and now, that the whole story about
Morgan's disappearance was planned by Morgan and Miller as a
publicity stunt.[8]

The governor of New York state, De Witt Clinton, was a Freemason. He expressed his indignation at Morgan's disappearance,
and issued a proclamation, offering a reward of 300 dollars for
any information about Morgan's whereabouts or about what had
happened to him. As the proclamation yielded no results, Clinton
issued a second proclamation, increasing the reward for information
to 2,000 dollars; but no one claimed the reward.[9] There seems to be
no doubt that Clinton and all the responsible masonic leaders were
angry at the disgraceful and foolish way in which the local Freemasons in Genesee county had acted; though some of these leaders
wished to hush up the scandal as far as possible in order to protect
the Freemasons' reputation.

Some weeks later, a body was washed up out of the River Niagara.
At the inquest it was identified as Morgan's, but on unsatisfactory
evidence, and rumours soon began to circulate that the corpse had
marks which showed that it was not Morgan's body. A second
inquest was held, but again the result was questioned. Then a Canadian woman came forward and said that she feared her husband
had been drowned in the River Niagara, and at a third inquest she
identified the corpse as being her husband, not Morgan. If, as seems
certain, it was in fact her husband, then Morgan's corpse was never
found.[10]

Meanwhile the outcry about Morgan was intensifying. If there
was no reliable evidence that he had been murdered, there was
plenty of evidence that he had been kidnapped and taken from
Canandaigua to Fort Niagara by Lawson, Chesebro, Sawyer and
Sheldon (another Freemason) and the High Sheriff, Eli Bruce. On 1
January 1827 Lawson, Chesebro, Sawyer and Sheldon were put on
trial, charged with kidnapping Morgan. At first they pleaded not

guilty, but then all except Sheldon changed their plea to guilty. This was thought to have been a skilful move by their lawyers, because it prevented evidence being given which might have implicated them in Morgan's murder.

Although the judge severely condemned their conduct, many people felt that he had been far too lenient in sentencing Lawson to two years' imprisonment, Chesebro to one year, and Sawyer and Sheldon to three months and one month.[11] But at this time kidnapping was only a misdemeanour in New York state. Three months later, Governor Clinton signed a bill to make it a felony punishable by imprisonment from three to fourteen years.[12] Clinton dismissed Eli Bruce from his position as Sheriff of Niagara county, and Bruce was afterwards tried and convicted of participating in the kidnapping of Morgan. He was sentenced to two years and four months' imprisonment.[13]

The protests about the Morgan case became stronger. On 4 July 1828, as part of the Independence Day celebrations, a meeting of anti-masons was held at Le Roy in New York state. The speakers were eloquent in their denunciation of the Freemasons who had 'set at defiance the laws both of God and of man' with their 'impious principles and blasphemous ceremonies'; and now Freemasonry had 'stained its kingly robes with the blood of a free citizen'.[14]

The rally was the start of an anti-masonic campaign which spread from New York state to most of the other states in the north-east. 'We war with the abominations of Masonry', said one of the speakers; and the meeting passed a resolution 'that it is the right and the duty of the citizens of these United Sates to use all lawful means to annihilate an institution which has shown itself capable of contriving, effecting and in a great degree concealing the crimes of kidnapping and murder'. They pledged themselves never to vote for any Freemason candidate in any election.[15]

While anti-masonic organizations as late as 1882 were erecting monuments to William Morgan, 'a Captain of the War of 1812, a respectable Citizen of Batavia and a Martyr to the Freedom of writing and speaking the Truth', who 'was abducted . . . by the Freemasons and murdered for revealing the secrets of their Order',[16] the Freemasons still today deny that he was murdered. They maintain that he made an agreement with his captors in Fort Niagara that they would pay him 500 dollars if he agreed not to publish his book and to disappear; and that he was then taken across the River Niagara to Canada, where the Canadian Freemasons helped him to vanish. There are various versions of what happened to him – that he lived the rest of his life in Canada, or near Albany in New York state; that he joined a native American tribe in the West; was seen in Smyrna in Turkey; became a pirate, and was hanged for piracy in Havana in Cuba; or that he went to the Cayman Islands, lived there for many years under another name, married another wife who bore him nine children, and died there aged 89 in 1864.[17] None of these stories can be substantiated, and all seem improbable.

The public indignation against the Freemasons over the Morgan case was used for political purposes. It was connected with the fact that Andrew Jackson, the leader of the Democratic Party and the most forceful and charismatic figure of his time, was a prominent Freemason who had been the Grand Master of the Tennessee lodges. Jackson was born in North Carolina in 1767, and was a teenager during the War of Independence. In 1781, when he was 14, the British army occupied the village where he was living. A British officer ordered the boy to clean his boots; young Andrew Jackson refused. The officer struck him a blow on the forehead with the hilt of his sword, leaving a scar which Andrew Jackson retained all his life. He also retained all his life a hatred of the British.

He became a lawyer, building up a good practice in Tennessee, holding minor judicial offices, and went into politics. He was elected to the state legislature and eventually to the United States Senate. He had a fiery temper which involved him in several duels; in one of them he received a serious wound. He fell in love with Mrs Rachel Robards, whose husband was in the process of divorcing her. Jackson and Rachel were married, as they believed, and started living together. They then found that her divorce from her husband had not been legally completed. When she was finally divorced from Robards, she and Jackson went through another marriage ceremony. The incident was used against Jackson by his political opponents, who accused him of committing adultery with another man's wife.

Although he had had no military training, he joined his local militia, and when the War of 1812 broke out the militia was incorporated into the army, and Jackson was given a military command. The war occurred because Britain claimed the right to stop American ships on the high seas and remove British sailors who had deserted. The discipline in the British navy was very severe, and was enforced by savage floggings; so many British sailors preferred to serve under the less severe discipline of the American navy. When the British navy stopped and searched American ships, they sometimes removed not only British deserters but also American citizens whom they mistakenly supposed were British deserters.

The war against Britain lasted for more than two years. Although the United States won some victories, especially in the fighting at sea, the Americans suffered more than Britain from the war, because it was fought on American soil. The British temporarily occupied Washington D.C., and burned the presidential mansion, the White House. After two years of war, the British and American representatives met at Ghent in the Netherlands to negotiate peace. The peace treaty was signed on 30 December 1814; but it took nearly a month for ships and news to cross the Atlantic, and when the British and American armies faced each other near New Orleans on 8 January 1815, they did not know that their two countries were no longer at war.

This ignorance enabled the United States to end the war on a triumphant note, and Andrew Jackson to win fame and popularity. He was in command of the American army in the Battle of New Orleans; it was a great victory for the United States. His next campaign was against the native Americans in Florida, who were instigated by the Spaniards to revolt against the rule of the United States. Two British agents were helping the native Americans. Jackson had them both hanged as spies.

By 1824 he had become the most famous politician in the Democratic Party, and he won the nomination to become the Democratic candidate in the presidential election. He had three opponents – the Whig candidate John Quincy Adams and the two independent candidates, W. H. Crawford and Henry Clay. Jackson received 99 votes in the electoral college against 64 for Adams, 41 for Crawford, and 37 for Clay; but as no candidate had an absolute majority, the decision passed to the House of Representatives, who elected Adams as President. It was only a temporary setback for Jackson, because the defeat did not weaken his position in his party, and he was adopted as the Democratic candidate in the presidential election of 1828.

By this time the anti-masonic movement had become an important political force in the states of New York, Pennsylvania and, especially, in Vermont and Rhode Island. It found a forceful leader in the journalist Thurlow Weed, for whom the Morgan case was a weapon to be used against Andrew Jackson. When all the evidence indicated that the corpse washed up out of the River Niagara was the missing Canadian, and not Morgan, Weed said that the body would be 'a good enough Morgan until after the election' in the autumn.[18] Weed was supported by a number of rising politicians, including Thaddeus Stevens. He afterwards became a champion of the Radicals in their campaign to pursue a harsh policy towards the former slave-owners in the South after the Civil War. William H. Seward, who was Abraham Lincoln's Secretary of State during the Civil War, was a prominent anti-mason in the 1830s.

The anti-masonic campaign did not prevent Andrew Jackson from winning the presidential election in 1828, defeating the Whig candidate, John Quincy Adams. It was seen as a victory for the democratic forces over the dignified, old-style politicians who had governed the United States since independence. On the evening of Jackson's inauguration as President of the United States on 4 March 1829, he gave a party at the White House at which supporters of the popular cause, admirers of Jackson, had the run of the building that had previously been frequented by the gentlemanly friends of John Adams, Jefferson, Madison and Monroe.

Andrew Jackson was a very popular President, and was much admired by the people, who remembered his victory in the Battle of New Orleans and loved his flamboyant and defiant personality; but the anti-masonic campaign was intensified during his presidency. Freemasonry was denounced as a conspiracy against the nation; an affront to the American ideal; as a sinister élite placing their members in positions of authority and privilege, violating the American principles of equality and fair play applied impartially to every citizen; as a secret society negating the open, honest government which was the pride of the American Constitution. The critics unearthed the anti-masonic writings and arguments of the defenders of the *ancien régime* in Europe, including the books of the Abbé Barruel and Professor Robison, to prove that Freemasonry was a threat to American democracy. With a flagrant disregard for historical truth, they denounced the Freemasons for betraying the ideals of the founding fathers of the American Constitution and 'the sainted name of Washington', and for threatening 'the government founded by a Washington, a Franklin, a Jefferson', without mentioning that Washington and Franklin were themselves Freemasons, like so many of their colleagues who made the American Revolution and the American Constitution which the anti-masons worshipped so highly.[19]

John Quincy Adams entered the fray with a denunciation of the Freemasons for having murdered William Morgan and for their improper influence in American political life. He hesitated to attack Andrew Jackson directly, for it might have aroused unfavourable comment if he had targeted the man who had defeated him in the election for the office of President of the United States. But he directly challenged Edward Livingston, who had drafted the legal code of the state of Louisiana before Jackson appointed him as Secretary of State in his government. Livingston was one of several Freemasons whom Jackson had included in his cabinet, which had led to suggestions of secret masonic influence and favouritism. Livingston was the Grand High Priest of the General Grand Royal Arch Chapter of the United States, just as Andrew Jackson had been Grand Master of the Tennessee Freemasons.

In an open letter to Livingston, dated 23 May 1833, Adams challenged him about the propriety of masonic oaths, which had led so many officials of the state of New York to fail in their duty to bring Morgan's murderers and abductors to justice; so

> what security can the country possess that they will not operate in the same manner upon a Secretary of State or a President of the United States? . . . If the President of the United States and the Secretary of State are bound by solemn oaths and under horrible penalties to befriend and favor one class of individuals in the community more than another . . . a privileged order is planted upon the community, more corrupting, more pernicious than the titles of nobility which our constitutions expressly prohibit . . . [20]

When Jackson stood for re-election in the presidential election of 1832, he found that he was opposed by an official Anti-Masonic candidate, William Wirt of Maryland, as well as the Whig candidate, Henry Clay. Jackson did not worry; he knew that he could rely on his great popularity with the electorate. During his election campaign he never mentioned the attacks on the Freemasons. His only recorded comment about the anti-masons is a confident remark which he made during the 1832 presidential election campaign, in a letter to his running mate, the candidate for the office of Vice-President, Martin Van Buren. At this time the anti-masonic movement was at its strongest. 'Everything is going well at present. Nullification* and anti-masonry are both declining fast, and will ere long be buried in oblivion.'[21]

His confidence was justified. He obtained 219 electoral votes against 49 for Clay and only 7 for Wirt, who did not win any state except Vermont. In the popular vote, Jackson's victory was not so overwhelming, but he received 701,780 votes against 484,205 for Clay and 100,715 for Wirt.[22] The chief effect of Wirt's candidature, and of the political activities of the anti-masons, was to help Jackson and his Democratic Party by splitting the opposition vote between the anti-masons and the Whigs.

By 1835 the Anti-Masonic party had ceased to operate in every state except Pennsylvania, and it ceased to be of any importance there soon afterwards.[23] The anti-masons drifted back into the Whig party, and the politicians who had made their name in anti-masonic politics found that there were other issues, such as the rising anti-slavery movement, in which they could gain more attention.

But if anti-masonry failed in terms of party politics, the campaign against the Freemasons, and the scandal caused by the case of William Morgan, did great harm to Freemasonry in the United States for more than twenty years. In several states, the state legislature set up commissions of inquiry to investigate the activities of the Freemasons; in Rhode Island legislation was passed banning extra-judicial oaths, including masonic oaths, and the Freemasons' charter was temporarily withdrawn.[24]

Many Freemasons left the society in disgust at the murder of Morgan or in fear of public hostility. In New York state there were 480 lodges and 20,000 members in 1825, the year before Morgan disappeared; by 1835 there were only 75 lodges with 3,000 active members. In Massachusetts the number of lodges fell from 107 in 1826 to 52 by 1844. In New Jersey, 29 lodges attended Grand Lodge in 1826; 5 came in 1835 and 4 in 1840. In Vermont the number fell from 47 in 1825 to zero in 1835. The collapse was less spectacular in Pennsylvania, where the number of lodges attending Grand Lodge

---

* This was the doctrine put forward by John C. Calhoun and the state of South Carolina, that a state was entitled to nullify an Act of Congress if it interfered with what they considered to be state rights. South Carolina had therefore refused to comply with the tariff imposed by Congress, and Jackson sent the Federal navy to seize the port of Charleston and collect the tariff by force. Nullification and anti-masonry had been made political issues by Jackson's opponents.

fell from 36 in 1825 to 21 in 1840, and in Ohio from 48 in 1825 to 26 in 1835.[25]

American Freemasonry did not begin to recover for nearly thirty years. By that time, slavery and the threat of the secession of the Southern states divided the nation, and absorbed attention to the exclusion of all other issues.

By 1856 the pro- and anti-slavery supporters were conducting an armed struggle in Kansas. The leader of the anti-slavery forces in Kansas was John Brown, who afterwards led an unsuccessful raid by white and black Abolitionists on the Federal arsenal at Harpers Ferry. He was captured and hanged for treason. His fate inspired an anonymous admirer to write the song 'John Brown's body lies a-mouldering in the grave, but his soul goes marching on'. It was the most popular song of the anti-slavery forces during the Civil War.

John Brown was a Freemason; he was initiated as a young man in Ohio in 1824. But after the William Morgan affair he left the society, and for a time joined the anti-masonic movement before devoting himself to the struggle against slavery. He said that he thought that the masonic initiation ceremony was ridiculous, and wrote to a newspaper edited by blacks: 'Another of the few errors of my life is that I have joined the Freemasons ... and a series of other secret societies instead of seeking the company of intelligent, wise and good men'.[26]

Senator Charles Sumner of Massachusetts had been active in the anti-masonic campaign of the 1830s: he declared that the cause of anti-masonry was 'great and good'.[27] He afterwards became a vigorous opponent of slavery and a leading spokesman for the Abolitionists. In 1856 he spoke in the Senate on the situation in Kansas, and denounced the pro-slavery forces there. Two days later, as he was sitting writing at his desk in the Senate, Congressman Preston S. Brooks of South Carolina, an ardent supporter of slavery and the Southern cause, came up to Sumner and beat him on the head with his stick so violently that Sumner fell bleeding and unconscious to the ground. He suffered for some years from the effects of his injury, which to his supporters was yet another example of Southern brutality. The United States was moving towards civil war. President James Buchanan, who was a Freemason,[28] was quite unable to handle the situation. He showed weakness, if not sympathy, towards the Southern slaveowners.

Joseph Henson was a black slave in Kentucky. He managed to

escape and to avoid recapture in the Northern states of the United States, where slavery had been abolished but escaping slaves were often seized by the authorities and returned to their Southern slave-owners to be flogged, or otherwise punished, and re-enslaved. He reached Canada, and became a Methodist minister. Henson was initiated as a Freemason in Ontario. He is said to have inspired Harriet Beecher Stowe to write her novel *Uncle Tom's Cabin*.[29]

In the presidential election of 1860, Abraham Lincoln was the candidate of the newly-formed Republican Party, standing on a platform of preventing the extension of slavery. He was opposed by three Democratic candidates who were split on important issues and could not unite against him. As a result, he was elected President of the United States, though he obtained only 40 per cent of the popular vote – the lowest percentage ever recorded by a successful candidate in the history of United States presidential elections. The three conflicting Democratic candidates were all Freemasons.[30] Of the four candidates in the election, Lincoln was the only one who was not a Freemason, though on several occasions he expressed a favourable opinion about them, saying that he thought that Freemasons did very good work.[31]

The lack of masonic solidarity among the three Freemason candidates had serious repercussions. It led to Lincoln's victory and to the outbreak of the Civil War which followed almost immediately, for the Southern states had warned that if Lincoln were elected, they would secede from the Union.

Freemasonry was not an issue in the Civil War. There were Freemasons on both sides as there had been in the American War of Independence and at Waterloo. A number of prominent generals in the Union and Confederate armies were Freemasons. General George B. McClellan was initiated as a Freemason in a military lodge when he was stationed in Oregon in 1853.[32] At the outbreak of the Civil War he was appointed commander-in-chief of the Union armies and was acclaimed by the press and public as the military genius who would rapidly conquer the South. The Northern soldiers and people sang about 'McClellan's our leader, he's valiant and strong' and 'McClellan again at the head of his men'. But as he led the Northern armies to a series of defeats or to victories which he failed to follow up and gain a decisive advantage, Lincoln at last lost patience and dismissed him. He revenged himself by standing against Lincoln in the presidential election of 1864, but was defeated. He had to console himself by becoming Governor of New Jersey after the war.

Admiral David G. Farragut was a Freemason.[33] His fleet inflicted a heavy blow on the South when it captured New Orleans in April 1862. General Benjamin F. Butler was then placed in command of the Northern army of occupation in the city. He was a Freemason.[34] Finding that the women of New Orleans insulted his soldiers, spitting at them and pouring their jerry pots over the heads of the soldiers who walked beneath their windows, he issued his notorious order that any woman of New Orleans who insulted a soldier in the United States army was to be treated like 'a woman of the town plying her avocation'.[35] He meant that these women were to be arrested and imprisoned like prostitutes in the local jails; but the Southern propagandists and their supporters, who violently denounced Butler, interpreted his order, without any justification, as inciting his soldiers to rape the insulting ladies of New Orleans. Faced with all the protests, Lincoln removed Butler from his command in New Orleans; but Butler continued to serve in leading positions in the Union army.

General Lew Wallace was a Freemason.[36] After service in the war against Mexico, and a successful career as a lawyer, he was appointed to a command in the Union forces in the Civil War. After the war he was a member of the court that tried the conspirators who had been accomplices in the assassination of Lincoln. He was also on the court that tried Major Henry Wirz, the commandant of the prison camp at Andersonville where Union prisoners had been brutally ill-treated during the Civil War. Wirz was convicted and hanged as a war criminal in the only war crimes trial that was held after the Civil War.

When Wallace retired from military and legal activity, he wrote a number of novels, including his very successful book, *Ben Hur*, a story of the sufferings of a Christian in the Roman Empire after the crucifixion of Christ. *Ben Hur* became a best-seller in many countries of the world, before being made into a very successful film in the twentieth century.

Congressman Clement L. Vallandigham of Ohio was a Freemason. During the Civil War he declared that anyone who attempted to change the war, which had originally been waged to preserve the Union, into a war for the abolition of slavery would be guilty of a crime against the Constitution. His opposition to the war in Union territory so incensed the military that General Burnside arrested and imprisoned him. Vallandigham obtained a writ of habeas corpus in the courts, which ruled that his imprisonment was illegal; but Lincoln

ordered the military authorities to ignore and defy the writ. Afterwards Lincoln sent Vallandigham through the enemy lines to the
South.

After the Civil War Vallandigham resumed his legal practice. In
1871 he appeared for the defence in a murder case, and demonstrated
in court to the jury how a gun might have been fired. He accidentally
fired a shot from the gun and killed himself.[37]

The most important figure in American masonry in the nineteenth
century was Albert Pike. With his books and other writings he made
the Scottish Rite the dominant form of masonry in the South of the
United States; it was said of him that 'he found the Scottish Rite in
a cabin and left it in a Temple'.[38] Before devoting himself to masonry,
Pike, a native of Boston, had become not only a successful lawyer
and administrator of Indian affairs in Oklahoma, but also a brigadier
general in the Confederate army in the Civil War, enlisting the native
Americans in Oklahoma to fight for the South.[39]

After the North had won the Civil War, and Lincoln had been
assassinated, the Radicals in Congress came into conflict with President Andrew Johnson about the policy to be adopted towards the
conquered South. The Radicals thought that the President was being
too soft towards the Southern slaveowners and was going too slowly
in granting rights to the blacks in the South. The dispute between
the President and Congress led to an attempt to impeach Johnson –
the only President of the United States to be subjected to impeachment proceedings until 1999. The Radical Republicans failed by one
vote to obtain the necessary two-thirds majority in the Senate to
impeach Johnson, who survived as President to the end of his term.

President Andrew Johnson was a Freemason.[40] The grounds given
for impeaching him were that he had illegally dismissed from office
the hardline anti-Southern Secretary of War, Edwin M. Stanton, who,
like the President, was a Freemason.[41] The impeachment proceedings
were led by the anti-mason Charles Sumner, the Freemason Congressman General Benjamin F. Butler, and the aged Thaddeus
Stevens; 35 years earlier Stevens had been more prominent than
Sumner in the Anti-Masonic Party at the time of the agitation which
followed Morgan's disappearance.[42] As usual, Freemasons and anti-
masons were divided on the great controversial issues of the day.

◆

CHAPTER 16

The Lautaro Lodge

A T the beginning of the nineteenth century the Spanish Empire stretched in an unbroken line up the west coast of South, Central and North America for nearly 7,000 miles and through 98 degrees of latitude, from Cape Horn to a line about 300 miles north of the small but thriving city of San Francisco. Here it bordered on the sparsely inhabited and largely unexplored region known as Oregon, so called after an imaginary River Oregon which was shown on all the maps but did not in fact exist. This territory of Oregon separated the Spanish Empire from Russian America (Alaska) which reached as far south as Sitka, some 600 miles to the north of the modern city of Vancouver. The Spanish Empire included California and a large part of the present United States to the west of the Rocky Mountains, as well as Texas and Florida and several islands in the Caribbean, including Cuba.

On the mainland of South America, only the Portuguese colony of Brazil, and the relatively small territories of Britain, France and Holland in Guiana and Honduras, did not belong to Spain. Brazil, stretching at its widest points for 2,000 miles from north to south and 3,000 miles from east to west, had been given to Portugal in an arbitration by the Pope in 1494, when he granted the rest of South and Central America to Spain.

In 1810 a revolution broke out in Buenos Aires which led to the proclamation of the independence of Argentina from Spain. During the next twenty years the rest of Spanish America revolted against Spain, and by 1830 the former Spanish Empire was divided into 16 independent republics which for many years waged war against each other and were engaged in civil wars.

Most of the men who led the revolution of 1810 in Buenos Aires were Freemasons – Carlos Maria de Alvear; Miguel de Azcuenaga; Antonio Luis Berutti; Juan José Castelli; Vincente Lopez y Planes, who wrote the words of the Argentine national anthem; Juan José Paso, who read out the Argentine declaration of independence when it was issued, a little belatedly, in 1816; and General Manuel Belgrano, who designed the flag of the Argentine Republic.[1] It is an irony that of all these names the best known in Britain today is Belgrano, not for what he did during his lifetime but because more than 150 years after his death a Right-wing dictatorship, of which he would almost certainly have disapproved, gave his name to a warship which was sunk by the British Navy in controversial circumstances during the Falklands War in 1982.

In the years after 1814, Chile and other parts of South America were liberated from Spain by a revolutionary army from Buenos Aires led by General José de San Martín, known today in Argentina as 'the Liberator'. Venezuela and the northern parts of South America were freed by a series of revolutions led by Simón Bolivar, who finally linked up with San Martín's victorious army in Guayaquil in what is today Ecuador. They were assisted in the liberation of Chile by Bernardo O'Higgins. He was the illegitimate son of a Creole* mother of good family and Ambrose O'Higgins, an Irishman who in the eighteenth century entered the service of the King of Spain, was created Marquis of Vallemar and Osórno, and appointed Spanish Viceroy of Peru. Young O'Higgins, Bolivar and San Martín were Freemasons. They belonged to the South American masonic society, the Lautaro Lodge, which was named after a South American Indian who led an unsuccessful revolt against Spanish rule in the sixteenth century.[2]

The South American revolutionaries were helped in their struggle against Spain by William Brown, an Irishman who emigrated as a young man to the United States, joined the U.S. merchant navy, and was captured at sea by one of the British warships which stopped American ships when searching for British deserters – one of the incidents which caused the war between Britain and the United States in 1812. Brown was forcibly pressed into the British navy, but served the British so well that he was made an officer. He was captured by the French and held as a prisoner-of-war, but twice escaped, on the

---

* A Creole is a person of Spanish origin who was born in the Spanish Empire in America.

second occasion reaching England via St Petersburg. He then went to Buenos Aires, joined the revolutionary struggle against Spain, and was appointed to command the Argentine fleet. Admiral Brown became a national hero in Argentina second only to San Martín. He was a Freemason.[3]

Another naval hero of South American independence was Thomas, Lord Cochrane (afterwards Earl of Dundonald). After a brilliant career of service in the British Navy in the war against Napoleon, he became a Radical MP; but he was wrongly accused of being involved in a financial fraud. He was tried before the Tory Lord Chief Justice, Lord Ellenborough, and convicted. He served a term of imprisonment, was discharged in disgrace from the Navy and expelled from the House of Commons. He then volunteered to fight in the Chilean navy in the war of independence against Spain. After he returned to England he was exonerated from the allegations against him, receiving a free pardon, and was restored to his position in the Navy and in society. Unlike Admiral Brown and so many of his other colleagues in South America, Cochrane was not a Freemason.

Although there is no doubt that all these South American Freemason revolutionaries were members of the Lautaro Lodge, there is controversy about the origin of the lodge. According to the Spanish Catholic anti-masonic propagandists, it was founded by Francisco Miranda, a native of Venezuela who enlisted in the French army and fought for the French on the side of the Americans in the American War of Independence. This gave him the idea that the people of South America might gain their freedom from Spain as the North Americans had won theirs from Britain. After the end of the American War of Independence he left the French service and went to London, and had several talks with the Prime Minister, William Pitt. Knowing that Spain had recently been at war with Britain, he suggested to Pitt that the British government might help the people of South America to win their independence from Spain; but Pitt, though interested, was non-commital.

Miranda returned to France after the French Revolution and fought bravely in the French revolutionary army against the Austrians in the Netherlands in the campaign of 1793. This did not prevent him from being arrested, like several other French revolutionary generals, on suspicion of treason and imprisoned by Robespierre; but he survived until the fall of Robespierre, and was released after 9 Thermidor. He tried to persuade the French Directory to help the struggle of South America against Spain; but as Spain became the ally of revolutionary France against Britain, Miranda went back to London and had further talks with Pitt, who still refused to take any action.

Miranda decided to act by himself. In 1806 he landed in Venezuela and tried to launch a revolution against Spanish rule; but he failed, and returned to London. He tried again in 1810, and this time had more success in Venezuela. He proclaimed the independence of Venezuela and New Granada (Colombia) from Spain, and stated that his ultimate aim was the unity of all South America in a federal republic; but after some initial successes, he failed again. He was not helped by the destruction of his army headquarters, along with many other buildings in Venezuela, in a great earthquake which cost thousands of lives. The Spanish Governor and the Roman Catholic Church declared that it was a sign that God was against Miranda.

After suffering several military defeats, Miranda surrendered to the Spanish authorities on condition that he would be allowed to go to the United States. The Spanish authorities broke the surrender terms. He was held in prison for six years, being moved from one dungeon to another, and after Ferdinand VII had established his autocratic rule in Spain, Miranda was transferred to a prison in Cadiz, where he died in 1816.

The story told by the Spanish Catholic anti-masons was that when Miranda was in London he joined two masonic lodges, one in Grafton Street and one in Fitzroy Square, and that it was the English Freemasons who incited him to found the Lautaro Lodge in Buenos Aires and to launch the revolution in South America and the movement for independence from Spain. This has been strongly denied by the English Freemasons. A learned English masonic historian, F. W. Seal-Coon, who in 1979 denounced what he called 'Spanish-American Revolutionary Pseudo-Masonry', has questioned whether Miranda was ever a Freemason.[4] Whether or not we share Brother Seal-Coon's disapproval of the 'pseudo-masonry' of the revolutionary Lautaro Lodge, we must certainly agree with him in repudiating the suggestion that the English Freemasons, under the Prince of Wales and the Earl of Moira, should have instigated revolution in any country in the world, and certainly not in the Spanish Empire after the Bourbon despot Ferdinand VII had become Britain's ally against Napoleon.

Mexico was by far the most valuable of the four vice-regalities into which the Spanish Empire in America was divided; people called it 'the jewel in the crown' of the King of Spain. It extended from the Isthmus of Panama to the frontier with Oregon, and was governed by the Viceroy in Mexico City. It was also the vice-regality in which the authorities had encountered most trouble from liberal revolutionaries, particularly after the repercussions of the French Revolution had been felt in Mexico. There had been a big drive by the government there against the Freemasons.

The revolutionary outbreaks in South America spread to Mexico. A revolt broke out in 1810 led by a Creole Catholic priest, Miguel Hidalgo, who was aged 57 and already bald, and had spent all his life caring for the Indians in his parish. He fought not only for Mexican independence but also for social justice. He denounced the rich as the oppressors of the poor, and demanded that their wealth be confiscated; some of their property should be distributed among the poor, and the rest given to the state.[5] He led his revolutionary followers under a banner of Our Lady of Guadalupe, the patron saint of Mexico; but he was a Freemason.[6]

The government sent General Calleja to suppress the revolt. Great savagery was shown by both sides in the conflict. When Hidalgo captured the town of Guanajuato he killed all the Creoles. When Calleja recaptured it, he did not wish to waste ammunition by shooting Hidalgo's men whom he had taken prisoner; so he ordered his men to cut the throats of 14,000 prisoners in the town square.[7]

After six months' fighting, the government forces captured Hidalgo. He was degraded from the priesthood and taken to Chihuahua for execution. He was tied, blindfolded, to a chair and the soldiers fired at him; but their first volley only shattered his arm and his belly, and did not kill him. The second volley broke his shoulder and spilled out his guts, but he still survived. Then the soldiers removed his blindfold, and saw that his eyes were full of tears, which so upset them that their third volley also failed to kill him. Then they walked up to him, placed the muzzles of their muskets on his heart, and at last fired the fatal shot.

The Inquisition ordered that anyone found with his portrait was to be excommunicated, in an attempt to blot out his memory. They succeeded in destroying all portraits of Hidalgo, so that no genuine portrait of him exists today; but they could not prevent the people from remembering him, and within a few years he was honoured as a hero of popular revolt against oppression, as he still is today in the celebrations in his honour in September every year.[8]

The next revolt in Mexico was led by another priest, José Morelos, who, unlike Hidalgo, was not a Freemason. His army was more disciplined than Hidalgo's, and did not commit any atrocities; but this did not prevent the government forces from shooting all their prisoners. Eventually Morelos was captured and shot. He too was degraded from the priesthood and excommunicated by the Church before his execution. One of the reasons for his excommunication was that he had a picture of Hidalgo in his possession.

The Spanish Liberal Freemason, Xavier Mina, had fought with the Spanish guerrillas against Napoleon, and supported the Liberal demand for the Constitution of 1812. He was almost certainly a Freemason. When Ferdinand VII returned to power in Spain and arrested Liberals and Freemasons in 1814, Mina escaped abroad. He went first to France and then to Cuba. There he met Mexican revolutionaries, and went to Mexico to fight for them against the Spanish authorities. He won a number of victories, but in 1817 he was captured by the government forces and shot.[9]

In Spain, more than in any other country in the world, Freemasonry really was the revolutionary conspiracy which the anti-masonic writers and the propagandists of the Catholic Church described. After Ferdinand VII suppressed them again in 1814, the illegal lodges became a very well-organized secret revolutionary society. They had some support among the aristocracy; but as in Naples and elsewhere in Italy they consisted largely of middle-class lawyers and journalists. They had far less support among the lower classes, who tended to be loyal to the King and the Catholic Church, particularly in the rural areas. But there was an important difference between the Spanish Free-masons and their brothers in France and Italy. In Spain the Freemasons had considerable support among army officers.

While many Freemasons were serving long terms of imprisonment, the Freemasons in the army organized a series of mutinies in Cadiz, especially in units waiting to be sent to suppress the revolts in Mexico. The mutinies were forestalled or suppressed by the government; but on 1 January 1820 an army officer, Rafael del Riego Nuñez, carried out a successful military coup in Cadiz. He had fought against Napoleon and had been taken prisoner by the French, and while a prisoner had been converted to liberalism by the French and had become a Freemason. As a result of Riego's coup, the Liberal Freemason politicians in Madrid were able to seize power and proclaim the Constitution of 1812. King Ferdinand was forced to accept them as his government. He swore an oath to observe the constitution, and issued a proclamation in which he declared: 'Let us advance frankly, myself leading the way, along the constitutional path'.[10] But he was dissembling, and had not the slightest intention of keeping his oath.

Almost immediately the Liberal revolutionaries, as usual, began to quarrel among themselves, and masonic solidarity did not hold them together. The Liberal politicians in Madrid – the Freemasons who had promulgated the Constitution of 1812 – were suspicious of Riego's army that had put them in power, and ordered it to be disbanded. Their fears increased when Riego came to Madrid and was received with enthusiastic demonstrations from his Radical supporters at banquets, receptions, and in the theatres. Riego and the revolutionary officers were suspicious of the Liberal politicians who tolerated the King and the counter-revolutionary plots in which he engaged with his supporters. Counter-revolutionary organizations like The Defenders of the Absolute King were formed in many districts.

The Liberal government, knowing that the Catholic Church was their enemy, passed legislation confiscating the property of the Church and suppressing monasteries. The King tried to veto this legislation, but was forced to give way and consent to it. A parish priest, Father Vinuesa, led an unsuccessful counter-revolution and was sentenced to a term of imprisonment. The Radicals thought that this sentence was much too light, and had been procured by corruption and the King's influence; so a revolutionary mob stormed the prison and murdered Vinuesa. King Ferdinand secretly approached King Louis XVIII of France and the powers of the Holy Alliance, asking them to intervene and restore him as an absolute monarch.

In 1821 a revolution broke out in Naples; it was organized by the Carbonari and the Freemasons. Metternich sent Austrian troops to suppress it. Next year the Holy Alliance met in Verona. Tsar Alexander proposed that they intervene by force to crush the Liberals in Spain, and that they authorize the French army to do the job. Metternich was a little cool towards the idea; he did not wish to see Russian and French influence extended to Spain. Lord Castlereagh, the British Foreign Secretary, and Wellington, on behalf of the British government, were even less enthusiastic; but neither Austria nor Britain were prepared to take active measures to prevent the French intervention, and at the insistence of the Tsar, Louis XVIII agreed rather reluctantly to send the Count of Artois' son, the Duke of Angoulême, with an army across the Pyrenees.

The Holy Alliance sent an ultimatum to the Spanish government ordering them to abolish the Constitution of 1812 and to restore Ferdinand as an absolute monarch. Britain tried to persuade the Spanish government to accept a compromise by which they would abolish the Constitution of 1812 but still retain some degree of constitutional government; but the Spanish Liberals were indignant at this attempt by the Holy Alliance to interfere in Spanish internal affairs, and to dictate their form of government. The fury of the Liberals made it politically impossible for the Spanish government to accept a compromise which would have been their only chance of survival, as the British Tory government, to the indignation of the British Liberals, refused to intervene to save Spain from the Holy Alliance.

Riego and the other revolutionary leaders carried on the resistance for some time, retreating before the advancing French; but eventually Riego was captured by counter-revolutionary Spanish Catholics who nearly lynched him. King Ferdinand then promised an amnesty to all Liberals who surrendered; but again he violated his oath, and carried out wholesale executions.

Riego was hanged in a public square in Madrid. He was regarded as a martyr by the Spanish republicans. His picture was displayed by them on many occasions in future years, and his 'Song of Riego' was still the song of the Left wing in Spain during the Spanish Civil War of 1936–9 and today.

The King was egged on by counter-revolutionary groups. There is supposed to have been a secret clerical organization called The Society of the Exterminating Angel which murdered Liberals and Freemasons; but if this society existed, it was hardly needed in view of the policy of King Ferdinand and his government. On 4 October 1822 the King issued a decree sentencing to death all who had supported the Liberal government, even if they had done nothing more than shout 'Viva Riego!' Hundreds of Freemasons were executed. The French and the other foreign governments expressed mild disapproval of the King's violation of his promise of amnesty, but did nothing effective to stop the executions.[11]

Events took a different course in Brazil. When Napoleon's armies invaded Portugal in 1807, the Portuguese royal family took refuge in Rio de Janeiro. King Juan VI liked Brazil so much that he remained there after the defeat of Napoleon and the restoration of Portugal to his government. He was there when a revolution broke out in Brazil in 1821, and independence from Portugal was proclaimed. King Juan was persuaded to go back to Portugal; but his son and heir, Dom Pedro, who was a Liberal and a Freemason, supported the national revolution in Brazil, placed himself at its head, and was chosen as the Emperor Pedro I of Brazil.

Although the British Tory government had reluctantly accepted the decision of the Holy Alliance at the Congress of Verona to intervene in Spain, the intervention marked the beginning of the divergence between Britain and the powers of the Holy Alliance, and Britain's decision to redress the balance of power in Europe by limiting the influence of Russia and Austria. The new British Foreign Secretary, George Canning, who was a Freemason, declared that he had called in the New World to help redress the balance of the Old. He gave diplomatic support to the revolutionary movements for independence in South America, and thereby discouraged the powers of the Holy Alliance from helping Spain and Portugal to suppress them. By 1830 both Portugal and Spain had given up all hope of recovering Brazil and the Spanish colonies in America.

The Emperor Pedro I ran into difficulties with influential circles in Brazil. He was too liberal for the conservative aristocracy. In 1831 he abdicated as Emperor in favour of his six-year-old son Pedro II, and returned to Portugal. His brother, Dom Miguel, had established a reactionary absolutist régime. As Pedro had abdicated the throne of Portugal when he became Emperor of Brazil, he now proclaimed his daughter Maria da Gloria as Queen of Portugal, and led the Liberal forces on her behalf.

A long and fierce civil war broke out in Portugal between the Liberals, led by Pedro, and the Conservatives led by Miguel. The Liberals were supported by the middle classes in the towns and by the revolutionary Radicals; the Catholic Church, the landowners and most of the army supported Miguel. There were many Freemasons among the leaders of the Queen's party. The British Foreign Secretary, Lord Palmerston, and the French government of Louis Philippe supported the Queen, despite considerable friction between Britain and France and between both governments and the Queen's Portuguese supporters; and as Metternich and Tsar Nicholas I of Russia were not in a position to help Miguel, the Liberals won in Portugal.

The civil war in Portugal spread into Spain. The persecution of

Liberals and Freemasons in Spain had continued until 1829, when King Ferdinand married Princess Maria Cristina of Naples. She was a beautiful woman, and the King fell deeply in love with her. As she was politically very sympathetic to the Liberals, she persuaded Ferdinand not only to relax his persecution of Liberals and Freemasons, but also to change the law of succession so as to allow her daughter Isabel to succeed him as Queen. When Ferdinand died, his brother Don Carlos, who was the champion of the extreme reactionary party, refused to recognize Isabel as Queen, and a savage civil war was fought in Spain between the Isabelinos and the Carlists.

It was a model for future civil wars in Spain. The Isabelinos were supported by the middle classes, the Liberals, and the revolutionaries of the extreme anti-clerical Left wing. Many of the leaders of the Isabelinos were Freemasons. The Carlists were supported by the Church, the large landowners, and the mass of the peasants. The anti-clerical revolutionary supporters of the Isabelinos attacked monasteries and murdered many Catholic monks and priests; the Carlists shot the wives of all the town mayors who supported the Isabelinos.

The Isabelinos were ultimately victorious. They were supported by Palmerston and by the British Legion of volunteers from Britain who went to fight on the Isabelino side. They were also supported by the government of Louis Philippe. Metternich and Tsar Nicholas were not in a position to help the Carlists.

After the independence of South America had been won, civil wars broke out in Brazil and Argentina, and they developed into wars between the independent republics. In these wars and civil wars there were Freemasons on both sides. In Argentina the country divided between the Liberal Unitarians and the nationalist Federalists. The Federalists were the party of the gauchos, whose only occupation was to slaughter the cattle on the pampas for dispatch to Buenos Aires or Montevideo for export to Europe. They were led by Juan Manuel de Rosas, who was in fact a politician from Buenos Aires but posed as the leader of the gauchos.

The Liberal Unitarians were supported by the middle class in Buenos Aires, who wished to develop international trade, industrialize the country, and introduce a liberal, constitutional régime. Many of their leaders were Freemasons. The struggle between Rosas and the Liberal Unitarians spread into Uruguay, where the Liberals were called Colorados. They overthrew the dictatorship of Rosas's friend General Manuel Oribe, whose supporters were called Blancos. Rosas then invaded Uruguay and reached the suburbs of Montevideo; but there he was stopped, and the defenders of the city held out for nine years.

The Italian revolutionary, Giuseppe Garibaldi, went to South America after he had been involved in an abortive insurrection in Genoa in 1834. He was a merchant seaman, and when he arrived in Rio de Janeiro he offered his services to the republican and mildly liberal government of the Brazilian province of Rio Grande do Sul in their struggle against the conservative government of the Emperor Pedro II. After fighting for four years for Rio Grande do Sul, Garibaldi went to Montevideo. Rio Grande do Sul was eventually conquered by the Brazilian imperial general, the Duke of Caixas, who was a Freemason.[12]

In Montevideo, Garibaldi led the Uruguayan navy in the struggle against Rosas and the Argentine Federalists. He became a Freemason in Montevideo, joining the revolutionary Lautaro lodge, like his colleague, the great Argentine Liberal leader Bartolomé Mitre, who had joined the Uruguayan Liberals in their fight for freedom against Rosas.

In his first campaign for Uruguay, Garibaldi fought a naval battle at Costa Brava on the River Paraná against his masonic brother, Admiral Brown, who at the age of 64 had been appointed commander-in-chief of Rosas's Argentine navy. It was a very bloody two-day battle. Garibaldi was outgunned by Brown, and lost two-thirds of his men. When he realized that he could no longer fight on, he blew up his ships and escaped overland. He found his way back to Montevideo, and played a leading part in the fight against Rosas both at sea and on land. He again fought against Admiral Brown in naval actions in Montevideo harbour.[13]

Garibaldi and Brown were the only commanders on the two sides who conducted the war with humanity. Usually it was waged with great savagery by armies of fewer than a thousand men on each side, who marched across the great spaces of the pampas for many days without encountering each other; when they did meet, they fought a war of extermination, for there were no facilities for taking prisoners. Any Uruguayan supporter of Oribe who was captured by the Liberals of Montevideo when he was fighting for Rosas was executed as a traitor.

In Rosas's army there was an NCO in each unit who was called the *degollador* (the cut-throat). It was his duty to kill the enemy prisoners after the battle. If the prisoner appeared to be nervous, the *degollador* put his arm comfortingly around his neck and told him that it would soon be over and would not hurt, and then cut the prisoner's throat. After a battle, if any of Garibaldi's men were too seriously wounded to walk, the wounded man would ask his comrades to shoot him to prevent him falling alive into enemy hands, and this was done on several occasions.[14]

Early in the war the Liberal leader General Juan Lavalle, who was a Freemason, captured Rosas's commander Manuel Dorrego, and ordered that he be immediately shot. This was used by Rosas's men to justify all their savagery towards their opponents during the war. Lavalle was duly defeated and captured by Rosas's men in 1841, and shot at once. One of the most savage of all Rosas's commanders was General Justo José Urquiza, the governor of the state of Corrientes. He was a Freemason, but his war against the Freemasons Mitre and Garibaldi was merciless.

In 1845 Admiral Brown retired from the Argentine service, and travelled to Europe. He was granted a safe-conduct to visit Montevideo on his journey, and he called on Garibaldi. The two old enemies had a very friendly talk.[15] Perhaps the fact that they were both Freemasons facilitated their get-together; but it is not unknown for enemy generals who are not Freemasons to meet after a war and to discuss their past battles, paying tribute to each other's courage and skill.

When the revolution of 1848 broke out in Europe, Garibaldi returned to Italy to take part in the struggle there. The siege of Montevideo continued for another four years. Then Brazil came into the war against Rosas's Argentina, and Urquiza changed sides and joined the Brazilians and the Unitarians of Montevideo. The three allies defeated Rosas at the Battle of Monte Caseros on 3 February 1852, and Rosas fled to England to spend his last days in a house near Southampton. It was not long before Urquiza fell out with his old enemies, the Unitarians, with whom he had made a temporary alliance against Rosas. The Unitarians defeated Urquiza, and Mitre became President of a Liberal republic in Argentina.

When he retired after eight years, he was succeeded by his colleague Domenico Sarmiento, who was also a constitutional Liberal President and wrote the history of the thirty-year struggle against Rosas. Sarmiento, like Mitre, was a Freemason. But after these two great Liberal

Presidents the peace of the River Plate was again disturbed by violent conflicts which have continued into the twentieth century.

In Mexico, independence was achieved not by a revolution but by a counter-revolution. When the generals and Conservatives, who had suppressed the revolts of Hidalgo, Morelos and Mina, found that a Liberal government had been established in Spain by the masonic Liberal revolution of 1820, they proclaimed the independence of Mexico, after they had made a coup in Mexico against the representatives of the Liberal government of Spain. The leader of the coup was General Agustín de Iturbide, who proclaimed himself the Emperor Agustín I of Mexico. He was a Freemason.[16] His Liberal brother-masons in Mexico did not approve of Iturbide proclaiming himself Emperor, and they persuaded one of his leading officers, General Antonio Lopez de Santa Anna, to overthrow him. Santa Anna, too, was a Freemason. Iturbide was allowed to go into exile; but when he returned and tried to carry out a second coup, the Liberals captured and shot him. Santa Anna then turned on the Liberals and made himself dictator.

Many citizens of the United States were settling in the Mexican province of Texas, and in 1835 a revolt broke out there. The immigrants demanded independence for Texas, but some of their leaders saw independence as a temporary stage, a stepping-stone to union with the United States. The revolutionary struggle against Santa Anna in Texas united two different groups – the Liberals, including Mexican-born Liberals, who fought against Santa Anna's dictatorship, and the slaveowners of the Southern states of the United States. They wished to introduce slavery into Texas; for though slavery had been abolished by the Liberal government of Mexico, it was flourishing in the Southern states of the USA. The Liberal leader of the Texan revolution, Sam Houston, was a Freemason; so were Stephen F. Austin, who first launched the campaign for independence; Mirabeau Bonaparte Lamar and Anson Jones, the second and the last Presidents of the independent state of Texas; and Captain William B. Travis, the commander of the garrison that held out at the siege of the Alamo. But Davy Crockett, who led the volunteers from the United States who went to fight for Texas, and was killed when Santa Anna captured the Alamo, was not a Freemason.[17]

The Texan defeat at the Alamo was followed by Houston's victory at the Battle of San Jacinto, where Santa Anna was defeated and taken prisoner. This was followed by the establishment of the independent state of Texas, and Houston and his Liberal followers found that they had won their heroic struggle in order to extend slavery. Texas remained an independent nation for only nine years; in 1845 it agreed to be annexed by the United States, becoming the twenty-eighth state of the Union. This led to war between the United States and Mexico, in which the Mexican army, commanded by Santa Anna, was defeated.

The annexation of Texas and the war against Mexico were due chiefly to the forward policy of President James K. Polk and his belief that it was the 'manifest destiny' of the United States to rule all the territory between the Atlantic and Pacific Oceans and from the Arctic snows to the tropics. Polk was a Freemason. So was General Winfield Scott, who commanded the army that captured Mexico City. It was widely believed that the other victorious United States commander, General Zachary Taylor, was a Freemason, but in fact he was not; nor was John C. Frémont, who led the United States force which won California from Mexico.[18]

In the course of twenty-five years, Santa Anna had betrayed and overthrown his commander-in-chief, Iturbide, who had appointed him to his military command; had installed Vincente Guerrero as the Liberal President of Mexico; had joined with Anastasio Bustamante to betray Guerrero, to capture him by a trick and execute him, and replace him with Bustamante as President; had betrayed and overthrown Bustamante; had defeated and killed Travis at the Alamo; had been defeated in his turn and taken prisoner by Houston at San Jacinto; and had lost a war and a large part of Mexican territory to Polk and Scott. Santa Anna, Iturbide, Guerrero, Bustamante, Travis, Houston, Polk and Scott were all masonic brothers.[19]

CHAPTER 17

The Nineteenth Century

AFTER the revolution of 1830 the French Freemasons in the Grand Orient were loyal to King Louis Philippe. The Conservative Prime Minister, François Guizot, was a Freemason, though he had allowed his membership to lapse. As the government policy, under Guizot, became more reactionary, some of the younger Freemasons turned against the régime and began to discuss how it could be overthrown. The police kept a close watch on the Freemasons. From time to time they reported that some masonic lodge was engaging in political activities. When the Grand Lodge of Grand Orient were informed about this, they expelled the revolutionary lodge.[1]

The writer Eugène Sue was a Freemason. In his novels, particularly in his *Les mystères de Paris*, he revealed the sufferings of the poor in the Paris slums. His book was treated with derision by the Conservatives and the middle classes, but helped to spread the sense of injustice felt by the working class, and the support for Socialism among Radical intellectuals.

In 1847 some Freemasons organized a number of banquets at which the speakers criticized the government. This was following the tradition of the masonic banquets held before the revolution of 1830 when La Fayette had criticized the government of Charles X. The chief speakers at the banquets of 1847 were Odilon Barrot and Adolphe Crémieux. They demanded the resignation of Guizot; but Crémieux was careful to state that he was not calling for revolution or for the establishment of a republic, for the Freemasons believed in constitutional monarchy.[2]

The first revolutionary outbreak of 1848 took place in Palermo in Sicily on 12 January. It was followed by the revolution in Paris on 24 February. On 15 March revolution broke out in Berlin, and on 19 March the people of Milan rose against the Austrian garrison and were victorious after five days' street fighting. The Carbonari and the Freemasons played the leading part in the revolution in Milan. There were revolutions in several parts of Germany – in Saxony, the Rhineland and in Baden. They were all eventually suppressed.

The outbreak of the revolution in Baden moved Dr Eduard Emil Eckert, an advocate practising in the courts of Saxony, to write a book, *The Order of Freemasons*, showing that the aim of the Freemasons was to overthrow the established religion and government in every country in the world. He warned his readers that 'Freemasonry is the mother of democracy', and cited an article in a German masonic journal of 1848: 'Democracy is a child of masonry, and we must recognize it as our child. It is our business to bring up this child to wisdom, strength and beauty'.[3]

After Louis Philippe had abdicated and fled to England, and the Second Republic had been proclaimed in France, the Grand Lodge of Grand Orient declared their support for the new régime, the republic, and the provisional government, which was headed by the moderate Liberal poet, Alphonse de Lamartine. He was not a Freemason. Serious political disagreements arose among the supporters of the provisional government. The Socialist Louis Blanc, who was a Freemason, and the Radical Alexandre Ledru-Rollin, who was not, went into opposition to the government; and in June 1848 the government's decision to close the workshops, where relief was given to the Paris poor, led to the street fighting of the 'June Days' between the Socialist revolutionaries and the government forces under General Louis Eugène Cavaignac. He replaced Lamartine as head of the government, with emergency powers. There is some evidence that Cavaignac may have been a Freemason, but this is doubtful.

For four days, from 23 to 26 June, the fighting continued, culminating in the storming of the barricade in the Faubourg St Antoine by Cavaignac's troops, who lost more officers than had fallen in any of Napoleon's battles. During the fighting the Archbishop of Paris, Monsignor Denis Auguste Affre, bearing his cross, walked out from the government lines towards the rebels on the barricade, but was shot and killed; both the government forces and the revolutionaries claimed that the other side had shot him. The revolutionaries were generally blamed for his death, and his martyrdom strengthened the position of the Catholic Church.

Cavaignac's victory was followed by the summary execution of thousands of revolutionaries, and many more were sent to prison camps in North Africa. His government then proceeded to pass laws restricting the right of public meeting, and banning secret political societies.

On 27 June, the day after the revolutionaries had been defeated, the Grand Orient issued a statement supporting Cavaignac. 'The hand of God has weighed upon us', but we all stood united 'against aberration, against folly, against the perversity of the conspirators and the anarchists, for the common welfare, for the welfare of the republic. The head of the Executive Power [Cavaignac] has led you, with a bleeding heart, to the combat; may God give him the strength to lead you to peace'.[4] It was not made clear, in the debates in the National Assembly of 24 and 25 July, whether the ban on political societies would extend to the Freemasons; but in practice the Freemasons were allowed to continue.

On 10 December 1848 the election was held for the new President of the Republic. The Freemasons' journal, *Le Franc-Maçon*, called on its readers to vote for Lamartine, because he believed in 'the sacred words, Liberty, Equality, Fraternity';[5] but Louis Napoleon Bonaparte (who would soon become the Emperor Napoleon III) was elected by a very large majority; he defeated Cavaignac, Ledru-Rollin, the Socialist François Raspail, and Lamartine, receiving 75 per cent of the votes cast, and coming top of the poll in all except four of the eighty-five departments of France. He was the son of Louis Bonaparte, King of Holland, and in his youth had been involved in the revolutionary movement in Italy in 1831. It has been suggested that he joined the Carbonari and the Freemasons in Italy, but this cannot be proved. He afterwards tried twice to make a revolution against Louis Philippe, and on the second occasion was sentenced to life imprisonment in the fortress at Ham near St Quentin in north-eastern France; but he made a sensational escape, took refuge in England, and returned to Paris to his electoral triumph in 1848.

Although he had been suspected at one time of being a Communist, as soon as he was elected President of the Republic he relied on the support of the Right wing and the Catholic Church. Young Radicals who flaunted red cravats, and shouted 'Long live the Social Republic!' were sentenced to several years' imprisonment. From time to time a

Freemasons' lodge was raided by the police, and warnings were sent by local officials to the government that 'members of the anarchist party' were planning to gain control of the masonic lodges in Paris and the provinces.[6]

The Grand Orient thought it would be wise to revise their constitution. In 1839, when they were living happily under Louis Philippe, they had stated that 'Masonry is a universal philanthropic association' and that one of their objectives was 'the examination and discussion of all social and economic questions which concern the happiness of humanity'. In August 1848, after the June Days and the legislation suppressing secret political societies, they changed this article in their constitution by deleting the words 'social and economic'; and a year later, on 10 August 1849, Grand Orient stated that all Freemasons must believe in God and in the immortality of the soul.[7]

In November 1848 a revolutionary mob in Rome murdered the Pope's Prime Minister, Count Pellegrino Rossi, on the steps of the Capitol because he had refused to support the movement to free Italy from Austrian domination. Pope Pius IX had pursued a liberal policy when he first became Pope; but after the murder of Rossi he fled to Gaeta in the Kingdom of Naples, called on the Catholic states to restore him to power in Rome, and henceforth was an extreme reactionary. In February 1849 Giuseppe Mazzini proclaimed the Roman Republic. Mazzini had originally been a member of the Carbonari, but had left them to form his own illegal revolutionary organization, Young Italy; he was probably a Freemason but it cannot be proved.

Louis Napoleon, seeking the support of the Catholic Church in France, sent an army to overthrow the Roman Republic and restore the Pope. The French army was commanded by General Charles Oudinot, who was a Freemason.[8] The Roman Republic was defended by an army of revolutionaries from many countries under the command of the Freemason Garibaldi. On 30 April Garibaldi defeated the French in the first battle; but later Oudinot captured an important strategic stronghold outside Rome, the Villa Corsini, by a trick when a truce had been agreed; and Garibaldi failed to recapture it in a bloody engagement.

After a month's fierce fighting, Oudinot captured Rome. Garibaldi retreated to the north, evading the pursuing French and Austrian armies. During the retreat his heroic wife Anita died, but Garibaldi reached the United States and resumed his career as a merchant seaman. During the fighting for Rome, Ledru-Rollin tried to help the Italian revolutionaries by organising a rising in Paris; but it was suppressed by Louis Napoleon. Ledru-Rollin fled to England.

On 2 December 1851 Louis Napoleon made a *coup d'état* and established his dictatorship. There was an attempt at resistance in Paris next day, led by the deputy Baudin, a Freemason;[9] but Baudin was shot dead on the barricade, and the resistance to the coup was suppressed. Radicals were arrested all over France and sent to detention camps in Algeria, where conditions were very harsh.

A week after the coup, on 10 December, Grand Orient ordered their lodges to suspend all meetings and activities until further notice.[10] Louis Napoleon held a plebiscite in which the people could vote Yes or No as to whether they wished him to continue as President of the Republic for ten years. The Grand Orient urged the Freemasons to vote Yes. On election day 7,439,216 voted Yes and 646,737 voted No.

On 17 February 1852 Louis Napoleon issued a decree which enabled the Minister of the Interior to close a newspaper after one initial warning and to imprison people without trial for ten years. Under this decree many opponents of the government were interned in the prison camps in Cayenne in the West Indies, both on the mainland and on Devil's Island. The Minister of the Interior who enforced the decree was Louis Napoleon's close collaborator, Jean Fiolin, Count of Persigny. He was a Freemason.

Some of Louis Napoleon's opponents escaped to Britain. The writer Victor Hugo, who was not a Freemason (though many people thought he was), settled in the Channel Islands. Many of the French refugees who joined Ledru-Rollin in London, unlike Ledru-Rollin himself, were Freemasons; and they joined a lodge in London, which was formed specially for French refugees.

The Grand Orient in France tried to ingratiate themselves with Louis Napoleon and his régime. They had functioned without a Grand Master for 38 years since Joseph Bonaparte refused to resign in 1814; but now they invited Prince Joachim Murat to be their Grand Master. He was the son of Napoleon's Marshal, the King of Naples, and was an ardent supporter and close associate of Louis Napoleon. He accepted the Freemasons' invitation, and was installed as Grand Master on 26 February 1852, when the winter feast of St John, which had been cancelled on 27 December 1851 because of the *coup dètat*, was belatedly celebrated.

On taking office, Murat issued a statement that the Freemasons would always avoid 'political passions' and that their motto was 'Charity, Fraternity'.[11] Next year he and the Grand Orient congratulated Louis Napoleon on establishing the Second Empire and taking the title of the Emperor Napoleon III.

In October 1854 Murat was re-elected Grand Master for a term of seven years, and the Grand Orient changed its constitution to transfer all authority from the Council of Grand Lodge to the Grand Master. The Constitution of 1854 declared that 'the Grand Master is the Supreme Head of the Order', its representative in its relations with foreign masonic bodies and with the government; 'he is the executive, administrative and directing power'.[12] Exercising his power as Grand Master, Murat suspended a number of masonic lodges in various parts of France on the grounds that they had been engaging in political discussions; and he arbitrarily dismissed several officials who had given many years of loyal service to the Grand Orient. In line with Napoleon III's policy towards the Church, Murat was eager to avoid antagonizing the Catholics. He congratulated the officials of a lodge at Caen for not wearing their masonic garments at the funeral of one of their brothers for fear that it might offend the local Catholic priest.[13]

In 1859 Napoleon III, making a complete political U-turn, went to war in alliance with King Victor Emmanuel of Piedmont against Austria. Victor Emmanuel, who was a Freemason, had become recognized by nearly all Italian revolutionaries as the leader of the movement for the reunification of Italy; to the Catholic Right wing, he represented 'the Revolution', the assault of revolutionary Freemasonry on the Catholic Church and civilization. Napoleon III's Radical and Socialist enemies cheered him as he rode at the head of his guard through the streets of Paris on his way to the railway station to join his army in Italy; his former allies, the Conservatives and the Catholic Church, were bitterly disappointed, and wondered whether he was a Freemason who had been waiting for an opportunity to help his Italian masonic and Carbonari brothers to liberate Italy from Austria and the Pope. But after his costly victory at Solferino, Napoleon III made peace with Austria, having given Lombardy and Tuscany to Victor Emmanuel in return for the cession by Piedmont of the province of Savoy and the port of Nice to France. He then reverted to his pro-Catholic policy, but relaxed his dictatorship to some extent after November 1860. His political opponents were now allowed some freedom, but the government was always liable suddenly to suppress their newspapers and imprison them without trial in Cayenne.

Murat's term as Grand Master would expire on 30 October 1861, and the meeting of the Assembly of the Grand Orient to elect a new Grand Master was due to be held in Paris on 20 May 1861. Those Freemasons who resented the rule of Napoleon III and Murat's actions as Grand Master, and who were more ready to defy the government since the relaxation of the dictatorship in November 1860, decided to invite Prince Napoleon to stand for Grand Master. Prince Napoleon was Napoleon III's cousin; he was the son of Jerome Bonaparte, King of Westphalia, and he was often referred to by his nickname of 'Plon-Plon'. He had become known as the leader of the Radical faction at Napoleon III's court, and because of this he was bitterly disliked by the Empress Eugénie, the Emperor's Spanish wife, who was a strong supporter of a reactionary Catholic policy. She could never forgive Prince Napoleon for his political attitude, although he had once been in love with her. To elect Prince Napoleon, instead of Murat, as Grand Master of the Grand Orient would be an act of defiance of the Emperor; but after Murat, following Napoleon's III's policy, voted in the Senate in favour of maintaining the temporal power of the Pope in Rome, the Radical Freemasons were more than ever determined to get rid of him.

When Prince Napoleon was invited to stand as Grand Master, he at first refused, saying that he did not wish to oppose his cousin, Prince Murat; but then he changed his mind and announced that he would stand, as he had been informed that in any case the majority of the members of the Assembly were intending to vote against Murat.[14]

The Assembly met on 20 May, and examined the delegates' credentials. Next day they re-assembled and were about to proceed to the election of the new Grand Master when they received a message from Murat, who was still Grand Master, adjourning the election till 24 May and ordering that the new Grand Master should be chosen not by the Assembly but by the existing Grand Master and his Council. The Assembly nevertheless remained in session, and elected Prince Napoleon as the new Grand Master by 120 votes out of 139; but the police then arrived and ejected them from the hall. On 23 May an order was issued by the Prefect of Police of the Seine district that as 'the election of a Grand Master of the Masonic Order is giving rise to an agitation of a nature which compromises public safety ... all Free Masons are forbidden to meet for the purpose of electing a Grand Master before the end of next October'.[15]

On the same day Murat issued an order dissolving the Assembly which had elected Prince Napoleon and forbidding any Freemason in Paris to meet for any purpose until further notice; and on 29 May he expelled from the society twenty-four masons who had played a leading part in Prince Napoleon's election. On 28 May Prince Napoleon issued a statement thanking the Freemasons for the confidence that they had shown him, but declaring that in view of the outcry which his candidature had aroused he would not stand for election as Grand Master.

On 29 September, a month before his term of office expired, Murat ordered the Assembly of the Grand Orient to meet in Paris on 14 October to elect a new Grand Master. Next day he announced that he would not be a candidate. On 10 October the Prefect of Police of the Seine district issued an order forbidding the Freemasons to meet to elect a Grand Master before May 1862. This greatly irritated the masonic delegates from the provinces who had already arrived in Paris for the election; but no further action was taken by the authorities till 28 October, when a deputation from the Grand Orient visited Persigny, the Minister of the Interior, and asked him to appoint a commission to run the affairs of the Grand Orient after Murat's term of office ended in two days' time until the election of the new Grand Master in May 1862; and Persigny appointed some officials of the Grand Orient who were considered trustworthy by the government.[16]

On 11 January 1862 Napoleon III issued an imperial decree. 'Napoleon, by the grace of God and the national will Emperor of the French' decreed that the Grand Master of the Grand Orient should be appointed by the Emperor, and he thereby appointed Marshal Bernard Magnan to be Grand Master.[17] This was in fact a compromise solution. Magnan was a non-controversial figure, and by appointing him Napoleon III was asserting his power over the Freemasons, but was removing the dictatorial Murat, who had caused so much resentment among many Freemasons. Magnan was quite conciliatory towards the Radical Freemasons who had come into conflict with Murat, and on issues on which they differed he usually gave way to them. He did not object when they repealed the Constitution of 1864 which had transferred all power from the Council of Grand Lodge to the Grand Master.

Magnan died on 29 May 1865. At his funeral in the Church of the Invalides in Paris, Monsignor Georges Darboy, the Archbishop of Paris, allowed masonic emblems to be displayed on the catafalque. Pope Pius IX was not pleased when he received Darboy's letter explaining why he had allowed this. Pius promptly issued another Bull condemning the Freemasons, and wrote on 26 October 1865 to Darboy: 'We cannot hide the fact, Venerable Brother, that our pain and surprise were extreme' when he heard about the masonic emblems on the catafalque.[18]

The Emperor permitted the Freemasons to elect their Grand Master after Magnan's death; they elected General Mellinet. He was as colourless and uncontroversial as Magnan, and did not become involved in controversy in the last days of the Second Empire. Many of the leaders of the opposition to Napoleon III, including Jules Favre, Adolphe Crémieux and Jules Simon, were Freemasons.

Henri de Rochefort was not a Freemason. He became the leading critic of Napoleon III and his family. In his newspaper *La Marseillaise* he criticized Prince Pierre Bonaparte, the Emperor's cousin. Pierre Bonaparte had joined the Carbonari as a young man in Italy, and had become a Freemason. After Rochefort's article was published, Pierre Bonaparte challenged Rochefort to a duel. Rochefort sent two of the journalists on his newspaper to Pierre Bonaparte's house in Paris; one of them was the son of a Jewish cobbler who wrote under the pseudonym Victor Noir. There was a contradiction in evidence as to what happened when they met in Pierre Bonaparte's house; but the encounter ended with Pierre Bonaparte shooting Victor Noir and killing him instantly.[19] Riots in Paris followed, as a result of which Rochefort was arrested for inciting disorder.

Pierre Bonaparte was put on trial for Noir's murder, but was found not guilty. The judge treated him with far more courtesy than he treated Rochefort, who was brought from prison to give evidence.[20] In the case of the murder of Victor Noir, it was the hero of the imperial establishment, Pierre Bonaparte, who was a Freemason, and the victims of Bonapartist oppression, Rochefort and Victor Noir, who were not.

The Freemasons played a prominent part in the revolution in Paris of 4 September 1870 after Napoleon III had been taken prisoner by the Germans at Sedan. Jules Favre, Jules Ferry, Louis Garnier-Pagès and Léon Gambetta, who led the revolution and proclaimed the Third Republic, were all Freemasons. When the German Chancellor,

Otto von Bismarck, continued the war after the fall of Napoleon III, and besieged Paris, Gambetta escaped from Paris in a balloon and organized the resistance to the Germans in the provinces.

The establishment of the Third Republic was followed by the Paris Commune. This was led chiefly by the survivors and heirs of the Red Republicans of 1848, many of whom had suffered years of imprisonment in harsh conditions in Cayenne. But it was also supported by Socialists and other revolutionaries, and from London by the German Socialist, Karl Marx, who wrote strongly in support of the Commune. The aged Louis Adolphe Thiers, who had been Foreign Minister under Louis Philippe and in opposition under Napoleon III, became Prime Minister of the government of the republic which was established at Versailles. He was not a Freemason. Negotiations with the Commune in Paris broke down, and Thiers sent the army to conquer Paris.

Several of the leaders of the Paris Commune were Freemasons Benoit Malon, who was a member of Marx's International Working Men's Association (later known as the First International); Felix Pyat; the songwriter Jean Baptiste Clément, who wrote the song 'Le Temps des Cerises' (Cherry Time) about the Commune; Zéphian Camélinat, who survived to become a member of the Communist Party in 1920; and another songwriter, Eugène Pottier, who wrote, among other poems and songs, the words of 'L'Internationale'.[21] But there were Freemasons on the other side. Louis Blanc condemned the Paris Commune, and remained in the National Assembly at Versailles; and from Italy Mazzini strongly condemned the Commune, though Garibaldi supported it.

On 29 April 1871 some Paris Freemasons set out from Paris to go to Versailles to discuss with Thiers ways of ending the civil war between the government and the Commune. They carried their masonic banners as they walked through the Porte Maillot. On this section of the battlefront the government army was commanded by General Montaudon, who was a Freemason. He ordered a ceasefire to allow the Freemasons from Paris to pass through his lines. They went on to Versailles, where their masonic brother, Jules Simon, took them to see Thiers; but Thiers insisted that Paris must submit unconditionally to the government at Versailles.[22]

The forces of the Versailles government were commanded by General Gaston, Marquis of Galliffet. He was not a Freemason. He had fought for Napoleon III in Mexico, and had established a reputation for reckless courage, gallantry with women, and merciless severity. When his troops captured Communard prisoners, Galliffet ordered that every tenth man should be immediately shot. The rest were taken as prisoners to Versailles, where they were forced to run the gauntlet of screaming middle-class ladies who struck them with their parasols, while the women among the Communard prisoners were seized by the hair and forced to grovel on the ground before the jeering crowd.[23] When the Commune in Paris heard of this, they arrested as hostages many people whom they considered to be sympathizers with Versailles, among them Archbishop Darboy.

As the Versailles troops fought their way into Paris, the Archbishop and many of the other hostages were shot. The Communards made a last stand in the cemetery of Père-Lachaise. The Versailles troops, after their victory, shot at least 20,000 of them.[24] Many other Communards were sent to prison camps in New Caledonia in the Pacific before being eventually released under an amnesty in 1880.

The revolution of 1848 in other countries led to less prolonged and turbulent events than those in France. The revolution in Vienna overthrew Metternich, but the old régime was re-established under a young Emperor, Franz Joseph, who was placed on the throne instead of his unsuitable uncle and father, at the age of 18 in December 1848, and reigned for 68 years. In the early years of his reign he re-established a Right-wing autocratic government. He suppressed the Freemasons, and forced every civil servant to sign a statement that he was not a Freemason and had no intention of becoming one.[25]

In Hungary the revolution was more threatening. It was led by Lajos Kossuth, a Freemason,[26] and it was suppressed only when Tsar Nicholas I sent Russian troops to help the Austrians crush the Hungarian resistance. Kossuth escaped to England, where he was received as a hero.

In 1867, after Austria had been defeated by Germany and Italy in the war of 1866, and the Russians had been defeated in the Crimean War, the Austrian government pursued a conciliatory policy in Hungary. The administration of Austria and Hungary was separated; an amnesty was granted to the Hungarian revolutionaries of 1849; and a more liberal régime was introduced in Hungary than in Austria. The Hungarian Liberal statesman, Count Gyula Andrassy, became Prime Minister of Hungary. He was a Freemason, and after 1867

masonic lodges were tolerated, and flourished, in Hungary. Freemasonry was still officially banned in Austria, but a society which
was in fact, though not in name, a masonic lodge was tolerated in
Bohemia after 1872.[27]

In Germany the revolutionary outbreaks of 1848 were defeated,
in some cases after prolonged fighting. Carl Schurz, at the age of 19,
fought in the revolution in his native Rhineland in 1848. After the
defeat of the revolution he escaped to Paris and became a journalist
before moving to London and working as a teacher in a school. In
1850 he secretly returned to Germany and organized the escape of
his friend and fellow-revolutionary Paul Kinker from Spandau prison
in Berlin.

In 1852 Schurz went to the United States, settling first in Philadelphia, where he became a Freemason. He then moved to Washington,
D.C., and practised law. By 1861 he was sufficiently prominent in
the Republican Party to be appointed United States ambassador to
Spain by Lincoln's government; but he resigned in order to join the
army, and was given a military command in the Civil War. After the
war he became the editor of various important newspapers and a
United States senator for Missouri, and was Secretary for the Interior
in the governments of Rutherford B. Hayes and General James A.
Garfield from 1877 to 1881.[28]It is a sad irony that this Radical
champion, after a lifetime of fighting for the cause of freedom, should
have been the Secretary for the Interior responsible for the ruthless
policy of extermination pursued in the West towards the native
Americans after Custer's defeat at Little Big Horn.

The first Greek masonic lodge was founded in Corfu in 1814, and
established itself in various parts of Greece. The Filiki Eteria (Friendly
Society) Lodge led the Greek revolution against Turkish rule in 1821
which won Greek independence in 1830.[29]

A Greek Freemason played a leading part in the movement of the
Young Turks which at the beginning of the twentieth century brought
about the modernization of Turkey and the overthrow of the despotic
rule of the Sultan. Cleanti Scalieris (Kleanti Skalyeri in Turkish)
was a wealthy Greek banker from a noble family who was born in
Constantinople in 1833. He was initiated in 1863 into a lodge which
had been established in Constantinople by the French Grand Orient.
He was friendly with Midhat Pasha, a high official in the Sultan's
government who was secretly the leader of the Young Turks. Midhat

Pasha had been initiated as a Freemason while he was a student in England. After he returned to Turkey he was appointed Governor of the Danube region, and established a régime in which there was no religious persecution. In 1872 he was for a short time Grand Vizier, the head of the Turkish government.

Scalieris and Midhat Pasha were able to exercise their influence on Prince Murad, the nephew of the Sultan Abd-Ul Aziz and the heir to the throne. Murad listened with sympathy to their progressive liberal views, and at their suggestion became a Freemason in 1872, joining a Greek-speaking lodge in Constantinople under the authority of the French Grand Orient. In 1876, while the Bulgarian revolt against Turkish rule was taking place and Russia was preparing to go to war with Turkey in support of the Bulgarians, Midhat Pasha carried out a coup, deposed Abd-Ul Aziz, and proclaimed Prince Murad as the Sultan Murad V.

A liberal-minded Freemason was now Sultan of Turkey; but within a few months he was deposed after another coup which placed the tyrannical Abd-Ul Hamid II on the throne. During his thirty-three-year reign he acquired international notoriety both by his despotic government and by the sexual excesses of his private life. At first he maintained Midhat Pasha as Grand Vizier, but then arranged for him to be assassinated. He kept Murad imprisoned in the palace. Scalieris tried to arrange for Murad to escape, but the rescue attempt failed. Murad died in 1904, having been kept as a prisoner in the palace for 28 years.[30]

Abd-Ul Hamid continued to reign until 1909, when he was deposed and imprisoned after the revolution of the Young Turks. The leader of the Young Turks was Talaat Bey, who afterwards took the name of Mehmet Talaat Pasha. He was a Freemason and became the Grand Master of the Turkish Grand Orient. He was appointed Grand Vizier in 1917 when Turkey and her allies, Germany and Austria, were beginning to lose the First World War. As a supporter of the Turkish government he was held responsible by the Armenians for the massacres and virtual extermination of the native population in the Turkish province of Armenia. Many of the Young Turks were Freemasons; but neither their progressive views on the modernization of Turkey, nor the principles of Freemasonry, prevented them from supporting the hideous programme of genocide in Armenia.

When Turkey lost the war, Mehmet Talaat Pasha was forced to resign as Grand Vizier in October 1918. Next year he left Turkey and went to live in Berlin. In 1921 he was assassinated in Berlin by an Armenian student who had not forgotten the massacres.[31]

The leader who emerged in Turkey from the disaster of defeat was Mustafa Kemal, who was called Kemal Ataturk. He was a Freemason; he was initiated into an Italian lodge in Macedonia.[32] He took command of the Turkish army when the victorious Allies – Britain eagerly, France more cautiously – authorized the Greek army to invade Turkey to compel the Turks to accept the Allied peace terms. The Greeks drove the Turks back 250 miles to the River Sakaria; there Mustafa Kemal stopped them, then drove them back all the way to the Mediterranean and out of Turkey. It was a disastrous intervention for the Greeks, who have never forgiven Kemal and the Turks for their ethnic cleansing of the Greek population in Smyrna, who were all driven out.

Kemal went on to abolish the rule of the Sultan and the Caliphate, to turn Turkey into a non-religious republic, and to bring prosperity to the country, keeping it free from wars and international alliances. After ruling as a dictator for 16 years and drinking a great deal of whisky, he died in power in 1938.

Nothing so dramatic or exciting happened to disturb the peace of the English Freemasons. Their worst experience was that, when the Duke of Sussex died in 1843, there was no member of the royal family willing to take his place as Grand Master. Queen Victoria did not approve of Freemasonry, because she associated it with the immoral lifestyle of her uncles; and her husband, Prince Albert, also disliked it, perhaps because, with his German background, he associated Freemasonry with revolution.

The Freemasons had to wait until Queen Victoria's son, Edward Albert, Prince of Wales, had come to manhood. He was initiated as a Freemason on a visit to Stockholm. Ever since the reign of Gustavus III, the Kings of Sweden had been patrons and Grand Masters of the Swedish Freemasons; and the Prince of Wales was initiated by King Oscar II of Sweden in Stockholm on Sunday 20 December 1868, passing through all ten degrees of the Swedish Rite.[33]

When he returned to England he joined various English lodges, and was installed as Grand Master at a great ceremony in the Albert Hall in London in 1875. In 1882, wearing his masonic dress, he led a deputation of Freemasons to Queen Victoria to congratulate her on having escaped an assassination attempt. When he became King he resigned as Grand Master and was succeeded by the Duke of Connaught, and he himself took the title of Protector of the Craft.[34]

During the nineteenth century, English Grand Lodge had continued to extend its lodges throughout the world. Lodges were established in Singapore by the daring and romantic Sir Stamford Raffles, the founder of the city and a Freemason.[35] It developed in Canada under the patronage of John Lambton, Earl of Durham. Lambton's political career in England, in opposition to Lord Liverpool's Tory government and as a member of Lord Grey's Whig government at the time of the struggle for the Reform Bill after 1830, was so passionately anti-Tory that he was given the nickname 'Radical Jack'. But when Palmerston appointed him ambassador to Russia, he was so captivated by the personal charm of Nicholas I that he became a virtual apologist for the foreign policy of the most reactionary 'Iron Tsar'. As Governor-General of Canada he pursued a wise and conciliatory policy after the rebellion of 1837. He was a Freemason, and encouraged the growth of Freemasonry in Canada.[36] Afterwards the first Prime Minister of Canada, Sir John Alexander Macdonald, was also a Freemason.[37]

The British introduced Freemasonry into Australia in the first years of colonization. The navigator of the South Seas, Captain James Cook, was a Freemason, and military lodges were formed in New South Wales soon after the British first went there in 1788. A lodge for civilians was established in 1820. In the early years, when the colony was under military government and a place to which convicts were deported from England, the Freemasons occasionally suffered, as they have done everywhere under authoritarian governments. On one occasion an army unit broke into a meeting of a Freemasons' lodge in Sydney and arrested the masons, because the Governor had thought that their meetings were illegal; but they were released after they had managed to persuade him that he had been wrong about this. The first masonic lodge in New Zealand was established in the first years after colonization in 1842.[38]

The British established lodges in India at an early stage, but they were much slower in admitting Indians to the lodges. When Manockjee Cursetjee applied to join a lodge in Bombay in 1841, the Provincial Grand Master of West India said that he was eligible; but the British members of the lodge refused to admit him because he was an Indian. Cursetjee then went to England, for he had heard that the Duke of Sussex was in favour of admitting Indians; but the

Duke was abroad, and in his absence Cursetjee could not find any English lodge that would have him. He then went to Paris, became friendly with the Duke Decazes, and was initiated as a Freemason in a lodge there. When he returned to India he applied to be admitted to a lodge in Bombay but was again rejected. In the end the Provincial Grand Master of West India, who had always been sympathetic to his application, founded a new lodge in Bombay, and Cursetjee was admitted as the first and only member at a ceremony in the Town Hall in Bombay on 15 December 1843.[39]

Even when the British Freemasons in India were prepared to admit Muslims, for whom the Muslim God Allah was the Great Architect of the Universe, they still objected to Hindus, on the grounds that they worshipped many gods, not one Great Architect. It was again the Duke of Sussex who intervened to order the British lodges in India to admit Hindus. He ruled 'that the various "gods" of the Hindus were not separate gods but personifications of characteristics of one central deity'.[40] Before the end of the nineteenth century Rudyard Kipling, who was an especially ardent Freemason and was first initiated as a mason in India, was claiming that the religious and racial quarrels which troubled British India disappeared inside the masonic lodges.[41]

But when the French Grand Orient in 1877 decided to remove all references to God and the Great Architect from their ceremonies, to remove the Bible from their lodges, and to admit agnostics and atheists, this was too much for English Grand Lodge. The Grand Orient argued that to admit atheists was the final step in the policy of religious toleration which the Freemasons had always supported; but English Grand Lodge broke off relations with the Grand Orient, as did the American Freemasons.[42] The Grand Orient declared that by their action 'English Grand Lodge has struck a blow against the cosmopolitan and universal spirit of Freemasonry'.[43]

The position with the Italian Grand Orient was not so clear. After Garibaldi had liberated Sicily in 1860, he was invited to become Grand Master of the Italian Grand Orient. He served in this office from 1862 to 1868, and showed considerable interest in the complicated details of the various masonic organizations in Italy.[44] Garibaldi's attitude towards religion was ambiguous; he sometimes attended religious services, and made statements which showed a belief in God; but on more than one occasion he openly stated that he was an atheist.

King Victor Emmanuel always claimed to be a good Catholic, and that his disagreements with the Papacy were not due to the fact that he was anti-religious, though he was repeatedly denounced by the Pope and the Catholic propagandists as the Freemason King who wished to overthrow the Church. In 1870, when Napoleon III had withdrawn his troops from Rome to fight in the Franco-German War, and had been defeated and taken prisoner at Sedan, Victor Emmanuel seized his opportunity and invaded the Papal States, which had already been reduced to a small area around Rome. Nothing was now left to the Pope except the Vatican City.

CHAPTER 18

The New Assault on Freemasonry

I N the last years of the nineteenth century, two new factors entered into the relationship of the Freemasons with their critics. Anti-masonry became more hysterical. Barruel, Robison and Eckert had exaggerated the role of the Freemasons in instigating the French Revolution of 1789 and the revolutions of 1848, but there was some basis of truth in their suggestion that the principles of Freemasonry encouraged men to believe in Liberty, Equality and Fraternity, and to work to overthrow the despotism of the absolute monarchies and the Catholic Church. In the United States in the 1830s, the anti-masons, after the case of William Morgan, had some excuse for alleging that Freemasons might conspire to get rid of their unfaithful brothers. But in the twentieth century the attack on the Freemasons has been quite divorced from reality; and the anti-masons have accused them of wholly imaginary conspiracies, and have transferred anti-masonry from the real world into the realms of fantasy.

The other phenomenon which has affected the position of the Freemasons is the rise in many countries during the 1880s of popular anti-Semitism. The action of the Catholic Church and the governments in many countries against the Jews in the eighteenth and early nineteenth centuries was taken on religious, not racial, grounds; Jews could always escape persecution by converting to Christianity. The anti-Semitism which developed after 1880 was racist.

Religious prejudice played a part in twentieth-century anti-Semitism. The anti-Semites justified their actions by saying that the Jews had killed Christ. Anti-Semitism was much stronger in Catholic than in Protestant countries; in Germany, where it played an important and sinister part, it was stronger in the Catholic south than in the Protestant north. It was strongest of all in the countries of the

Orthodox Church. But it was directed against all Jews, whatever religion they professed; and it was accompanied in many countries by popular violence against Jews which had not been seen since the pogroms at the time of the Crusades in the eleventh and twelfth centuries and during the Black Death in 1348–50.

The Freemasons were affected by the anti-Semitism of the twentieth century. To some extent it took the heat off them, as the Jews, not the Freemasons, became the chief target for reactionary Right-wing attacks. Masonry remained the great enemy of the reactionaries only in countries like Spain and the Latin American states where there were very few Jews, and where Jews did not play an important part in politics. But anti-Semitic propaganda brought in the Freemasons, who were accused of being accomplices and pawns of the Jews in the Jewish campaign against civilization; and the Freemasons suffered the consequences of this, though to a lesser extent than the Jews.

While the British Freemasons rigidly adhered to their rule that Freemasonry must not become involved in politics, the French Freemasons in the Grand Orient not only took part in political activity but went so far as to become closely involved with one political party, the Republican Party, which later became the Radical Socialist Party. This party was not, as its name might imply in other countries, a party of Socialist extremists, but a moderate party of the Centre-Left corresponding most closely to the Liberal Party in Britain.

Before the general election in France in 1877 the Right-wing parties and press launched a campaign against the Freemasons, whom they accused of being revolutionaries and Communards; in some parts of France, Right-wing prefects prevented masonic lodges from meeting.[1] A victory for the Republican Party in the general election became essential for the Freemasons if they were to survive as a lawful organization. The Liberal leader and prominent Freemason Emmanuel Arago denounced the Conservative and Right-wing parties as 'the irreconcilable and dangerous enemy of the masons, the enemy of knowledge, of freedom of conscience, of the light, and of the true rights of man'.[2] The Republican victory in the general election saved Freemasonry in France.

The hysterical element was introduced into anti-masonry by Gabriel Jogand-Pagès, who wrote his books and articles under the pseudonym Leo Taxil.[3] He was a French Freemason, a member of the Grand Orient. He began his polemical career by writing books which were published by the Anti-Clerical League. His first pamphlet in 1879, *Down with the Clergy*, led to his prosecution for libel; but he was acquitted, and in 1881 published a scandalous book *The Secret Love Life of Pius IX*, who had died in 1878. The Grand Orient thought that Taxil's libellous attacks on the Pope were discrediting Freemasonry, and expelled him from the Grand Orient. Pius IX's successor, Leo XIII, opposed Freemasonry as strongly as Pius had done. In 1884 Leo issued a new Bull in which he declared that the Freemasons 'follow the Evil One' and aim at 'overthrowing all the religious and social orders introduced by Christianity'.[4] He followed this with another denunciation of Freemasonry in 1891.

In 1885, after six years' writing activity for the Anti-Clerical League, Taxil announced that he had repented and had become a good Catholic. He proceeded to write a series of books and pamphlets attacking Freemasonry and revealing the nefarious activities of the Grand Orient. Taxil referred to the part played by women in Freemasonry. A feminist movement in France in the 1880s had asked for women to be admitted as Freemasons. The Grand Orient refused this request, but did not object when women's lodges and mixed lodges of both sexes were formed.[5] These women's and mixed lodges did not develop to any great extent. Taxil wrote about the sexual orgies that took place in masonic lodges, and that the Freemasons provided women for the gratification of the lusts of their members.

Taxil attacked these women's lodges in his books *Are there Women in Freemasonry?* and *The Evidence of Women's Lodges*. He also published *The Three-Pointed Brothers*, a reference to the masonic emblem of the three points; *Masonic France: New Revelations*; and *The Masonic Murders*, in which he blamed the Freemasons for the murders of the Princess of Lamballe and the other victims during the French Revolution; of Tsar Paul I of Russia; of Charles X's son, the Duke of Berry, in 1820; of several policemen; and, of course, of William Morgan, who had been 'tortured in a cave by the monsters of the Rochester lodge'.[6] He also alleged that it was the Freemasons who had arranged for their former Grand Master, Philippe Egalité, to be guillotined; and he published a picture of the Grand Council of the Grand Orient sentencing Philippe Egalité to death. Taxil's books were translated into many languages.

Taxil was acclaimed by the Catholic Church. In 1887 he was granted a private audience by Pope Leo XIII, who praised his work.

The Bishop of Grenoble, Monsignor Armand Joseph Fava, wrote to Taxil on 3 August 1891 to congratulate him on his services to the Church. The Bishop denounced the Freemasons for teaching 'that the Holy Virgin does not deserve this name, that Jesus Christ is not the Son of God made Man . . . Satan is there; he presides at their sacrilegious orgies, enjoying dragging in the mud the living image of God'.[7]

Taxil wrote about the wicked plans of Albert Pike in the United States to subvert Christianity, and claimed that Pike had sent his agents to France for this purpose. Taxil and his German colleague Hacks, who called himself Dr Bataille, revealed this in their book *The Devil in the Nineteenth Century*, which was serialized in their newspaper in 240 parts in the course of one year. More sensational revelations followed in July 1895 when Taxil published *Memoirs of an Ex-Pallandist by Miss Diana Vaughan*, in 24 instalments. She revealed that Pike had founded a secret organization, the Palladium, and that she was one of its secret agents, but had now repented. She wrote that the Freemasons in the Palladium engaged in satanic rituals, and that when Pike died, his successor as the head of the Palladium was Adriano Lemmi, the Grand Master of the Italian Grand Orient in Rome.

Taxil's success culminated in a great anti-masonic congress which was held in Trent in the Austrian Empire in September 1896. The 700 delegates who attended the congress included thirty-six bishops.[8]

The congress at Trent led to several attacks on Freemasons throughout the Austrian Empire; but some of the delegates at Trent were beginning to be a little sceptical about Diana Vaughan, and asked if Taxil could arrange for her to appear in person at some anti-masonic gathering. Taxil said that this was impossible, for her life would be in danger from the Freemasons if she appeared in public, and she must remain in hiding. But the pressure on Taxil to produce Diana Vaughan increased, and he eventually promised that she would appear at a meeting at the Geographical Society in Paris on 19 April 1897.

Taxil appeared at the Geographical Society on 19 April, and told the truth to the crowded audience. He said that Diana Vaughan was the name of his secretary, and that she had never had anything to do with Freemasonry; he had invented the whole story. 'The Palladium exists no more. I created it and I have destroyed it. You have nothing more to fear from its sinister influence'. He then quickly left the hall by a rear door before the astounded audience could protest.[9]

In the 1880s there were pogroms of Jews in Russia. In 1905 a Russian, Sergei Nilus, published a book in Russia, *The Protocols of the Elders of Zion*. He claimed that it was a document drawn up by the governing body of the international Jews, and in the preface he explained how he had got hold of the manuscript; but in fact he had written it himself. The Protocols purported to be a plan by the Jewish leaders to conquer the Gentiles and rule the world; and they intended to accomplish this by making use of Gentile dupes. 'From all ends of the world, the words "Liberty, Equality, Fraternity" brought whole legions into our ranks'; and 'there are blind agents carrying our flag with delight' today. 'Masonry acts as a blind mask' for the achievement of the plan for Jewish world domination.[10]

After the Russian Revolution of 1917 the Protocols were translated and published in many countries of the world. The title of the English edition, published in 1920, was *The Jewish Peril*. The London Conservative newspaper, the *Morning Post*, published a long review of the book under the heading 'The Jewish Peril. Have the Bolsheviks a Masonic Origin? Plan of World Conquest'.[11]

In the Austrian Empire and Bohemia, anti-masonry flared up at the beginning of the twentieth century. But a great Czech Liberal, Tomáš Garrigue Masaryk, condemned the Catholic Church for believing the lies of Taxil and for its hysterical denunciations of the Freemasons. In an article in his monthly journal, *Naše Doba* (Our Times), in 1906 he traced the development of Freemasonry after the formation of English Grand Lodge in 1717, but thought that although it represented a movement in favour of religious toleration, it no longer had great importance in the modern world. The Catholic attitude towards the Freemasons showed that 'Freemasonry is the guilty conscience of the Catholic Church'.[12]

When Masaryk became President of the new state of Czechoslovakia after the First World War, Freemasonry flourished there. He never became a Freemason himself, but his chief collaborator, Edvard Beneš, who succeeded him as President, and his son, Jan Masaryk, both joined masonic lodges in Prague.[13]

In France in 1894 Captain Alfred Dreyfus, a Jew serving in the French army, was falsely accused of having betrayed military secrets to the German government. He had been framed by anti-Semitic army officers. He was convicted and sentenced to imprisonment in terrible conditions on Devil's Island in Cayenne, before he was at last released and vindicated after a controversy which for twelve years divided French society into Dreyfusards and anti-Dreyfusards. The Right wing insisted that Dreyfus was guilty, even when they knew he was not, in order to uphold the honour of the army; the Dreyfusards demanded his release and vindication as part of their struggle against the injustice of the Right wing, the Church and the army leadership. Many of the Dreyfusards were Freemasons, but the most eminent of them were not. Neither Emile Zola nor Georges Clemenceau were Freemasons; nor were those other leading Left-wing anticlerical authors, Victor Hugo, Ernest Renan and Anatole France. But the French Right wing continued to denounce Free-masonry as a revolutionary Left-wing conspiracy. At the time of the Dreyfus affair 80,000 Right-wing sympathizers signed a petition demanding that the Freemasons be suppressed.[14]

The French Freemasons were so closely associated with the Radical Party that some of them tended to look askance at Socialists who wished to become Freemasons. After the French Socialist Party, the SFIO, was formed in 1905, there were applications from Socialists who wished to join. Despite the objections of these old Radical Party hacks, the Grand Orient agreed to admit Socialists, and lowered the admission fees and the subscription which had previously been too high for members of the working class who would have liked to join. At the beginning of the twentieth century several prominent Socialists – Jean Longuet, Jean Monnet, Roger Salengro, and Vincent Auriol – were Freemasons; but the two greatest French Socialists of the twentieth century, Jean Jaurès and Léon Blum, were not.[15]

Many schoolteachers were Freemasons, and often came into con-flict with the local Catholic priest. In 1910 the Catholics were com-plaining that at least 10,000 schoolteachers were Freemasons.[16] The army and the Church continued to regard the Freemasons as a sub-versive organization; but Marshal Joseph Joffre, the commander-in-chief of the French army in the early years of the First World War, was a Freemason.[17]

Two prominent members of the French Communist Party, Marcel Cachin and André Marty, were Freemasons. Marty was a sailor in the French navy and was sent to the Black Sea in 1919 to help the Russian counter-revolutionary armies overthrow the Bolshevik régime. He tried to organize a mutiny in the navy, and was sentenced to imprisonment. His supporters among the French Freemasons tried to persuade their brothers to launch a campaign to grant him an amnesty. When a motion in favour of an amnesty was defeated in the Chamber of Deputies, Marty's supporters demanded that the Grand Orient take disciplinary action against those Freemason deputies who had voted in the Chamber against the amnesty; but again, as always, political loyalties were stronger than masonic loyalty. In the end the Grand Orient supported a campaign in favour of a general amnesty, and on all occasions urged a conciliatory and merciful policy. They opposed the dismissal and victimization of those who had taken part in the general strike of 1920.[18]

The attempt to enlist masonic solidarity in favour of an amnesty for Marty was ironical, because the Fourth Congress of the Communist International in 1922 condemned Freemasonry and directed all Communists to resign from their lodges. In Russia Freemasonry had been prohibited throughout the nineteenth century, as every Tsar, including the liberal Alexander II, had maintained the ban on the Freemasons that had been imposed by Alexander I and Nicholas I. But Russian Liberals and Socialists joined illegal masonic lodges.

At the outbreak of the First World War in August 1914 the moderate Russian Socialists (the Mensheviks) supported the war, although it had been an accepted principle of the Socialist International, ever since the days of Marx and Engels, that the Russian and the international Socialist movement would always oppose any war in which Tsarist Russia, the 'gendarme of Europe', was involved. Only Lenin's Bolshevik group in Russia opposed the 'imperialist war'. It is said that the Russian Mensheviks supported the war because of the influence of the Russian Freemasons, who were persuaded by their masonic brothers in the French Radical and Socialist parties to come to the aid of France, Russia's ally. But there was no need for the Freemasons to arouse the national patriotism, or the 'social chauvinism' as Lenin called it, of the Socialist parties and the working class in every belligerent country in 1914.

Several of the leaders who came to power in Russia after the revolution of March 1917, including the most important member of the government, Alexander Kerensky, are said to have been Freemasons; but there is no reliable evidence of this. It is said that two French Freemasons, Cachin and the Socialist Minister of Agriculture, Albert Thomas, were sent to St Petersburg in the summer of 1917 and begged Kerensky, on their knees, not to abandon his French masonic brothers and to launch the June offensive which failed so disastrously and was probably the chief cause of Lenin's triumph; but this depends on the story told by Kerensky's bodyguard, an anti-masonic Russian colonel; and there was plenty of non-masonic allied pressure on Kerensky to launch the offensive.[19] Kerensky was overthrown by the Bolshevik revolution of November 1917. Neither Vladimir Ilyich Ulyanov, who took the name of Lenin; Lev Davidovich Bronstein (Trotsky); Josef Visarionovich Djugashvili (Stalin), or any of the Bolshevik leaders, were Freemasons.

The resolution of the Communist International in 1922 stated that Freemasonry was a petty bourgeois movement which at various times in the past had gained the support of the Radical and dissatisfied section of the bourgeoisie and had fulfilled a revolutionary role, but was now opposed to the revolutionary action of the proletariat and must be repudiated by Communists.[20] But there was no serious persecution of Freemasons in the Communist Soviet Union. The Russian Freemason and political dissident, Dr Lovin, who spent twenty years as a prisoner in Soviet labour camps between 1929 and 1954, has stated that during all his time in the camps he did not meet another Freemason, and was never questioned by the Soviet secret police – which was called successively the OGPU, the NKVD, and the KGB – about his masonic activities.[21]

In France the Freemasons continued their association with the Radical Party. The electoral victory of the Cartel des Gauches (the Left Coalition) in 1924 led to the establishment of a Radical government under Edouard Herriot. Many members of the Cabinet were Freemasons, though Herriot himself was not.[22]

The French Right wing renewed their attack on the Freemasons after the Stavisky scandal. Serge Alexandre Stavisky, the son of a Jewish dentist, had led an adventurous life and had several times been under observation by the police, but had kept out of serious trouble while he amassed a fortune of nearly 800 million francs by a series of financial frauds. When the frauds were exposed in January 1934, the Prime Minister was the Radical Camille Chautemps. He was a Freemason, and the Right-wing parties alleged that the masons had used their influence in high places to hush up the scandal and protect Stavisky. Before Stavisky could be arrested, he committed suicide.

The government appointed a councillor of the Court of Appeal,

Albert Prince, to investigate the Stavisky case; but a few days later Prince was found dead on a railway line where he had apparently fallen and had been decapitated by a passing train. Some people thought he had committed suicide because of the strain under which his inquiries had placed him; but the Right wing said that he was already dead when his body was placed on the line, and that he had been murdered by the Freemasons to prevent him revealing how they had been involved in Stavisky's frauds. Prince's death remains a mystery which has not been satisfactorily explained by some secret documents which were published thirty years later.[23]

In Germany General Erich von Ludendorff introduced a new element of insanity into the debate about Freemasonry. He had been Chief of Staff to Field Marshal Paul von Hindenburg during the First World War, and was responsible for the German victory over the Russians at Tannenberg in East Prussia in August 1914. He later directed operations on the Western Front. After the war he joined Adolf Hitler in leading an unsuccessful Right-wing revolt in Munich in 1923. In 1927 he published a book, *The Destruction of Freemasonry through the Disclosure of its Secrets*.

He revealed that 'the secret of Freemasonry everywhere is – the Jew'. The Freemasons were agents of the Jews; when they talked about their 'brothers in the society' they meant the Jews. It was irrelevant whether the Jew had been converted to Christianity and baptized as a Christian, for the Jew does not change his blood by being baptized any more than a Negro changes the colour of his skin when he converts to Christianity: 'a baptized Jew remains a Jew'. The Jews were in favour of Liberty and Brotherhood because if they could persuade the Gentiles to believe in these ideals, then the Gentiles would grant liberty to the Jews first to enter, and then to dominate, political and social life in every country of the world; and people who believed in brotherhood would welcome Jews. The masonic rituals all had a Jewish origin; and Freemasons wore aprons to conceal the fact that, being Jews, they had been circumcized.[24]

Ludendorff's views were developed in 1931 by one of Hitler's Nazi supporters who wrote under the pseudonym of Dr Custos, in his book *The Freemason, the World Vampire*. Ludendorff and Custos distorted the facts in order to uphold their preposterous theories. They wrote that the sinister hand of the British Freemasons and the Jews had been at work in the Balkans. The revolution of the Young

Turks was planned in 1900 in the masonic lodges in Salonika, where there were 70,000 Jews out of a total population of 110,000. The First World War had been planned by the Freemasons in order to destroy Germany. The French and English Freemasons paid £5 million to the Serbs to murder the Archduke Franz Ferdinand in Sarajevo in 1914, and the murder took place on 28 June, which was one of the Freemasons' feast days. This was of course an error; the Freemasons' summer festival of St John is on St John the Baptist's Day, 24 June.

It was the Freemasons who had brought the United States into the war against Germany, for President Woodrow Wilson and General John J. Pershing, the commander-in-chief of the United States expeditionary force to Europe in 1918, were Freemasons; and the movement for the destruction of the Austrian Empire had been led by the Freemason T. G. Masaryk. Custos wrote that when the Freemasons had succeeded in defeating Germany, they imposed the Treaty of Versailles on 28 June 1919 – the Freemasons' feast day. There were more errors here, for apart from repeating the mistake that 28 June, not 24 June, was the masonic feast day, neither President Wilson nor Masaryk were Freemasons, though General Pershing was.

As for Bolshevism, Custos wrote that Lenin and Trotsky, the leaders of the Bolshevik revolution in Russia, were Jewish Freemasons.[25] In fact, Lenin was not a Jew, though Trotsky was, and neither was a Freemason. The Nazi line was developed in another publication, *Freemasonry, the Road to Jewish World Domination*.

The Left and the Centre Left in France, confronted with the Fascist threat from the growing anti-Semitic and anti-masonic movement, formed in 1935 the People's Front of the Communists, the Socialists and the Radicals. The Freemasons were suspicious of the Communists, who had denounced Freemasonry at the Fourth Congress of the Communist International in 1922; and the strength of the Freemasons in the Radical Party meant that it would be difficult to persuade the Radicals to support the People's Front unless the Freemasons could be won over. So the Communist leader, Maurice Thorez, went to the headquarters of the Grand Orient and addressed a meeting of the leading Freemasons.[26] He succeeded in persuading them to support the People's Front, which won the general election of May 1936 and formed a government under Léon Blum. The Communists did not enter Blum's government but supported it in the Chamber of Deputies.

The Spanish Civil War led to new attacks on Freemasonry. General Francisco Franco and his supporters followed the tradition of the Right wing in Spain in denouncing *masoneria* as the sinister force behind revolutionary movements, and the French Right wing suggested that the French Freemasons were helping their Spanish brothers to make their revolution in Spain. The French Grand Orient confined themselves during the Spanish Civil War to campaigning for charitable aid for the Spanish refugee children who came to France, and to organizing charitable help for the suffering people of Spain.[27]

The People's Front in France broke up when Hitler and Stalin signed their pact in August 1939. The French Communist Party was suppressed, many Communists were imprisoned, and Communists were ejected from local government councils. The Communist Party opposed the war against Germany, which they called an imperialist war. The Freemasons gave their full support to the war.

The attitude of the Socialist president of the Council of the Grand Orient, Arthur Groussier, during the Second World War and the years of German occupation was condemned by many Freemasons as a servile and sycophantic effort to ingratiate the Grand Orient with each successive government that came to power. When the Germans invaded France in May 1940, Groussier wrote to the Prime Minister, Paul Reynaud, assuring him of the full support of the Grand Orient at this time 'when France summons all her strength to triumph over the invader', and mentioning that Gambetta and 'the victor of the Marne' (Joffre) had been Freemasons.[28] But a month later the French defeat brought to power the aged Marshal Philippe Pétain and his government of Vichy. Pétain hated Freemasons even more than most French generals did. In this he was fully supported by General Maxime Weygand. Like Pétain, Weygand had won a reputation as a great military leader in the First World War.

Weygand had been appointed commander-in-chief by Reynaud during the German invasion in May 1940; but after the armistice with Germany he gave his full support to Pétain and the Vichy régime. On 23 June 1940, a few days after Pétain became head of state in France and signed the armistice with the Germans, Weygand drafted a statement, which Pétain approved, declaring that 'the old order of things, that is to say, the political régime of masonic, capitalist and internationalist abandonment of principles, has led us to where we are. France wants no more of this'.[29]

On 13 August 1940 Pétain issued a decree suppressing secret societies. It did not expressly mention the Freemasons, but it was directed chiefly against them. Six days earlier Groussier, knowing that Pétain was intending to issue the decree, had written him a letter in the most respectful terms. He assured the Marshal that the Grand Orient was prepared to make any sacrifice at this time of national revival, but hoped that it would not be required to sacrifice its very existence. He referred to the fact that Joffre had been a Freemason.

By now the alliance between Britain and France had been severed. The British navy had bombarded the French fleet at Oran in North Africa to prevent it from being surrendered to the Germans, and relations between the government of Vichy and Churchill's government in Britain were very bad. Groussier therefore emphasized, in his letter to Pétain, that the Grand Orient had had no relations with English Grand Lodge since 1877. He ended the letter by assuring Pétain that the Freemasons would work loyally for the regeneration of France under Pétain's leadership. Pétain did not reply to Groussier's letter.[30]

Under the decree of 13 August 1940, a Service for Secret Societies was established with Bernard Fay as chairman. He was an intellectual who had written a number of books about Freemasonry, including his erudite *Freemasonry and the Intellectual Revolution of the Eighteenth Century*. His first action was to require all civil servants to sign a declaration that they were not, and had never been, a member of a secret society, which included the Freemasons, or that, if they had been Freemasons, they had decisively broken with the society. Fay then proceeded to publish a list of the names of all Freemasons. This labelled them and signalled them out for victimization by the authorities.[31]

In his work against the Freemasons, Fay cooperated with the German occupation authorities. Freemasonry had been banned in Nazi Germany in 1934, when Wilhelm Frick, the Minister of the Interior, declared that it was 'inappropriate that a secret society with obscure aims should continue to exist in the Third Reich'.[32] But Fay found that the German Nazis were less eager than he was to take action against the Freemasons; they were much more interested in rounding up Jews and sending them to the extermination camps in Poland.

Groussier was doing his best to remain on good terms with the German occupation authorities. He found that Otto Abetz, the German ambassador in Paris, was not unsympathetic; some people said that Abetz had himself been a Freemason in Germany before the Freemasons were suppressed there.[33]

There was a difference in emphasis in the attitude of the men of Vichy towards the Freemasons. Pétain himself was strongly against them. He was a devout Catholic, and had never forgiven them for their attacks on the Church at the end of the nineteenth century when Pétain was young. In January 1943 he wrote to Fay congratulating him on his work in the Service for Secret Societies, and told him that 'Freemasonry is chiefly responsible for our misfortunes; it is Freemasonry which lied to the French and taught them the habit of telling lies'. On 25 May 1943 Pétain told the Rector of the Catholic Institute of Paris that Freemasonry still threatened France because, though the Freemasons had been driven underground, 'Freemasonry still reigns'. Pétain thought that the Freemasons were worse than the Jews. 'A Jew cannot help his origin' he said to Fay, 'but a Freemason has chosen to become one.'[34]

But the Vichy Prime Minister, Pierre Laval, who happily handed over foreign Jews in France, including the children, to the Germans to be deported and murdered in the extermination camps in Poland, had nothing against the Freemasons. He disapproved of the campaign against them, and did what he could to protect them.[35]

Many Freemasons were members of the resistance movement, and could not forgive Groussier for his submissive attitude towards the Germans. After the war Groussier tried to justify his action. He said that he wished to prevent the Germans from treating the Freemasons as they treated the Jews, and claimed that he had succeeded, because the Freemasons were not murdered in the gas chambers; any Freemason who was executed by the Germans was executed for having been active in the resistance movement, not because he was a Freemason.[36] This argument did not impress the Freemasons who had taken part in the resistance.

Many Freemasons played an active part in the resistance. Of the 50,000 Freemasons in France in 1939, 6,000 were arrested and interrogated by the Germans on suspicion of being members of the resistance; 989 were deported to concentration camps in Germany or Poland; and 545 were executed or died in German concentration camps.[37] These included the resistance hero, Jean Moulin, who died under torture at the hands of the Gestapo in Lyons in 1943, and the German Jew, Eduard Ignaze Engel, who was known by his pseudonym Plantagenet. After playing an active part against the Nazis as a journalist in Paris, and being Master of the Goethe Lodge, the only German-speaking lodge in France, he joined the French resistance movement in 1940. He was arrested by the Germans in October 1943 and executed in Buchenwald concentration camp in Germany on Christmas Day 1943.[38]

Several Freemasons took part in the liberation of Paris in August 1944.[39] After the victory, the General Council of the Grand Orient wrote to General de Gaulle as they had written to Pétain in August 1940. They expressed their 'profound admiration' for de Gaulle's actions 'which have permitted France to recover her ideal of liberty', and praised him for abolishing the illegal anti-masonic laws of Vichy. De Gaulle disliked Freemasons as much as other French generals did; like Pétain in 1940, he did not reply to the Grand Orient's letter.[40]

The part played in the resistance movement by both Freemasons and Catholics raised the possibility of at last putting an end to the 200 years of conflict between the Continental Freemasons and the Catholic Church. A secret meeting was arranged in a street in Toulouse between the Freemason resistance leader Marc Rucart and Henri Frenay, of the Catholic resistance movement. 'I have just come out of prison', said Rucart. 'I spent nearly a year in Fresnes. Have you been in prison yet?' 'Not yet', replied Frenay, 'I've been lucky'.[41] It was the first step in a reconciliation between the Freemasons and the Catholic Church. It was not easy for these fellow-members of the resistance movement to persuade their leaders to forget the old antagonisms between Freemasonry and the Papacy; but despite difficulties and setbacks, relations have greatly improved in view of the more tolerant Catholic attitude which followed the Second Vatican Council in 1962–5.[42]

CHAPTER 19

Freemasonry in the World

In Italy, when Mussolini came to power in 1922, he condemned the Freemasons, despite the part they had played in the Risorgimento in the nineteenth century. Like all other dictators, he could not tolerate the existence of a secret society which might conceivably become a revolutionary organization. He ordered all Fascists who were Freemasons to resign from their masonic lodges. Some of them only pretended to do so, and continued secretly to be Freemasons. King Victor Emmanuel III, like his grandfather Victor Emmanuel II, was a Freemason.

In July 1943 a majority of the members of the Fascist Grand Council, realizing that Mussolini was losing the war, overthrew him, and the King ordered his arrest. Hitler sent German paratroopers to rescue him, and he continued for another eighteen months as the head of a Fascist government in the north, in the territory under German occupation. Today some Italian Fascist sympathizers blame the Freemasons for having organized the coup which deposed Mussolini in July 1943. As usual, the role of the Freemasons had been exaggerated. Count Dino Grandi, who played the leading part in organizing the revolt against Mussolini on the Fascist Grand Council, was not a Freemason,[1] though the King was certainly a member of the society. It was not Freemasonry, but the fact that Mussolini was losing the war, that brought about his downfall.

In Norway the first Freemasons' lodge was founded in 1745.[2] As long as Norway was part of Sweden, Freemasonry flourished there under the patronage of their Grand Master, the King of Sweden; and when Norway peacefully separated from Sweden in 1905 and became an independent kingdom, the Freemasons continued to prosper. But in 1940 the Germans invaded Norway and entrusted the government of the country to Major Vidkun Quisling, who has given his name to a new word in the English language, meaning 'traitor'.

Quisling had been an intelligence officer in Russia during the First World War, and later was Minister of Defence in the Norwegian government. He was filled with a deep hatred of Bolsheviks, Jews and Freemasons. He was convinced that the Jews and Freemasons were behind the Bolsheviks, and that only Adolf Hitler could lead the crusade to destroy Jewish masonic Bolshevism.

As ruler of Norway, he requisitioned the splendid Masonic Temple in Oslo and turned it into offices for his staff, making structural alterations which ruined the building architecturally. He sent the extensive library of the Temple to Germany; but there were Freemasons working in the Norwegian resistance movement, and they intercepted the books on their way to Germany and saved them.

After the war Quisling was put on trial for treason by the Norwegian government. Ironically, the trial was held in a building which had been used before the war as a masonic lodge. He was convicted, sentenced to death and shot.[3]

After the Second World War, when South Africa was ruled by the Nationalist apartheid government, the Freemasons came under suspicion. Having suppressed the Communist Party and the African National Congress, and arrested Nelson Mandela and his colleagues, the government, on 28 July 1964, appointed Mr Justice D. H. Botha as the sole member of a commission of inquiry into secret organizations. The South African Freemasons had never taken part in the struggle against apartheid; they were as respectable and law-abiding as the British Freemasons. But they were accused by certain members of the Dutch Reformed Church of aiming at establishing 'a world government and a world religion' which would replace the authority of the government of an independent South Africa. Mr Justice Botha reported that there was no evidence 'that Freemasonry in South Africa actively interests itself in the establishment of a world state with a world government, or that through its conduct it in any way weakens the will of the South African nation to fight for its survival'.[4]

The Freemasons came under a more serious attack in Switzerland. Colonel Emile Sonderegger had a long record of fighting against extremist and revolutionary activity. He had commanded the troops who had broken the general strike in 1918, and had become the leader of an anti-masonic movement in Switzerland. A great demonstration against the Freemasons was held in Geneva on 9 November 1932, which led to violence in which a number of demonstrators were wounded; but the movement grew stronger a few months later after Hitler had come to power in Germany. On 22 April 1933 Sonderegger spoke at a great anti-masonic rally in Zurich, and denounced Freemasonry as an anti-patriotic organization controlled by Bolsheviks and Jews. In 1933 and 1934 anti-masonic demonstrations, and counter-demonstrations by anti-Fascist supporters, were held in Berne.

Sonderegger won the support of the Catholic peasants in some of the country districts, and he obtained the necessary number of signatures to demand a referendum on a proposal to amend the federal constitution by banning Freemasonry. He was opposed, not only by the Freemasons and their sympathizers, but also by all Liberals who objected to a proposal which would interfere with the right of free speech and freedom of assembly of the members of a law-abiding society. In the referendum which was held on Sunday 28 November 1937 the proposal to ban Freemasonry was defeated by 515,000 votes against 235,000. After this defeat, Sonderegger's anti-masonic movement rapidly collapsed.[5]

The Freemasons encountered difficulties in Japan. The first masonic lodge established there was a British military lodge in Yokohama in 1864. Other lodges were formed by British and American residents in Japan; but the Japanese government forbade any Japanese to become a Freemason. The government thought that Freemasonry was a foreign movement which would introduce foreign influence into Japan and conflict with Japanese social and religious traditions. But a few Japanese intellectuals abroad became Freemasons in London and other foreign cities.

To add to the difficulties of Japanese Freemasons, a French Roman Catholic priest, Father F. Ligneul, who lived in Japan as the head of a French Catholic mission from 1880 to 1912, began an anti-masonic agitation. In 1900 he published a book, *Mimitsu Kessha* (The Secret Society). It warned that Freemasonry was a movement which believed in absolute freedom and equality, and would therefore destroy any social system based on hierarchical authority; Freemasons, he argued, carried their belief in freedom and equality to the point of working to overthrow all established governments.

The Japanese diplomat, Count Tadasu Hayashi, was stationed at the Japanese embassy in London from 1900 to 1906. He played a part in the negotiations which led to the alliance between Britain and Japan in 1902. In 1903 he was initiated as a Freemason in a lodge in London; and he negotiated a renewal of the British-Japanese treaty in 1905. In 1906 he returned to Japan and was appointed Foreign Minister; but his political opponents in Japan discovered that he had become a Freemason in London, and Hayashi was expelled from the Japanese Privy Council on the grounds that he was a Freemason. He therefore resigned from his London Lodge, which made it possible for him to continue his political career in Japan.

The opposition to Freemasonry in Japan was increased by the Japanese hatred of Jews. There were only 2,000 Jews in Japan, but they were regarded with great suspicion after Japan had intervened against the Bolsheviks in the Russian Civil War of 1918–20. The Jews were denounced as Bolshevik agents. A Japanese translation of *The Protocols of the Elders of Zion* was published in 1919, and Jews and Freemasons were regarded as dangerous Communist revolutionaries. The denunciation of Jews and Freemasons redoubled when the League of Nations condemned the Japanese attack on Manchuria in 1931. An official Japanese government spokesman declared that 'the anti-Japanese activities in England are all instigated by Jewish Freemasons'. The naval cadets were informed that 'a gang of Masonic Jews have incessantly been masterminding international intrigues against Japan behind the scenes in Britain, the United States, China and Russia'. The *Japanese Chronicle* in April 1938 denounced 'the secret league of Freemasons . . . engaged in the struggle behind the World Revolution'.[6]

On 7 December 1941 Japanese aeroplanes attacked the United States fleet at Pearl Harbor, and Japan entered the Second World War. The secret police proceeded to arrest Freemasons, who were persecuted more fiercely than they were in Nazi-occupied countries in Europe. Under the Nazis, a Freemason, though excluded from office and employment, was not normally arrested unless he happened also to be a Jew or a member of the resistance; in Japan, Freemasons were arrested merely for the crime of being Freemasons, and were interrogated, often under torture. When they fainted from lack of sleep, or from the effect of torture, their interrogators revived them by throwing buckets of cold water over them, and began torturing them again.

Organizations which were thought to be associated with Freemasonry, or under foreign influence, like the Rotary Club and the Boy Scouts, were also suppressed; they were accused of being agents of the Freemasons. In the House of Peers, the nobleman Tokutaro Higuchi spoke against the suppression of the Rotary Club, which he claimed was a harmless and loyal organization. He was promptly arrested and charged with treason.

The persecution of Freemasons was extended into all the countries which were conquered by Japan – Korea, Manchuria, China, Hongkong, the Philippines and Singapore.

After the defeat and surrender of Japan in 1945, Freemasonry was able to exist there. The American commander-in-chief and Governor of Japan, General Douglas MacArthur, was a Freemason, and he gave every assistance to the Japanese Freemasons. For the first time native Japanese were allowed to become Freemasons. Freemasonry played its part in the democratic Western-looking country that Japan has become since the Second World War.[7]

In Spain, Portugal and Latin America, the Freemasons in the twentieth century have been hated, feared and persecuted by the Catholic Church and the Right-wing parties. In Spain, one of many tentative Anarchist risings took place in Barcelona in 1909 against the government of King Alfonso XIII. The government declared martial law and suppressed the rising. The military authorities arrested Francisco Ferrer, an intellectual who was a theoretical Anarchist, had written books criticizing the Catholic Church, and had founded independent schools in which there was no religious teaching. He was a Freemason. He was accused of having instigated the revolt in Barcelona, was tried by court martial, sentenced to death and shot. The Ferrer case shocked Liberal opinion all over Europe.[8]

The Freemasons were banned under the Right-wing dictatorship of General Primo de Rivera in the 1920s, and tolerated after the revolution of 1931, the abdication of King Alfonso and the fall of the monarchy. But the Freemasons were about to encounter their most savage persecutor. When General Francisco Franco made his attempted coup in July 1936 and began the Civil War, he declared that he was fighting to liberate Spain from Communism and Freemasonry. In September 1936 he issued a decree banning Freemasons in the territory which his armies occupied. The victories of his soldiers and the capture of towns from the Republican government was usually followed by massacres of Republican prisoners, and any of the prisoners who were identified as Freemasons were invariably shot.

In February 1939, after he had captured Barcelona and was on the verge of final victory, Franco issued his Law of Political Responsibilities, containing a long list of organizations and individuals who were to be punished for their responsibility for the political woes of Spain. The Freemasons were expressly named in the decree, and all masonic lodges were banned. Apparently Franco at one time considered issuing an order that all Freemasons were to be executed, but he was persuaded that this would contravene the surrender terms which he had granted to the defeated Republicans.

Having won the civil war and established himself as dictator of all Spain, and deftly keeping out of the Second World War, Franco issued another draconian decree against the Freemasons in March 1940. It set up a Tribunal for the Suppression of Masonry, made it a criminal offence to be, or ever to have been, a Freemason, and decreed that the relatives of Freemasons could be punished for having permitted a member of their family to join a masonic lodge. Several thousand Freemasons were tried before this tribunal and sentenced to long terms of imprisonment.

Despite the denunciations of Freemasons as Communist revolutionaries, it was possible in the twentieth century, as it had been in the eighteenth century, for a Freemason to be a political supporter of the Right wing. General Manuel Presa Alamo was initiated as a Freemason in 1929, but in view of the drive against the Freemasons he resigned from the society in 1933. He fought for Franco in the civil war, and was appointed Chief of the Air Force. This did not save him from being brought before the Tribunal for the Suppression of Masonry when it was discovered that, ten years before, he had been a Freemason for four years.

General Aranda was another Right-wing Freemason. He fought for Franco in the Civil War and was decorated as a war hero. But he too had to appear before the tribunal. In view of their services to Franco, both Alamo and Aranda were treated leniently; neither was sentenced to imprisonment, but both were placed on the reserve list. After Franco's death and the accession of King Juan Carlos,

General Aranda was restored by royal decree to the active service list in 1976, when he was aged 86.

In 1963 it was announced that the Tribunal for the Suppression of Masonry would be abolished because it had completed its task and had rooted out Freemasonry in Spain; but in case there were still some Freemasons left, who were not in prison, the functions of the tribunal would be transferred to the Tribunal of Public Order.[9]

Franco also attached great importance to informing the people about the dangers of Freemasonry, and personally participated in the propaganda campaign. He wrote fifty articles about Freemasonry which were published in the journal of the Falange movement, *Arriba*, at various dates between 14 December 1946 and 3 May 1951. In 1952 they were published in a book, *Masoneria* by J. Boor, which was Franco's pseudonym. After Franco's death the book was reprinted in 1982, and it was stated that Franco was the author.

Franco was a little more rational than Ludendorff, Custos or Nilus. He pointed out that Communism, Freemasonry, and the Judaism revealed in *The Protocols of the Elders of Zion*, were three different phenomena. The Communists and the Freemasons were bitter enemies; the Communists were anti-capitalist, while the Freemasons supported capitalism. But they had united against Spain, and the 33 degree Norwegian mason, Trygve Lie, the 33 degree Belgian mason Paul Henri Spaak, the 33 degree Spanish mason, Giral, and the 33 degree Mexican mason, Padilla, were for the moment eager allies of the Communists. Nor did Franco believe that international Free-masonry was a united force, for he wrote that the appointment of the Vichy Admiral Darlan as ruler of North Africa by President Roosevelt and the American Freemasons after the Allied landing there in November 1942, and Darlan's assassination soon afterwards by an agent of General de Gaulle, was an incident in the struggle between the American and British Freemasons.

Franco went back into history to show that the Freemasons have always plotted against Spain. The first Spanish lodge was formed in Madrid in 1731 by the Duke of Wharton, whom the British had banished from England because of his treason and immorality, and had sent him to Spain to corrupt Spanish life by founding Free-masonry. But Franco saw the French Freemasons as the chief enemy of Spain. They acted in the traditional French belief that 'a strong Spain is a stranglehold around the neck of France'.

Franco repeatedly harped on Francisco Ferrer, who had been

executed as an Anarchist in Barcelona in 1909 when Franco was a young man, and had been glorified as a martyr by the French and Belgian Freemasons. Franco wrote that Ferrer had plotted in France with the French Freemasons to destroy Spain, and had been caught and rightly punished when he returned to Spain to carry out his mission. It was the Freemasons who destroyed the Spanish Empire, and their skill and experience as secret agents made them the most efficient of the British spies. Freemasons dominated among the officials of the League of Nations, the United Nations, and the British BBC. Worst of all the enemies of Spain was President Franklin D. Roosevelt's widow, 'the picturesque Mrs Roosevelt, the well-known woman mason'. Franco certainly went astray when he accused the Freemason Ernest Bevin, the British Labour Foreign Secretary, and the Freemason Léon Blum, the French Socialist Prime Minister, of thwarting the beneficial plan of General George Marshall, the United States Secretary of State, to give economic assistance to Spain. In fact, neither Bevin nor Blum was a Freemason, but Marshall was an active one.

Writing under the pseudonym of Boor made it easier for Franco to assert that the Spanish people had replied to the conspiracies of the Freemasons with the slogan 'With Franco to the death!'[10]

The suppression of Freemasonry in Spain continued throughout Franco's lifetime, though in the case of learned intellectual books the censorship was relaxed during his last years. The historian professor José A. Ferrer Benemeli was able to publish his book, *Spanish Masonry in the Eighteenth Century* in 1974,[11] a year before Franco died. Benemeli was not a Freemason, but he wrote with great sympathy about the liberal ideas of the eighteenth-century Freemasons, and how they endured persecution.

After Franco's death in 1975, King Juan Carlos immediately introduced political democracy in Spain. The ban on Freemasonry was abolished, and the Freemasons were allowed to meet freely and legally. Their lodges are not centres of revolution in democratic Spain.

It was a similar story in Portugal. The Freemasons were suppressed under the dictatorship of Dr Oliveira Salazar, though Salazar was so successful in preventing revolution and averting civil war that no large-scale massacres and executions of Freemasons took place in Portugal as they did in Spain. After Salazar's death, democracy was restored in Portugal and Freemasons' lodges were permitted. They are no more revolutionary today than they are in Spain.

*

The Lautaro Lodge continued to play an active part in Mexican politics. After the fall of Santa Anna, the Liberal President Ignacio Comonfort came to power. He was a Freemason.[12] His government was overthrown by a military coup. His Minister of Justice, the Indian Benito Juárez, led the Liberal forces in a savage civil war against the Right-wing military dictator, General Miguel Miramon. Juárez was a Freemason.[13] The Catholic Church denounced Juárez, the Liberals and the Freemasons, and supported the Right-wing military dictators. The slogan of the Right wing was 'Religion and Order'. The Liberals fought for 'God and Liberty'.

The most ferocious of the Right-wing military leaders was General Leonardo Márquez. After he had defeated the Liberals at Tacubaya in 1859 he sent his men into the hospital to kill all the wounded Liberal soldiers. They also killed all the doctors in the hospital who had treated the wounded Liberals, and were therefore considered guilty as accessories in the Liberal masonic conspiracy. After this exploit Márquez boasted of his nickname 'the Tiger of Tacubaya'.[14]

The civil war lasted for three years before Juárez won and entered Mexico City; but immediately Napoleon III, using the excuse that the Mexican government had been unable to repay the debts that it owed to its French creditors, invaded Mexico and installed the Archduke Maximilian of Austria, the brother of the Austrian Emperor Franz Joseph, as Emperor of Mexico. Maximilian had mildly Liberal ideas, and it was said that before he went to Mexico, when he was Viceroy of Lombardy and Venetia for his brother, he had become a Freemason; but this cannot be proved.[15]

Maximilian hesitated for some time as to whether he should accept the throne of Mexico; but he was encouraged to accept by his father-in-law, King Leopold I of the Belgians, who was a Freemason.[16] Leopold is best known to British readers as Queen Victoria's 'Uncle Leopold' to whom she turned for advice. He was known as the 'Nestor of Europe' because of his diplomacy and wise judgment; but he was not as wise as usual when he encouraged Maximilian to go to Mexico.[17]

The French occupied Mexico City, placed Maximilian on the throne there, and drove Juárez to the very limit of Mexican territory on the frontier with the United States at El Paso del Norte (today Ciudad Juárez). But Juárez doggedly held on, while his Liberal supporters waged a guerrilla war against the French, who executed many of them. The Liberals were finally victorious when, at the end of the

American Civil War, the United States threatened to intervene unless Napoleon III withdrew his army from Mexico. So Napoleon III left Maximilian to his fate.

Maximilian remained in Mexico after the French withdrew, and was taken prisoner by the Liberals at Querétaro, sentenced to death by a court martial, and executed by a firing squad. There were rumours that Juárez would pardon Maximilian because they were both Freemasons;[18] but even if Maximilian was in fact a Freemason, this point was never raised in any of the unsuccessful attempts to persuade Juárez to commute the death sentence.[19]

Juárez was a great leader and a wise statesman, and deserves the title of the Liberator of his Country and the position which he still holds today in the memory of Mexicans. The resentment felt by his followers about the cruelties committed by the French and by the Mexican Right Wing made it politically impossible for him to pardon Maximilian; but there were very few other executions after the Liberal victory, despite all that they had suffered at the hands of the Right-wing and clerical parties in the previous ten years.

Juárez's most able and daring commander was Porfirio Díaz. After the departure of the French, Díaz captured Mexico City from the Right-wing forces in the last battle of the war. When Juárez died in 1872, civil war broke out between his followers, and Díaz, after a series of hairbreadth escapes, emerged victorious. He made himself President of Mexico, and contrived to be regularly re-elected and to rule as dictator for 35 years, from 1876 to 1911. Díaz was a Freemason. It is not certain when he was initiated, but as President of Mexico he accepted the position of Grand Master of one of several Mexican masonic organizations, though he never attended a meeting of Mexican Grand Lodge.[20]

Díaz's dictatorship was appreciated by the merchants, investors and governments of Europe, for he succeeded in securing law and order in Mexico and the safety of the lives of the foreign residents there. At the time of the execution of Maximilian in 1867 Queen Victoria had written in great indignation: 'It would be an eternal disgrace to us were we to entertain any diplomatic relations with such a bloodstained Government as that of the monster Juarez and his adherents'.[21] But in 1906 her son, Edward VII, made his masonic brother President Díaz a Knight Commander of the Order of the Bath because of what Díaz had done for the benefit of British merchants in Mexico.

But Díaz's dictatorship was viewed more favourably by the politicians and businessmen in London than by the peasants and the Liberal intellectuals in Mexico. The peasants worked long hours in harsh conditions which were enforced by Díaz's brutal police; and for the Liberals Díaz, the thirty-five-year-old revolutionary of 1865, had become the eighty-year-old reactionary dictator of 1910. He was overthrown by a revolution in 1911 and fled to Paris, where he died in exile. The Liberals were led by the moderate intellectual professor, Francisco Madero, who was a Freemason.[22] He was supported by the more extreme revolutionary peasant leaders, Pancho Villa and Emiliano Zapata, who were not Freemasons.

Madero was assassinated by General Victoriano Huerta; Huerta was overthrown by Venustiano Carranza; and eventually General A. Obregon came to power. Mexico settled down to stable government after more than ten years of civil war. Several of the twentieth-century Presidents of Mexico were Freemasons.

The Freemasons were active in other parts of Latin America. That adventurous young man, William G. Walker, born in Nashville, Tennessee, in 1824, studied law and practised as a lawyer in Nashville, but then decided to go to Europe and studied medicine at the universities of Edinburgh in Scotland and Heidelberg in Germany. Having qualified as a doctor, he practised medicine in Philadelphia and in New Orleans, but then became a journalist in San Francisco. While in California he was initiated as a Freemason. In 1855 he took it into his head that he would like to be dictator of Nicaragua, and went there with 56 followers. After several unsuccessful attempts he captured Granada and declared that he was the head of the government of Nicaragua. His government was recognized by the United States; but he had annoyed the British by upsetting their relations with Honduras. So the British sent a naval unit which defeated and captured Walker. The British handed him over to the authorities in Honduras, who tried him by court-martial and shot him on 12 September 1860.[23]

Throughout the nineteenth and twentieth centuries the Lautaro Freemasons pursued their revolutionary activity in Latin America. They played a leading part in liberating Cuba from Spanish rule. Anarciso Lopez, who led an unsuccessful revolt in Cuba in 1851 and was captured and shot by the Spanish authorities, was a Freemason; so were José Julio Marti, the 'Apostle of the Liberation of Cuba', who led the revolt of 1875; Calosto Garcia-Iniguez, who fought for Cuban independence for twenty years; and Nasciso Valdes, who raised the Cuban flag over the lighthouse at Morro Castle in Havana in the hour of victory in 1902. The dictator General Machado, who was overthrown by the revolution of 1933, was a Freemason;[24] but Fidel Castro, who seized power in the revolution of 1959 and has governed Cuba for forty years, is not a Freemason, and, like other heads of authoritarian governments, views the activities of the Freemasons with some suspicion. His follower Che Guevara, the Argentine revolutionary who for young Radicals throughout the world became a hero, an example and a martyr, was not a Freemason.

The Chilean Socialist, Salvador Allende, was a Freemason.[25] After a lifetime of political activity which showed that he was very close to the Communist Party, he came to power in Chile by a democratic election in 1970. The Right-wing parties organized a campaign of passive resistance and strikes, including a doctors' strike, which reduced Chile to chaos and led to violent clashes between supporters of the government and the opposition. Allende, finding himself unable to cope with the situation, and acting on the advice of his Communist Party supporters, invited General Augusto Pinochet to enter his government as Minister of Defence in the hope of appeasing the Right-wing opposition; but in September 1973 Pinochet overthrew the government by a coup, in the course of which Allende was shot. In the ensuing years of Pinochet's dictatorship, thousands of Allende's Left-wing supporters were arrested, tortured and executed. In 1990 Pinochet agreed to end his dictatorship and allow a democratic régime to be restored in Chile on condition that he was granted immunity from prosecution for any crimes that he might have committed during his years as dictator.*

The Freemasons played an important part in winning the independence of the Philippines from Spain. José Rizal, the hero of the independence movement, was a Freemason. He was captured and

---

* In 1998 Pinochet came to London for medical treatment, and was detained while legal proceedings were brought to extradite him to Spain to answer charges of having murdered and tortured Spanish subjects while he was ruler of Chile. The proceedings led to conflicting decisions in the High Court, the Court of Appeal and the House of Lords, and at the time when I am writing (August 1999) the case has not yet been decided.[26]

shot by the Spanish government on the field of Bagumbayan on 30 December 1896, at the beginning of the final struggle which won independence two years later.[27]

The history of Freemasonry in the Balkans is difficult to unravel because it has been protected by secrecy and confused by the wildest allegations. The Freemasons in Croatia, Slovenia, Bosnia, Serbia, Montenegro and Macedonia, as in other countries, were influenced by liberal ideas. They consisted almost exclusively of middle-class intellectuals, and supported, not very successfully, the weak liberal trends in their countries. It is not surprising that in Yugoslavia, even more than elsewhere, they have been accused by reactionary propagandists of committing the most bizarre and dreadful crimes and of being responsible for all the miseries from which the people of the Balkans have suffered in the terrible twentieth century.

The attack on the Freemasons has been particularly vehement in Croatia, where the Roman Catholic Church has persecuted its revolutionary, liberal and unorthodox critics with a ferocity which has not been equalled anywhere except in Spain. The Freemasons have been repeatedly denounced in the press, on the last occasion as recently as May 1999.[28]

Already before the First World War people were accusing the Freemasons of being agents both of English Grand Lodge and of the British Secret Service, who were working to throw the Balkans into chaos so that the British government could take advantage of the situation. It was generally known that Edward VII had been Grand Master of English Grand Lodge, and he was seen as the master mind linking the British government with the Freemasons. Croatian writers, as well as the Germans Ludendorff and Custos, accused the Freemasons of organizing the assassination of the Archduke Franz Ferdinand in Sarajevo in 1914 in order to begin the First World War and destroy Germany and her allies.

A more subtle and complicated anti-masonic line, particularly in Croatia, has been to argue that the British Freemasons are responsible for the wars that have raged in the Balkans since 1991 because of their actions nearly ninety years earlier. In 1903 Serbia was ruled by King Alexander Obrenović. The Obrenović dynasty had led the struggle for Serbian independence from Turkey after Milosh Obrenović had murdered his rival for the leadership, Karageorge, in his sleep in 1817. King Alexander married a woman, Draga, who was certainly of lower-class origin, even if it was an exaggeration to call her a Belgrade prostitute. In 1903 the supporters of the Karageorge family broke into the palace, murdered King Alexander and Queen Draga, threw their bodies out of the window for them to be trampled on by the crowd, and proclaimed Peter Karageorge as King.

Under the Obrenović dynasty, Serbia had been the ally of Austria, to which the Serbs looked to protect them against their neighbour, Bulgaria, and the Bulgarian's protector, Russia. So it was thought that Edward VII and the British Freemasons, who controlled British foreign policy, wished to overthrow the Obrenović dynasty and place the Karageorge family on the throne in their place. The British government professed to be shocked at the murder; They withdrew their ambassador from Belgrade and refused to send a representative to the new King's coronation; but their ambassador returned to Belgrade after a year, and Britain established far more friendly relations with Serbia than she had done with the Obrenović Kings.

This, say the critics today, was the cause of all the killings of the 1990s. If the British Freemason Edward VII had not overthrown the Obrenović dynasty, Serbia would have been fighting as Austria's ally in the First World War, as all her Balkan neighbours did; Serbia would not have been rewarded by the victorious Allies in 1918 by the creation of a new nation, Yugoslavia, under Serbian domination; Serbia would not have been able to resist the German pressure in 1941 and would not have entered the Second World War on Britain's side; the victorious Allies at Yalta in 1945 would not have imposed a Communist Yugoslavia; and the separate governments of all parts of the Balkans would have been peacefully accepted by everyone in 1991.[29] There might be some truth in all this if it did not include the Freemasons. Although British Foreign Secretaries have sometimes hypocritically denied this, the British government, like all other governments, ever since the days of Cardinal Wolsey and Queen Elizabeth I in the sixteenth century, have acted on the principle laid down by the Italian statesman, Cavour: 'If we did for ourselves what we do for our country, what scoundrels we should be'. But although British, as well as other diplomats, follow this maxim, they did not learn it in British Freemasons' lodges.

When the Freemasons in Japan were arrested after Pearl Harbor in December 1941, they were accused by their Japanese interrogators of being spies. In the case of one British Freemason, when he denied being a spy, his interrogator asked him if he was a patriotic Englishman. 'Yes', replied the Freemason. 'Well, then', said the Japanese interrogator, 'all Japanese abroad are expected to spy for Japan; so you, as a patriotic Englishman in Japan, must be willing to act as a spy for England.'[30] If the British Freemason made any further reply, it is not recorded.

The Japanese interrogator had a point here. Most British Freemasons, if asked to spy for Britain abroad in wartime, or even in peacetime, would think it was their patriotic duty to do so. But most patriotic Englishmen who are not Freemasons would also agree to spy for Britain if asked to do so by the British government. On the other hand, in every war in which Britain has been engaged since 1717, there have been some British Freemasons who have opposed the war and their government's policy, just as there have been nonmasons who have done this. As always, when political crimes and questions of war and peace are involved, Freemasonry is irrelevant.

The establishment of the Karageorgević dynasty did in fact lead to a reversal of alliances in the Balkans; Serbia became the ally of Russia, and Bulgaria passed into the Austrian and German camp. The Archduke Franz Ferdinand was murdered in Sarajevo not by the masons but by members of a secret Serbian nationalist group. It is very unlikely that they had any farseeing design to cause a European war; they probably acted merely out of hatred of Austria, which had annexed Bosnia and Herzegovina six years before.

The Austrian government thought that this was a good opportunity to annex Serbia, and sent a threatening ultimatum, imposing such humiliating terms that they thought that the Serbian government would certainly refuse to comply; this would give Austria the excuse to go to war. Serbia agreed to most of the Austrian demands, but hedged on a few of them, and Austria declared war. We now know that the Serbian government had decided to accept all the Austrian demands, but were persuaded by the Russian Foreign Office to reject the most outrageous of the terms, after Serbia had received a secret pledge of Russian support in the event of war. A French writer has suggested that a secret Serbian organization which had its contacts in the Russian government was responsible for the Serbian decision which was the cause of the First World War.[31]

The Serbs fought bravely on the Allied side, and suffered heavy losses. The British press wrote admiringly of 'gallant little Serbia' repulsing the Austrian and German armies, and praised the heroism of the Serbian soldiers in their retreat through the snow to the safety of the French fleet in the Adriatic. Serbian children came as refugees to England, and their plight aroused great sympathy.

The victorious Allies created the new state of Yugoslavia. The King of Serbia became King of Yugoslavia* and was soon succeeded by his son, Prince Alexander, who had served with distinction in the Serbian army during the war. The Croatians, Slovenes, Bosnians, Montenegrins and Macedonians in Yugoslavia were dominated by the Serbs, which they greatly resented; and as Yugoslavia was a member of the coalition formed by the Allies against Bolshevik Russia, the Communists as well as the Croatian nationalists – the Ustaše – opposed the Yugoslav government, and were suppressed. In January 1929 King Alexander established his dictatorship, with the approval of *The Times* and the British government.[32] The Communists and the Ustaše both suffered in the torture chambers of King Alexander's police and in the internment camps.

In October 1934 King Alexander went on a state visit to France. As he drove through the streets of Marseilles with the French Foreign Minister, Louis Barthou, a man in the crowd fired with his revolver at Alexander and Barthou, and killed them. The assassin was probably one of the Ustaše refugees in Hungary, though the Ustaše leader, Ante Pavelić, had recently moved from Hungary to Mussolini's Italy. The Yugoslav government held Hungary responsible for Alexander's death, and Yugoslavia and her allies threatened to go to war but Mussolini supported Hungary. There were widespread fears that a European war might break out; but Mussolini was preparing to invade Abyssinia, and did not want a war in Europe. The dispute ended peaceably.[33]

The Croatians have always denied that the assassin was an Ustaše, and believe that King Alexander was murdered by the V.M.R.D., a secret society of Macedonians who, like the Croatians, resented Serbian domination. But a new theory has been put forward in Croatia – that Alexander was murdered by the Freemasons. According to this story, Alexander was the Master of a masonic lodge. He decided to build a railway in Bosnia, and asked the Freemasons to pay for it. His masonic brothers refused, and Alexander was forced to borrow the money from foreign bankers at a high rate of interest.

* From 1918 to 1929, the new kingdom was officially called 'the Kingdom of Serbs, Croats and Slovenes', though it was popularly known as 'Yugoslavia'. The name was officially changed to the 'Kingdom of Yugoslavia' after King Alexander established his dictatorship in January 1929.

He was so angry that he resigned from his lodge. The Freemasons regarded him as a defaulting brother who had broken his masonic oaths by leaving the society, and murdered him.[34]

When Hitler invaded Yugoslavia in 1941, he was welcomed by the Ustaše in Croatia, and Pavelić was installed as the dictator of an independent Croatian state. The tenth of April, the day on which the state was proclaimed and the German troops entered Zagreb, is once again celebrated by the Ustaše in Croatia.

Pavelić's Ustaše government, with the support of the Croatian Catholic Church, killed the enemies of the Catholic faith – Orthodox Serbs, Jews, and Communist atheists. They began murdering Jews three months before Hitler and the Germans did. The Serbs today claim that during the Second World War the Ustaše killed 750,000 Serbs; the Croatian authorities say that the number of victims was fewer than 70,000. Impartial historians have estimated that the figure was probably about 330,000. The Ustaše murdered many of them in the Jasenovac concentration camp, but also went into the villages, accompanied by Catholic priests, and slaughtered all Orthodox Serbs who refused to convert to Roman Catholicism. They asked the children to make the sign of the cross. If the children crossed themselves, in the Roman Catholic manner, from left to right, they were spared; if they did it from right to left, in the manner of the Serbian Orthodox Church, they were murdered.[35]

The Ustaše also persecuted the Freemasons, but, like the Nazis in Germany, they treated the Freemasons less severely than the Jews and the Communists. Freemasonry was repeatedly denounced in government propaganda, and the press published lists of the names of Freemasons, thus exposing them to public hatred, just as Fay's Service for Secret Societies in Vichy France published the names of the French Freemasons.[36] But the Freemasons were not exterminated in Croatia, like the Jews and gypsies.

There was also an anti-masonic campaign in Serbia, where the German occupation authorities installed a pro-German puppet government under General Nedić and Dimitrije Ljotić. Ljotić and the Germans organized an exhibition in Belgrade in 1941, showing how Freemasonry was a revolutionary movement associated with Communism.[37]

After the war, the Croatian Josip Broz Tito became the Communist ruler of Yugoslavia. He had led the victorious war of liberation waged by his Partisans against the Germans and their collaborators

in 1941–45. During the war he had called for the unity of all nation-
alities in Yugoslavia; his Partisans had protected the Serbs from being
murdered by Croatian Fascists, and the Muslims in Bosnia from
being murdered by the Serbian nationalists.

From 1920, when he joined the Yugoslav Communist Party, Tito
loyally followed the party line laid down by Stalin and the Communist International in Moscow; but after he came to power in Yugoslavia in 1945 he resented the dictatorial attitude towards Yugoslavia
adopted by Stalin and the Communist Party of the Soviet Union,
and he eventually rebelled against Soviet domination.

The Communist International was dissolved in 1943, but a new
organization, the Cominform (Informbureau) was founded in 1947;
it consisted of the eleven most important Communist Parties, including the Communist Party of the Soviet Union and the Communist
Party of Yugoslavia. In 1948 the Communist Party of Yugoslavia
was expelled from the Cominform. Although the great majority of
Yugoslav Communists supported Tito against Stalin, a few of them
sympathised with Stalin and the Cominform. Tito's secret police,
which was under the control of the Minister of the Interior, Alek-
sander Ranković, kept a close watch on these Cominform supporters,
and imprisoned many of them in very harsh conditions in the concentration camp on the island of Goli Otok in the Adriatic. Tito suppressed them in Yugoslavia as ruthlessly as Communists accused of
'Titoism' were suppressed in other Communist countries.[38]

One of Tito's closest collaborators was the veteran Communist
Moša Pijade, a middle-class Jew from Belgrade. He was the leading
Marxist theoretician in the Yugoslav Communist Party, for which
he had worked loyally for thirty years in King Alexander's prisons
and as a partisan fighter during the Second World War. He strongly
supported Tito against Stalin. But, according to recent anti-masonic
writers in Croatia, the secret police investigated him in 1948, along
with all other Party members, to make sure that he had no links
with the Cominform. In the course of these investigations they discovered that Pijade was a Freemason. These Croatian anti-masonic
writers do not fail to point out that he was also a Jew.[39]

As ruler of Yugoslavia, Tito pursued a policy of balancing national-
ities against each other, and the hardliners against the more liberal
members of his government and the Communist Party. In the 1950s
he disciplined and arrested the liberal Milovan Djilas; in 1966 he
dismissed the hardline Ranković, the head of the secret police, and

his supporters. For five years, from 1966 to 1971, the rigour of the dictatorship was relaxed in Yugoslavia until the outbreak of the movement for independence in Croatia in 1971 drove Tito to reintroduce a more repressive régime.

Some people today in Yugoslavia and in the former Yugoslavia believe that Tito was a Freemason. There are two reasons why they believe this. The first is because on his tomb in Belgrade there is only the simple inscription 'Josip Broz Tito 1892–1980', with no further words or adornment, which is known to be a custom among Freemasons; but in fact Tito directed that his tomb should be marked in this way because he had been impressed by the tomb of Franklin D. Roosevelt in the United States, which bears the solitary inscription 'Franklin Delano Roosevelt 1882–1945'. Roosevelt was a Freemason,[40] and this may well be the reason why his tomb bears only his name and the dates of his birth and death; but Tito wished his tomb to be marked in the same way, not because he was a Freemason but because he liked Roosevelt's tomb.

The second reason is because of his decision to dismiss Ranković and the hardliners in 1966. This decision was certainly taken on political grounds, because Tito believed that it was now possible and desirable to relax the dictatorship; but as Ranković and many of his lieutenants were Serbs, they believed then – and are even more convinced today – that they were dismissed because the Croatian Tito did not like Serbs. They also believe that the Freemasons were behind the decision to overthrow Ranković and the hardliners. Ranković's ally Živadin Simić, the leading figure in the Serbian secret police, was certain that Tito was a Freemason.[41]

There is no doubt that it would have been in accordance with the traditional policy of the Freemasons for them to have supported the move towards liberalization and a relaxation of the dictatorship in 1966; but there is no proof that Tito was a secret Freemason, and it is very unlikely. The Communist International had condemned Freemasonry in 1922, and it is hard to believe that Tito, who loyally followed the line of the Communist International from 1920 till his breach with the Cominform and Stalin in 1948, would have defied Party discipline and become a Freemason. Apart from this, from what we know of Tito's character, it would not be surprising if, like Napoleon, Clemenceau and other forceful leaders who might well have been Freemasons, he had decided not to join the society himself.

After the proclamation of the independence of Slovenia and

Croatia in 1991 and of Bosnia in 1992, the invasion of Croatia and Bosnia by the Serbian army, and the atrocities committed by the Serbs in Vukovar and Sarajevo, new stories were published in Croatia incriminating the Freemasons. It was said that all the trouble in Yugoslavia had been planned by Lawrence S. Engelburger, the United States Assistant Secretary of State in President George Bush's administration; by the Italian Foreign Minister, Gianni De Michelis (a former Prime Minister); and by Hans Van Den Broek, the Dutch Foreign Minister, who afterwards became a leading official of the European Union. De Michelis was a member of the masonic P2 lodge of the Italian Grand Orient; in 1995 he was convicted of corruption, and sentenced to four years' imprisonment. Engelburger and Van Den Broek, as well as De Michelis, are supposed to be Freemasons.

When the fighting in Croatia and Bosnia began, the United Nations sent observers to Yugoslavia to report on what was happening there. For many months they took no action against the Serbs, and were accused by the Croatians and Bosnians of being pro-Serb. Eventually they recommended that drastic economic sanctions be imposed against Serbia, and the United Nations acted on their recommendation. All this is said to have been a masonic plot: by taking no action in the early stages, and later imposing sanctions, the Freemasons ensured that the fighting would continue and that Serbia would be economically crippled, thus causing war and chaos which the Freemasons could exploit to their own advantage.

The latest shots in the anti-masonic campaign came in May 1999, when the Croatian newspaper *Globus* alleged that Nenad Porges, the Minister for the Economy in the Croatian government, was a Freemason.[42] At the time when I am writing we do not know whether this article in *Globus* will have any repercussions.

In March 1999 the United States and its Nato allies announced that unless the government of Slobodan Milošević in Belgrade agreed to allow Nato troops to enter Kosovo to protect the Albanians from the Serbs, Nato would bomb Yugoslavia, including Kosovo; and in preparation for the start of the bombing campaign, United Nations' observers would be withdrawn from Kosovo. The Serbian nationalist extremists had announced that if Nato bombed Yugoslavia they would enter Kosovo and exterminate the Albanians there; and, as President Bill Clinton and his allies might have foreseen, when the UN observers were withdrawn from Kosovo, the Serbian nationalists carried out their threats. Soon after the Nato bombing began, Slavko Čuruvija, the editor of the opposition newspaper, *Dnevni Telegraf* in Belgrade, was murdered. As he had regularly criticised Milošević's government, he was generally regarded as the victim of the Serbian nationalist extremists. But, not surprisingly, another explanation has now been put forward: in 1998 Čuruvija had published several articles about Freemasonry in his newspaper. It was therefore suggested that he had been murdered by the Freemasons.

None of these allegations can be verified; none is supported by any reliable evidence; and they are all improbable. There is no need to bring in the Freemasons in order to explain why an opponent of the Serbian nationalists should have been murdered, or why the United States and its Nato allies, throughout the 1990s, have consistently worked to bring about the defeat, the dismemberment, and the economic ruin of Serbia, Russia's ally in the Balkans.

◆

CHAPTER 20

Modern Freemasonry in Britain

W HILE Freemasons in Spain, Japan and Nazi-occupied
Europe were being savagely persecuted, the English Freemasons were still living in the happy atmosphere of the
days of Edward VII. English and Continental masonry had taken
two completely different roads. The Continental Freemasons saw
themselves as engaged in a great political struggle, as Emmanuel
Arago had expressed it in 1877, against 'the enemy of the Masons,
the enemy of knowledge, of freedom of conscience, of the light and
the true rights of man'.[1] The English Freemasons were strictly non-
political, and had established lodges in which political discussions
were banned and where men of strongly differing political views
could meet in friendship, including men whom Arago would have
characterized as the enemies of knowledge, freedom of conscience,
of the light, and of the true rights of man.

The British Freemasons included among their brothers a large number of men of the highest eminence in their professions and walks of
life. Artists from Hogarth and Sir John Soane in the eighteenth century;
musicians from Thomas Arne, who wrote *Rule Britannia!*, to Sir Arthur
Sullivan; and, on the lighter side, Lionel Monckton;* actors from David
Garrick and Edmund Kean to Sir Henry Irving (who in 1895 became
the first English actor to be given a knighthood), Sir Herbert Beerbohm
Tree, Sir Harry Lauder, Sir Donald Wolfit and Peter Sellers.

---

* In the twentieth century, the Russia artist, Marc Chagall, who was a Freemason,
worked in England. The Freemason musicians in Europe, apart from Mozart and
Haydn, included John Christian Bach, Franz Liszt, Giacomo Meyerbeer, and Jean
Sibelius, who was one of the founders of the first masonic lodge in Finland in 1922.
Among the masonic lighter musicians in the United States were John P. Sousa and
Irving Berlin.

There were writers from Alexander Pope, Jonathan Swift, Edward Gibbon, James Boswell, Robert Burns, Richard Brinsley Sheridan, Sir Walter Scott, Captain Frederick Marryat, and James Hogg (the 'Ettrick Shepherd') to Anthony Trollope, W. S. Gilbert (who collaborated in the operettas with his masonic brother Arthur Sullivan), Oscar Wilde, Rafael Sabatini, Sir Arthur Conan Doyle, who did many things during his life apart from inventing Sherlock Holmes; and that great Freemason, Rudyard Kipling. There were the scientists and medical men – from Edward Jenner, the inventor of vaccination, and the great eighteenth-century surgeon and dentist, the Chevalier Bartholemew Ruspini, who emigrated from Bayonne to London, became the Prince Regent's dentist, and showed such kindness to Italian and other foreign visitors to London that Pope Pius VII made him a Chevalier and a Knight of the Golden Spur, although he knew that he was a Freemason; and in the twentieth century Sir Bernard Spilsbury and Sir Alexander Fleming, the discoverer of penicillin.

Many of the leading military commanders in the late nineteenth and twentieth centuries were Freemasons – Lord Roberts of Kandahar, Lord Kitchener, Sir John French (later Earl of Ypres); Earl Haig; Sir Claude Auchinleck; and Earl Alexander of Tunis.* There were the politicians from Canning to Lord Randolph Churchill, Cecil Rhodes, Leopold Amery, the Labour Prime Minister Clement Attlee, his colleague Arthur Greenwood, and Gerald, Lord Gardiner, Harold Wilson's very progressive and outstandingly upright Labour Lord Chancellor in the 1960s.[2]

Sir Winston Churchill joined the Freemasons when he was aged 26; he was initiated into a lodge at the Café Royal in London on 24 May 1901, just after he had first become a Conservative MP. He resigned from the Freemasons in July 1912, when he was Home Secretary in the Liberal government because pressure of work made it impossible for him to attend lodge meetings.[3]

As Prince of Wales, Edward VII was an ideal Grand Master for the English Freemasons. Easy going, pleasure-loving and tolerant, as a young man he had shocked his serious and high-minded father,

---

* The French had only one masonic general, Marshal Joseph Jacques Césaire Joffre; but the Germans had several, from Field Marshal Karl Wilhelm Duke of Brunswick, Field Marshal Gebhard Leberecht von Blücher, General Count August Gneisenau, General Gerhard von Scharnhorst and King Frederick William IV of Prussia to Admiral Alfred von Tirpitz and General Count Alfred von Schlieffen, who invented the Schlieffen Plan for an attack on France at the beginning of the First World War.

Prince Albert, by his rough, boisterous pranks. He once poured wine over one of the servants, ruining the new livery of which the servant was very proud; but he stopped indulging in this type of unkind behaviour at an early age.

His father and mother were even more shocked when they discovered that while he was attending army manoeuvres at the Curragh in Ireland when he was aged 19 a young woman, a prostitute, was smuggled into his quarters during the night. Soon afterwards, Prince Albert died from typhoid fever which he contracted from the bad drains in Windsor Castle. Queen Victoria was convinced that her beloved husband had died as a result of the distress which Edward's conduct had caused him.

Where women were concerned, Edward did not reform his ways as he grew older. He continued to make love to beautiful women wherever he went: to the opera singer Hortense Schneider when he saw her in Jacques Offenbach's *La Grande Duchesse de Gérolstein* during the Paris Exhibition of 1867; to the society beauty, Mrs Lillie Langtry; to Lady Mordaunt, whose husband Sir Charles Mordaunt, unlike most society gentlemen, objected and involved Edward in the scandal of a divorce case; to the Socialist bluestocking Lady Brooke (later the Countess of Warwick); to the Honourable Mrs Alice Keppel of Polesden Lacey, near Dorking; but probably not to the famous head-hunting society hostess Mrs James of West Dean Park in Sussex. Hilaire Belloc was almost certainly libelling this lady when he wrote in his famous poem that she had given another meaning to the word 'entertain' when it was announced that 'Mrs James will entertain the King'.[4]

But he conducted all his love affairs discreetly, and usually avoided scandal. He was able to do this because, though the middle and lower classes expected him to be a faithful husband and pretended to themselves that they believed that he was, the upper-class society nobility and gentry among whom he lived knew that he, like themselves, had mistresses.

He was also helped by his beautiful wife, Princess Alexandra of Denmark, who knew that she must accept the duties, if she was to be entitled to enjoy the privileges, of her royal position; and that one of her duties, as the wife of the Prince of Wales and later as his Queen, was not to object if he made love to other women, though she herself would always remain a chaste and faithful wife. He, in return, always treated her with the respect due to her position as

Princess of Wales and as Queen, and expected his mistresses, too, to show due deference to her, which they always did. This was especially so in the case of Mrs Keppel. Queen Alexandra even asked her to visit Edward when he was dying, because she knew that this was what Edward and Mrs Keppel would have wished.

He could not always avoid scandal. After the Mordaunt divorce in 1870 there was the Tranby Croft, or the baccarat, scandal of 1891.[5] Edward was a member of a house party at Tranby Croft in Yorkshire, the home of Sir William Gordon-Cummings, baronet, at which the guests gambled at the illegal French card game, baccarat. Their host was accused of cheating, and this led to a libel action in the High Court in London in which Edward appeared as a witness. It was regrettable that it became known that the Prince of Wales had played baccarat; and it was unfortunate that it transpired that when the Prince travelled in the royal train, he always carried a pack of cards in his pocket and played an illegal French card-game with his companions. The public was as shocked as the Queen, and the press was very critical. The Liberal *Daily Chronicle* wrote that the Prince of Wales's 'taste for the lowest type of gambling . . . has profoundly shocked, we may even say disgusted, the people who may one day be asked to submit to his rule'.[6] But the Freemasons remained loyal to him, and their faith in their Grand Master was unimpaired.

He was friendly with all men, whatever their political views – in France with General de Galliffet, the butcher of the Paris Commune, as well as with the Radical Gambetta. He showed his broadmindedness and lack of exclusiveness by inviting one of the handful of new Labour MPs, Henry Broadhurst, to stay at his country house at Sandringham in Norfolk, which had been built for Edward. But when he discovered that Broadhurst did not possess evening dress, he arranged for him to have dinner privately in his room.[7]

In politics he was a Conservative to the core. He liked sleeping with the Countess of Warwick, but thought that her Socialist political views were ridiculous. He did not favour inviting Indians to join British social clubs in India; he discouraged this because he thought that it was bound to lead to trouble. But he liked Jews, and was friendly with several Jewish financiers.

As King, Edward played a part in international diplomacy. This did provide a grain of truth for the accusation which was subsequently made by Ludendorff, Custos and the Nazi writers that the Freemason Edward VII was planning to make war on Germany and destroy her. He helped to form the new international alignments by which Britain abandoned her policy of neutrality in foreign wars, which she had pursued since Palmerston's death, and formed the new Entente Cordiale, an alliance with France and Russia against Germany. To achieve this, he visited his cousin Tsar Nicholas II on his yacht at Reval in what is today Estonia but was then in the Russian Empire. This was an unpopular move at the time, because British public opinion was very hostile to Russian Tsarism; articles about the tyranny of the Tsar and the ill-treatment of the peasants, the political prisoners exiled to Siberia, and particularly about the Poles and Jews, were constantly appearing in the British press. But Edward was determined to build the anti-German alliance with France and Russia. When two Labour MPs criticised his visit to the Tsar, he withdrew his invitation to them to attend the royal garden party.[8]

Neither British Socialists nor foreign anti-masons could discredit Edward in the eyes of the great majority of the British people. When they heard about his efforts to improve relations by his talks with foreign statesmen whom he met during his summer holidays at Biarritz in France and at Marienbad in Bohemia in the Austrian Empire (today Marianske Lažne in the Czech Republic) they called him 'Edward the Peacemaker' and made up a song about him which was sung in the music halls:

> There'll be no war,
> Not while we've got a King like good King Edward,
> There'll be no war
> For he hates that sort of thing.
> There'll be no war,
> Peace with honour, that's what he's after,
> So let's all sing together, boys,
> Sing God save the King.

Edward was not happy about the far-reaching political and social reforms introduced by his Liberal government after 1906. He particularly disapproved of those two young Radical firebrands, David Lloyd George and Winston Churchill, who went around the country winning Radical applause by their attacks on the aristocracy and the House of Lords. Edward spoke to them about this, and showed his disapproval; but he knew that he could not stop them from making these speeches. He died in the middle of the constitutional crisis of 1910, leaving the restriction on the powers of the House of Lords, which Edward had strongly opposed, to be dealt with by his successor, George V.

The British Freemasons continued to bask in the royal favour. After Edward VII there were other members of the royal family who continued their link with the Freemasons. The Duke of Connaught became Grand Master when Edward VII succeeded to the throne. Then came Edward VIII, George VI – a particularly active Freemason – and Philip, Duke of Edinburgh. Today the Duke of Kent is Grand Master.

The Freemasons increased their opulence and wealth and the splendid size of their operations. They decided to build a new hall – the third building on the site in Covent Garden where they had first met in a simple inn in 1717 and had built an impressive hall in the 1870s. They raised money for the third building by holding the largest masonic meeting ever known, at Olympia on 8 August 1925. The Grand Master, the Duke of Connaught, attended with the Prince of Wales (afterwards King Edward VIII) and the Duke of York (afterwards King George VI). The tables at which the members sat for lunch extended for a total of five miles; the guests were served by 1,300 waitresses, ate 600 pairs of best end of lamb, 3,000 lbs of salmon, 1,500 chickens and 250 gallons of ice-cream. The members paid for their lunch a total of £826,014 11s.6d. which contributed to the cost of building the new hall.[9] It was opened in 1933.

On 24 June 1967 the Freemasons celebrated the two hundred and fiftieth anniversary of the foundation of Grand Lodge by a great rally at the Albert Hall in London. Seven thousand members attended, and the Duke of Kent was installed as Grand Master.[10] Today there are more than 8,000 masonic lodges in England and Wales.[11]

In the First World War, the Freemasons performed their duty as patriotic Englishmen, as they did during the Second World War. At the outbreak of the First World War, Field Marshal Sir John French was commander-in-chief of the British Army; but in December 1915 he was replaced by General Sir Douglas Haig. The story of the intrigues which were conducted to get rid of French and install Haig was only revealed after the war. Among other methods, Haig used the position of his wife, who was one of the Queen's ladies-in-waiting, and Lady Haig intervened with the King in her husband's favour. When people subsequently read about it, they were shocked that while the soldiers were fighting and dying at the front, such plotting for personal advancement should go on among the High Command. French and Haig were both Freemasons. There was no question here of a meeting of a masonic lodge arranging to find a good job for both brothers while non-masons were excluded.

The split between the English and the Continental Freemasons was accentuated when English Grand Lodge in 1929 issued a statement explaining the conditions under which it would recognize and co-operate with foreign Freemasons. It would only do so with Free-masons who were under a rigid central authority of a Grand Lodge and did not allow local branches the liberty to develop their own policies; if belief in God was a condition of membership; if the members undertook to perform their obligations on an open Volume of the Sacred Law – that is to say, on the Bible or the Koran or the equivalent book of some other religion; if women were excluded; and if 'the discussion of religion and politics within the lodge was strictly prohibited'. The condition excluding women was strongly worded: 'that the membership of the Grand Lodge and individual lodges shall be composed exclusively of men, and that each Grand Lodge shall have no masonic intercourse of any kind with mixed lodges or bodies which admit women to membership'.[12]

At a time when Freemasons in many countries were confronted with the rise of Fascism and the greatest threat that there had ever been to Freemasonry and to the principles of toleration in which Freemasons believe; when local lodges were taking independent action to resist this threat in the face of the hesitation and subservi-ence of their Grand Lodge; when women were beginning to demand equal rights with men; English Grand Lodge chose this moment to insist that they would have no dealings with any Freemasons who extended religious toleration to atheists, who were prepared at least to have dealings with women's and mixed lodges, who allowed local lodges to have any independence from their faltering Grand Lodge, and who were prepared to introduce politics into lodge meetings by referring to the Fascist threat that was confronting them.

CHAPTER 21

Modern Freemasonry in the United States

B Y THE middle of the twentieth century Freemasonry had become more firmly established in the United States than in any other country. At one time, more than half the Freemasons in the world were in the United States. Freemasonry did not originate in America; it was imported from Britain before the American Revolution. But the principles of Freemasonry had a strong appeal to a nation brought up in the American tradition. The idea of a band of equals and brothers joined together in a non-sectarian but nevertheless religious deism was welcomed by a people whose earliest traditions go back to the religious nonconformity of their founders, the Pilgrim Fathers of 1620; where many more people attend some kind of church service every Sunday than in Great Britain; and where ideas of brotherhood, equality and solidarity were strong, even if it was originally, and for many years, the brotherhood, equality and solidarity of white males, to the exclusion of women and the black and coloured races.

The Freemasons in the United States, like the Freemasons in Britain, deny that they are a religion. However, an organisation which insists that its members believe in God – though they call him the Great Architect of the Universe to show that he may be either the Roman Catholic, Protestant, Jewish, Muslim, Hindu or any other God – is clearly an organisation of deists.

The United States is a popular democracy where the will of the majority prevails. At times this popular majority has persecuted an unpopular minority, subjecting them to discrimination, ostracism, oppression and sometimes to violence culminating in murder. In theory the rights of the minority are protected by the Constitution of the United States with its important constitutional amendments;

but in practice, at times of popular hysteria against a minority, the state and federal judges, who should have protected these minorities, have failed to do so, and have allowed themselves to be influenced by the mass hysteria.

Since the beginning of the nineteenth century many groups have been the victims of these outbursts of popular fury: Native Americans, Mormons, Freemasons, anti-slavery Abolitionists, champions of the rights of African-Americans in the South and the victims of the Ku Klux Klan after the Civil War. In the early twentieth century, Irish immigrants and immigrants from Eastern Europe and from Mexico became targets, along with pacifists, anarchists and pro-Germans during the First World War; the Japanese Americans during the Second World War; and the Communists and pro-Communist fellow-travellers during the Cold War. For many years the state and federal courts, as well as the Supreme Court of the United States, did nothing to protect the rights of these persecuted minorities.

The Freemasons were the victims of one of these popular outbursts in the 1820s and 1830s, and they suffered severely from it. In some states Freemasonry completely ceased to function; in all states their membership fell. It took thirty years before they began to revive. In 1850 they still had only 66,000 members in the United States; but then other burning issues of the day made people forget about the Freemasons.[1] The issue of the abolition of slavery in the years leading up to the Civil War, the Civil War itself, and the struggle between the champions of the rights of the African-Americans and the supporters of white supremacy during Reconstruction divided the nation. The Freemasons were able to become what the speculative Freemasons in England in the early eighteenth century had intended Freemasonry to be – an organisation in which men of conflicting opinions could meet in friendship despite their differences on the burning issues of the day.

The Freemasons in America at the end of the nineteenth century succeeded in doing this only because they strictly enforced the rule banning political arguments in the lodges. It was a remarkable achievement to form an organisation in which men who had played a prominent part in these bitter disputes and had fought in a civil war on opposite sides could meet in friendship. But one result was that Freemasonry in the United States, unlike anywhere else in the world, enforced racial segregation. At a time when German lodges had been persuaded to admit Jews, and when British lodges in India, under pressure from the Duke of Sussex and other leaders of English Grand Lodge, reluctantly agreed to admit Indians to white lodges, the lodges in the United States excluded African-Americans. If they had admitted them, the former slaveowners and the supporters of white supremacy would have denounced the Freemasons as a band of Radical revolutionaries and 'nigger-lovers'; and the Freemasons in the South would again have become victims of violent attacks, including lynchings, from reactionaries.

During the American War of Independence, when American liberals in the North worked with slaveowners in the South in the struggle against Britain, the British, although they themselves owned black slaves in the West Indies and were engaged in the slave trade, encouraged the slaves of the revolutionaries in Georgia and South Carolina to escape from their masters and join the British garrisons in the ports they held, to work there as labourers. They accepted some of these runaway slaves as members of a British military Freemasons' lodge, though no African-American had been allowed to join any American lodge.

But the man who played the leading part in developing Freemasonry among African-Americans was not a slave. Prince Hall was the son of an English officer and a African-American woman of French descent who had been freed from slavery. He was born in Massachusetts in 1748 and became a Methodist minister in Cambridge, Massachusetts. In 1775 he was accepted as a member of a British military lodge, the first African-American to become a Freemason. Despite this, Prince Hall supported the struggle for American independence against the British; and when George Washington and the American military leaders allowed slaves to enlist in the Revolutionary army, promising them their freedom if they did, Prince Hall encouraged African-Americans to enlist, and may possibly have done so himself. In 1791 the first Grand Lodge of African-Americans was formed, with Prince Hall as Grand Master. After his death in 1807, the African-American lodges were named after him.[2]

For many years there was no collaboration between the mainstream and Prince Hall lodges; but after the movement in favour of equal rights for African-Americans developed in the 1960s, several mainstream white lodges entered into visiting relations with Prince Hall lodges. Others refused to do so, however, and no step was taken towards merging the lodges of the two masonic organisations.[3]

In most countries of the world there have at times been divisions and splits between Freemasons' lodges which have led to the creation of two rival Grand Lodges; but in the United States the number of Grand Lodges far exceeds any other country's. Apart from the divisions between the mainstream lodges for whites only, and the Prince Hall lodges for African-Americans, the American respect for states' rights has led them to organise Freemasonry on a state, not a federal, basis. Whereas in Great Britain all the English lodges are under English Grand Lodge, with separate Grand Lodges for Scotland and Ireland, in the United States every state has its own Grand Lodge. They are, however, linked together by the system that Albert Pike created at the end of the nineteenth century.

Pike's system was based on the so-called Scottish Rite* with thirty-three degrees. There were to be two Supreme Councils, one for the Northern Jurisdiction and another for the Southern Jurisdiction. The names Northern and Southern Jurisdictions were not strictly accurate, for the Northern Jurisdiction was restricted not only to the Grand Lodges north of the Mason-Dixon line but also to those east of the Ohio River, with all the Grand Lodges to the south and west of this area being in the Southern Jurisdiction.

Although the majority of the white mainstream lodges adopt Pike's Scottish Rite, others adopt the York Rite; these lodges are in friendly relations with the lodges of the Scottish Rite. There is also an organisation officially called 'The Ancient Arabic Order of Nobles of the Mystic Shrine', which is popularly called 'The Shriners'. It was founded in the state of New York in 1870. Only Freemasons who have reached the thirty-second degree in the Scottish Rite, or who have become Knights Templars in the York Rite, are eligible to join the Shriners. It is considered to be the highest form of masonry in the United States, but it is not recognised by English Grand Lodge or any foreign Grand Lodge, which do not maintain visiting relations with it.

There is a Grand Lodge of Ancient, Free and Accepted Masons (the mainstream white lodge) in every state. In most states, though not in all, there is 'The Most Worshipful Prince Hall Grand Lodge of Free and Accepted Masons'. There are 18 additional Grand Lodges in New York, 14 in Texas, 12 in California, 9 in Louisiana, 7 in Georgia, 6 in Ohio, 5 in Pennsylvania, and at least 2 others, apart from the Scottish Rite and the Prince Hall Grand Lodge, in each of

* For the origin of the term 'Scottish Rite', see *supra*, p. 72.

all except nine of the other states. Whereas in England there is one United Grand Lodge, in the United States there are 246 Grand Lodges, perhaps more.[4]

By 1903 – twelve years after Pike's death – the number of Freemasons in the United States had risen from 66,142 in 1850 to 860,128.[5] They were about to enter the period of their greatest influence.

At the end of the nineteenth and the beginning of the twentieth century, the British Freemasons produced a vivid figure, King Edward VII. At the same time the American Freemasons produced a quite different but equally vivid figure, Theodore Roosevelt. He was born into the wealthy and respected New York State family of the Roosevelts, who had been prominent in New York life and society for two hundred years. Born in New York City in 1858, he spent most of his childhood on his father's estate in Oyster Bay on Long Island Sound, where he engaged in sports involving vigorous physical exercise, swimming, rowing and horseback riding. At Harvard University, he became prominent as a boxer. After graduation, he went to England, where he joined the Alpine Club in London, and later, in Switzerland, climbed the Jungfrau and the Matterhorn before returning to New York to practise law. He entered politics and became prominent in the Republican Party. When the Republican William McKinley was elected President of the United States in 1896 he appointed Roosevelt to be Assistant Secretary of the Navy.

The administration was confronted with the threat of war between the United States and Spain as a result of their conflict of interests in Cuba, and Roosevelt, who strongly supported the war, prepared the navy for action. When war began, he enlisted in a cavalry regiment from New York and went to Cuba, attaining the rank of colonel. He was in command of the regiment at the Battle of San Juan Hill; he dismounted from his horse and led the infantry in a charge up the hill, which the Americans captured after suffering heavy losses. This exploit confirmed the popularity he had already acquired by his colourful personality. The British historian James Bryce, who knew Roosevelt and was appointed British ambassador in Washington when Roosevelt was President, wrote that he was 'a figure throbbing with life who becomes the hero, almost the personal friend, of a multitude who admire his force and love his breezy ways'.[6]

When McKinley ran for his second term as President in 1900

Theodore Roosevelt was elected as his Vice-President. McKinley was assassinated by an Italian anarchist in September 1901, and Roosevelt became the youngest President of the United States at the age of forty-three. At the end of his term he was re-elected in 1904 with the largest popular vote that any U. S. President had ever received; yet he announced he would not run for a second term in 1908, and supported the candidature of his Secretary of War, William Howard Taft. After Taft succeeded him as President in March 1909, Roosevelt went on a visit to England and Africa.

Theodore Roosevelt, like McKinley and Taft, was a Freemason, and an active one. In several public statements he emphasized the link that Freemasonry provided between important public figures and the ordinary middle-class American. He wrote in 1898: 'I enjoy going to some little lodge where I meet the plain hard-working people on a basis of genuine equality. . . . It is the equality of moral men'; and he made an almost identical statement twenty years later.[7]

But as always, masonic solidarity did not prevent bitter rivalry between two Freemasons who were ambitious politicians. Theodore Roosevelt had supported Taft in the presidential election of 1908, but four years later, after he returned from his tour of England and Africa, he ran against Taft for the nomination as Republican candidate for president at the Chicago Convention. A bitter conflict at the Convention led to a split in the Republican Party, with Roosevelt running against Taft as an Independent Republican. The Democratic candidate, Woodrow Wilson, beat both Taft and Roosevelt, and Roosevelt went off on a visit to South America.

After the outbreak of the First World War, Roosevelt energetically supported the campaign to bring the United States into the war on the side of the Allies. He denounced the pro-Germans and the isolationists and President Wilson's policy of neutrality. When the United States declared war on Germany he supported the war, but criticised Wilson's administration for its unpreparedness. His flamboyant career ended when he died in his sleep on 6 January 1919 at the age of sixty.

By the 1930s there were over two million Freemasons in the United States; the claim that they numbered 3,303,660, amounting to 12% of the male white population, may be an exaggeration. It has been suggested that the Freemasons' strength and influence reached its peak at this time and has declined in the last seventy years.[8] This may be a case of statistics being misleading. It is true that the rise in the number of Freemasons has not kept pace with the growth of the population of the United States. It is also true that if the office of President of the United States is taken as the test of masonic influence, their position in the first half of the twentieth century was much more impressive than in earlier or later times. In the 108 years between 1789 and 1897, eight of the 23 presidents were Freemasons – Washington, Madison,* Monroe, Andrew Jackson, Polk, Buchanan, Andrew Johnson and Garfield. In the fifty-six years between 1897 and 1953, seven of the nine presidents were Freemasons – McKinley, Theodore Roosevelt, Taft, Harding, Hoover, Franklin D. Roosevelt and Harry S. Truman. Only Woodrow Wilson and Calvin Coolidge were not Freemasons. In the forty-eight years since 1953 only two of the ten presidents – Lyndon Johnson and Gerald Ford – were Freemasons.

But these figures can be misleading. When the Freemason McKinley was elected President in 1896, he defeated the Democratic candidate, the Freemason William Jennings Bryan. Bryan was again defeated by McKinley in the 1900 election, and by the Freemason Taft in 1908, but was appointed Secretary of State by the non-mason Woodrow Wilson, after Wilson had defeated Taft and Theodore Roosevelt in 1912. The Freemason Thomas R. Marshall was Wilson's Vice-President from 1913 to 1921. Eisenhower was not a Freemason, but he appointed the Freemason James McKay to be his Secretary of the Interior.

During the twentieth century there were Freemasons on the Right, in the Centre, and on the Left of American politics. On the Right there was J. Edgar Hoover, the head of the Federal Bureau of Investigation, and General Douglas MacArthur; in the Centre Truman and Wendell Wilkie; on the Left, Franklin D. Roosevelt and his Vice-President Henry A. Wallace, who was denounced as a pro-Communist fellow-traveller after 1950.

Fiorello H. La Guardia, who was three times Mayor of New York City from 1934 to 1946, was a Freemason. He was denounced as a traitor by Mussolini because he, an Italian by origin, had strongly supported the United Nations and the Allied cause during the Second World War.

The list of eminent American citizens who have been Freemasons is so long that one is tempted to think that it would be quicker to

* For Madison, see *supra*, p. 108n.

name those who have not been Freemasons. The lists are not always reliable. Freemasons have sometimes claimed that distinguished men were their brothers when in fact they were not; and anti-masons have wrongly accused their enemies of being masons. The sons of famous men have sometimes denied, not always truthfully, that their father was a Freemason. Mistakes have been made because lodge records have been lost, and famous figures have sometimes been claimed as Freemasons because they have been confused with other people with the same name. But after all these factors have been taken into consideration, the list is impressive.

There have been generals – John J. Pershing in the First World War, and Omar Bradley and Mark Clark in the Second World War, as well as George Marshall of the Marshall Plan, and Douglas MacArthur.

There have been important business executives – the financier John Jacob Astor at the beginning of the nineteenth century, and in the twentieth century the motor car manufacturers Henry Ford, Walter P. Chrysler and Ransom E. Olds, who built the first three-wheeled 'horseless carriage' in 1886 and the first four-wheeled one in 1893; the inventor of the safety razor, King C. Gillette, president of the Gillette Safety Razor Company; Alexander J. Horlick, whose family firm invented malted milk and who became president of Horlick's Malted Milk Corporation; Andrew W. Mellon, President of Mellon National Bank; the businessman Melvin Jones, who founded the Lions charitable organisation in 1917; the pencil manufacturer Eberhard Faber, head of the Eberhard Faber Pencil Company of New York; James C. Penney, the founder of the large department store chain; and David Sarnoff, the radio and television executive.

And many more prominent Americans have been Freemasons:

John Fitch, who invented the speedboat at the end of the eighteenth century, though its importance was not recognised at the time and it was developed later by others; and Richard M. Hoe, inventor of the rotary press and the wet press for printing newspapers in 1847.

Charles Lindbergh, the first man to fly alone across the Atlantic Ocean in 1927, who became notorious for his pro-German sympathies during the Second World War; Edward V. Rickenbacker, who won fame as an airman in both the First and Second World Wars; the astronauts John Glenn, the first man to encircle the world in space in 1962 and who became a U.S. Senator for Ohio; James B. Irwin, the fourth man to land on the moon in 1971; and Virgil 'Gus' Grissom and Leroy Gordon Cooper.

Arctic explorers Dr Elisha Kent Kane, the young physician who went on two expeditions to the Arctic to search for Sir John Franklin in the 1850s; Robert E. Peary, who began exploring the Arctic from Greenland in 1896 and eventually became the first man to reach the North Pole in 1909; and Admiral Richard E. Byrd, who was the first to fly over the North Pole in 1926 and who led several Antarctic expeditions after 1928.

Armament manufacturers Samuel Colt, the inventor of the Colt rifle in 1835, and Richard J. Gatling, who invented the Gatling gun in 1862.

Samuel Gompers, the founder and first president of the powerful trade union the American Federation of Labor; the physicist Albert A. Michelson, who measured the speed of light in 1882; Manly P. Hall, the writer on metaphysics who founded the Philosophical Research Society in 1919; the early nineteenth-century architects James Hoban, who built the first White House and rebuilt it after it had been burned by the British in the War of 1812, and Benjamin H. Latrobe, who built the Roman Catholic cathedral in Baltimore, helped rebuild the White House, and installed the first water system in Philadelphia; the Austrian physician Franz Anton Mesmer, who introduced mesmerism, a form of hypnosis, as a medical treatment in Paris in 1778 before emigrating to the United States and joining a masonic lodge in Philadelphia; Dr Arthur T. Still, who lost three of his children from spinal meningitis in 1864 and ten years later adopted osteopathy as a form of medical treatment for the disease.

In the twentieth century there were the dermatologist Charles F. Pabst, who invented the term 'athlete's foot'; the eminent physician Dr Charles H. Mayo; and the psychiatrist Karl A. Menninger.

Edwin L. Drake, who first drilled for oil at Titusville, Pennsylvania, in 1859 for the Pennsylvania Rock Oil Company, the oldest petroleum company in the world; George M. Pullman, the engineer who built the first sleeping car for trains in 1858 and the first dining car ten years later; Charles C. Hilton, who, after managing hotels in Chicago, opened the first of his Hilton Hotels at the end of the nineteenth century; and Oscar Tschirsky, who as a twenty-seven-year-old immigrant from Switzerland became the *chef* at the Waldorf-Astoria Hotel in New York in 1893; the popular nineteenth-century journalist Richard A. Locke; Cornelius Hedges, who founded the first National Park in the United States at Yellowstone in Wyoming in 1872; Booker T. Washington, the African-American who at the end of the nineteenth and beginning of the twentieth centuries did so much to educate the members of his race and preach racial harmony; Daniel C. Beard, who started the Boy Pioneers in the United States in 1905, two years before Baden Powell began the Boy Scouts in Britain; and Christopher Diehl, who started the first masonic library in the United States.

In the twentieth century there was the sculptor and painter Gutzon Borglum, who began carving the gigantic National Monument at Mount Rushmore in South Dakota which would be completed by his son; the photographer Alvin L. Coburn; the horticulturist Luther Burbank; Hubert Eaton, who first replaced tombstones in cemeteries by tablets level with the ground; and Thomas Lowell, the popular author who wrote of his travels in India and the Middle East.

In the hundred years since moving pictures were invented Freemasons have played a leading part in the American film industry, as executives, producers, directors, scriptwriters and actors. The producers include Cecil B. DeMille, whose film *The Squaw Man* was the first major film to be made in Hollywood; Louis B. Meyer, of Metro-Goldwyn-Meyer; Florenz Ziegfeld; Darryl F. Zanuck, the cofounder of Twentieth Century Fox; and Jack L. Warner, the last survivor of the Warner Brothers, who first produced sound pictures in 1927. David W. Griffith outraged the liberals by directing *The Birth of a Nation* in 1915, which glorified the Ku Klux Klan and the supporters of white supremacy in the South after the Civil War; but he won liberal sympathy with his next film *Intolerance* in 1916, in which he attacked the oppressors of peoples throughout history, including a twentieth-century lawyer who in order to further his political career frames an innocent victim in a trial that is a miscarriage of justice.

The actors have included many native-born Americans and immigrants from Europe, both in the early silent films and in later talking pictures. Harold Lloyd, W. C. Fields, Douglas Fairbanks Sr, Al Jolson, Clark Gable, Tom Mix, Oliver Hardy of the Laurel and Hardy films, Ernest Borgnine and Eddie Cantor; Elmo Lincoln, the first actor to play Tarzan of the Apes in a film; Audie Murphy, who played the frightened soldier in *The Red Badge of Courage*, and in real life was the most decorated hero of the Second World War; the comedians and television stars Arthur Godfrey and Red Skelton; Roy Rogers; and John Wayne.

Many composers of popular music have been Freemasons: the

composer of famous military marches, John Philip Sousa; Irving Berlin, who in a long career composed 'Alexander's Ragtime Band', the music for *Top Hat* and other Fred Astaire and Ginger Rogers films, and many other well-known pieces; George M. Cohan, who composed 'Yankee Doodle Dandy' and the patriotic song 'Over There (The Yanks are Coming)', which aroused support for the intervention of the United States in the First World War; and the African-American jazz composers, musicians and band leaders Louis Armstrong, Duke Ellington, Nat King Cole, Paul Whiteman and William 'Count' Basie.

In sport there are the boxer Jack Dempsey and African-American boxers Jack Johnson and Sugar Ray Robinson; and the baseball players Ty Cobb, Rogers Hornsby and Branch Rickey.

The smallest and tallest men on record were Freemasons. In the nineteenth century the midget Charles S. Stratton, who was exhibited by the circus manager P. T. Barnum as 'General Tom Thumb', was two feet in height. Robert Pershing Wadlow, who was nearly nine feet tall, died at the age of twenty-two in 1940. In circus entertainment, the six Ringling brothers, who developed the performance that became known as *The Greatest Show on Earth*, were masons.

Some of the traditional heroes of the American West in the nineteenth century were Freemasons – Kit Carson and William F. Cody (Buffalo Bill), who became a member of the legislature in Nebraska. So was the famous nineteenth-century journalist Richard A. Locke; and in the twentieth century Norman Vincent Peale, the famous Protestant clergyman, preacher and best-selling author; the performer Houdini, with his vanishing conjuring trick; and the cartoonist George McManus.

The Freemasons can claim to have had several distinguished judges among their brothers. The most eminent is undoubtedly John Marshall, who was Chief Justice of the U.S. Supreme Court for thirty-four years from 1801 to 1835, when he died at the age of seventy-seven. He did more than anyone to mould the Constitution of the United States and to establish the role of the Supreme Court as the upholder of the constitutional rights of American citizens. More recently Earl Warren was Chief Justice, from 1953 to 1969, playing the leading part in a series of judicial decisions that established the rights of the African-Americans and other minority groups.[9]

Whatever may be said about the fall in masonic influence in the last seventy years, the Freemasons in the United States are still more numerous, wealthier and more secure than in any other country. In 1998 there were 12,841 mainstream lodges with 2,066,216 Freemasons, and in addition 4,243 Prince Hall lodges with 200,817 members.[10] This is still nearly half of all the Freemasons in the world. The Freemasons, so many of whom are successful businessmen, are wealthy. This is shown by the splendid halls where their lodges meet. In England Freemasons' Hall in London, the headquarters of English Grand Lodge, is a magnificent building, though there is no other masonic building in England of comparable grandeur. The ordinary Freemason lodge meets, in some cases, in small, old, dilapidated buildings where they first convened in the seventeenth and eighteenth centuries; in other cases they meet in expensive hotels and restaurants which the Freemasons regularly patronise, and occasionally in medium-sized modern buildings belonging to the lodge. Many lodges in the United States are almost as impressive as Freemasons' Hall in London.

The expense of maintaining these splendid buildings is one of the reasons why Freemasons' lodges in the United States are much larger than in Britain. There are several lodges in the United States with more than a thousand members, whereas in Britain very few lodges have more than a hundred members. In the United States, when the membership of a lodge falls to a hundred, they consider the possibility of amalgamating with another lodge.

In 1920, as the result of a campaign waged by influential groups who disapproved of drinking alcohol, a constitutional amendment was created that prohibited the drinking of alcohol throughout the United States. This would not have suited the English Freemasons. They no longer indulge in the heavy drinking of their forebears in the eighteenth century, when it was said that one of the Freemasons' secrets was the name of the brother who had succeeded in drinking the other brothers under the table at the last lodge dinner; but the English Freemasons still normally drink the Queen's health and other toasts at their dinners in champagne and other wines. The Freemasons in the United States happily accepted Prohibition; several lodges had already given up drinking alcohol and joined the campaign that led to the imposition of Prohibition.

Now most Freemasons' lodges in the United States drink toasts in wine, either during or after the dinner. There are regular toasts – 'To our country', followed by a pledge of loyalty to the flag of the

United States; to the President of the United States; to their Grand Lodge; to the brothers who are serving in the armed forces; to the departed brothers.

The Freemasons in the United States are as eager as the British Freemasons to dissociate themselves from the revolutionary Freemasons of the Grand Orient and the Lautaro lodges of France, Italy, Spain and South America. Both in Britain and in the United States the Freemasons are closely identified with the Establishment; but while in Britain this is done through their association with the aristocracy and the royal family, in the United States it is shown by devotion to the national flag. In Britain and the United States a copy of the Volume of the Sacred Law – which in Christian lodges is the Bible, but in other lodges can be the Koran of the Muslims or the sacred book of any other religion – must lie open throughout the proceedings; but in the United States the Stars and Stripes must also always be displayed. There is nothing like this in a British lodge; having the Queen's cousin as their Grand Master, they can dispense with the Union Jack.

Both the British and the American lodges place great emphasis on the fact that they ban all political discussion in the lodges; but just as the English Freemasons, when they drafted Anderson's Constitutions in 1723, combined a ban on political discussion with declarations of loyalty to George I, the House of Hanover and the Protestant Succession, so the Freemasons in the United States combine a ban on political discussion with expressions of devotion to country and flag. Not only must the Stars and Stripes be displayed at every lodge meeting, but periodically in every lodge, and at every meeting of a Grand Lodge, Freemasons perform what is colloquially called 'the Flag Ceremony', officially known as 'The Reception of the Flag of our Country'. Some lodge members leave the room and return carrying the Stars and Stripes which they hand to the lodge master, who leads the members in pledging their loyalty to the flag to the accompaniment of the singing of 'America' or 'The Star Spangled Banner'.[11]

The American Freemasons are as much an organisation of the Establishment as the British Freemasons; but the Establishment in Britain is different from the Establishment in the United States. In Britain the Establishment is a hereditary monarchy and a hereditary aristocracy; in the United States it consists of self-made businessmen, or, if they are people who have inherited their wealth from self-made men of an earlier generation, are successful entrepreneurs. In Britain increasing numbers of people are coming to regard the royal family and the hereditary aristocracy as obsolete, or at least as out-of-date; in the United States, the successful businessman is still admired. He is much less likely than the British aristocrat or member of the royal family to be the object of popular hostility.

The American Freemasons have not been immune from attack, but their critics are not taken very seriously. The media millionaire Pat Robertson, who made an unsuccessful attempt to become President of the United States when he ran in the Republican primaries in 1988, has attacked them in his book *The New World Order* which he published in 1991, and on many other occasions. The Baptist minister Dr John Ankerberg, president of the Ankerberg Theological Research Institute, who has attacked homosexuals, the supporters of abortion, and other dissident groups, also denounced the Freemasons in his 1990 pamphlet *The Secret Teachings of the Masonic Lodge: A Christian Perspective*. A Texan physician, Dr James L. Holly, joined in the attack. But though Pat Robertson is a well-known public figure, able to give himself widespread television coverage, there is no reason to believe that his attacks on the Freemasons are taken seriously by the viewers who watch his television programmes. The Freemasons have had no difficulty in exposing the weakness of the arguments of Pat Robertson, Askerberg and Holly. Some of them go back more than a hundred years and revive the allegations that Taxil made against Pike and his Scottish Rite in the days of Diana Vaughan.[12]

The Freemasons in the United States, with their deep roots in the American way of life and widespread influence among their fellow-citizens, need not worry unduly if they form a smaller percentage of the total population than they did seventy years ago, or if fewer Freemasons have been President of the United States in the second than in the first half of the twentieth century. They have more cause to be anxious about the decline of their influence among African-Americans. Prince Hall Freemasonry has lost its influence among the younger generation. In several states, Prince Hall Grand Lodges have closed down and the number of Prince Hall Freemasons is falling.

But the Freemasons need not be unduly alarmed. Their position in the United States is much more secure than in any other country. In Croatia and France, with their traditions of Right-wing Catholic attacks on revolutionary Freemasonry, the anti-masonic campaign is reviving. In April 2001 a book was published in France that received great publicity. Ghislaine Ottenheimer and Renaud Lecadre, in *Les Frères invisibles*, renewed all the accusations against 'the invisible brothers', the Freemasons, which had been made by the anti-masons from the time of Barruel in the eighteenth century to Fay and Pétain under the Vichy regime sixty years ago. They write of how Philippe Egalité voted for the death of his cousin Louis XVI; of how the Freemasons were encouraged by Napoleon; how in the early days of the Third Republic Freemasons plotted against the conservatives at the time of the Dreyfus case. Turning to the present day, every recent financial scandal and Left-wing political development is said to have been planned at secret meetings of Freemasons, and prominent French and foreign politicians, who have never been Freemasons, are accused of having been secretly admitted into a Freemasons' lodge. Ottenheimer and Lecadre would have their readers believe that the sinister influence of the Freemasons constitutes a threat to democracy and public life in France.[13]

In Britain the attack on the Freemasons is more likely to come from Radical and Left-wing circles. There is public suspicion of Freemasons, which the English Grand Lodge policy of revealing their activities has not been able to dispel entirely. There are demands from official bodies that men employed in certain occupations, particularly the police, should be forced to declare whether or not they are Freemasons.

This could not happen in America today. It is difficult to believe that any federal or state authority in the United States would issue orders to compel a man to declare whether or not he is a Freemason, even without the knowledge that any such action would be banned by the courts as a violation of the Freemasons' constitutional rights. In America Freemasons are generally respected, not hated or feared. Whoever may be the victims of the next outburst of popular hysteria in the United States, it will not be the Freemasons. One hundred and seventy-five years after the disappearance of William Morgan, the Freemasons are safe. They will not be the target of the next witchhunt, but will watch it complacently from the sidelines, since discussion about it will be banned in the lodges under the 'no politics' rule.

CHAPTER 22

Are the Freemasons a Menace?

ENGLISH Freemasonry was unable to continue in its comfortable Edwardian past without being involved in controversy. In the second half of the twentieth century Freemasonry came under attack. The first assault came from the Reverend Walton Hannah, a clergyman of the Church of England who soon afterwards became a Roman Catholic, chiefly because the Roman Catholic Church was less tolerant than the Church of England towards Freemasonry. In his book *Darkness Visible* he attacked the Freemasons; but although he made a few allegations which hinted at a masonic conspiracy – he wrote about attempts to bribe him not to publish the book, and of threats to his publisher – his criticism of the Freemasons was chiefly theological. He argued that the Freemasons' Great Architect of the Universe was not the Christian God, and that therefore Christians, particularly bishops of the Church of England, should not be Freemasons. *Darkness Visible* and Hannah's next book, *Christian by Degrees*, greatly annoyed those Anglican clergymen who had become Freemasons; but Hannah did not succeed in weakening Freemasonry, and his books were soon forgotten, perhaps because his arguments were too theological and intellectual.

A more threatening and successful attack on the Freemasons was launched in the 1980s by the popular writer Stephen Knight. He claimed that he was exposing Freemasonry as a conspiracy by the Freemasons to help each other against the rest of the world. According to Knight, Freemasons in official positions, having sworn to do this by their fearful masonic oaths, with the bloodcurdling penalties for breaking their oaths, place their loyalty to their masonic brothers above their public duties. They help each other to obtain employment and promotion, so that in some organisations, like the City of

London with its livery companies and the governing bodies of the corporation, it is virtually impossible for anyone who is not a Freemason to be appointed to influential positions. Freemasons recognize each other by their secret signs and phrases; and when a Freemason recognizes a masonic brother who has made a secret sign to him, he will help him instead of doing his duty.

Knight and his supporters assert that a Freemason who is a policeman will allow a criminal to evade justice if the criminal has identified himself as a Freemason by a secret sign; and stories are told of judges who, when trying a case in court, gave judgment in favour of a Freemason who made a secret sign to the judge. The anti-masons argue that from this it follows that the enforcement of law and order, and the administration of justice, is thwarted when policemen and judges are Freemasons. All Freemasons should be compelled by law to identify themselves to the general public, so that their actions can be scrutinised by the public, and the extent of their influence revealed.

Knight began his campaign to expose the Freemasons in a book *Jack the Ripper: the Final Solution*, which he published in 1976, about the murders committed by the killer known as Jack the Ripper which shocked London in 1888.[1] The murderer, who wrote taunting letters to the police signed 'Jack the Ripper' and claiming to be the murderer, killed five, or probably six, prostitutes in the very poor working-class district of Whitechapel in the East End of London, and disembowelled them in a manner not dissimilar from the form of killing referred to in the initiation proceedings in masonic lodges. The murders were committed at night, sometimes in the victim's house and sometimes in the street. The first woman was killed on 31 August 1888, and the second on 8 September. On 30 September two women were killed on the same night within about an hour of each other. The fifth murder was committed on 9 November. It then seemed as if the murderer had stopped, but a very similar type of murder of a prostitute was committed on 18 July 1889. This was the last of the killings.

Jack the Ripper was never caught, and his identity is still a mystery. Several books have been written giving the author's opinion as to who he was; he is usually identified as a man who was afterwards caught and executed for another murder which had no connection with the Ripper killings. But none of these solutions can be proved. There was a popular belief in the 1890s that an eccentric clergyman who held open-air revivalist prayer meetings on the beach at Margate in the summer was Jack the Ripper; but there was probably no truth at all in this story.

Stephen Knight, in *Jack the Ripper: The Final Solution*, put forward the most far-fetched theory of all – that the murders were committed by the Freemasons at the instigation of Queen Victoria's Freemason doctor, Sir William Gull, and with the connivance of the Freemason Chief of the Metropolitan Police, Sir Charles Warren. Knight asserted that Prince Albert Edward, Duke of Clarence, the weak-minded son of the Prince of Wales (the future Edward VII) who was, after his father, the heir to the throne, had secretly married a Roman Catholic woman without the consent of his grandmother the Queen, which was legally required by the Royal Marriages Act. This woman bore him a child.

The Prime Minister, Lord Salisbury, asked Gull to arrange for this Roman Catholic woman to be imprisoned in a private lunatic asylum. But five prostitutes knew about this, and Salisbury asked Dr Gull to silence them. Gull, being a Freemason, considered that the prostitutes were traitors to the nation and should therefore be disposed of as if they were Freemasons who had betrayed masonic secrets. So he sent two Freemasons to murder the five prostitutes and disembowel them in the traditional masonic manner.

An incident occurred in connection with the second of the two murders committed on 30 September 1888. A policeman walked through Mitre Square in Whitechapel at 1.25 a.m. and saw nothing unusual there; but when he went there again a quarter of an hour later, at 1.40 a.m., he found the disembowelled body of a prostitute. He also saw that someone had chalked on the wall in the square: 'The Jewes are The Men That will not be blamed for nothing'.

When Sir Charles Warren was told about the writing on the wall, he ordered it to be washed off. He gave as his reason that he feared that if it were seen by passers-by, it might trigger off anti-Jewish riots in the East End; but Warren was criticized for erasing the writing, because the handwriting might have revealed clues as to the murderer's identity which would have enabled him to be caught. Knight, in his book, stated that 'the Jews' is a phrase used by Freemasons to refer to Jubela, Jubelo and Jubelum, who figure in the story about the murder of Hiram Abiff at the time of the building of Solomon's temple. Sir Charles Warren, being a Freemason, realized that the inscription on the wall about the Jews referred to Jubela, Jubelo and Jubelum, and that it meant that the Freemasons had committed the Jack the Ripper murders. This was why he ordered the writing to be washed off. Knight stated that the inscription about the Jews, and the fact that Warren ordered it to be erased, was kept secret for nearly 90 years until Knight discovered it in the secret files of Scotland Yard in the 1970s. He also stated that Warren never gave any explanation as to why he ordered the writing on the wall to be washed out.

But Knight's assertions about this are untrue. The existence of the writing on the wall, and the fact that Warren ordered it to be erased, was not kept secret for 90 years, but was discussed in several books about Jack the Ripper in the 1930s, where the reason that Warren gave for erasing the writing – that he feared that it might cause anti-Jewish riots – was also discussed. But this did not prevent Knight from further developing his theory about the Freemasons and Jack the Ripper in his book *The Brotherhood* in 1984. He wrote that 'Warren impeded the Ripper investigation at every stage', and that this shows there was 'an official cover-up of immense proportions that confirms that Freemasonry really was the unseen power behind the throne and government alike'.[2]

Knight's story collapses at every stage. Jubela, Jubelo and Jubelum are not referred to as 'the Jews' by Freemasons. The existence of the writing on the wall, and Warren's reason for erasing it, were not kept secret for 90 years. Knight does not explain how the five murdered prostitutes found out about the Duke of Clarence's marriage, or why Gull should have thought that their action in revealing it should be punished as if they had been Freemasons who had revealed masonic secrets. Nor does he give any explanation as to why the murderers should have written the inscription about the Jews on the wall, thus identifying the Freemasons – if Knight's theory were correct – as the murderers, when they presumably would have wished to keep this a deathly secret.

Lord Salisbury, an easygoing statesman and a very devout member of the Church of England, is very unlikely to have participated in murder, even in order to hush up a scandal involving the royal family. Nor is there any reason to believe that Sir William Gull would have ordered Freemasons to murder anyone. As for Sir Charles Warren, this was not the only occasion on which he was criticized for an error of judgement in his actions as Chief of the Metropolitan Police; but all historians, not only masonic historians, owe him a debt of gratitude for his part in founding that most learned historical society, the Freemasons' Ars Quatuor Coronatorum lodge, and the journal in which they publish their most informative and balanced articles on masonic history.

Knight's book *The Brotherhood* in 1984 was followed by Martin Short's even more fanciful books *Inside the Brotherhood: Further Secrets of the Freemasons* in 1989 and *Lundy: the Destruction of Scotland Yard's Finest Detective* in 1991. By the time *Inside the Brotherhood* was published, Stephen Knight had died at the age of 33 from epilepsy brought on by being struck on the head with a bat while playing cricket. Short just – but only just – refrains from saying that Knight was murdered by the Freemasons because he had criticized them in *The Brotherhood*; but he says that many Freemasons firmly believe that their masonic brothers murdered him.[3] In *Lundy: the Destruction of Scotland Yard's Finest Detective* Short alleges that Lundy, a Scotland Yard detective, was framed and dismissed from his post because he refused to participate in a plot by the Freemasons at Scotland Yard to help their masonic brothers escape justice.

In reading the books of Knight and Short, two points must be borne in mind. The first is that some policemen are corrupt, and some judges give legal decisions that are sometimes very difficult to understand and explain. In the case of the police, it is inevitable, and indeed desirable and necessary, that detectives meet criminals, talk to them and have drinks with them, and at least pretend to become friendly with them, in the hope of obtaining useful information. They may, must and often do go further and make bargains, though they publicly deny this to avoid criticism from judges and from public opinion.

The second point is that detectives, barristers and judges tend to have a somewhat cynical sense of humour, and often make jokes in private at their own expense and about their profession which should not be taken too seriously, even by writers of popular books about Freemasons. When members of the public believe, and politicians and other persons who appear on television state, that our British police force is the best in the world, experienced policemen know that, while it may perhaps be the best in the world, it is nevertheless much less good than it ought to be. When these same politicians and television personalities indignantly reject the suggestion that Libyans accused of committing acts of terrorism should be tried in a neutral country and not in Scotland – because this would imply that British justice is not perfect and infallible – experienced barristers and judges know that it may be fairer than in other countries, but that it is not unknown for innocent people to be convicted in British courts; and because they cannot, or do not wish to, say this in public, they are all the more likely to say so in private.

It is those policemen and judges who make these remarks in a jocular and cynical manner who disapprove most strongly of the corruption and injustice, and are most likely to try their best to stamp them out; while those politicians and opinion-formers who denounce most loudly the corruption and racial prejudice in the police force are usually the same as those who yesterday placed restrictions on the power of the police authorities to punish corrupt and racially-prejudiced policemen by introducing safeguards to ensure a fair hearing for the accused policeman, out of sympathy for, or fear of, the police and other trade unions.

In his book about Lundy, Short described a dinner held at the Royal Lancaster Hotel in 1980 by a masonic lodge which consists almost exclusively of policemen who are Freemasons. The brothers were, as usual, allowed to bring a guest, and one policeman brought as his guest a well-known criminal. During the dinner a raffle was held, and the well-known criminal won the first prize, which was a TV set. As he went to collect the prize, another policeman present whispered to his neighbour that this was the first TV set that the criminal had acquired without stealing it. Everything about this story rings very true; but when Short draws the conclusion that some masonic lodges are not 'a column of mutual defence and support' as the Freemasons claim, but 'cells of crime and corruption', we should ask him if he is sure that corrupt, or honest, policemen have never taken a criminal as their guest to some dinner that had nothing whatever to do with the Freemasons.[4]

The famous story has often been told about the trial of the poisoner Frederick Seddon before Mr Justice Bucknill in 1912 for the murder of Mrs Barrow. When Seddon had been found guilty and was asked if he had anything that he wished to say before the judge passed sentence, he swore that he was not guilty 'by the Great Architect of the Universe'. Mr Justice Bucknill was a well-known Freemason, and he realised from Seddon's words that Seddon too was a Freemason. Bucknill was old and ill, and had shown signs during the trial of being emotionally affected by the strain of summing-up; and in passing sentence of death on Seddon he said that Seddon's words showed that they were both members of the same praiseworthy society, and that, though this would increase his distress at sentencing Seddon to death, it could not prevent him from doing his duty. Knight turns on its head this story, which has so often been cited in favour of the Freemasons, and argues that the judge's distress was caused by his sorrow that Seddon had not revealed that he was a Freemason at an earlier stage in the trial; if he had, Mr Justice Bucknill could have summed up in his favour and handled the trial in such a way that the jury would not have returned a verdict of guilty.[5]

Short tells many stories of incidents which were told to him by High Court judges who made him promise not to reveal their names. One judge mentioned a case when another judge was hearing a petition for custody of the children in divorce proceedings between husband and wife. The judge intervened during the husband's examination and cross-examination by counsel in such a way as to show that he was strongly in favour of the wife, until the husband brushed his hand through his hair, turning his hand as he did so. This was a masonic secret sign, and as soon as the judge saw it, he immediately changed his attitude, and after a few more questions gave judgment for the husband, awarding him the custody of the children.

This sounds an unlikely incident, and the anonymous judge who spoke to Short was probably just telling a good story. It is not at all unusual for a judge who is not a Freemason to give the impression during a trial of being in favour of one of the parties when he has in fact decided to give judgment against him. Judges do this in order to show, or to give the impression, that they have not been biased from the beginning against the litigant who loses.

Short is on safer and stronger ground when he writes in *Inside the Brotherhood*[6] about the case of the Italian Freemasons in the P2 lodge and the death of Roberto Calvi. The P2 lodge of the Italian Grant Orient was founded by Lucio Gelli. He had been an active Fascist fighting for Mussolini's Italian Social Republic in the north against the Communist Partisans in 1944. He led raids by the Fascists to defeat and capture the Partisans, who were then invariably executed; but Gelli, like other Fascists in the same position, thought that it was possible that the Allies might win the war, and that the Communist Partisans would then be able to revenge themselves on the Fascists. So he thought that it would be prudent to keep in with them; and when he led the Fascists in their raids on the Partisans, he secretly tipped off the Partisans that he and his Fascists were coming. This enabled the Partisans to escape before the Fascists arrived; but it was not enough to enable Gelli to convince the Communists and the anti-Fascist tribunals after the war that he had always really been a member of the resistance movement, and he ran away to Argentina in 1945. After he had spent some years in Argentina, he returned to Italy on an Argentine diplomatic passport, and was soon able to take advantage of an amnesty which exempted him from prosecution for his Fascist activities in 1943–45.

He became a shady business man, dealing particularly in trade with Romania at the height of the Cold War, when the borderline between legal and black-market transactions with Eastern Europe was sometimes difficult to determine. These trading activities brought him into contact with financiers and export managers, and with politicians both of the extreme Right, the Liberal Centre, and the Italian Communists. He formed a new masonic lodge which was called the P2 lodge of the Grand Orient. The members of the lodge included 43 MPs, among them 3 Cabinet ministers; 43 generals, 8 admirals, many heads of the government civil service, 24 journalists, and the most important people in Italian television. When the financial frauds in which Gelli had been involved with the Romanians became known, there was an uproar, and the incident was used to discredit the Freemasons. The Italian Grand Orient put forward the usual and plausible masonic excuse that there are always a few bad apples in any barrel; they expelled the P2 lodge from the Grand Orient. This did not, of course, appease the critics, who said that the expulsion was a sham, and that really P2 continued to work closely with the Grand Orient.

Gelli was convicted of fraud in Switzerland, and sentenced to a term of imprisonment in a Swiss jail; but he escaped in 1985 and fled to Uruguay. He later voluntarily returned to Italy to face trial there on various charges of fraud, and managed to drag out the proceedings, for many years. Eventually, in April 1992, he was found guilty and sentenced to eighteen years and six months imprisonment; but he was immediately released from custody pending the hearing of his appeal. The proceedings are still continuing.[7]

It was perhaps because the Italian Parliamentary report on the P2 scandal was published in 1984, so soon after the Calvi affair, that people hastened to connect the Freemasons with Calvi's death. Calvi was the chairman of an important and exclusive private bank, the Banco Ambrosiano, which had some important clients, including both Gelli and the Vatican. In June 1982 Calvi was told that the Bank of Italy wished to question him about $1,400 million which had disappeared, and he decided to leave immediately for London. He had many friends in England; some of them were Freemasons.

On the night of 19 June 1982 Calvi's body was found hanging on the railings of Blackfriars Bridge in London from a noose around his neck. The coroner's inquest returned a verdict that he had committed suicide by hanging himself. But then a number of curious facts emerged and were published in the Italian press. He had in his pocket some stones and straw, and enough drugs to enable him to take a lethal dose. People wrote articles and spoke on television, asking pertinent questions: if he had wished to commit suicide, why did he not simply swallow an overdose of the drugs in the house in Hampstead where he was staying, rather than going to Blackfriars Bridge and hanging himself there. And why did he have stones and straw in his pocket?

Articles were published in the Italian press criticising and ridiculing the suicide verdict. As it was clear that the inquest had been superficial and unsatisfactory – as inquests so often are today – a second inquest was held in June 1983. The verdict of the first inquest was overruled, and a new verdict was returned – an open verdict of death from causes unknown. But the matter did not rest there; *The Times* sent a reporter to question the foreman of the coroner's jury – another phenomenon of modern times. The foreman said he was sure that if the second jury had been told all the facts that he now knew, they would have returned a verdict of murder.

More and more people believed that murder was much the most likely explanation. The evidence indicated that Calvi was kidnapped by hired killers, taken out in a boat on the Thames, murdered in the boat, and that his body was then heaved up from the boat with a rope around his neck after he was dead, and his corpse left hanging on the bridge.

So far the arguments are convincing; but at this point the Freemasons enter the story, and with them enter nonsense and hysteria. As Gelli was one of the customers at Calvi's bank, P2 and the Freemasons must have been involved; and Calvi had told his friends that on a previous visit to London he had attended a masonic lodge. The members of this lodge included not only a very wealthy business man, Peter de Savary, but also several members of the royal family.

As the only members of the royal family who were active Freemasons in 1982 were the Duke of Kent and Prince Michael of Kent, and they both belonged to Royal Alpha Number 16 Lodge, this must have been the lodge which Calvi visited (unless he was referring to a visit to London in earlier years, when King George VI and Prince Philip, Duke of Edinburgh, belonged to a Navy Lodge Number 2612).

Short and his anti-masonic colleagues do not consider a third possibility – that Calvi, who was an absconding chairman of a bank and had been accused of embezzling nearly $1.5 billion, might have invented the whole story about attending a lodge and meeting a millionaire and several members of the royal family.

The anti-masons discovered other evidence incriminating the Freemasons. Calvi's killers had hanged him, after they had already murdered him, because the noose around his neck resembled the cabletow which is hung around the new mason's neck in the ceremony when he is first initiated as a Freemason. They put the stones and straw in his pockets because Freemasons believe that when a man is first initiated, he is like a rough uncut stone, and that he is gradually hewn into a 'Perfect Ashler'. They hanged him from Blackfriars Bridge because the Freemasons in the Italian P2 lodge perform their ceremonies dressed up in black cassocks like Dominican friars, who are known in history as the Black Friars. The bridge is just within the jurisdiction of the City of London Police force, who are, in Short's words, 'steeped in Freemasonry'; and the bridge is within sight of the Temple Gardens, which is most significant, as the Freemasons are descended from the Knights Templars of the fourteenth century.

Finally, Short brings out his last and conclusive argument. Calvi must have been murdered either by the Mafia or by the Italian Freemasons; but no one has suggested that the Mafia have any links in London, whereas two Italian Freemasons named Florio Carboni and Sylvano Vittot accompanied Calvi on his visit to London. Carboni had contact with a British Freemason while he was in London with Calvi. Short then draws the conclusion: 'No evidence links any British masons with a plot to kill Calvi, but . . .'[8]

I have referred at some length to Short's book because it seems to me that, like the writings of his friend Stephen Knight, it is an excellent example of the point which I made in Chapter 18: that while there was at least some basis in fact for the anti-masonic arguments of Prichard, Le Franc, Barruel and Robison in the eighteenth century, and of Eckert, Bernard and John Quincy Adams in the nineteenth, the enemies of Freemasonry in the last 120 years – Taxil, Nilus, Ludendorff, Custos and the latest batch of English popular writers and their counterparts on television, have taken anti-masonry into the realms of fantasy. There were certainly Freemasons in the P2 lodge, and perhaps Italian Freemasons in other lodges, who would have been glad to get rid of Calvi; there were people in the Vatican who would have been equally glad to see him out of the way. It is certainly not impossible that some of them might have hired a professional killer to carry out the murder. It is possible that they hired killers in the Mafia; and it is possible, in the days of air travel and the links between the countries of the European Union, that professional hitmen could travel from Italy to London to commit the murder even if, unlike the Italian Freemasons, they did not have Mafiosi brothers in London.

It is even possible that many of these incriminating facts have been invented, or greatly exaggerated; that Calvi did in fact commit suicide – he had reason to do so – and that there is some other explanation which has not yet been put forward of the facts which conflict with suicide. It is possible that these clues of the rope, the stones and the straw were deliberately planted in order to incriminate the Freemasons. But the thing that is most difficult to believe is that even the coolest and most professional of hitmen would make no mistakes at all, and would remember, as they hastened to depart after murdering Calvi, that the Dominicans were known as the Black Friars and that the Temple Gardens were once the home of the Knights Templars who were the ancestors of the Freemasons.

The Freemasons are the first to admit that some masons are evil, fraudulent and corrupt; but other men who are not Freemasons are sometimes evil, fraudulent and corrupt. There have been brilliant young financial wizards who were not Freemasons who thought that they would 'borrow' money from their company or bank and play about with it on the stock exchanges, make a great profit, and then repay the money; but the value of the shares unexpectedly fell, and they found that they could not repay it. There have been criminals of every nationality engaged in illicit traffic in drugs, or stealing gold bars, who have hired hitmen to murder their rivals. We can be sure that none of these criminals was a Freemason, for we would certainly have been told if they were.

The Freemasons also admit that forty or fifty years ago, and also more recently, some brothers have joined the craft, as they put it, 'for the wrong reasons'. They mean that these Freemasons joined because they thought that they would get some benefit from joining, not in order to do good and improve themselves and to contribute to the many charitable foundations, both masonic and non-masonic, to which the Freemasons give a large part of their great wealth, as even their opponents admit.

Organizations tend to become what their opponents accuse them of being. When the Catholic Church in the eighteenth century accused the Freemasons of plotting revolution in their lodges, many young revolutionaries joined the Freemasons, and in due course the masonic lodges really did become the centres of revolutionary agitation. In the first half of the twentieth century, everybody said that the Freemasons were a mutual aid society where the members helped each other to get good jobs, even if they did not help brothers who committed crimes. The people who wanted to get good jobs and to have influential friends became Freemasons. There are many men today in their sixties and seventies – and no doubt some younger ones – who were advised by their parents, uncles or schoolmasters to become Freemasons.

The Freemasons also point out that it is not only in masonic lodges that people meet useful friends who give them the good jobs that they do not give to people whom they have not met socially. They say that in this they are no different from a golf club. In one sense this is true, but it is not the whole truth. Members of golf clubs do not take oaths not to reveal the secrets of the club. They do not insist that all members of the club believe in God, though until recently in Britain, and still today in parts of the United States, they do insist that no Jew shall be admitted as a member. Above all, members of golf clubs have not allowed a mantle of secrecy to be placed around them.

It is the secrecy which still today, as always, is the trouble. Edward VII, when Prince of Wales and Grand Master, said that the Freemasons were a secret society, but not a dangerous one[9]; but this is too subtle a distinction to impress their critics or the general public. The Freemasons today insist that they are not a secret society; that they publish a year-book with the list of the names of their Grand Master and the officials of Grand Lodge and of thousands of other masters of lodges all over England and Wales; that they have even published, and put on sale, books in which their former secret rituals and 'mason words' are published; that they have shown part of their ceremonies in a video which is on sale to the public; that many of their secret phrases – 'on the square' is only one example – have become part of the English language; that in the books in which they reveal their ritual only a few especially sacred words – the name of God, Jahbulon, is one of them – have been left blank; and that these missing words have in any case often been disclosed to the world by deserting brothers.

But if a non-mason, a 'cowan' as they call him, begins asking questions, he will find that only the highest officials of Grand Lodge are really responsive. At only a slightly lower level, the master and officials of the district and the local lodges will reply to inquiries either by evasion or by silence.

In the 1720s there were sceptics who thought that the only secrets that the Freemasons had were the names of the society ladies whom they had seduced, and the identity of the brother who had succeeded in drinking the other brothers under the table at the last lodge meeting. There is less heavy drinking today, though masons still enjoy good food and wine. Is it true, as has so often been suggested, that, as in G. K. Chesterton's Father Brown story *The Purple Wig*, the great secret revealed when the wig was removed was that the wearer of the wig had nothing to hide? This has probably always been true of English Freemasonry since 1717, though it was, of course, not true – and is still not true – of the revolutionaries in the Lautaro lodges, or those who today are facing the most cruel persecution, torture and death in the illegal lodges in Iran, Afghanistan and other countries where the Muslim Fundamentalists have come to power.

The Freemasons always insist that they are not a religion. It is easy to see why they are so insistent about this: if Freemasonry is a religion, the Archbishop of Canterbury and his bishops, the Chief Rabbi and a few Catholic Freemasons should not be attending meetings of a religion which is a different one from that of which they are prominent leaders. Yet Freemasons talk about their meetings and their ritual, which is a joke to many cowans, in the reverend tones which a Roman Catholic adopts in the confessional or during Mass.

When I was researching for this book, a leading Freemason told me he was sure that a higher percentage of Freemasons than of the general public go to church on Sundays, which may well be true in a country in which so few people regularly attend church every week.

Not everyone will think this is the best criterion by which a man's virtue and morals should be judged; but however this may be, the Freemason can certainly claim to be one of the few organizations where words like 'virtue' and 'morals' are taken seriously, and are not regarded only as something ridiculous which interferes with the sacred pursuit of making money.

The Freemasons' attitude towards women seems extraordinarily out of date. They are outstandingly kind to their wives and to their female employees, who are far less likely to encounter harassment or disrespect from Freemasons than from many employers or higher business executives. But the Freemasons not merely exclude women from their own ranks but also refuse to have any dealings with any other society that accepts women. They are not violating the Sex Discrimination Act, which allow members of private clubs to exclude people because of their sex; and most women, and most wives, say that they do not object if men, including their husbands, wish to spend an afternoon or evening from time to time with other men at lunches or dinners from which women are excluded. Most women do not enjoy – to the extent that men do – dressing up in uniforms and taking part in ceremonies that are hundreds of years out of date. For this reason, most women do not wish to join either masonic lodges or City livery companies, and are perfectly happy to go to an occasional guest night, letting their husbands attend the other dinners and functions with other men only.

But even in the reign of George I, in the days of Hogarth and *The Beggar's Opera*, people commented adversely on the fact that the Freemasons excluded women; and this seems even more strange today, when women are playing an increasingly important part in the professions, in commerce, in big business – to say nothing of the literary and showbiz world. Already in the last year of the century and the Millennium, a great and powerful multinational organization suffers less dislocation (save in some exceptional cases) if the chairman has a heart attack than if his secretary takes her annual holiday or goes into hospital to have a baby; and a young lady who appears regularly on television and is not only beautiful, but also gives the impression of being caring and kind, exercises far more political and public influence than the members of any Freemasons' lodge. Perhaps it is a sound instinct of self-preservation which makes the Freemasons exclude women; for by the year 2030, if not earlier, no one will believe that a society which excludes women, and consists solely of old and middle-aged men, can possibly exercise any influence in political or public life, either for good or for evil.

But in 1999 many people still believe all the stories, however ridiculous, that are told about Freemasons, and are calling for legislation to restrict Freemasons' rights. At present they do not call for the suppression of Freemasonry; but if it was possible 62 years ago in a country with democratic traditions as strong as those of Switzerland, for nearly one-third of the population to vote in a referendum in favour of a constitutional amendment to suppress the Freemasons; if it is possible in England today for MPs to demand that members of organizations and professions should be compelled by law to disclose whether or not they are Freemasons; then it is only one step further to demand that Freemasonry be made illegal; for the history of Great Britain and, even more, the history of the United States should remind us that it is not only absolute monarchs and dictators but also popular majorities and their democratically-elected representatives in a free Parliament, who can persecute unpopular minorities.

The silliest factor in the situation is that until 1967 Freemasons were required by law to give a list of their members, and the time and place of their meetings, to their local JPs. This had been enacted by the Unlawful Societies Act 1799. The Freemasons usually complied with the Act, though some lodges sometimes forgot to do so; but the Unlawful Societies Act was repealed by the Criminal Law Act 1967, at a time when the Statute Law Revision Acts were abolishing many Acts on the statute book that had not been enforced for many years and were now regarded as obsolete.

The Unlawful Societies Act, like the Unlawful Oaths Act, had been passed to destroy the Radicals and trade unions. The Unlawful Oaths Act was used in 1834 to prosecute the six agricultural labourers at Tolpuddle in Dorset who were referred to at the time as 'the Dorchester labourers' and are today called 'the Tolpuddle Martyrs'. The six men had sworn an oath not to reveal what had taken place at their trade union meetings. This was enough to send them to transportation to Australia and the living hell of the convict ships and the penal settlements of New South Wales and Van Diemen's Land (Tasmania).

These Acts were therefore regarded as notoriously evil by Harold Wilson's Labour MPs of 1967; They rushed to repeal them without realizing that thirty years later they would be demanding that Freemasons should once again be forced to register with the JPs or some other similar body. It is typical of the attitude of the popular anti-masonic writers that Stephen Knight in *The Brotherhood* should accuse the Freemasons of failing to give the names of their members to JPs, with violating the Unlawful Societies Act, and with using their masonic influence in high places to escape prosecution for their offence. Knight did not realize that the Act had been repealed seventeen years before his book was published.

The Freemasons were quite prepared to give their names to JPs under the Act of 1799; but they object now to legislation which would compel them to do so, because this would be singling them out as compared with other organizations. Their comparison with a golf club is, as we have seen, a little unsound; but they can rightly point out what an outcry there would be if members of the police force and the judges were required by law to declare which of them were Roman Catholics, which of them had voted Labour or Conservative at the last general election, and which of them had made donations to Israel during one of the Arab-Israeli wars of 1948, 1967 or 1973.

Meanwhile, until the legislation can be forced through the House of Commons and the House of Lords, the new Anti-Masonic Party resorts to that body which has so often in history been the instrument of persecution: the Parliamentary Committee of Inquiry. Officers of Grand Lodge and of the police forces are ordered to appear before the Committee and tell them how many members of the West Midlands Police Force are Freemasons. They are warned that if they do not come, they will be locked up in the Clock Tower below Big Ben in Westminster for as long as the House of Commons cares to keep them there. We have not yet seen a head-on conflict between the judges and the House of Commons such as has occurred several times throughout history. The last time was in 1840, when the law courts committed to prison, for contempt of court, those servants of the House of Commons who defied their injunctions; and the House of Commons committed to the Clock Tower, for contempt of the House, the Sheriff of Middlesex who attempted to enforce the order of imprisonment for contempt of court. Will such a conflict come again? It is certainly not impossible in view of the attitude of the judges and the House of Commons today.

The Home Secretary adopts a position which, at least on the surface, is fair and reasonable. He points out that people say that there is no smoke without fire; and as there is plenty of smoke coming from Freemasons' Hall, there is need for an inquiry to condemn or vindicate the Freemasons. But is there not also smoke emanating from other places – from the offices of the road hauliers who run vehicles and buses; from the public utility companies; from Harrods; from the Director of Public Prosecutions; from Kensington Palace; from the Crown Prosecution Service, from the PROs of many multinational corporations; from the Millennium Dome; from the Fraud Squad; from Balmoral and the Prince of Wales's entourage; from many Labour town halls; and from the Lord Chancellor's official residence? Are not criminal prosecutions stopped, not only when Freemasons are involved, but when judges or the Director of Public Prosecutions stop the case from going to the jury, and prevent the prosecution of men whom most people believe to be guilty? Is it not because of a reaction – perhaps a reaction which has gone too far – against the stern hanging judges of the days of Lord Goddard and Mr Justice Avory, in favour of judges who fall over backwards to protect a suspected criminal, when there is no question of Freemasons being involved?

It is easy to see why the Freemasons are chosen for harassment. They are seen as a privileged, wealthy, middle-class group; like City livery companies they can be attacked with impunity because they have tended to ignore criticism and do not wish to lower themselves by replying to it. The critics have to be a little careful about whom they criticize. The blacks in Brixton – like the Asians in Bradford and the Jews in Golders Green – may strike back. In the famous words of Anatole France, they are very wicked animals; if they are attacked, they defend themselves. They may start a riot, or burn down the offices of publishers of books which criticize their religion; and the Jews of Israel, too, know how to punish their enemies. But the Freemasons, like the leaders of the ethnic minorities, rightly restrain their members from retaliation, from forming vigilante groups; and, unlike the blacks and the Asians, they are not protected by a government which is determined to enforce law and order.

Is it not time that the Freemasons were left alone to hold their dinners and their lodge meetings in peace? For the Freemasons, these meetings are inspiring rituals; for others, they are nothing worse than harmless play-acting and silly nonsense. Sixty years ago it was fashionable, in British intellectual circles, to laugh at and criticize the Jews. Today, in most of Western Europe, the only people who make anti-Semitic jokes are the Jews themselves. Anti-Jewish remarks from anyone else are considered to be inappropriate since six million Jews were killed in the Holocaust by German, Croatian, Lithuanian, Latvian and other Fascists. Let us hope that it will not be necessary for six million Freemasons to be slaughtered before it becomes unfashionable to denounce them.

Notes and References

Chapter 1 – The Masons

1. Gimpel, *The Cathedral Builders*, 7.
2. Ibid., 52.
3. Ibid., 51, 97.
4. Ibid., 68–69.
5. Ibid., 65.
6. Hutton, 'Sandgate Castle A.D.1519–1540', in *Archaeologia Cantiana*, xx.235; Knoop and Jones, *Genesis of Freemasonry*, 121.
7. No records of the Masons' Company of London earlier than the seventeenth century have survived; but see *The Worshipful Company of Masons*, 324.
8. Lane, *The Outwith London Guilds of Great Britain*, 5, 9, 17–18.
9. Ibid., 25–26, 28–29, 32–33.
10. *Statues of the Realm*, 23 Edw.III, c.5–7; 25 Edw.III, c.1, 2; 12 Ric.II, c.4; 3 Hen.VI, c.2, 3; 11 Hen.VII, c.22; 6 Hen.VIII, c.1, 3; 7 Hen.-VIII, c.6; 24 Hen.VIII, c.13; 33 Hen.VIII, c.9; 2 & 3 Edw.VI, c.19; 1 & 2 Ph. and Mary, c.2; 5 Eliz., c.4.
11. *Early Masonic Pamphlets*, 80; Piatikorsky, *Who's Afraid of Freemasons?*, 50; *Statutes of the Realm*, 33 Hen.VIII, c.9.
12. *Statutes of the Realm*, 23 Edw.III, c.5–7; 25 Edw.III, c.1, 2.
13. Knoop and Jones, *Genesis of Freemasonry*, 29.
14. Ibid., 118–21.
15. Markham, 'Further Views on the Origins of Freemasonry in England', in *Ars Quatuor Coronatorum*, ciii.82.
16. *Statutes of the Realm*, 3 Hen.VI, c.2–5.
17. Vibert, 'The Compagnonnage' (*AQC*, xxxiii.191–228, especially pp. 198–9.)
18. Findel, *History of Freemasonry*, 62, 71.
19. For the date and origin of the Mason Word, see Knoop and Jones, *Genesis of Freemasonry*, 92, 103–7; Knoop, 'The Mason Word';

Knoop and Jones, 'Prolegomena to the Mason Word'; Draffen, 'The Mason Word' (*AQC*, li.194–211; lii.139–59; lxv.54).

Chapter 2 – The Heretics

1. Horne, 'The Saints John in the Masonic Tradition'; Note on St Barbara (*AQC*, lxxv.76–102; lxxvi.227); Knoop, Jones and Hamer, *The Two Earliest Masonic MSS.*, 44–45.
2. Lane, 5, 17.
3. *The Complete Works of St Thomas More*, viii.29.
4. As in the case of the burning of John Hooper, the Protestant Bishop of Gloucester, by order of Queen Mary Tudor, on 9 Feb. 1555; see also the burning of Nicholas Ridley, the Protestant Bishop of London, under Mary Tudor, on 16 Oct. 1555 (Foxe, *Acts and Monuments*, vi.659; vii.550–1).
5. *Wriothesley's Chronicle*, i.107–8.
6. Mozley, *John Foxe and his Book*, 86–87.
7. Hilles to Bullinger, (1541), 18 Sept. 1541, 10 May, 18 Dec. 1542, 26 Sept. 1543, 15 Apr. 1545, 28 Jan., 30 Apr. 1546, 26 Jan. 1547 (*Original Letters relative to the English Reformation*, i. 200–21, 224–38, 240–2, 246–56).
8. Barden Papers, 45; Read, *Lord Burghley and Queen Elizabeth*, 346–7.
9. Motley, *The Rise of the Dutch Republic*, iii.445–7; *For. Cal. Eliz.*, xviii. 715, 721, 725, 728, 768.
10. Tharaud, *La tragédie de Ravaillac*, 226, 251, 255.
11. For the Rosicrucians, see 'the three Rosicrucian Manifestoes', *Allgemeine und General Reformation der ganzen weiten Welt* (Kassel, 1614), *Fama Fraternitatis* and *Die Chemische Hochzeit* (Kassel, 1615). See also Waite, *The Real History of the Rosicrucians* (London, 1887); and Yates, *The Rosicrucian Enlightenment* (London, 1972).
12. For Fludd, see Jackson, 'Rosicrucianism and its Effect on Craft Masonry' (*AQC*, xcvii.122–3).

Chapter 3 – The Seventeenth Century

1. Knoop and Jones, *Genesis of Freemasonry*, 130–1.
2. Ibid. 97; Lane, 27, 31.
3. Matt. xvi.18.
4. Geneva Bible, notes to 1 Sam.xxvi.9.
5. 2 Chron., chaps. ii–viii.
6. Knoop and Jones, *Genesis of Freemasonry*, 90.

7. Piatigorsky, 46–48, 59, 61, 63, 92–102.
8. White, *Isaac Newton*, 158–62; Peters, 'Sir Isaac Newton and "The Oldest Catholic Religion"'; Peters, 'Sir Isaac Newton and the Holy Flame' (*AQC*, c.192–6; ci.207–13).
9. *Early Masonic Pamphlets*, 30, 79.
10. Knoop and Jones, *Genesis of Freemasonry*, 92.
11. Jackson, 'Rosicrucianism and its Effect on Craft Masonry' (*AQC*, xcvii.124).
12. Ibid.; Hamill and Gilbert, *Freemasonry: A Celebration of the Craft*, 20.
13. Hamill and Gilbert, *Freemasonry: A Celebration of the Craft*. 254; Knoop and Jones, *Genesis of Freemasonry*, 132; Rogers, 'The Lodge of Elias Ashmole' (*AQC*, lxv.38).
14. Plot, *The Natural History of Stafford-shire*, 316; *Early Masonic Pamphlets*, 31.
15. Williamson and Baigent, 'Sir Christopher Wren and Freemasonry: New Evidence' (*AQC*, cix.188–90).
16. Castells, *English Freemasonry in the Period of Transition*, 36; Knoop and Jones, *Genesis of Freemasonry*, 144.
17. For the proceedings against the Templars, see Castle, 'Proceedings against the Templars' (*AQC*, xx.47–70, 112–42, 269–342).
18. Barruel, *Mémoires pour servir à l'histoire du Jacobinisme*, ii.376.
19. For the many theories of the story of the Knights Templars in Scotland, see especially Robinson, *Born in Blood*, passim.
20. Barruel, ii.344–86.
21. Ibid., ii.369.
22. Larudan, *Les Francs Maçons écrasés* (Amsterdam, 1747), and the English translation, *The Freemasons Crushed*.
23. Knight and Lomas, *The Second Messiah*, 155–261, especially pp. 236–7.
24. For the possible links between the Knights Templars and the Freemasons, see Hooker, 'The Knights Templars – Fact & Fiction' (*AQC*, xcvi.204–11); for the important differences between them, see Hamill and Gilbert, *Freemasonry: a celebration of the Craft*, 18.

Chapter 4 – Grand Lodge

1. Findel, 126.
2. *To all Godly People in the Citie of London*; Knoop and Jones, 'An Anti-Masonic leaflet of 1698' (*A.Q.C.*, lv.152–4).
3. Knoop and Jones, *Genesis of Freemasonry*, 134.
4. Calvert, *The Grand Lodge of England*, 4–7, 250–1.
5. Knoop and Jones, *Genesis of Freemasonry*, 159; Crawley, 'The Rev.

Dr Anderson's Non-Masonic Writings 1702–1739'; Robbins, 'Dr Anderson of the "Constitutions"' (*AQC*, xviii.28–42; xxiii.6–34).

6. For Desaguliers, see Knoop and Jones, *Genesis of Freemasonry*, 173–4; Calvert, 21; Fay, *La Franc-Maçonnerie et la révotution intellectuelle du XVIIIe siècle*, 76–87.

7. Knoop and Jones, *Genesis of Freemasonry*, 181.

8. Calvert, 250.

9. Ibid., 252.

10. Fisher, 'John Montague, second Duke of Montagu' (*AQC*, lxxix.69–89.

11. For Wharton, see Calvert, 61–68; Fay, 101–8.

12. Knoop and Jones, *Genesis of Freemasonry*, 296.

13. Ibid., 180.

14. Rottenbury, 'The Pre-Eminence of the Great Architect in Freemasonry' (*AQC*, xcvii.193).

15. Knoop and Jones, *Genesis of Freemasonry*, 183 and n.

16. Ibid., 178.

17. Ibid., 179.

18. 'Freemasons at Canterbury in 1732' (*AQC*, xxxiii.186–7).

19. *Early Masonic Pamphlets*, 25, 209.

20. Knoop, Jones and Hamer published an expurgated version of this obscene and disgusting poem in *Early Masonic Pamphlets*, pp. 83–90, in 1945. It is to the credit of the Freemasons' historical lodge, the Ars Quatuor Coronatorum, that their scholastic integrity led them to publish the full unexpurgated text in 1994 (McLeod, 'The Hudibrastic Poem of 1723', in *AQC*, cvii.9–52. The text of the poem is on pp. 13–20.)

21. *The Free-Masons' Accusation and Defence* (*Early Masonic Pamphlets*, 157–76.)

22. *A Full Vindication of the Ancient and Honourable Society of Free and Accepted Masons* (London, 1726) (in ibid., 176–85).

23. Calvert, 30; Fay, 81; *AQC*, xxv.278.

24. Findel, 241.

25. Calvert, 29; Robbins, 'Frederick, Prince of Wales, as a Freemason' (*AQC*, xxix.326, 329).

26. Calvert, 29.

27. Williams, 'Alexander Pope and Freemasonry' (*AQC*, xxxviii.127).

28. Jones and Clarke, 'A chaplain in a lodge in Liverpool in 1754'; Clarke, 'John Locke and Freemasonry' (*AQC*, lxxvii.144, 168).

29. *The Free Mason's Health*, or *The Enter'd Prentice Song* (*Early Masonic Pamphlets*, 39–40).

30. Songs sung at the Theatre Royal, Dublin, for Masons, on 29 Nov. 1733 (ibid., 295).

31. Ibid., 298.
32. *Ode to the Grand Khaibal* (1726) (ibid., 191).
33. *The Master Mason's Ballad* (1730) (ibid., 232).
34. *A Song sung by a Mason occasioned by a report that they were guilty of Sodomitical practices* (ibid., 249).
35. For Rouget de Lisle and Pottier, see Hamill and Gilbert, *Freemasonry: A Celebration of the Craft*, 242; Chevallier, *Histoire de la Franc-Maçonnerie française*, ii.516; Denslow, *10,000 Famous Freemasons*, iii.360.

Chapter 5 – The Pope's Bull

1. Proclamation of the Council at The Hague, 12 Dec. 1735 (*Early Masonic Pamphlets*, 333–4).
2. Pamphlet by Philorangielo, 30 Dec. 1735 (ibid.).
3. Clement XII's Bull '*In eminenti*', 28 Apr. 1738 (Hamill and Gilbert, *World Freemasonry*, 78–81).
4. Ibid., 82.
5. Ibid.; Vatcher, 'John Coustos and the Portuguese Inquisition' (*AQC*, lxxxi.9).
6. For Crudeli's case, see Hamill and Gilbert, *World Freemasonry*, 81–82; Vatcher, ibid. (*AQC*, lxxxi.9–87).
7. For Freemasonry in the Austrian Empire, and the attitude of the Emperor Francis I, see Malazovich, 'A Sketch of the earlier History of Masonry in Austria and Hungary'; Bradley, 'Bro. Mozart and Some of his Masonic Friends'; Winterburgh, 'Prague: A Centre of Freemasonry' (*AQC*, iv.20–24, 181–93; v.15–19; vii.77–82, 184–9; ix.129–44; xxvi.242).
8. Du Vigneau's report to Lodge Absalom at Hamburg, 5 Aug. 1743 (in Malazovich, *AQC*, iv.189–90).
9. For Coustos, see Vatcher, in *AQC*, lxxxi.9–87; Hamill and Gilbert, *World Freemasonry*, 84.
10. Hamill and Gilbert, *World Freemasonry*, 84.
11. Report by Henrique, Varajāo, Moller and Abranches, 25 Apr. 1744 (in *AQC*, lxxxi.67–68).
12. Coustos's promise of secrecy, 23 June 1744 (ibid., 73).
13. Lande and others to the Holy Office, 22 Sept. 1744 (ibid., 73).
14. Hamill and Gilbert, *World Freemasonry*, 84.
15. For Radclyffe and the Jacobite Freemasons, see ibid., 44, 47; Tuckett, 'The Early History of Freemasonry in France'; Vatcher, 'A Lodge of Irishmen at Lisbon, 1738'; Mellor, 'The Roman Catholic Church and the Craft'; Read, 'The Church of Rome and Freemasonry' (*AQC*,

xxxi.7–30; lxxxiv.75–109; lxxxix.60–69; civ.51–56); Chevallier, i.171).

16. Chevallier, ibid.; Denslow, i.309.

Chapter 6 – Germany and France

1. For the initiation of Frederick the Great, see Gottschall, *Deutsche Originalcharactere des achtzehnten Jahrhunderts* (1897), vol. iv; translation in Cerf, 'How Frederick the Great of Prussia became a Freemason' (*AQC*, x. 188).

2. For the government policy towards Freemasonry in France in the years 1737–45, see Chevallier, i.9–120; Fay, 132–51; Hamill and Gilbert, *World Freemasonry*, 49–50; Findel, 200–15; Tuckett, 'The early history of Freemasonry in France'; Hills, 'Women in Freemasonry'; Vibert, 'The Compagnonnage'; Smith, 'The so-called "Exposures" of Freemasonry of the Mid-Eighteenth Century'; Bathem, 'Chevallier Ramsay: a new appreciation'; Batham, 'The Compagnonnage and the emergence of Craft Masonry in France'; Bernheim, 'Notes on early Freemasonry in Bordeaux (1732–1769)'; Read, 'The Church of Rome and Freemasonry'; Litvine, 'Anti-Masonry: a neglected Source' (*AQC*, xxxi.7–30; xxxiii.71; 231; lvi.4–36; lxxiv.51–52; lxxxi.280–315; lxxxvi.1–28; ci.33–132; civ.51–56, 121–38).

3. Hamer and Clarke, 'An Anti-Masonic "Deliberation" by Six Doctors of the Sorbonne in 1745' (*AQC*, lxxxvi.29–34).

4. Tallentyre, *The Friends of Voltaire*, 199.

5. Saintsbury, 'Voltaire' (*Encyclopaedia Britannica*, (11th edn.), xxviii, 204).

Chapter 7 – English Grand Lodge: 'Wilkes and Liberty'

1. Calvert, 31, 43. citing the report in the *London Daily Post* of 29 May 1739 of Anderson's death on 28 May 1739, and in the *London Evening Post* of 2 June 1739 of his funeral on 1 June 1739. Calvert states that Desaguliers died on 29 November 1743, and was buried on 6 March 1744, and refers to his obituary in the *General Evening Post* of 2 March 1744. The delay between his death and his obituary and funeral seems surprising, and Calvert gives no explanation of this. Other authorities, perhaps more plausibly, state that Desaguliers died in 1744.

2. Ibid., 17.

3. Ibid., 18.

4. Beck, 'Anthony Sayer, gentleman: the truth at last' (*AQC*, lxxxviii.69).
5. Calvert, 18, citing *London Evening Post*, 16 Jan.1741–2.
6. For Dunckerley, see Calvert, 171–2.
7. Piatigorsky, 146.
8. For Ramsay, see Hamill and Gilbert, *Freemasonry: A Celebration of the Craft*, 17; Hamill and Gilbert, *World Freemasonry*, 19; Crawley, 'The Templar Legends in Freemasonry'; Batham, 'Chevalier Ramsay: A new appreciation' (*AQC*, xxvi.62; lxxxi.280–315.)
9. For the origin of the Royal Arch, see *History of English Freemasonry*, 14; Ough, 'The Origin and Development of Royal Arch Masonry' (*AQC*, cvii.188–95).
10. See Exod., xx.2, 3, 5; Num., xxxi.14, 15, 17, 18.
11. Hamill and Gilbert, *Freemasonry: A Celebration of the Craft*, 40.
12. Denslow, iv. 89–90; Hamill and Gilbert, *World Freemasonry*, 35; Conder, 'The Hon. Miss St Leger and Freemasonry' (*AQC*, viii.16–23).
13. Hills, 'Women and Freemasonry' (*AQC*, xxxiii.63–77); Denslow, iv.177–8. For women in masonic lodges in 18th-century France, see Chevallier, i.200–6.
14. Hamill and Gilbert, *Freemasonry: A Celebration of the Craft*, 245; Denslow, iv.309–10; and see Crawley, 'The Hon. A. Wesley and the lodge at Trim' (*AQC*, xv.108–24).
15. For the split between the Ancients and the Moderns, see *History of English Freemasonry*, 10; Hamill and Gilbert, *Freemasonry: A Celebration of the Craft*, 35; Hamill and Gilbert, *World Freemasonry*, 36.
16. For Wilkes's admission as a Freemason and the ensuing controversy, see Calvert, 195.
17. Ibid.
18. Ibid., 196.

Chapter 8 – Troubles and Scandals

1. For Dodd's case, see Calvert, 179–83; Birkenhead, *Famous Trials of History*, 149–58.
2. Calvert, 182.
3. Ibid., 183.
4. 'The Masonic Certificate of Edward Gibbon'; Mackay, 'Sir Walter Scott as a Freemason'; Clarke and Jones, 'Why was James Boswell a Freemason?' Webb, 'Robert Burns, poet and freemason' (*AQC*, xvii.22; xx.209–20; lxxix.90–92; ciii.213–29).
5. Wonnacott, 'Doctor Dodd, Grand Chaplain' (*AQC*, xx.352–5).
6. Birkenhead, 150.

7. For the Chevalier d'Éon, see Crawley, 'The Chevalier d'Éon' (*AQC*, xvi.231–51); Calvert. 186–92.
8. Crawley, op. cit., (AQC, xvi.247).
9. Crawley, ibid. (*AQC*, xvi.245).
10. Ibid., 247–8.

Chapter 9 – The American Revolution

1. Rosenthal, *Salem Story*, 67, 71, 76, 85, 87, 105–6, 115, 120, 124, 147, 152, 155.
2. Hamill and Gilbert, *World Freemasonry*, 97.
3. Ibid., 86–87; Fenton, 'The Military Services and Freemasonry'; Rogers, 'Lancashire Military Lodges' (*AQC*, lx.5; lxxvi.101–20).
4. Hamill and Gilbert, *World Freemasonry*, 97–98.
5. *The Autobiography of Benjamin Franklin*, 93, 97, 99, 105–6.
6. Voorhis, 'Benjamin Franklin's Reprint of Anderson's Constitutions of 1723' (*AQC*, lxxxiv.69).
7. Aldridge, *Benjamin Franklin, Philosopher and Man*, 44–45.
8. Bullock, *Revolutionary Brotherhood*, 50–52; Cerza, 'Anti-Masonry' (*AQC*, lxxx.243).
9. Smyth, 'Worshipful Brother George Washington of Virginia' (*AQC*, lxxxviii.182–3).
10. Hamill and Gilbert, *World Freemasonry*, 98, 101.
11. Ibid., 101; Hamill and Gilbert, *Freemasonry: A Celebration of the Craft*, 43; 'Signers of the Constitution of the United States' (in Whitney, *Founders of Freedom in America*, pp.vii–x); Cerza, 'The American War of Independence and Freemasonry' (*AQC*, lxxxix.174).
12. Heaton, *Masonic Membership of the Founding Fathers*, p.xvi.
13. Cerza, 'The Boston Tea Party and Freemasonry' (*AQC*, xcviii.208).
14. Ibid.; Nasser, 'The Boston Tea Party' (*AQC*, xcviii.207–9; cii.248–9).
15. *Journals of Congress, September 5, 1774, to January 1, 1776*, 3, 68; Neustadt, *Carpenters' Hall*, 16–23.
16. Charles and Nancy Cook, *Blueprint for a Revolution*, 11, 13–14, 29, 37–38.
17. Fenton, 'Richard Carlile' (*AQC*, xlix.97).
18. Denslow, ii.173–4.
19. Hamill and Gilbert, *World Freemasonry*, 101.
20. Denslow, ii.92, who states that Joseph Galloway was a member of the masonic Philadelphia Lodge No.2; but he may be confusing him with another Joseph Galloway who became a master mason in Washington Lodge No.59, Pennsylvania, in June 1796, after the other Joseph Galloway had fled to England (Heaton, 124).

21. Haywood, *Famous Masons and Masonic Presidents*, 285.
22. Denslow, i.126.
23. Ibid., ii.307–8.
24. Ibid., i.163–4.
25. Ibid., iii.156, 178.
26. Ibid., i.120.
27. Ibid., i.163–4.
28. Hamill and Gilbert, *Freemasonry: A Celebration of the Craft*, 43; Sherman, 'The "Negro" on "Compact" Grand Lodge' (*AQC*, xcii. 48–71).
29. Fleming, *Liberty! The American Revolution*, 302–3.
30. Denslow, ii.162.
31. Ibid., i.30–31, 54; iii.282, 312–13.
32. Lafontaine, 'Paul Jones' (*AQC*, xliv.203–7).
33. Ibid., 208.
34. Ibid., 209–13.
35. Denslow, iii.120–1.

Chapter 10 – The Magic Flute

1. Chevallier, i.39, 47, 161–2.
2. Ibid., i.197.
3. Ibid., i.194.
4. Ibid., i.275.
5. Benemeli, *La Masoneria Española en el Siglo XVIII*, 97.
6. Ibid., 107, 118–20. For the difference between the two Papal Bulls of 1738 and 1751, see Read, 'The Church of Rome and Freemasonry' (*AQC*, civ.57).
7. For Mozart's masonic music and his connection with the lodge in Vienna, see Bradley, 'Bro. Mozart and some of his Masonic Friends' (*A.Q.C.*, xxvi.244–6). See also Sharp, 'Mozart's Masonic Music'; Smyth, 'Brother Mozart of Vienna'; Webb, 'Joseph Haydn, Freemason and Musician' (*AQC*, lxix.15–30; lxxxvii.37–78; xciv.61–82).
8. Francovich, *Storia della Massoneria in Italia*, 130–1.
9. For the Illuminati, see Hamill and Gilbert, *World Freemasonry*, 74–78. See also Ferminger, 'The Romances of Robison and Barruel' (*AQC*, 1.161 and n.)
10. See Nesta H. Webster, *World Revolution: The Plot against Civilization* (London, 1921); Nesta H. Webster, *Secret Societies and Subversive Movements* (London, 1924).
11. Churchill's unpublished article, 'Zionism versus Bolshevism', 8 Feb. 1920, (in Churchill Archives, CHAR 8/36, pp.92–93).

12. For the text of the edict, see Reinalter, *Joseph II und die Freimaurerei*, 64–66.
13. Barruel, *Mémoires pour servir à l'histoire du Jacobinisme*, ii.261–4.
14. Marie Antoinette to Leopold II, 17 Aug. 1790 (*Lettres de Marie-Antoinette*, ii.192.
15. For Mozart's reluctance to compose *The Magic Flute*, and its production, see Bradley, 'Bro. Mozart and some of his Masonic Friends' (*AQC*, xxvi.249–50).
16. Ibid., 250–1.
17. Ibid., 250.

Chapter 11 – The French Revolution

1. Denslow, iv.89.
2. Ibid., i.89; Chevallier, i.288.
3. Francovich, 145–6.
4. Casanova's account of his escape, in Yeats-Brown, *Escape*, 681–743.
5. Hamill and Gilbert, World Freemasonry, 73–74; Francovich, 436, 439, 441; Ivanoff, 'Cagliostro in Eastern Europe' (*AQC*, xl.45–80).
6. Francovich, 440.
7. Ibid., 446–7.
8. Ibid., 461–2, 464.
9. Ibid., 464.
10. Ibid., 468,
11. Ibid., 468–70.
12. Ibid., 472.
13. Chevallier, i.312.
14. Cabanès, *Marat inconnu*, 46–83.
15. Chevallier, i.367.
16. Cabanès, 48–49.
17. Ibid., 83–113.
18. Benemeli, 301–3.
19. Ibid., 304.
20. Telepneff, 'Freemasonry in Russia' (*AQC*, xxxv.277).
21. ibid., 261–79.
22. Ferminger, 'The Romances of Robison and Barruel' (*AQC*, i.42).
23. Lefebvre, Guyot and Sagnac, *La Révolution Française*, 119.
24. Chevallier, i.206.
25. Goethe, 'Campagne in Frankreich 1792' (*Goethes Werke*, xxxiii.75).
26. Lefebvre, Guyot and Sagnac, 150.

Chapter 12 – Loyalist and Revolutionary Freemasons

1. Findel, 182, 387.
2. Ibid., 388.
3. Chevallier, i.367.
4. Findel, 430–1.
5. Keane, *Tom Paine*, 413–14.
6. Robison, *Proofs of a Conspiracy*, 382.
7. Barruel, *Mémoires pour servir à l'Histoire du Jacobinisme*, i., p.i.
8. Ibid., i.i.
9. Ibid., i.11.
10. Ibid., ii.260–1.
11. ibid., ii. 258.
12. Robison, 9–11; PS to 2nd edn., 26.
13. Berry, 'Some historical Episodes in Irish Freemasonry' (*AQC*, xxvi.197).
14. Ibid., 199.
15. Ibid.
16. Ibid.
17. *Statutes at Large*, 37 Geo.III, c.123; 39 Geo.III, c.79; R. v. Loveless and others (Carrington and Payne, vi.596).
18. Denslow, iii.213–14; Calvert, 203. For a contrary view about the date of Moira's initiation, see Hamill, 'The Earl of Moira' (*AQC*, xciii.32).
19. Hamill, 'The Earl of Moira' (*AQC*, xciii.47).
20. Ibid., 34.
21. Francovich, 190–1.
22. Nelson to Paoli, 8 Feb. 1794 (*Despatches and Letters of Nelson*, i.351).
23. Stolper, 'Freemasonry in Naples in the Eighteenth Century' (*AQC*, xciii.72); Villari, 'Caracciolo'; Villari, 'Naples, Kingdom of' (*Encyclopaedia Britannica* (11th edn.), v.299; xix.186); Holland Rose, 'The Second Coalition' (*Cambridge Modern History* (1907–10 edn.), viii.658).
24. Holland Rose, ibid.

Chapter 13 – Napoleon

1. Napoleon I to Champagny, 13 Sept. 1805 (Chevallier, ii.85).
2. Chevallier, ii.23.
3. 'Napoleon I and Freemasonry'; Tuckett, 'Napoleon I and Freemasonry' (*AQC*, viii.188; xxvii.115).
4. Chevallier, ii.19.

5. O'Meara, *Napoleon at St Helena*, i.170; see also Chevallier, ii.17.
6. Chevallier, ii.12, 14, 23, 26.
7. Ibid., ii.15, 46; Tuckett (in *AQC*, xxvii.98–99).
8. Chevallier, ii.90–91; Tuckett (in *AQC*, xxvii.107).
9. Chevallier, ii.48.
10. Ibid., ii.30–31.
11. Report into Freemasonry (1811) (ibid., ii.36–42).
12. Ibid., 40, 157–62; Crowe, 'A Curious Carbonari Certificate'; Radice, 'Introduction to the History of the Carbonari'; Radice, 'The French Charbonnerie in the Nineteenth Century' (*AQC*, xvi.163–70; liii.48–143; liv.35–67, 122–77; lx.106–16).
13. Chevallier, ii.95–97.
14. Tarlé, *Bonaparte*, 20.
15. Chevallier, ii.96.
16. Wellington to Peacocke, 4 Jan. 1810 (*Wellington at War*, 182–3). See also Wellington's Order of the Day, 5 Jan. 1810 (*Wellington's Supplementary Despatches*, vi.467).
17. Wellington to Carleton, 13 Aug. 1838; Wellington to Walsh, 13 Oct. 1851; Walsh to *Freemasons' Quarterly Magazine*, 6 Mar. 1854 (in Crawley, 'The Hon. A. Wesley and the Lodge at Trim' (*AQC*, xv.108–24).

Chapter 14 – The Restoration

1. Chevallier, ii.52.
2. Ibid.
3. Ibid., ii.103.
4. Ibid., ii.52.
5. Ibid., ii.53.
6. Ibid., ii.24–25, 53–54.
7. Ibid., ii.53.
8. Denslow, i.108.
9. Chevallier, ii.54.
10. Ibid., ii.47.
11. Kurtz, *The Trial of Marshal Ney*, 269–70; Wellington to Angela Burdett Coutts, 1 Sept. 1849 (ibid., 314–15).
12. Chevallier, ii.189.
13. Kurtz, 203–5.
14. Ibid., 316.
15. Chevallier, ii.111–13.
16. Ibid., ii.105–9.
17. Ibid., ii.23.
18. Ibid., ii.109–12.

19. Ibid., ii.192
20. Ibid., ii.193–5.
21. Ibid., ii.197–9.
22. Ibid., ii.199.
23. Radice, 'Introduction to the History of the Carbonari'; Radice, 'The French Charbonnerie in the Nineteenth Century'; Stolper, '"Napoleonic" Freemasonry in Italy' (AQC, liii.48–143; liv.35–7, 122–77; lx.106–16; c.164–78).
24. Winterburgh, 'Prague: A Centre of Freemasonry'; Reinalter, 'Freemasonry in Austria in the Eighteenth Century' (AQC, lxxvii.68–70; c.206).
25. Telepneff, 'Russian Freemasonry during the Reign of Alexander I' (AQC, xxxviii.6–21, 35).
26. Telepneff, 'Polish Freemasonry' (AQC, lix.192–5).
27. Kushelev's report (June 1821) in Telepneff, 'Russian Freemasonry during the Reign of Alexander I' (AQC, xxxviii.43–50).
28. Telepneff, 'Russian Freemasonry during the Reign of Alexander I'; Telepneff, 'Polish Freemasonry' (AQC, xxxviii.29–66; lix.195).
29. History of English Freemasonry, 18; Hamill and Gilbert, Freemasonry: A Celebration of the Craft, 39; Hamill and Gilbert, World Freemasonry, 107, 109, 111, 117.
30. Denslow, i.136.
31. Simmons, A Letter to His Grace the Duke of Northumberland, 5–7, 29–30.
32. The Life of Robert Owen written by himself, i.224–5.
33. Fenton, 'Richard Carlile' (AQC, xlix.94–103).
34. Ibid., 91.
35. Holyoake, 'Carlile, Richard' (Dictionary of National Biography, iii.1011).

Chapter 15 – The Case of William Morgan

1. Bernard, Light on Masonry, 379n.
2. Hamill and Gilbert, World Freemasonry, 190.
3. Bernard, 370.
4. Ibid., 372.
5. Ibid., 373.
6. Ibid., 372, 377.
7. Ibid., 379–91.
8. Hamill and Gilbert, World Freemasonry, 194.
9. De Witt Clinton's proclamations, 26 Oct. 1826 and 19 Mar. 1827 (Bernard, App.25–26).

10. Muir, 'The Morgan affair' (*AQC*, cv.227–9); Hamill and Gilbert, *World Freemasonry*, 193.
11. Muir (in *AQC*, cv.224); Vaughn, *The Anti-Masonic Party in the United States*, 7.
12. Vaughn, 7.
13. Bernard, 388, 479–86; Muir (in *AQC*, cv.225).
14. Herbert A. Read's speech, 4 July, 1828 (Bernard, 451).
15. T. F. Talbot's speech, 2–6 Aug. 1828; resolution of meeting of 4–6 Aug. 1828 (ibid., 476, 465).
16. Muir, 'The Morgan affair' (*AQC*, cvi.139).
17. Ibid., 135; Voorhis, 'The Morgan Affair of 1826' (*AQC*, lxxvi.202).
18. Muir (*AQC*, cv.228.).
19. Bernard, App. 33; 393.
20. John Quincy Adams to Livingston, 23 May 1833 (John Quincy Adams, *Letters on the Masonic Institution*, 163–5.)
21. Vaughn, 67.
22. Ibid., 68.
23. Ibid., 100, 126.
24. Ibid., 140–1, 145–6.
25. Voorhis (in *AQC*, lxxvi.201).
26. Denslow, i. 139–40.
27. Ibid., iv.208.
28. Ibid., i.149.
29. Ibid., ii. 217; Hamill and Gilbert, *Freemasonry: A Celebration of the Craft*, 238.
30. Denslow, i.78–79, 137–8, 324–5 (John Bell, Breckinridge, Douglas).
31. Ibid., iii.86.
32. Ibid., iii.163.
33. Ibid., ii.35–36.
34. Ibid., i.162–3.
35. Butler's General Order No. 28, May 1862 (Ward, *The Civil War*, 126).
36. Denslow, iv.291–2.
37. Ibid., iv.268–9.
38. Hamill and Gilbert, *Freemasonry: A Celebration of the Craft*, 45.
39. Hamill and Gilbert, *World Freemasonry*, 201–6; Denslow, iii. 340–1.
40. Denslow, ii.298–9.
41. Ibid., iv.180–1.
42. For Thaddeus Stevens's part in the anti-masonic campaign, see Vaughn, 90–111; Cerza, 'Anti-Masonry' (*AQC*, lxxx.247).

Chapter 16 – The Lautaro Lodge

1. Denslow, i.19, 41, 78, 90, 191; iii.102.
2. Ibid., iv.95–96; Seal-Coon, 'Spanish-American Revolutionary Masonry' (*AQC*, xciv.98–103); *Enciclopedia Vniversal Ilvstrada*, xxix.1131–2.
3. For Admiral Brown, see Ratto, *Almirante Guillermo Brown*, passim; *Biografias Navales*, 13–21; Mulhall, *The English in South America*, 144–54; Levi-Castillo, 'Admiral William Brown' (*AQC*, xcii.16–24).
4. Hall-Johnson, 'A Century of English Freemasonry in Argentina'; Seal-Coon, 'Spanish-American Revolutionary Masonry' (*AQC*, lxv.98; xciv.93).
5. Timmons, 'José Maria Morelos' (*Hispano-American Historical Review*, xlv.183–95).
6. Denslow, i.254.
7. Domenech, *L'Empire au Mexique*, 22.
8. Roeder, *Juárez and his Mexico*, 31.
9. Denslow, iii.208.
10. Altamira, 'Spain' (*Cambridge Modern History*, x.218).
11. Ibid., x.214–30.
12. Denslow, i.194.
13. Ridley, *Garibaldi*, 119–26, 142–3, 174–5; Stolper, 'Garibaldi: Freemason' (*AQC*, cii.7).
14. Garibaldi, *Clelia*, 458n.; Ridley, *Garibaldi*, 198.
15. Ridley, *Garibaldi*, 220.
16. Denslow, ii.281.
17. Ibid., i.39–40, 267; ii.257–8, 311–12; iii.49.
18. Ibid., ii.82; iii.353–4; iv.115, 223–4.
19. Ibid., i.162; ii.150–1, 251–2, 257–8, 281; iii.353–4; iv.96–97.

Chapter 17 – The Nineteenth Century

1. Chevallier, ii.255–7, 283.
2. Ibid., ii.289–92.
3. Eckert, *Die Freimaurer-Orden*, 281, 288–9.
4. Chevallier, ii.305.
5. Ibid., ii.322.
6. Ibid., ii.315, 342–8.
7. Ibid., ii.336.
8. Denslow, iii.296.
9. Chevallier, ii.356.

10. Ibid., ii.355.
11. Ibid., ii.358.
12. Ibid., ii.371.
13. Ibid., ii.380.
14. Ibid., ii.398–9.
15. Ibid., ii.402.
16. Ibid., ii.403–6.
17. Ibid., ii.408.
18. Ibid., ii.441.
19. *Le Constitutionnel*, 11 Jan. 1870; Eugénie de Grèce, *Pierre Napoléon Bonaparte*, 314–26.
20. *The Times*, 22, 23, 24, 25, 26, 28, 29, 31 Mar. 1870; Eugénie de Grèce, 353–76.
21. Chevallier, ii.492–3.
22. Ibid., ii.504–5, 516–17.
23. Jellinek, *The Paris Commune of 1871*, 195, 366; *The Times*, 26 May 1871.
24. Jellinek, 370.
25. Winterburgh, 'Prague, a Centre of Freemasonry' (*AQC*, lxxvii.69).
26. Hamill and Gilbert, *Freemasonry: A Celebration of the Craft*, 236.
27. Winterburgh, in *AQC*, lxxvii.69–70.
28. Denslow, iv.111.
29. Philor, 'Freemasonry in Greece'; Rizopoulos, 'Sultan Murad V and Freemasonry' (*AQC*, xi.100; civ.188).
30. Rizopoulos, op. cit. Layiktez, 'Sultan Murad V' (*AQC*, civ.189–95; cvii.230–2).
31. Denslow, iv.216–17.
32. Hamill and Gilbert, *Freemasonry: A Celebration of the Craft*, 226.
33. Batham; 'Note'; Khambatta, 'The Influence of the Prince of Wales (Edward VII)' (*AQC*, xci.226; cviii.84).
34. Hughan, 'King Edward VII (*AQC*, xxiii.102–3).
35. Hamill and Gilbert, *Freemasonry: A Celebration of the Craft*, 241.
36. Webb, 'John George Lambton, The First Earl of Durham' (*AQC*, cix.115–53).
37. Denslow, iii.112–13.
38. Sharp, 'Some Aspects of Operative Masonry in New South Wales'; Sharp, 'Australia's Oldest Masonic Document' (*AQC*, c.208–19; cix.250–65); Hamill and Gilbert, *Freemasonry: A Celebration of the Craft*, 55.
39. Musa, 'The First Indian Freemason' (*AQC*, lxxxi.317–21).
40. Hamill and Gilbert, *World Freemasonry*, 146.
41. Ibid.
42. Ibid., 171.

43. Chevallier, ii.546.
44. Stolper, 'Garibaldi: Freemason' (*AQC*, cii.5–12, 14–21).

Chapter 18 – The New Assault on Freemasonry

1. Chevallier, ii.531–2.
2. Ibid., ii.550.
3. For Taxil, see Hamill and Gilbert, *World Freemasonry*, 173–6; Cerza, 'Anti-Masonry'; Seal-Coon, 'Modern Anti-Masonry at Home and Abroad' (*AQC*, lxxx.250; cii.172–4.
4. Hamill and Gilbert, *World Freemasonry*, 171, 173.
5. Chevallier, iii.12.
6. Taxil and Verdun, *Les Assassinats Maçonniques*, 157.
7. Fava to Taxil, 3 Aug. 1891 (in *L'Existence des Loges de Femmes*, 6).
8. Winterburgh, 'Prague: A Centre of Freemasonry' (*AQC*, lxxvii.70).
9. Hamill and Gilbert, *World Freemasonry*, 178.
10. Nilus, *Protocols of the Wise Men of Zion*, 16.
11. *Morning Post*, 28 May 1920.
12. T. G. Masaryk, 'Svobodní zednáři' (in *Naše Doba*, xiii.30–35).
13. Hamill and Gilbert, *Freemasonry: A Celebration of the Craft*, 227, 238.
14. Chevallier, iii.11, 54.
15. Ibid., iii.12, 21, 34.
16. Ibid., iii.10.
17. Ibid., iii.201.
18. Ibid., iii.51–52.
19. Piatigorsky, 371–3.
20. Hamill and Gilbert, *World Freemasonry*, 181.
21. Piatigorsky, 263.
22. Chevallier, iii.121.
23. For the Stavisky case and the death of Prince, see ibid., iii.233–63.
24. Ludendorff, *Vernichtung der Freimaurerei durch Enthüllung ihrer Geheimnisse*, 6, 14, 76.
25. Custos, *Freimaurer der Weltvampyr*, 8, 34–36, 43–44.
26. Chevallier, iii.284.
27. Ibid., iii.288.
28. Groussier to Reynaud, 21 May 1940 (ibid., iii.307–8).
29. Weygand, *Rappelé au service*, 298–9.
30. Groussier to Pétain, 7 Aug. 1940 (Chevallier, iii.316–18).
31. Ibid., iii.333, 335, 351–3.
32. Hamill and Gilbert, *Freemasonry: A Celebration of the Craft*, 182.
33. Chevallier, iii.326.

34. Ibid., iii.312–14; De Brinon to Goebbels, 11 May 1943 (ibid., iii.359); Ousby, *Occupation: The Ordeal of France 1940–1944*, 98.
35. *Laval parle*, 106–9.
36. Chevallier, iii.320.
37. Ibid., iii.370.
38. Denslow, iv.409.
39. For the part played by Freemasons in the resistance in France, see Chevallier, iii.373–93.
40. Grand Orient to de Gaulle, 18 Oct. 1944 (ibid., iii.399–400).
41. Ibid., 387.
42. For the attitude of the Catholic Church to the Freemasons since Vatican II, see Read, 'The Church of Rome and Freemasonry' (*A.Q.C.*, civ.51–94).

Chapter 19 – Freemasonry in the World

1. Information from Signor Salvatore Spinello of the Italian Grand Orient.
2. Lange, 'A Sketch of Norwegian Masonic History' (*AQC*, xiii.35).
3. Denslow, iv.3.
4. 'The South African Commission of Enquiry into Secret Organizations' (*AQC*, lxxviii.74–82).
5. Muller-Ruegg, 'Swiss Freemasonry's Fight for Life' (*AQC*, lx.211–22).
6. Washizu, 'Anti-Masonry in Japan' (*AQC*, cvii.50–51).
7. For anti-masonry in Japan, see ibid., *AQC* cvii.85–116.
8. Ibid., ii.43.
9. For Freemasonry in Spain, see Cerza, 'Anti-Masonry'; Seal-Coon, 'Modern Anti-Masonry' (*AQC*, lxxx.253; cii.175, 177).
10. Boor, *Masoneria*, 11–15, 28–29, 31–32, 34–35, 43, 47, 51, 53–55, 65, 183, 214, 219, 323.
11. Benemeli, *La Masoneria Española en el Siglo XVIII* (Madrid, 1974).
12. Denslow, i.240–1.
13. Ibid., ii.321–2,
14. *Libro Rojo*, 200–14; Gagern, *Todte und Lebende*, i.276; Garcia and Pereyra, *Paredes y Arrillaga*, 291.
15. Denslow, iii.153–4.
16. Ibid., ii.77.
17. For King Leopold's position about Maximilian becoming Emperor of Mexico, see Ridley, *Maximilian and Juárez*, 76–77, 79, 92–93, 141, 149.
18. Denslow, ii.352.
19. For the attempts to persuade Juárez to pardon Maximilian, see Ridley, *Maximilian and Juárez*, 272–6.
20. Gould, 'Freemasonry in Mexico' (*AQC*, x.68–69).

21. Queen Victoria to Stanley, 18 July 1867 (RA: VIC/J 102/102).
22. Denslow, iii.120.
23. Ibid., iv.290.
24. Ibid., i.95; iii.101–2, 115, 141–2; iv.268.
25. Hamill and Gilbert, *Freemasonry: A Celebration of the Craft*, 226.
26. 'R. v. Bow Street Metropolitan Stipendiary Magistrate and others, ex parte Pinochet Ugarte (Amnesty International and others intervening)' (*All-England Law Reports*, 1998, iv.897–947; 1999, i.577–99; ii.97–192.)
27. Denslow, iv.43–44.
28. *Globus*, 14 May 1999.
29. Information from Dr Emina Kurtagić.
30. Washizu, 'Anti-Masonry in Japan' (*AQC*, cvii.95).
31. Spalajkovich to Pašić, 12/25 July 1914; Petrovitch, 'The Story of the Black Hand and the Great War' (in Pozzi, *Black Hand over Europe*, 248–67).
32. *The Times*, 8 Jan. 1929.
33. Avon, *Facing the Dictators*, 111–12, 123; Pozzi, pp. xvi–xix; Ridley, *Mussolini*, 243–4.
34. Information from Branko Markić.
35. Hory and Broszat, *Der kroatische Ustasche Staat*, 84–106; A. Djilas, *The Contested Country*, 118–27, 210 (n.38), 212 (n.58); *France*, 13 Oct. 1941; *Never Again*, passim; *Crime without Punishment*, 17–23; Ridley, *Tito*, 163–6.
36. Information from Branko Markić.
37. Cerza, 'Anti-Masonry' (*AQC*, lxxx.253).
38. See Ridley, *Tito*, 282–9, 296–9.
39. Information from Branko Markić.
40. Denslow, iv.65–68.
41. Information from Simić's daughter, Ljubica Simić.
42. *Globus*, 14 May 1999.

Chapter 20 – Modern Freemasonry in Britain

1. Chevallier, ii.550.
2. For the eminent Freemasons mentioned, see *History of English Freemasonry*, 32; Hamill and Gilbert, *Freemasonry: A Celebration of the Craft*, 226–45; Denslow, vols. i–iv.
3. Denslow, i.212.
4. Magnus, *King Edward the Seventh*, 268.
5. For the Tranby Croft case, see Shore, *The Baccarat Case*, passim.
6. Shore, p.vi.

7. *Henry Broadhurst MP: Told by Himself*, 146–53.
8. Magnus, 405–6.
9. Hamill, *The Craft*, 84–85.
10. *History of English Freemasonry*, 29.
11. Ibid., 20.
12. Hamill and Gilbert, *World Freemasonry*, 129.

Chapter 21 – Modern Freemasonry in the United States

1. Gould, *A Concise History of Freemasonry*, 423.
2. For Prince Hall, see Wesley, *Prince Hall, Life and Legacy*, passim; Sherman, review of Wesley's *Prince Hall, Life and Legacy*, in *AQC*, xc.306–22; Hamill and Gilbert, *Freemasonry: A Celebration of the Craft*, 233; Denslow, *10,000 Famous Freemasons*, ii.165.
3. Henderson and Pope, *Freemasonry Universal*, i.23–24.
4. Henderson and Pope, i.84–210.
5. Gould, 423, 426.
6. Bryce, *Modern Democracies*, i.118.
7. Piatigorsky, *Who's Afraid of Freemasons?*, 179–80, 186.
8. Piatigorsky, 190, 197.
9. For the list of Freemasons who played a prominent part in the public life of the United States, see Hamill and Gilbert, *Freemasonry: A Celebration of the Craft*, 226–45; Denslow, vols. i–iv, passim.
10. For the figures of the numbers of Freemasons' lodges and of Freemasons, in the mainstream and Prince Hall lodges, see Henderson and Pope, i.84–210; ii.421–4.
11. For the Flag Ceremony, see Henderson and Pope, i.66.
12. Robinson, *A Pilgrim's Path*, 61–109; 'The Official Site of Pat Robertson' (Internet); 'Biography of Dr John F. Ankerberg (Ankerberg Theological Research Institute)' (Internet).
13. Ottenheimer and Lecadre, *Les Frères invisibles*, passim; *L'Express*, Apr. 2001.

Chapter 22 – Are the Freemasons a Menace?

1. For Jack the Ripper, see Knight, *Jack the Ripper*, passim; Knight, *The Brotherhood*, 52–55; Adam, *Trial of George Chapman*, 45–50.
2. Knight, *The Brotherhood*, 55.
3. Short, *Inside the Brotherhood*, 16–21.
4. Short, *Lundy*, 332.
5. Knight, *The Brotherhood*, 161–6.

6. For Gelli and P2, see Short, *Inside the Brotherhood*, 397, 402, 414; information from Signor Spinello.
7. *The Times*, 17 Apr., 13 Oct. 1992; 28 Dec. 1993.
8. For Calvi's case, see Short, *Inside the Brotherhood*, 411–15.
9. Hughan, 'King Edward VII' (*AQC*, xxiii.103).

Bibliography

ADAM, Hargreave L. *Trial of George Chapman* (Edinburgh and London, 1930).

ADAMS, John Quincy. *Letters on the Masonic Institution* (Boston, 1847).

AHIMAN REZON. *The Constitutions of Freemasony: or Ahiman Rezon: The Antient Charges of the Free and Accepted Masons* (Dublin, 1858).

AKERREN, B. O. Y. 'The Swedish Rite in England and HRH Albert Edward Prince of Wales, a member of the Grand Orient of Sweden' (*AQC*, cx. 208–20) (London, 1998).

ALDRIDGE, A. O. *Benjamin Franklin, Philosopher and Man* (Philadelphia and New York, 1965).

The All-England Law Reports (London, 1998–9).

Allgemeine und General Reformation der ganzen weiten Welt (Kassel, 1614).

ALTAMIRA, R. 'Spain' (in *Cambridge Modern History*, x. 205–43) (Cambridge, 1907–10).

ANDERSON, J. *The Constitutions of the Free-Masons Containing the History, Charges, Regulations etc of that most Ancient and Right Worshipful Fraternity* (London, 1723).

Ars Quatuor Coronatorum (Transactions of Quatuor Coronati Lodge No. 2076), vols i–cx (London, 1884–1998).

AVON, Earl of. *The Eden Memoirs: Facing the Dictators* (London, 1952).

The Bardon Papers: Documents relating to the Imprisonment & Trial of Mary Queen of Scots (ed. Conyers Read) (London, 1909).

BARRETT, D. V. *Secret Societies* (London, 1997).

BARRUEL, Abbé. *Mémoires pour servir à l'histoire du Jacobinisme* (London, 1797–8).

BATHAM, C. N. 'Chevalier Ramsay: A new appreciation' (*AQC*, lxxxi. 280–315) (London, 1969).

— 'The Compagnonnage and the Emergence of Craft Masonry in France' (*AQC*, lxxxvi. 1–28) (London, 1974).

— 'More about the Compagnonnage' (*AQC*, lxxxvii. 242–6) (London, 1975).

— 'Note on Edward VII's initiation as a Freemason' (*AQC*, xci. 10–27) (London, 1979).

— 'The Origin of Freemasonry (A New Theory)' (*AQC*, cvi. 16–50) (London, 1994).

BECK, R. T. 'Anthony Sayer, Gentleman: the truth at last' (*AQC*, lxxxviii. 65–84) (London, 1976).

BENEMELI, J. A. F. *La Masoneria Española en el Siglo XVIII* (Madrid, 1974).

BERNARD, E. D. *Light on Masonry* (Utica, 1829).

BERNHEIM, A. 'The *Mémoire Justificatif* of La Chausée and Freemasonry in Paris until 1773' (*AQC*. civ., 95–120) (London, 1992).

— 'Note on Early Freemasonry in Bordeaux (1732–1769)' (*AQC*, ci. 33–132) (London, 1989).

BERRY, H. E. 'Some Historical Episodes in Irish Freemasonry 1790–1830' (*AQC*, xxvi. 241–70) (London, 1913).

The Bible. The Geneva Bible. *The Bible and Holy Scriptvres conteyned in the Olde and Newe Testament . . . With moste profitable annotations vpon all the hard places, and other things of great importance* (Geneva, 1560).

Biografias Navales (Buenos Aires, 1963).

BIRKENHEAD, F. E. Smith, Earl of. *Famous Trials of History* (London, 1926).

BOOR, J. (General Franco). *Masoneria* (Madrid, 1952).

BRADLEY, H. 'Bro. Mozart and some of his Masonic Friends' (*AQC*, xxvi. 41–70) (London, 1913).

BROADHURST, H. *Henry Broadhurst MP.: The Story of his Life from a stonemason's bench to the Treasury bench. Told by Himself* (London, 1901).

BRODSKY, M. L. 'Eugène Goblet D'Alviella: Freemason & Statesman: Belgium's Foremost Freemason of the XIXth Century (*AQC*, c. 61–87) (London, 1988).

BRYCE, J. (VISCOUNT BRYCE). *Modern Democracies* (London, 1921).

BULLOCK, S. C. *Revolutionary Brotherhood: Freemasonry and the Transformation of the American Social Order 1730–1840* (Williamsburg, Va., 1996).

BULTZO, A. C. J. 'English Masonry in Greece' (*AQC*, lxxxi. 225–7) (London, 1969).

CABANÈS, Dr. *Marat Inconnu* (Paris, 1891).

Calendar of State Papers (Foreign Series) of the reign of Elizabeth (1558–1589) (ed. J. Stevenson, E. R. Wernham, etc.) (London, 1863–1950) (cited as 'For.Cal.Eliz.'), vol. xviii).

CALLAWAY, M., Jr. 'Benedict Arnold and Freemasonry: correction of a long-standing error' (*AQC*, lxxx. 120–2) (London, 1968).

CALLEJAS, R. F. 'A Report on Masonry in Cuba in 1969' (*AQC*, lxxxii. 101–3) (London, 1970).

CALVERT, A. P. *The Grand Lodge of England 1717–1917* (London, 1917).

Cambridge Modern History (ed. A. W. Ward, C. W. Prothero, S. Leathes) (Cambridge, 1907–10).

CARR, H. 'The Foundation of the Great Lodge of Iran' (*AQC*, lxxxi. 266–79) (London, 1969).

— 'Review of Professor Jacob Katz's book *Jews and Freemasons in Europe 1723–1939*' (*AQC*, lxxxiii. 322–8) (London, 1971).

CARRINGTON, F. A. and PAYNE, J. *Reports of Cases argued and Ruled at Nisi Prices* (London, 1827–41).

CASTELLS, F. de P. *English Freemasonry in the Period of Transition AD 1600–1700* (London, 1931).

CASTLE, E. J. 'Proceedings against the Templars in France and England for Heresy etc. AD 1307–11' (*AQC*, xx. 47–70) (London, 1907).

CAYWOOD, D. 'Freemasonry and the Knights of Malta: A Post Preface?' (*AQC*, cvi. 186–96) (London, 1994).

CERF, A. J. W. 'How Frederick the Great of Prussia became a Freemason' (*AQC*, x. 188) (London, 1897).

CERZA, A. 'The American War of Independence and Freemasonry' (*AQC*, lxxxix. 169–75) (London, 1977).

— 'Anti-Masonry' (*AQC*, lxxx. 241–70) (London, 1962).

— 'The Boston Tea Party and Freemasonry' (*AQC*, xcviii. 207–9) (London, 1986).

CHEVALLIER, P. *Histoire de la Franc-Maçonnerie Française* (Paris, 1974–5).

CHURCHILL, W. S. 'Zionism versus Bolshevism', 8 Feb. 1920 (unpublished article in Churchill Archives CHAR 8/36, pp. 92–93).

CLARKE, J. R. 'The Change from Christianity to Deism in Freemasonry' (*AQC*, lxxviii. 49–73) (London, 1966).

— 'The Establishment of the Premier Grand Lodge: why in London and why in 1717?' (*AQC*, lxxxi. 1–9) (London, 1969).

— 'John Locke and Freemasonry' (*AQC*, lxxviii. 168–71) (London, 1966).

— 'Was Sir Christopher Wren a Freemason? A re-appraisal of the evidence' (*AQC*, lxxviii. 201–6) (London, 1966).

CLARKE, J. R., and JONES, G. P. 'Why was James Boswell a Freemason?' (*AQC*, lxxix. 90–92) (London, 1967). See also Jones, G. P.

CONDER, E. 'The Hon. Miss St Leger and Freemasonry' (*AQC*, viii. 16–23) (London, 1895).

CONDER, E., Jr. *Records of the Hole Crafte and Fellowship of Masons with a Chronicle of the History of the Worshipful Company of Masons of the City of London* (New York, 1894).

Le Constitutionnel (Paris, 1870).

COOK, C. and N. *Blueprint for Revolution* (Thomaston, 1996).

CRAWLEY, W. J. C. 'The Chevalier d'Éon' (*AQC*, xvi. 231–51) (London, 1903).

— 'The Hon. A. Wesley and the Lodge at Trim' (*AQC*, xv. 108–24) (London, 1902).

— 'The Rev. Dr Anderson's Non-Masonic Writings 1702–1739' (*AQC*, xviii. 28–42) (London, 1905).

— 'The Templar Legends in Freemasonry' (*AQC*, xxvi. 45–70) (London, 1913).

— 'General George Washington and Lodge No. 227' (*AQC*, xxiii. 95–97) (London, 1910).

Crime without Punishment: Genocide against the Serbs (Belgrade, 1991).

CROWE, F. J. W. 'A Curious Carbonari Certificate' (*AQC*, xvi. 163–70) (London, 1903).

CRYER, B. 'The Church's Concern with Freemasonry' (*AQC*, xcv. 1–20) (London, 1983).

— The De-Christianizing of the Craft' (*AQC*, xcvii. 34–74) (London, 1985).

CUSTOS, Dr. *Freimaurer der Weltvampyr* (Berlin, 1931).

D'ALVIELLA, Count G. *Fifty Years of Masonic Life in Belgium (1870–1920)* (*AQC*, xxxiii. 231–41) (London, 1920).

— 'The Papal Bulls of Freemasonry in Belgium' (*AQC*, xxv. 81–87) (London, 1912).

DAWSON, F. J. 'The Chevalier Bartholomew Ruspini 1728–1813' (*AQC*, lxxxvi. 87–89) (London, 1974).

DENSLOW, W. R. *10,000 Famous Freemasons* (Columbia, Missouri, 1957–60).

DJILAS, A. *The Contested Country* (Cambridge, Mass., 1991).

DODSLEY, D. R. 'Doctor Edward Jenner and some other eminent physicians and surgeons in Freemasonry' (*AQC*, civ. 139–49) (London, 1992).

DOMENECH, E. *L'empire au Mexique et la candidature d'un Prince Bonaparte au trône mexicain* (Paris, 1862).

DRAFFEN, G. 'Prince Hall Freemasonry' (*AQC*, lxxxix. 70–91) (London, 1977).

DRAFFEN, G. S. 'The Mason Word' (*AQC*, lxv. 54) (London, 1953).

DURR, A. 'Ritual of Associations and the Organizations of the German People' (*AQC*, c. 88–108) (London, 1988).

DYER, C. F. W. 'The Women have their Way: Ladies Nights etc of the 1790s' (*AQC*, lxxxviii. 193–4) (London, 1976).

Early Masonic Pamphlets (ed. D. Knoop, G. P. Jones and D. Hamer) (Manchester, 1945).

ECKERT, E. E. *Der Freimaurer-Orden in seiner wahren Bedeutung* (Dresden, 1852).

Enciclopedia Vniversal Ilvstrada Evropa-Americana (Barcelona, 1887–99).

Encyclopaedia Britannica (11th edn.) (London and New York, 1910).

EUGÉNIE DE GRÈCE, Princess. *Pierre Napoléon Bonaparte* (Paris, 1963).

Fama Fraternitatis und Die Chemische Hochzeit (Kassel, 1615).

FAVA, Mgr A. J., and TAXIL, L. *L'Existence des Loges de Femmes affirmée par Mgr Fava Évêque de Grenoble et par Léo Taxil* (Paris, 1892). See Taxil.

FAY, B. *La Franc-Maçonnerie et la révolution intellectuelle du XVIIIe siècle* (Paris, 1961 edn.)

FENTON, S. J. 'The Military Services and Freemasonry' (*AQC*, lx. 3–25) (London, 1950).

— 'Richard Carlile: His Life and Masonic Writings' (*AQC*, xlix. 83–121) (London, 1939).

FERMINGER, W. K. 'The Romances of Robison and Barruel' (*AQC*, l. 31–69) (London, 1940).

FINDEL, J. G. *The History of Freemasonry* (2nd edn., London, 1869).

FISHER, W. G. 'John Montague, second Duke of Montagu: the first noble Grand Master' (*AQC*, lxxix. 90–92) (London, 1967).

FLEMING, T. *Liberty! The American Revolution* (New York, 1997).

FLYNN, K. 'Freemasons at War' (*AQC*, cv. 172–82) (London, 1993).

FOOTTIT, C. R. S. 'English Royal Freemasons' (*AQC*, cv. 172–82) (London, 1993).

For.Cal.Eliz. See Calendar of State Papers.

FOXE, J. *The Acts and Monuments of John Foxe* (ed. J. Pratt) (London, 1877, and New York, 1965) (The Book of Martyrs).

France (London, 1941).

FRANCO, Generalissimo Francisco. See Boor.

FRANCOVICH, C. *Storia della Massoneria in Italia dalla origine alla Rivoluzione Francese* (Florence, 1974).

FRANKLIN, B. *The Autobiography of Benjamin Franklin* (New Haven, 1964).

Freemasonry: An Approach to Life (United Grand Lodge of England, London, 1999).

'Freemasons at Canterbury in 1732' (*AQC*, xxxiii. 186–7) (London, 1920).

GAGERN, C. von. *Todte und Lebende* (Berlin, 1884).

GARCIA, G., and PEREYRA, C. *El Gral. Paredes y Arrillaga: los Gobiernes de Alvarez y Comonfort* (Mexico City, 1974).

GARIBALDI, G. *Clelia ovvero Il governo del monaco* (Milan, 1870).

GAUNA, E. 'Review of *Giuseppe Mazzini Uomo Universale* by Carlo Gentile (*AQC*, lxxxvi. 298–300) (London, 1983).

The Gentleman's Magazine, Feb. 1798, pp. 140–8 (London, 1798).

Gibbon, E. 'The Masonic Certificate of Edward Gibbon' (*AQC*, xvii. 22) (London, 1904).

GILLESPIE, H. W. 'Goethe in Zürich' (*AQC*, xc. 284–6) (London, 1978).

GIMPEL, J. *The Cathedral Builders* (London, 1983).

Globus (Zagreb, 1999).

GOETHE, J. W. von. 'Campagne in Frankreich 1792' (*Goethes Werke* (Weimar, 1887–1916)).

GOTCH, C. 'The Role of the Innkeeper in Masonry' (*AQC*, ci. 213–23) (London, 1989).

GOULD, F. R. *A Concise History of Freemasonry* (London, 1903).

— 'Freemasonry in Mexico' (*AQC*, x. 16–69) (London, 1897).

GRUNDMANN, R. R. 'Some Aspects of Freemasonry on Polish Soil' (*AQC*, civ. 205–15) (London, 1992).

HALL-JOHNSON, A. S. 'A Century of English Freemasonry in Argentina' (*AQC*, lxv. 98–106) (London, 1953).

HAMER, D., and CLARKE, J. R. 'An Anti-Masonic Declaration by Six Doctors of the Sorbonne in 1745' (*AQR*, lxxxvi. 20–34) (London, 1974).

HAMILL, J. *The Craft* (Wellingborough, 1985).

— 'The Earl of Moira, Acting Grand Master 1790–1813' (*AQC*, xciii. 31–48) (London, 1981).

— '"The Sins of our Masonic Fathers"' (*AQC*, ci. 133–59) (London, 1989).

HAMILL, J., and GILBERT, R. *Freemasonry: A Celebration of the Craft* (London, 1992).

— *World Freemasonry* (London, 1991).

HANNAH, W. *Christians by Degrees* (London, 1954).

— *Darkness Visible* (London, 1952).

HAYWOOD, H. L. *Famous Masons and Masonic Presidents* (Richmond, Virginia, 1945).

HEATON, R. E. *Masonic Membership of the Founding Fathers* (Silver Spring, Maryland, 1974).

HEINEMAN, J. W. 'An Early Pronouncement of the Church A. D. 1326?' (*AQC*, lxxxvii. 239–42) (London, 1975).

HENDERSON, K., and POPE, T. *Freemasonry Universal: A New Guide to the Masonic World* (Williamstown, Victoria, Australia, 1998–2000).

HERTLING, S. 'A Brief History of Danish Freemasonry' (*AQC*, xc. 277–83) (London, 1978).

HEWITT, A. R. 'Craftsmen in Captivity: Masonic Activities of Prisoners of War in World War I, World War II in Europe and the Far East' (*AQC*, lxxvii. 79–108) (London, 1965).

HILLS, P. G. 'Women and Freemasonry' (*AQC*, xxxiii. 63–77) (London, 1920).

The History of English Freemasonry: A Souvenir of a permanent exhibition in the Library and Museum of the United Grand Lodge of England at Freemasons' Hall, London (London, 1986).

History of Grand Master's Lodge No. 1 (London, 1958).

HOBBS, J. W. 'An Irish Lodge Minute Book 1782–1797' (*AQC*, xxxiv. 74–124) (London, 1921).

HOLYOAKE, G. J. 'Carlile, Richard' (*Dictionary of National Biography*, iii. 1011).

HOOKER, A. H. 'The Knights Templars – Fact & Fiction' (*AQC*, xcvi. 204–11) (London, 1984).

HORNE, A. 'The Saints John in the Masonic Tradition' (*AQC*, lxv. 76–102) (London, 1953).

HORY, L., and BROSZAT, M. *Der kroatische Ustascha-Staat 1941–1945* (Stuttgart, 1964).

HOWE, H. 'The Collapse of Freemasonry in Nazi Germany 1933–5' (*AQC*, xcv. 23–36) (London, 1983).

HUGHAN, W. J. 'King Edward VII Past Grand Master and Protector of the Craft' (*AQC*, xxiii. 101–3) (London, 1910).

IVANOFF, B. 'Cagliostro in Eastern Europe (Courland, Russia & Poland)' (*AQC*, xl. 45–80) (London, 1928).

JACKSON, A. C. P. 'Our Predecessors: Scottish Masons of about 1660' (*AQC*, xci. 10–27) (London, 1979).

— 'Rosicrucianism and its effects on Craft Masonry' (*AQC*, xcvii. 115–50) (London, 1985).

JARVIS, C. M. *Grand Stewards 1728–1978* (London, 1978).

JELLINEK, F. *The Paris Commune of 1871* (London, 1937).

JOHNSTON, S. P. 'Seventeenth Century Descriptions of Solomon's Temple' (*AQC*, xii, 135–49) (London, 1899).

JONES, G. P., and CLARKE, J. R. 'A Chaplain in a Lodge in Liverpool in 1754' (*AQC*, lxxvii. 143–4) (London, 1965). See Clarke and Jones.

Journals of Congress containing their Proceedings from September 5, 1774, to January 1, 1776 (Philadelphia, 1800).

KAULBACK, M. S. 'The First Knights Templars in the United States' (*AQC*, cvii. 224–7) (London, 1995).

KEANE, J. *Tom Paine* (London, 1995).

KENDALL, G. ' "Crimean Simpson": War Artist and Freemason' (*AQC*, cv. 195–201) (London, 1993).

— 'Freemasonry during the Anglo Boer War 1899–1902' (*AQC*, xcvii, 20–33) (London, 1985).

KENNEDY, W. 'Freemasonry: a possible origin' (*AQC*, cvii. 196–200) (London, 1995).

KHAMBATTA, R. B. 'The Influence of the Prince of Wales (Edward VII) on the Administration and Development of the Craft' (*AQC*, cviii. 81–121) (London, 1996).

KNIGHT, C., and LOMAS, R. *The Second Messiah* (London, 1997).

KNIGHT, S. *The Brotherhood: The Secret World of the Freemasons* (London, 1984).

— *Jack the Ripper: The Final Solution* (London, 1976).

KNOOP, D. 'The Mason Word' (*AQC*, li. 194–211) (London, 1940).

KNOOP, D., and JONES, G. P. 'An Anti-Masonic Leaflet of 1698' (*AQC*, lv. 152–4) (London, 1944).

— *The Genesis of Freemasonry* (Manchester, 1947).

— 'Prolegomera to the Mason Word' (*AQC*, lii. 139–59) (London, 1941).

KNOOP, D., JONES, G. P., and HAMER, D. *The Two Earliest Masonic MSS* (Manchester, 1938).

KURTZ, H. *The Trial of Marshal Ney* (London, 1957).

LAFONTAINE, E. C. de. 'Paul Jones' (*AQC*, xliv. 203–22) (London, 1934).

LANE, R. F. *The Outwith London Guilds of Great Britain* (London, 1994).

LANGE, A. J. 'A Sketch of Norwegian Masonic History' (*AQC*, xiii. 35–36) (London, 1900).

LARUDAN, Abbé. *Les Francs-Maçons ecrasés* (Amsterdam, 1747).

LAVAL, P. *Laval parle* (ed. Josée de Chambrun, his daughter) (Paris, 1948).

LAYIKTEZ, C. 'Sultan Murad V, Kleanti Skalyeri, Sultan Abdulhamit II: Young Turks and Freemasons' (*AQC*, cvii. 230–2) (London, 1995).

LEFEBVRE, G., GUYOT, R., and SAGNAC, P. *La Révolution Française* (Paris, 1930).

LE FRANC, Abbé. *Le voile levé pour les curieux, ou Le secret de la révolution revélé à l'aide de la franc-maçonnerie* (Paris, 1791).

— *Le voile levé poir les Curieux, ou Histoire de la Franc-Maconnerie depuis ses origines jusqu'à nos jours, par M. l'Abbé Lefranc . . . tombé sous la hache des assassins à Paris le 2 septembre 1792* (Liége, 1826).

LEVI-CASTILLO, J. R. 'Admiral William Brown: His capture and masonic rescue in Guayaquil' (*AQC*, xcii. 16–24) (London, 1980).

L'Express (Paris, Apr. 2001)

El Libro Rojo 1520–1867 (ed. V. E. Palacio, M. Payno, F. A. Mateos and F. M. de la Torre) (Mexico City, 1905–6).

LINNECAR, R. 'Studies in Masonry' (*The Miscellaneous Works of Richard Linnacar of Wakefield*, 247–62) (Leeds, 1769).

LITVINE, J. 'Anti-Masonry: A Neglected Source' (*AQC*, civ. 121–38) (London, 1992).

LUDENDORFF, E. *Vernichtung der Freimaurerei durch Enthüllung ihrer Geheimnisse* (Munich, 1927).

LUZIO, A. *La Massoneria e il Risorgimento Italiano* (Bologna, 1925).

McDOWELL, B. *The Revolutionary War* (Washington, D.C., 1967).

MACKAY, A. M. 'Sir Walter Scott as a Freemason' (*AQC*, xx. 209–20) (London, 1907).

McLEOD, W. 'The Hudibrastic Poem of 1723' (*AQC*, cvii. 9–52) (London, 1995).

MAGNUS, P. *King Edward the Seventh* (London, 1964).

MALCZOVICH, L. de. 'A Sketch of the earlier history of Masonry in Austria and Hungary' (*AQC*, iv. 20–24, 181–93; v. 15–19, 187–92; vi. 85–91; vii. 18–24, 77–82, 184–9; viii. 180–8; ix. 129–44) (London, 1891–6).

MARIE ANTOINETTE. *Lettres de Marie-Antoinette* (Paris, 1896).

MARIS, L. G. 'English Freeemasonry in Germany (1821–1929, 1945–71)' (*AQC*, lxxxiii. 274–300) (London, 1971).

MARKHAM, A. G. 'Further Views on the Origins of Freemasonry in England' (*AQC*, ciii. 78–123) (London, 1991).

— 'Some Problems of English Masonic History' (*AQC*, cx. 1–19) (London, 1998).

MASARYK, T. G. 'Svobodní zednáři' (*Naše Doba*, xiii. 30–35) (Prague, 1906).

MELLOR, A. 'Eighteenth-Century French Freemasonry and the French Revolution' (*AQC*, xcvii. 105–14) (London, 1985).

— 'The Roman Catholic Church and the Craft' (*AQC*, lxxxix. 60–69) (London, 1977).

MORE, T. *The Complete Works of St Thomas More* (New Haven and London, 1963–79).

Morning Post (London, 1920).

MOTLEY, J. L. *The Rise of the Dutch Republic* (London, 1861 edn.)

MOZLEY, J. F. *John Foxe and his Book* (London, 1940).

MUIR, R. F. 'The Morgan Affair and its Effect on Freemasonry' (*AQC*, cv. 217–34; cvi. 131–40) (London, 1993–4).

MULHALL, M. G. *The English in South America* (Buenos Aires, 1878).

MULLER-RUEGG, E. 'Swiss Freemasonry's Fight for Life 1933–1937' (*AQC*, lx. 211–26) (London, 1950).

MUSA, F. B. 'The First Indian Freemason, Rt. Wor. Bro. Manockjee Cursetjee' (*AQC*, lxxxi. 317–21) (London, 1969).

NASSER, C. J. 'The Boston Tea Party' (*AQC*, cii. 248–9) (London, 1990).

NAUDON, P. *Histoire générale de la Franc-Maçonnerie* (Paris, 2nd edn. 1987).

NELSON, Claire M. 'The Masonic Connections of Haydn's Impresario Johann Peter Solomon' (*AQC*, cx. 177–91) (London, 1998).

NELSON, Horatio, Lord. *The Despatches and Letters of Vice Admiral Lord Viscount Nelson* (ed. Sir N. H. Nicolas) (London, 1845–6).

NEUSTADT, Katherine D. *Carperters' Hall: Meeting Place of History* (Philadelphia, 1981).

Never Again (ed. M. Bulajić, A. Miletić, D. Laskić) (Belgrade, 1991).

NEWMAN, A. 'Politics and Freemasonry in the Eighteenth Century' (*AQC*, civ. 32–54) (London, 1992).

NILUS, S. *The Protocols of the Wise Men of Zion* (New York, 1920).

O'MEARA, B. E. *Napoleon at St Helena* (London, 1888).

Original Letters relative to the English Reformation (ed. H. Robinson) (Cambridge, 1846–7).

OTTENHEIMER, G., and LECADRE, R. *Les Frères invisibles* (Paris, 2001).

OUGH, A. 'The Origin and Development of Royal Arch Masonry (*AQC*, cviii. 188–95) (London, 1996).

OUSBY, I. *Occupation: The Ordeal of France 1940–1944* (London, 1997).

OWEN, R. *The Life of Robert Owen written by Himself* (London, 1858).

PARRY, D. L. L. 'Friends in High Places: the Favours sought by the Freemasons of Orléans, 1890–1914' (*French History*, xii(ii). 195–212) (Oxford, 1998).

— 'The Political Culture of the Third Republic' (unpublished manuscript).

PATRICK, W. D. 'Making a Mason at Sight' (*AQC*, xcix. 196) (London, 1987).

PEARMAIN, A. 'Music and Masonry' (*AQC*, ciii. 130–4) (London, 1991).

PETERS, H. 'Sir Isaac Newton and the Holy Flame' (*AQC*, ci. 207–13) (London, 1989).

— 'Sir Isaac Newton and "The Oldest Catholic Religion"' (*AQC*, c. 192–6) (London, 1988).

PETROVITCH, W. M. 'The Story of the Black Hand and the Great War'. See Pozzi.

PEYRE, D. C. Van. 'Prince Frederick (Great Master 1816–1831) and the Higher Degrees in the Netherlands' (*AQC*, cx. 95–105) (London, 1998).

PHILON, N. 'Freemasonry in Greece' (*AQC*, xi. 100–1) (London, 1898).

PIATIGORSKY, A. *Who's Afraid of Freemasons?* (London, 1997).

PLOT, R. *The Natural History of Stafford-shire* (Oxford, 1686).

POZZI, H. *Black Hand over Europe* (Zagreb, 1994 edn) (first published 1935).

PRICHARD, S. *Masonry Dissected* (London, 1730).

QUISTGAARD, H. 'King Charles XIV John of Sweden as a Freemason' (*AQC*, lxxiv. 71–72) (London, 1962).

RABES, L. 'Beethoven and his Masonic Song "Maurerfragen"' (*AQC*, lxxx. 144–50) (London, 1968).

RADICE, F. R. 'The French Charbonnerie in the Nineteenth Century' (*AQC*, lx. 106–16) (London, 1950).

— 'An Introduction to the History of the Carbonari' (*AQC*, li. 63–136; lii. 63–136; liii. 48–143; liv. 35–67, 122–77) (London, 1940–3).

RATTO, H. R. *Almirante Guillermo Brown* (Buenos Aires, 1961).

READ, CONYERS. Lord Burghley and Queen Elizabeth (London, 1960).

READ, W. The Church of Rome and Freemasonry (1738 ... 1917 ... 1983)' (*AQC*, civ. 51–94) (London, 1992).

REINALTER, H. 'Freemasonry in Austria in the Eighteenth Century' (*AQC*, c. 197–207) (London, 1988).

— *Joseph II und die Freimaurerei* (Vienna, 1987).

RIDLEY, J. *Garibaldi* (London, 1974).

— *Maximilian and Juárez* (New York, 1992).

— *Mussolini* (London, 1997).

— *Tito* (London, 1994).

RIEGELMANN, H. *Die Europäischen Dynastien in ihrem Verhältnis zur Freimauerei* (Berlin, 1943).

RIZOPOULOS, A. C. 'Lord Byron: Freemason' (*AQC*, cix. 247–9) (London, 1997).

— 'Sultan Murad V and Freemasonry: A Political Dream of the Nineteenth Century' (*AQC*, civ. 187–95) (London, 1992).

ROBBINS, A. F. 'Dr Anderson of the "Constitutions"' (*AQC*, xxiii. 6–34) (London, 1910).

— 'The Earliest Years of English Organized Freemasonry' (*AQC*, xxii. 67–89) (London, 1909).

— 'Frederick, Prince of Wales, as a Freemason' (*AQC*, xxix. 326–9) (London, 1916).

ROBINSON, J. J. *Born in Blood: the Lost Secrets of Freemasonry* (London, 1990).

— *A Pilgrim's Path: Freemasonry and the Religious Right* (New York, 1993).

ROBISON, J. *Proofs of a Conspiracy against all the Religions and Governments of Europe carried on in the secret meetings of Free Masons, Illuminati and Reading Societies* (Edinburgh and London, 1797).

— 2nd edn (London and Edinburgh, 1797).

— 4th edn (London and Edinburgh, 1798).

ROEDER R. *Juárez and his Mexico* (New York, 1947).

ROGERS, N. 'Lancashire Military Lodges' (*AQC*, lxxvi. 101–20) (London, 1964).

— 'The Lodge of Elias Ashmole, 1646' (*AQC*, lxv. 35–53) (London, 1953).

ROSE, C. *Freye Bemerkungen über die politische Verfassung des Ordens der freyen Maurer von dem Bruder Christian Rose* (Leipzig, 1787).

ROSE, H. 'The Second Coalition' (*Cambridge Modern History*, viii. 633–64) (Cambridge, 1907–10).

ROSENTHAL, B. *Salem Story: Reading the Witch Trials of 1692* (Cambridge, 1995).

ROTTENBURY, R. H. S. 'The Pre-Eminence of the Great Architect in Freemasonry' (*AQC*, xcvii. 34–74) (London, 1985).

Royal Archives: RA: VIC/J 102/102.

RUNCIMAN, R. T. 'Sir Arthur Conan Doyle, Sherlock Holmes and Freemasonry' (*AQC*, civ. 178–87) (London, 1992).

RUTTON, W. L. 'Sandgate Castle AD 1539–40' (*Archaeologia Cantiana*, xx. 228–57) (London, 1893).

SAINTSBURY, G. 'Voltaire' (*Encyclopaedia Britannica* (11th edn, xxviii. 199–205) (London and New York, 1910).

SEAL-COON, F. W. 'The Birth of Freemasonry (Another Theory)' (*AQC*, xcii. 199–202) (London, 1980).
— 'Modern Anti-Masonry at Home and Abroad' (*AQC*, cii.170–7) (London, 1990).
— 'Simon Bolivar, Freemason' (*AQC*, xc. 231–48) (London, 1978).
— 'Spanish-American Revolutionary Masonry: the Mythical Masonry of Francisco de Miranda' (*AQC*, xciv. 83–106) (London, 1982).
SHARP, ALLAN M. 'Australia's Oldest Masonic Document: A Factual Interpretation' (*AQC*, civ. 150–65) (London, 1992).
— 'Some Aspects of Operative Masonry in New South Wales, Australia: 1788–1850' (*AQC*, c. 208–19) (London, 1988).
SHARP, ARTHUR 'Masonic Songs and Song Books of the late Eighteenth Century' (*AQC*, lxv. 84–95) (London, 1953).
— 'Mozart's Masonic Music' (*AQC*, lxix. 15–30) (London, 1957).
SHERMAN, J. M. 'The Negro "National" or "Compact" Grand Lodge' (*AQC*, xcii. 148–71) (London, 1980).
— Review of C. H. Wesley's *Prince Hall: Life and Legacy* (*AQC*, xc. 306–22) (London, 1978).
SHORE, W. T. *The Baccarat Case* (Edinburgh and London, 1932).
SHORT, M. *Inside the Brotherhood: Further Secrets of the Freemasons* (London, 1989).
— *Lundy: the Destruction of Scotland Yard's Finest Detective* (London, 1991).
The Signers of the Constitution of the United States (Bloomington, Ill., 1976).
SIMMONS, J. *A letter to His Grace the Duke of Northumberland on the very Extraordinary Transactions of the Society for the Encouragement of Arts, Manufactures, and Commerce Relative to His Royal Highness the Duke of Sussex* (London, 1824).
SMITH, S. N. 'The so-called "Exposure" of Freemasonry of the Mid-Eighteenth Century' (*AQC*, lvi. 4–36) (London, 1946).
SMYTH, F. 'Brother Mozart of Vienna' (*AQC*, lxxxvii. 37–75) (London, 1975).
— 'Freemasonry in Finland' (*AQC*, lxxvii. 87–98) (London, 1965).
— 'Worshipful Brother George Washington of Virginia' (*AQC*, lxxxviii. 181–4) (London, 1976).
SOLF, H. H. 'The Revival of Freemasonry in Post-War Germany' (*AQC*, xcvii. 1–17) (London, 1985).
'The South African Commission of Enquiry into Secret Organizations' (*AQC*, lxxviii. 74–82) (London, 1966).
S.P. *The Secrets of Masonry Made known to all Men by S.P., late Member of a Constituted Lodge* (London, 1737/8).
SPURR, M. 'William Stukeley: Antiquarian and Freemason' (*AQC*, c. 113–30) (London, 1988).

STARR, M. P. 'Alastair Crawley: Freemason!' (*AQC*, cviii. 150–61) (London, 1996).

Statutes at Large, vols xvii, xviii (London, 1798–1800).

The Statutes of the Realm, vols i–iv(i) (London, 1810–19).

STEMPER, W. M. 'Conflicts and Developments in Eighteenth-Century Freemasonry: the American Context' (*AQC*, civ. 198–205) (London, 1992).

STOLPER, E. E. 'Freemasonry in Naples in the Eighteenth Century' (*AQC*, xciii. 77–97) (London, 1981).

— 'Garibaldi: Freemason' (*AQC*, cii. 1–23) (London, 1990).

— '"Napoleonic" Freemasonry in Italy' (*AQC*, c. 164–78) (London, 1988).

TALLENTYRE, S. G. *The Friends of Voltaire* (London, 1906)

TARLÉ, E. *Bonaparte* (London, 1937).

TATSCH, J. H. 'An American Masonic Crisis: the Morgan Incident of 1826 and its Aftermath' (*AQC*, xxxiv. 196–209) (London, 1921).

TAXIL, L. *Le Culte du Grand Architecte* (Paris, 1886).

— *La France Maçonnique: Nouvelles divulgations* (Paris, 1888).

— *Les Frères Trois-Points* (Paris, 1886).

TAXIL, L., and VERDUN, P. *Les Assassinats Maçonniques* (Paris, 1889). See FAVA.

TEKTON LODGE No. 4696. *Consecration by VW Bro. Colville Smith CVO Grand Secretary ... at Carpenters' Hall, Throgmorton Avenue, EC2, on Thursday, 29th January, 1925* (London, 1925).

TELEPNEFF, B. 'A Short Note on Polish Freemasonry' (*AQC*, lix. 192–5) (London, 1948).

— 'Freemasonry in Russia' (*AQC*, xxxv. 261–92) (London, 1922).

— 'Some Aspects of Russian Freemasonry during the reign of the Emperor Alexander I' (*AQC*, xxxviii. 6–66) (London, 1925).

THARAUD, J. and J. *La tragédie de Ravaillac* (Paris, 1913).

THORP, J. T. 'An Early Will of Philip, Duke of Wharton' (*AQC*, xxxi. 160–8) (London, 1918).

The Times (London, 1870–1999).

TIMMONS. W. H. 'José Maria Morelos: Agrarian Reformer' (*Hispano-American Historical Review*, xlv. 183–95 (Durham, North Carolina, 1965).

To All Godly People in the Citie of London (London, 1698).

TUCKETT, J. E. S. 'The Early History of Freemasonry in France' (*AQC*, xxxi. 7–30) (London, 1918).

— 'Napoleon I and Freemasonry' (*AQC*, xxvii. 96–141) (London, 1914).

TUNBRIDGE, P. 'The Climate of European Freemasonry 1730 to 1750' (*AQC*, lxxxi. 88–128) (London, 1969).

— 'Field Marshal the Duke of Kent as a Freemason' (*AQC*, lxxviii. 17–48) (London, 1966).

VATCHER, S. 'A Lodge of Irishmen at Lisbon, 1738: An Early Record of Inquisition Proceedings' (*AQC*, lxxxiv. 75–109) (London, 1972).

— 'John Coustos and the Portuguese Inquisition' (*AQC*, lxxxi. 9–87) (London, 1969).

VAUGHN, W. P. *The Anti-Masonic Party in the United States 1826–1843* (Lexington, Kentucky, 1983).

VIBERT, L. 'The Compagnonnage' (*AQC*, xxxiii. 191–228) (London, 1920).

VILLARI, L. 'Caracciolo' (*Encyclopaedia Britannica*, 11th edn, v. 299–300) (London and New York, 1910).

— 'Naples, Kingdom of' (*Encyclopaedia Britannica*, 11th edn, xix. 182–90) (London, and New York, 1910).

VINCENT, E. S. *A Record of Freemasonry in the Province of Cornwall 1751–1959* (Truro, 1960).

VOORHIS, H. V. R. 'Benjamin Franklin's Reprint of Anderson's Constitutions of 1723' (*AQC*, lxxxiv. 69–74) (London, 1972).

— 'The Morgan Affair of 1826 in the USA' (*AQC*, lxxvi. 197–203) (London, 1964).

WAITE, A. E. *The Real History of the Rosicrucians* (London, 1887).

WARD, E. 'Anderson's Freemasonry not Deistic' (*AQC*, lxxx. 36–57) (London, 1968).

— 'William Hogarth and his Freemasonry' (*AQC*, lxxvii. 1–20) (London, 1965).

WARD, G. C. *The Civil War* (New York, 1990).

WASHIZU, Y. 'Anti-Masonry in Japan: Past and Present' (*AQC*, cvii. 85–116) (London, 1995).

WEBB, J. 'John George Lambton, the First Earl of Durham' (*AQC*, cix. 115–53) (London, 1997).

— 'Joseph Haydn: Freemason and Musician' (*AQC*, xciv. 83–106) (London, 1982).

— 'Robert Burns, Poet and Freemason' (*AQC*, ciii. 213–29) (London, 1991).

— *Rudyard Kipling: Man, Poet, Mason* (Addlestone, 1988).

WEBSTER, NESTA. *Secret Societies and Subversive Movements* (London, 1924).

— *World Revolution: the Plot against Civilization* (London, 1921).

WELLINGTON, ARTHUR WELLESLEY, Duke of. *Supplementary Despatches* (London, 1858–72).

— *Wellington at War: A Selection of his Wartime Letters* (ed. A. Brett-James) (London, 1961).

WESLEY, C. H. *Prince Hall: Life and Legacy* (Washington, D.C., and Philadelphia, 1977).

WEYGAND, M. *Mémoires: Rappelé au Service* (Paris, 1950).

WHITE, M. *Isaac Newton: the Last Sorcerer* (London, 1997).

WILLIAMS, W. J. 'Alexander Pope and Freemasonry' (*AQC*, xxxviii. 111–46) (London, 1925).

WILLIAMSON, B., and BAIGENT, M. 'Sir Christopher Wren and Freemasonry: New Evidence' (*AQC*, cix. 188–90) (London, 1997).

WILSON, H. C. BRUCE. 'Mirabeau's Scheme for the Political Penetration of Freemasonry' (*AQC*, lvii. 138–94) (London, 1947).

WINTERBURGH, E. 'Prague: a Centre of Freemasonry' (*AQC*, lxxvii. 65–78) (London, 1965).

WONNACOTT, W. 'Doctor Dodd, Grand Chaplain' (*AQC*, xx. 382–5) (London, 1907).

The Worshipful Company of Masons (London, 1989).

The Worshipful Society of Free Masons. *An Introduction to the Society* (London, 1997).

— *Constitutions, Rules and Regulations* (London, 1998).

Wriothesley, C. *A Chronicle of England during the reigns of the Tudors* (London, 1875–7).

YATES, FRANCES. *The Rosicrucian Enlightenment* (London, 1972).

YEATS-BROWN, F. *Escape* (London, 1933).

Index